A Biblical Theology of Worship
Dr. Ian A. Fair

HCU Media LLC
Accra, Ghana ◆ Frisco, TX

A Biblical Theology of Worship

HCU Media LLC

Published and Copyright © 2020
By Dr. Ian A. Fair & HCU Media LLC

ISBN-13: 978-1-939468-13-0 (Paperback Edition)

Also available in Kindle Format

ALL RIGHTS RESERVED

No part of this publication may be reproduced, sored in a retrieval system, or transmitted in any form by any means – electronic, mechanical, photocopying, recording or otherwise – without prior consent from publishers.

Scripture quotations, unless otherwise noted, are from The Holy Bible, Revised Standard Version, copyright 1971, Zondervan Bible Publishers.

Cover Design by Dale Henry - www.dalehenrydesign.com

First Edition August 2020
10 9 8 7 6 5 4 3 2 1

Dedicated to all my brothers and sisters in Christ
in
Africa and the United States of America
who have patiently and graciously
listened to my teaching and preaching for the past 60
years
and who have encouraged me
to keep studying

May all the glory, praise, and worship
be to
our heavenly Father
and
our Lord Jesus Christ

Soli Deo Gloria

CONTENTS

Preface & Postscript i

Credits……...……………...………..xvii

Bibliography xxiii

Chapter 1: Some Initial Thoughts...1

Chapter 2: Some Thoughts from the Early Centuries of Christianity 25

Chapter 3: Introduction to Terminology...................................33

Chapter 4: What is a Theology of Worship? 45

Chapter 5: The Prolegomena Focus, and Essential Elements of Worship 61

Chapter 6: A Theology of Church 93

Chapter 7: A Theology of Church and Worship 105

Chapter 8: Types of Christian Assemblies in the 1st Century ...127

Chapter 9: Discussion of The Lord's Supper, or the Eucharist.155

Chapter 10: The Lord's Supper in Scripture 175

Chapter 11: Prayer..211

Chapter 12: Scripture..223

Chapter 13: Preaching and Homily 233

Chapter 14: Singing in the Worship Assembly 249

Chapter 15: The Fellowship or *Agapē* Love Feast 285

Chapter 16: Christian Worship in the Second Century 291

Chapter 17: Worship Since the Second Century 297

Chapter 18: Defining and Understanding a Contemporary Theology of Worship 301

Addendum 1: Gordon D. Fee, *Paul, the Spirit, and the People of God*...307

Addendum 2: Clinton Arnold, *Ephesians* 311

Addendum 3: Peter O'Brien, *The Letter to the Ephesians*.........315

Addendum 4: *Exegetical Studies on Singing in Worship*..........317

AUTHOR 351

WHO WE ARE 353

Preface & Postscript[1]

As I begin this project, I must confess that my reason for engaging in this study of worship is intensely personal. Too often I have succumbed to either my body carrying out an activity in worship, like singing, while my mind is barely on the words and less on their meaning. I have fussed over the songs we have chosen to sing without seriously contemplating their message. Often my mind is focused on other activities while I carry out the physical acts of the worship. Furthermore, at times activities have been included in the worship liturgy which barely relate to worship and I have comfortably followed along with the group. On occasion I have left the worship service with the feeling that I have not really worshipped God as he deserves to be worshipped, but have had a good experience of fellowship. A Moses "holy ground" experience of God's presence has on many occasions been little more than a distant memory of an ancient Sinai desert recollection!

Recently, I was engaged in a study of the Old Testament book of Exodus. I noticed a radical difference in the attitude on both YHWH's[2] and Moses' part when they met. An early life changing experience occurred for Moses when he encountered YHWH in a burning bush somewhere near Mount Sinai. In this life changing experience YHWH instructed Moses regarding his plans to redeem Israel out of Egyptian slavery. Emphasizing the importance of this encounter YHWH ordered Moses to take off his sandals because he was standing on holy ground! What made

---

[1] The postscript comments were added after discovering David F. Wells' writings on Evangelical Theology.

[2] I am using the Jewish Tetragrammaton YHWH (Jewish four-letter spelling) to refer to God since it involves more than merely the word god or God whichever way you choose to spell it. In order to carry this meaning forward the early Jews, ca 270 BCE, who translated the Hebrew Pentateuch into Greek, which we call the Septuagint, used the word *kúrios* for the Hebrew Tetragrammaton YHWH. Our English translations render this as LORD all in capitals to signify its importance and difference from Lord. YHWH is the form of referring to God that He chose to be known by. In English we refer to this as Jehovah, but I am not satisfied with this English spelling and prefer to refer to it by the Tetragrammaton YHWH to retain its holiness, greatness, and sovereignty.

the ground holy? Certainly not the impressive mountain where YHWH met Moses, since it was merely one mountain among many. It was the *real presence* of YHWH that made the ground holy! Then sometime later, Moses was again at Mount Sinai to meet with YHWH and receive what we know as the Ten Commandments. The significant occasion was not simply to give Moses and Israel Ten Commandments, for YHWH could have revealed these to Moses by any other means. *The significance was YHWH coming to meet with and be with Moses and Israel in a new and intensely personal way.* The mountain was described as holy; it burned with fire, it shook like an earthquake, it was covered by a cloud of dark smoke! *YHWH was there*! This got Moses' and Israel's attention! *It was holy ground because of YHWH's presence!* YHWH instructed Moses to warn the people not to move up into the mountain to be too near to YHWH. Failure to obey this command would result in instant death. Strict boundaries were set by YHWH for how far the people could approach the mountain, and how they should react to YHWH's presence (Ex 19:16ff).

In his epistle to the Philippians, in similar manner, Paul instructed the Philippians to respond to God in *fear and trembling* since God wanted to be present in their lives to assist them to work out their own salvation, meaning to work with them to activate or bring their own salvation to maturity, Phil 2:12:

> *Therefore, my beloved, as you have always obeyed, so now, not only as in my presence but much more in my absence, work out your own salvation with fear and trembling;* [13] *for God is at work in you, both to will and to work for his good pleasure.*

The real presence of YHWH should invoke an awesome attitude of awe and reverent worship in which one realizes one is "on holy ground" and in the presence of the most powerful force imaginable! Scripture often speaks of *worship* as *prostrating* oneself before YHWH. The Greek word used on such occasions is *proskuneō* meaning to either prostrate oneself before someone, to worship someone, to venerate someone, and to recognize someone as a sovereign supernatural being. The word and concept are found all over the New Testament in regard to Christian worship of God and Christ.[3]

One could answer that things changed radically after the death of Christ and images drawn from the Old Testament are not relevant today! After all, it is said by some, we are under grace and God is no longer the lofty or remote YHWH whom we should fear, but who is now our Father whom we can approach with boldness through Christ. Certainly, the graceful loving fatherhood is a biblical teaching and one to be treasured, but that does not imply reducing God to our human level and diminishing our approach to God to remote Jewish experience! Ignoring the holiness of the almighty Father in a mundane attitude is simply immature theology and even blasphemy! It is interesting that YHWH throughout his tumultuous history with Israel still considered Israel to be His children, and Himself their Father! Simply read the Book of Revelation and note how the Almighty God is reverenced and worshipped by the 24 elders prostrating themselves before the Holy One on the Throne in the Holy of Holies. Notice Rev 4:1ff!

> [1] *After this I looked, and lo, in heaven an open door! And the first voice, which I had heard speaking to me like a trumpet, said, "Come up hither, and I will show you what must take place after this."* [2] *At once I was in the Spirit, and lo, a throne stood in heaven, with one seated on the throne!* [3] *And he who sat there appeared like jasper and carnelian, and round the throne was a rainbow that looked like an emerald.* [4] *Round the throne were twenty-four thrones, and seated on the thrones were twenty-four elders, clad in white garments, with golden crowns upon their heads.* [5] *From the throne issue flashes of lightning, and voices and peals of thunder, and before the throne burn seven torches of fire, which are the seven spirits of God;* [6] *and before the throne there is as it were a sea of glass, like crystal.*
>
> *And round the throne, on each side of the throne, are four living creatures, full of eyes in front and behind:* [7] *the*

---

[3] Cf. Bauer, *A Greek English Lexicon.*

> *first living creature like a lion, the second living creature like an ox, the third living creature with the face of a man, and the fourth living creature like a flying eagle. [8] And the four living creatures, each of them with six wings, are full of eyes all round and within, and day and night they never cease to sing,*
>
>> *"Holy, holy, holy, is the Lord God Almighty, who was and is and is to come!"*
>
> *[9] And whenever the living creatures give glory and honor and thanks to him who is seated on the throne, who lives for ever and ever, [10] the twenty-four elders fall down before him who is seated on the throne and worship him who lives for ever and ever; they cast their crowns before the throne, singing,*
>
>> *[11] "Worthy art thou, our Lord and God, to receive glory and honor and power, for thou didst create all things, and by thy will they existed and were created."*

This study is therefore intended to be a study of a *biblical theology of worship* in which we explore the full meaning of *reverence and worship* before an almighty God who still is YHWH, who is still the great I AM, the ground of all being, who is the one who always was and is and always will be, and whose presence makes the ground on which we stand holy, whether it is on a mountain in Arabia or a church building in suburbia!

A point to consider here! The church building itself is not a holy place, but when God is present in worship it becomes a holy sanctuary and experience!

This study hopefully will not be a discussion of a liturgical *structure* of worship in which one determines a *fixed or preferred form or dogmatic pattern of worship*. The way I will be using the word liturgy relates to the ingredients, the theology, and the attitude of the formal worship service of God and Christ. I am exploring a reverent attitude that a religious group should adopt in its formal worship service as in a Sunday worship service when a congregation gathers to worship its deity, and in the case of the Christian assembly where one gathers with God in a sacred meal. The English word *liturgy* derives from the Latin *liturgia*, which in turn derives from the Greek *leitourgia* which refers to activity in a public worship service.[4]

Obviously, in a theology of worship one must examine the ingredients or components involved in the liturgy but only in so far as they define and express the theology of the action involved.

It is too easy to fall into the trap of determining a fixed form or order of worship that everyone should adopt. A fixed dogmatic form or schedule of worship will, I hope, not be the outcome of this study. I trust I will navigate safely the turbulent seas of contemporary worship, not having lost my theological compass, and not having succumbed to the danger of dogmatic demands regarding a set form of worship. My focus will be on *what* takes place in, and the *focus or direction* of the worship of God, and *not the order in which* this should be done. Time will tell how well I succeed in this! I have tried not to be too scholarly and technical, but to be scholarly enough to support my arguments and conclusions.

It is my opinion that each congregation or house church group should design its own worship service liturgy *within the parameters of a sound biblical theology of worship that meets the Scriptural and spiritual definition of Christian worship in the assembly of the saints.* I hope this study will be seen as an attempt to define a theology of worship that will guide our worship deliberations.

What I imply with this statement and the freedoms we have in deciding our worship liturgy and practice, for example, is that each group needs to decide for its own community and culture the time on the Lord's Day in which it will meet for worship, and the content and suitable order of the worship service. Essentially, the worship service and liturgy should be both Biblically and theologically grounded and culturally relevant in regard to language and style. For example, for centuries the Roman Catholic Church required that the language of the liturgy should be Latin, regardless of the vernacular of the local community. However, in the dialogues subsequent to the Second Vatican Council, (Vatican II)

---

[4] Cf. *Oxford English Dictionary*.

ca 1962 the local vernacular was permitted in localities where this was necessary. Worship must be understood and appreciated by the worshippers (cf. 1 Cor 14: 13 ff, where Paul instructed the Corinthians to sing and pray with the spirit and understanding) and be relevant and meaningful to the local culture. I hope to enlarge on this as our study develops.

In the process of this study we will examine the *praxis*[5] and relevant acts of worship in which the early church engaged in worship of God and Jesus. In the case of each worshipping act we will also attempt to develop a biblical theology for each worshipful act such as in the reading and preaching of Scripture, prayer, the Lord's Supper, benevolent giving, and singing.

By a theology of worship, I have in mind seeking first to understand the principles and mindset that lay behind the worship of the early church as revealed in Scripture. We will seek to understand why the early church worshipped and why they worshipped the way they did. We will explore the dynamic for the worship in regard to its relationship to God, Jesus, the local congregation/house church, and the Jewish and Gentile communities in which the congregation or house church found itself witnessing to the marvelous redemptive work of God in Jesus. In other words, we will explore and seek to determine the principles and mindset that should lie behind and control all Christian worship services. We will seek to explore a suitable spiritual dynamic that should motivate and guide all worship, whether in a church Sunday worship assembly on the Lord's Day, or in life in general.

By proposing a theology of worship, I have in mind the biblical and theological principles, mindsets, and dynamics driving the worship and not merely the socio/cultural contexts in which the worship takes place. This does not mean that a theology of worship should not be sensitive to the socio/cultural context of the worshippers. By speaking of a theology of worship I am in-

---

[5] *Praxis* refers to the process by which a principle, lesson, or skill is enacted, embodied, or realized in a living context. *Praxis* may also refer to the act of engaging, applying, exercising, realizing, or practicing ideas.

ferring that the *driving force* behind the worship should be biblically and theologically grounded and driven and not sociologically or culturally defined and driven. Christian worship should be culturally and sociologically relevant and not defined or driven by sociological, anthropological, or cultural principles.

I will hold that although there is a thin line between a theological biblical foundation to worship and a culturally sensitive worship, this thin line should not be erased or surrendered to where the driving force in worship is more culturally sensitive than biblically and theologically defined and grounded.

Postscript

When I began writing this book I was unaware of the challenging research and writing of David F. Wells as he examined our contemporary Christian world, Church, and Theological context. I have found much of my concerns echoed in Wells' writings and have been accouraged to learn that there are others who have similar concerns for theology and church in the secular culture in which we find ourselves seeking to find our theological center and church meaning and purpose. Although my primary concern has been to explore a pure non-partisan biblical theology of worship, I find Wells' thoughts[6] regarding the theological challenges of the Protestant Reformation[7] running parallel to my concerns regarding understanding a Restoration Movement[8] Church of Christ understanding of theology, church, and worship.

Like Wells, I regret the tendency of some churches to seek relevance with contemporary culture rather than with the concept of *Sola Scriptura*. Culturally relevant is achieved by reaching out to our cultural neighbors and post-modern society in a manner

---

[6] David Falconer Wells is a Distinguished Senior Research Professor at Gordon-Conwell Theological Seminary. He is the author of several books in which his evangelical theology engages with the modern world. He has taught at Trinity Evangelical Divinity School and has served as the Academic Dean at Gordon-Conwell Theological Seminary's Charlotte Campus.

[7] Cf. Martin Luther and his attempt to reform the Roman Catholic Church. I have found Eric Metaxas' study, *Martin Luther*, to be most helpful.

[8] Cf. Thomas Campbell, Alexander Campbell, Barton W. Scott, Leroy Garrett, cf. Foster, *et al*, eds., *The Stone-Campbell Movement*, Hughes, *Reviving the Ancient Faith*.

which Marva Dawn described as *dumbing down* our theology to the level of our post-modern cultural environment![9] Someone has described this tendency as the choice between *Sola Scriptura*[10] and *sola cultura,* with *sola cultura* winning out!

I close this postscript with a few pertinent comments on David Wells' pivotal study, *The Courage to Be Protestant: Reformation Faith in Today's World,* and his other challenging work *No Place for Truth: or Whatever Happened to Evangelical Theology?* Wells asks the thought provoking question "has something indeed happened to traditional theology and to modern churches that has changed the direction and focus of our Christian faith and worship?" I too fear that *something* has happened among contemporary Churches of Christ. In regard to his concept of fellowship and "Evangelicalism," Wells claims:

> Today, quite a few churches have made their peace with our affluent and postmodern culture. The customers want ease, comfort, and something that is both contemporary and easy on the mind. That is what they are getting. *The experience of reverence and awe has become quite rare.* And the consequence of all of this is that the center in evangelical faith is crumbling. That center was God and his Word.[11]

According to Wells, the evidence indicates that many contemporary pastors have abandoned their traditional role as *ministers of the Word* to become *therapists and "managers of the small enterprises we call churches."* Along with their parishioners, they

---

[9] Dawn, *Reaching Out*.

[10] I understand *Sola Scriptura* after the thought of Martin Luther as *theology and church practice grounded in Scripture Only* rather than grounded in church dogma, church tradition, or cultural interests and norms. I read this in similar fashion to Thomas Campbell (1809) who based his "church restoration plea" on his oft cited *Declaration and Address* which stated that we should speak where the Bible speaks and be silent where the Bible is silent in regard to church doctrine and theology. I fully recognize that church theology and worship should be relevant and sensitive to contemporary culture, but this is radically different from theology and worship being driven by or based on contemporary norms.

[11] Wells, *The Courage to Be Protestant,* emphasis mine, IAF.

have abandoned genuine theology and biblical truth in favor of the sort of inner-directed experiential, culturally relevant religion that now pervades Western society.

Specifically, Wells deplores the wholesale disappearance of biblical doctrine and theology in the church, the academy, and modern culture. Western culture as a whole, Wells argues, has been transformed by modernity, and the church has simply gone with the flow. The new environment in which we live, with its huge cities, triumphant capitalism, invasive technology, and pervasive amusements, has vanquished and homogenized the entire world. While the modern world has produced astonishing abundance, it has also taken a toll on the human spirit, emptying it of enduring meaning and morality.

Wells charges that seeking respite from the corrosive tendencies of modernity, people today have increasingly turned to religions and therapies centered on the self and cultural relevance. The shift has been from *Thou to me*, and from *Thou to cultural relevance*! Whether consciously or not, an increasing number of churches have taken the same path, refashioning their faith into a religion of the self and cultural relevance. They have been co-opted by modernity, have "sold their soul for a mess of pottage." According to Wells, they have lost the truth that God stands outside all human experience, in which God still summons sinners to repentance and belief regardless of their self-image, and that he calls his church to stand fast in *his word of truth* against the blandishments of a godless secular world.

Well's *No Place for Truth* is a contemporary cry, a clarion call to all church leaders to note well the crisis they have come to in capitulating to modernity, what a risk they are running by abandoning historic orthodoxy. It is provocative reading for scholars, ministers, seminary students, and all theologically concerned individuals.[12]

---

[12] Pertinent summary of relevant concerns and reviews relating to Wells' *No Place for Truth*.

I simply cannot escape reference to a few comments by renowned scholars and theologians who have read and been moved by *Well's No Place for Truth.*[13]

James Davis Hunter[14]: "In this book David Wells boldly nails his theses of biblical Christianity to the doors of modernity. This may be the most provocative book evangelical pastors and laypeople ever read."

Carl F. H. Henry[15]: "A penetrating appraisal of the state of religion in America, a discerning plea for its recovery of intellectual properties and an outline of new directions if evangelicalism is to escape cultural captivity."

Os Guinness[16]: "Well's trenchant analysis is a devastating CAT scan of American evangelism. Unless it is responded to as well as read, the diagnosis might as well be postmortem, for evangelicalism has no future if this condition is not remedied. Evangelicalism can only remain evangelical if it is passionately serious about truth and theology."

In view of my appreciation of David Wells' criticism of modern evangelicalism, and my heritage in the role of the Restoration Movement in many Churches of Christ, I find it necessary to clarify my understanding of Restoration Theology among

---

[13] Cf. the back cover of *No Place for Truth.*
[14] James Davison Hunter is an American sociologist who is the LaBrosse-Levinson Distinguished Professor of Religion, Culture, and Social Theory at the University of Virginia and the founder and executive director of UVA's Institute for Advanced Studies in Culture. Hunter is a prominent figure in the sociology of religion and the sociology of culture, with much of his work dedicated to the study of evangelicalism and cultural change. He is also notable for popularizing the term culture war.
[15] Carl Ferdinand Howard Henry was an American evangelical Christian theologian who provided intellectual and institutional leadership to the neo-evangelical movement in the mid-to-late 20th century. He was and still is widely published and respected in his criticism of much evangelical theology.
[16] Os Guinness is an English author and social critic. Guinness has written or edited more than 30 books that offer valuable insight into the cultural, political, and social contexts in which we all live.

Churches of Christ in the broader picture of Evangelical Theology.[17]

Evangelicalism and Evangelical Theology

Evangelicalism is a broad term used to define or explain conservative movements among Protestant churches which eschew synodal and creedal fellowship categories that define or limit Christian fellowship. The concept is based on a heavy emphasis of the plenary inspiration of Scripture, the origin or development of faith, a world lost in sin and needing regeneration, conversion, salvation, a spiritual new birth, and the role of the Holy Spirit in regeneration. Evangelical movements fall somewhere between a more liberal relationship with Scripture and an extreme literalist interpretation of Scripture. All claim the allegiance to *Sola Scriptura* with degrees of hermeneutic application.

A major thesis of Evangelical Theology hinges around the role of the Holy Spirit. Churches with a Calvinistic heritage hold that man in his natural state has a mind either spiritually destroyed or seriously impaired by sin, either inherited sin or personal sin. Before man in his unregenerate state is able to understand God's atonement his spiritual reasoning needs regeneration by God who through the initiative of the Holy Spirit regenerates this. Man's regenerated mind can then reflect on Scripture and be led by the regenerating power of the Holy Spirit through his regeneration, new birth, and sanctification.

A prominent feature in evangelical theology, faith is not the result of a rational reflection on *Sola Scripture,* but is a faith generated by the Holy Spirit. In an unfortunate misguided hermeneutic of Eph 2:8 it is argued that faith is the gift of God, not man's rational deliberations. The emphasis on the role of the Holy Spirit varies in different models of evangelicalism.

However, in all evangelical theology the Holy Spirit, the grace of God, and Spirit initiated faith plays a heavy role in redemption and regeneration.

---

[17] For a good discussion seeking to understand the relationship of Churches of Christ with Evangelical Theology I recommend William R. Baker, *Evangelicalism and the Stone-Campbell Movement,* and Robert D. Cornwall, "Evangelical," in Foster, *et al*, eds, *Encyclopedia of the Stone-Campbell Movement.*

Repentance and baptism in most views of evangelical theology are not understood to be regenerative but the result of a regenerated faith and new birth.

Churches of Christ Restorationist Thinking and Evangelical Theology

Most Churches of Christ, inclusive of Christian Churches, find their roots in the Stone-Campbell Restoration movement initiated in the USA by Thomas Campbell, 1809, his son Alexander Campbell, ca. 1820, and Barton W. Stone ca. 1820, in Philadelphia, Kentucky, Virginia, and the Great Awakening movement of that era.[18]

Restoration theology places great significance on God's gracious concern for humankind who are lost and estranged from God through sin. They place significant emphasis on restoring the church and church doctrine as found in Scripture. Out of his loving kindness and grace God provided redemption for man through his Son, Jesus the Messiah, who in atonement for man's sins died on a cross, redeeming mankind from slavery to sin, and uniting them together in one body in Christ through his death and resurrection. Restoration faith is thus understood to be the result of faithful preaching and hearing the Gospel message.

Faith, repentance, and baptism are understood to form the regenerative process in which God and the Holy Spirit create a new birth into the family of God. Baptism alone does not save nor regenerate the believer! It is God who saves and regenerates the believer through their obedient faith in Jesus' redeeming and atoning sacrifice on the cross. The regenerative power in baptism is the working of God through his Holy Spirit, not man's efforts! Cf. Acts 2:37-38; Col 2:10-14; Gal 3:24-29, Eph 2:4-10.

In keeping with the general mindset of evangelical theology, Christians in Churches of Christ share the view that mankind is estranged from God through sin and needs forgiveness. This forgiveness takes place through faith in the redeeming atonement of Jesus' death and redemption. Upon a rational faith in God and the redeeming work of Jesus on the cross the believer responds in

---

[18] For biographical resources cf. Foster, *et al*, eds., *Encyclopedia of the Stone-Campbell Movement*,.

repentance for sin and obedience in baptism *for* the remission of sin, at which point the believer is regenerated, experiences the new birth, and through the power of the Holy Spirit is forgiven and born into the family of God. The indwelling Holy Spirit abides within the believer empowering them to live lives that bring glory to God through Jesus and the church. Cf. Eph 3:14-21.

Common features with evangelical theology are grace, faith in *Sola Scriptura*, faith in Jesus' redeeming death and resurrection, a new regenerating birth in baptism, the work of the Holy Spirit in sanctification, and a dedicated life based on faith in sound doctrine seen as faithful teaching of Scripture, not credal systems.

Evangelical Theology, David Wells, and Ian Fair

Thus, I share with Wells an intense faith in Scripture and Scriptural doctrine as a basis for life in Christianity and the church. Likewise, I share concern for the decline of doctrine and faith in *Sola Scriptura*, and concern over the inroads of culture and a corporate mindset in the future of the church and evangelicalism. As a Restorationist I share concern for the restoration of church life based in Scripture, doctrine, and sound biblical hermeneutic and theology. I deplore the inroads of sociological motives and cultural norms in Christian theology and worship.

I trust the study I have pursued in this book reflects the same concerns I find in Wells' critical analysis of contemporary trends which I also see in many Churches of Christ in the USA. Time will tell!

A Preamble of Sorts

In order to set my concerns for a Theology of Worship in some form of historical-theological narrative I am inserting here an extract from David Wells' study, *The Courage to Be Protestant: Reformation Faith in Today's World*.[19] He sings my song although in a slightly different storyline or tune than mine! He writes:

---

[19] Wells, *The Courage to Be Protestant*, pp. 3-7.

I am beginning this story, not with the Book of Acts, or even with the birth of Protestantism. I am going back no further than the end of the Second World War (1939–1945). What took shape immediately after this war, both in Europe and in the United States, was a resurgence in evangelical believing. Here are the most immediate roots of contemporary evangelical believing.

Seven decades have now passed since this resurgence began. In this time, evangelicalism has matured in many ways and some of what has been achieved has been nothing less than spectacular. However, along with all of this astonishing growth there are also signs, as I have suggested, of internal weakness and decay. This is seen in many ways, but here I want to focus on just one of these. *It is the decline in the role that biblical doctrine once played.*[20] But this decline, of course, involves much more than just the doctrine itself. *It is really about a diminished interest in the Word of God in the life of the church. It is about not being able to hear that Word without hearing it as if it were endorsing our way of life today, our cultural expectations, and our priorities.* The reality, of course, is that the truth of God's Word is often in sharp antithesis to what is taken as being "normal" in our culture. *To hear this Word, then, is to see that the Christ of this Word is against the culture in quite a few important ways.* It is this sense of antithesis that has been lost. *Once this is lost we cannot hear God's Word on its own terms. We are hearing it as a "word" that comes from God but that, in fact, is partly coming from our own culture. We are therefore not meeting with God as he is but, rather, with him the way we want him to be.*

Most profoundly, then, what has also been diminished through our lost appetite for the teaching of Scripture is a vision of God in his greatness, in his transcendence and holiness, as he stands over against the world in its sinfulness. This is always what is secured in the

---

[20] Emphases here and below are mine, IAF.

church's understanding when doctrine has its proper place in Christian understanding. The reason is that God's truth comes from God and when it is heard as he gave it, it takes us back to our center, to God as triune, to God in his greatness. *To hear God's Word as the Word from this God is inevitably to become God-centered.* But it is this center that has become blurry, and this God-centeredness that is much scarcer. But let me begin where this resurgence itself began ...

There are still many who think evangelicals should be doctrinally shaped, who love the Word of God, who value biblical preaching, who want to be God-centered in their thought and life, who live upright lives, and who are not ashamed of their roots in the Reformation. They are the ones who are so important in sustaining the missionary enterprise today, and the ones in whom one finds an older, and quite admirable, piety.

It would be quite unrealistic to think that evangelicalism today could look exactly as it did fifty years ago, or a hundred, or five hundred. *At the same time, the truth by which it is constituted never changes because God, whose truth it is, never changes. There should therefore be threads of continuity that bind real Christian believing in all ages. It is some of those threads, I believe, that are now being lost.*

The result of this, then, was that beginning in the 1970s and 1980s two large constituencies in the evangelical coalition, the church marketers and the emergents, began to drift away. And each was capitalizing on what had become critical, in-house weaknesses. *The main weakness was that, unlike the fundamentalists, evangelicals have often sat a little loose on the institution of the church. The reason, of course, was that the place of Scripture was changing. The place of doctrinal thinking was becoming more uncertain. This gave the opening and, indeed, the freedom to the church marketers in the 1970s, 1980s, and 1990s to see building the church less in biblical terms and more as a venture in capitalism. As in any business venture, they began by identifying the market. Then they designed a product to meet the identified needs.*

But this was not the only outcome to a lost function of biblical authority. A different outcome was soon seen in the emergents, *who quickly showed that they were more culturally oriented intellectually than biblically disciplined.* For them, it quickly became a case of *sola cultura* rather than *sola scriptura*.

Thank you, David Wells, for so succinctly expressing and confirming my concerns!

Credits

I feel compelled to mention how deeply I am indebted to several outstanding scholars for the thoughts that I will be pursuing and outlining in this study. My summarization of their magisterial thoughts may not do them justice, but they certainly have pointed my thinking in a certain direction regarding theology, worship, and the Church. To mention one who immediately stands out, I am beholden to Gerhard Delling's definitive study, *Worship in the New Testament*. Delling in Chapter 1 writes:

> The New Testament knows that the heathen world, in whose midst it stands, also seeks to serve God (fn. Acts 17:23), erects altars to Him, recognizes in the presence of particular men the approach of the gods, and offers sacrifices. The New Testament acknowledges in heathen Worship an undertaking that is genuine according to its lights. It even states that in reality God is near to those who do not know Him (fn. Acts 17:22-27). *The New Testament, none the less, pronounces an adverse judgment on this Worship, yet not simply because it is inadequate but because it does not take God seriously at all, because it does not reach God because man, who has rendered himself guilty (fn. Rom 1:20 ff), can no more on his own initiative enter into relationship with God* (italics mine, IAF).[1]

I am also indebted to the following scholars and theologians whose writings and reflections on theology and worship have likewise challenged and engaged my thoughts and studies regarding the theology of worship: Oscar Cullmann, *Early Christian Worship* and *The Early Church*; Ralph P. Martin, *Worship in the Early Church*; Marva J. Dawn, *Reaching out Without Dumbing Down*; Franklin M. Segler and Randall Bradley, *Christian Worship: Its Theology and Practice*, Michael F. Bird, *Evangelical Theology*; Wayne Grudem, *Systematic Theology*; and David F.

---

[1] Delling, *Worship in the New Testament*, p. 1.

Wells, *The Courage to be Protestant, Reformation Faith in Today's World.*²

I am deeply grateful to six of my former professors and two colleagues in the academy of scholars at Abilene Christian University; the first, Professor Abraham J. Malherbe who taught us to approach the biblical text with a sound biblical critical exegetical model. In Malherbe's classes careless and incomplete scholarship was not acceptable! Failure to set and maintain exegetical studies deeply within a biblical critical process was unthinkable and soundly criticized. I was indeed blessed by being able to study under Professor Malherbe, a fellow South African, who in his academic career reached the pinnacle of international respect and academic success. I take the liberty here of including a comment from a tribute to Malherbe by a highly respected international scholar, Professor Cilliers Breytenback of Humbolt-Universität in Berlin.

Professor Breytenback:

> With great pride I remember the meeting of the Studiorum Novi Testament Societas in 1989. The late Abe Malherbe, then still Buckingham Professor for New Testament Textual Criticism and Literature at Yale Divinity School, gave a main paper. The Societas (SNTS) is the elite organization of NT scholars in the world. And you must have written two scholarly books to be considered as a new member. Since I became a member in 1987 and attended the first conference in 1988 in the UK, this was my second meeting listening to papers from senior scholars, primarily from Europe, the UK and occasionally the USA.
>
> *But that summer was special. Abe gave a superb, very learned paper on "'Pastoral Care' in the Thessalonian Church." And I was proud. Here was somebody from South Africa, like me, somebody from Huguenot family like my mother's family, Cilliers. And this was somebody to whom I could speak in my mother tongue Afrikaans. And he gave the best paper on the conference.*

---

² For a more thorough list of scholarly works that have guided my thinking cf. the more detailed Bibliography listed below.

> *With great acumen he took the audience through the Greek background of the expressions, conceptions and rhetorical strategies of Paul's first letter to the Thessalonians ... The unforgettable display of sophisticated learning by Malherbe at the SNTS is something the Christian institutions that supported his career can take pride in ... (notably Abilene Christian University).*
>
> *In 2000 I was in South Africa and invited to join the academic procession of the convocation of the University of Pretoria at the main event of the annual graduation. The honorary guest was the seventy-year-old Abraham Malherbe: the degree of Doctor Divinitatis honoris causa (the highest honor an academic community can bestow) was conferred upon him by the University of Pretoria.[3]*

Alongside Professor Malherbe stands Professor Everett Ferguson, who like Malherbe was a graduate with the PhD from Harvard University. Ferguson is an internationally recognized historian of early church life. Ferguson insisted that scholars of the New Testament keep their studies enriched by the background and foreground of the New Testament text. Ferguson left a deep impression on me and countless other fellow students and colleagues. When we enter the field of early church history few today equal the monumental scholarly studies and writings of Professor Ferguson. A glance at the bibliography of his lifetime work and this study will reveal the depth and breadth of Professor Ferguson's work and my indebtedness to him. In appreciation of the internationally recognized works of Professor Ferguson I am also taking the liberty of including a few comments of international scholars regarding Professor Ferguson's lifetime of work. I might emphasize here that what I am attempting in this study lies deeply rooted in the specific field and expertise of Professor Ferguson's monumental, detailed, and scholarly studies.

Professor Alan Kreider, Anabaptist Mennonite Biblical Seminary on Ferguson's *The Early Church and Today*:

---

[3] Professor Cilliers Breytenback, "Abraham Malherbe," *Restoration Quarterly*, vol. 56/3, 2014.

> "The Early Church and Today is a fitting monument to Everett Ferguson's distinguished career. "Ferguson is one of his generation's premier patristics scholars, and this book shows why – Unrivalled knowledge of early Christian writings; judicious interpretation; orderly presentation ..."

Professor Pauline Allen, University of Pretoria, South Africa, regarding Ferguson's *Early Church*

> "This is a fine collection of integrated essays produced by an internationally distinguished scholar in the field of Christian studies ..."

Professor Jeff Christian, Distinguished Professor of Early Christian Literature, Abilene Christian University,

> "The academic world knows Everett Ferguson as one of the finest patristic scholars of our time. Everett's friends and community of faith know him as a deeply committed churchman ..."

Professor Lee Martin McDonald, Acadia Divinity College, Nova Scotia, President of the Institute for Biblical Research:

> "Ferguson's erudite collection of articles on the church, its history, mission, and ministries is the work of a master scholar who is well informed, articulate, and sensitive to the needs and concerns relevant to the church ..."

I am likewise thankful to Professor Neil R. Lightfoot, Distinguished Professor of New Testament at Abilene Christian University who stressed that scholars should always do hermeneutics with a keen awareness of the several contexts of the text: historical, grammatical, literary, sociological, and theological.

Professor Tom Olbricht, Distinguished Professor of Biblical Theology, Abilene Christian University and Pepperdine University, taught us to think theologically rather than simply in a book, chapter, and verse concordance approach.

Professor J W Roberts professor of Greek and New Testament at Abilene Christian University instilled in us a keen awareness of working primarily out of the Greek text.

Professor Anthony Lee Ash emphasized not overlooking the Old Testament in understanding the New.

Professor Mark Hamilton, Distinguished Professor of Old Testament and Ancient Near East languages at Abilene Christian University emboldened me to have another look at the Old Testament.

Professor Andrei Orlov, Distinguished Professor of Old Testament and Intertestamental Theology and Jewish Mysticism at Marquette University challenged me to see Judaism and Christianity through the lens of Mystical Judaism and not simply through contemporary traditional Christian and Jewish lenses.

When attempting to write a theology of worship we have an almost 2000-year history of resources available. Regarding this I find solace in a comment by Professor N. T. Wright of St. Andrew's University in his magisterial work *Paul and the Faithfulness of God*. Wright is obviously not engaging the topic of Worship which is the burden of this study, but his sentiments regarding biblical research and resources are *apropos*.

> *The subject we are here investigating is of course immense. So is the body of scholarship that surrounds it. This is nothing new. Virgil, writing over two thousand years ago to the emperor Augustus, declared that his subject was so vast that he must have been almost out of his mind to have begun the work in the first place; and that was long before printing and the internet. Modern scholars in many fields express what I have found day after day in writing the present work: The bibliography ... is enormous, and I could have increased the size of this book two- or threefold by debating divergent views. In every paragraph, if not in every sentence, I could have argued explicitly for or against the opinions of several scholars. I recall in this connection the dour Scot who was assigned the three-day task of packing up my books when we moved from Auckland Castle to the Fife coast in the summer of 2010. 'What I cannae get my mind around,' he declared, 'is – all them books, all on the one subject!' There is a serious point here. We are long past the time when one could read, or even skim-read, 'everything'. As in many other fields, so with biblical scholarship, one has to choose certain conversation partners,*

and that is what I have done in this book. There are moments when, at particularly crucial turns in the road, I have tried to be a little more comprehensive, but for much of the time I have concentrated on expounding themes and passages with a fairly light touch on the footnotes. I apologize to friends, colleagues and indeed experts in the field whose work receives less attention than I would have liked.[4]

Wright adds:

> *Another problem with any thematic treatment of any writer is the necessary repetition. Either one must write a set of commentaries on all the texts from end to end, in which case one must repeat the necessary general statements on key topics every time they come up (or collect them into 'excursuses'); or one must expound one's chosen themes, in which case one must perforce repeat elements of the exegesis of this or that passage. I have chosen the latter route ... I regret the occasional overlap, but those who come to this book for a treatment of a particular topic may be glad to find the relevant material in one place.*[5]

I find solace in other shared concerns with Wright in that I am given to repetition especially regarding significant biblical texts, but I find this necessary to keep the topics discussed related to their theological roots, and in dynamic tension with the relevant biblical texts.

On a totally different level, but equally important, I am indebted to my faithful copy editor, Christi Romeo, who proofread the manuscript on too many occasions, all necessary, in an effort to make my words and thoughts readable and reasonable. Grammatical, theological, and typological "infractions" are all mine! Thank you, Christi!

To God be the glory for ever and ever!

---

[4] Wright, *Paul and the Faithfulness of God*, Kindle locations 553-566.
[5] Wright, *Paul and the Faithfulness of God*, Kindle locations 570-576.

Bibliography

The following bibliography will provide some idea of those scholars and theologians who have challenged me and shaped my thinking. The list of resources includes books on doing Theology, books on Worship, commentaries related to Worship, and Lexicons and Theological Dictionaries.

In the references to these sources in the body of the study I will merely refer to the author unless he/she has authored more than one book. In that case I may merely present a brief title to the book. On occasion when I think this will be helpful, I will document fully the source in a footnote.

I find support in Wright's comments above that the library of resources covering religious and theological topics is enormous and far beyond the scope of this study or bibliography, but I hope the references provided will enrich our study of the topic of a theology of Christian worship.

General Bibliography

Allison, Greg R., *Historical Theology*, Grand Rapids: Zondervan, 2011.

Anderson, Hugh, *The Gospel of Mark*, Grand Rapids: Wm. B. Anderson, 1976.

Aricheas, Daniel C., and Howard A. Hilton, *1 Timothy: A Handbook on Paul's First Letter to Timothy*, UBS, 1995.

Arnold, Clinton E., *Ephesians*, Grand Rapids: Zondervan Exegetical Commentary on the New Testament, Kindle Edition, 2011.

Ash, Anthony Lee, *Pray Always: What the New Testament Teaches About Prayer*, Abilene: Leafwood Publishers, 2008.

Baker, William R. ed., *Evangelicalism and the Stone-Campbell Movement*, Downers Grove: InterVarsity Press, 2002.

Bales, James, *Instrumental Music and New Testament Worship*, Searcy: James D. Bales, 1973.

Barth, Karl, *Protestant Theology in the Nineteenth Century*, London: SCM Press, 1972.

Barth, Karl, *Evangelical Theology*, London: Collins Fontana, 1965.

Barth, Markus, *Colossians*, The Anchor Yale Bible Commentaries, 1994.

Barth, Markus, *Ephesians 4-6*, The Anchor Yale Bible Commentaries, 1960.

Bauckham, R. J., *2 Peter, Jude*, Word Biblical Commentary, Dallas: Word, Incorporated, 1998.

Beale, G. K., *A New Testament Biblical Theology: The Unfolding of the Old in the New*, Grand Rapids: Baker Academic, 2013.

Beasley-Murray, G. R., *Baptism in the New Testament*, Grand Rapids: Wm. B. Eerdmans, 1962.

Beasley-Murray, George, R., *John*, Word Biblical Commentary, Dallas: Word Books, 1999.

Bird, Michael F. *Colossians and Philemon*, Cambridge: Lutterworth Press, 2009.

Bird, Michael F., *Evangelical Theology: A Biblical and Systematic Introduction*, Grand Rapids: Zondervan, 2013.

Bloesch, Donald G., *Essentials of Evangelical Theology*, Vols 1 and 2, New York: Harper and Row, 1978.

Blomberg, Craig, *1 Corinthians*: *The NIV Application Commentary*, Grand Rapids: Zondervan, Kindle Edition, 1994.

Bock, Darrell L. *Acts*, Grand Rapids: Baker Academics, 2007.

Bowden, John, *Karl Barth*, London: SCM Press, 1971.

Bratcher, Robert G. and Eugene Nida, *Handbook on Paul's Letter to the Ephesians*, New York: United Bible Societies, 1982.

Bruce, F. F., *The New Testament Documents, Are They Reliable?* Stellar Books, 2013, originally published by Tyndale Publishers, 1959.

Bruce, F. F., *The Book of Acts*, Grand Rapids: Wm. B. Eerdmans, 1988.

Bruce, F. F., *The Epistle to the Ephesians*, Kindle Edition, 1939-1946.

Brueggemann, Walter, *Old Testament Theology,* Nashville: Abingdon Press, 2008.

Carson, D. A., *The Gospel of John*, Grand Rapids: Wm B. Eerdmans, 1991.

Charlesworth. M. J., *Anselm of Canterbury, Proslogion*, trans. in The Major Works, ed. Brian Davies and G. R. Evans, NY: Oxford University Press, 1998.

Ciampa, Roy E. and Brian S. Rosner, *The First Letter to the Corinthians,* Grand Rapids: Eerdmans Publishing, Kindle Edition, 2010.

Cullmann, Oscar and F. Leenhardt, *Essays on the Lord's Supper*, Lutterworth Press, 1958.

Cullmann, Oscar, *Early Christian Worship*, London: SCM Press, 1953, 1973.

Culver, Robert, *Systematic Theology: Biblical and Historical*, Ross-Shire: Mentor, 2005.

Davis, W. D., and Dale C. Allison, *Matthew*, Vol. II, Edinburgh: T & T Clark, 1991.

Dawn, Marva, *Reaching Out without Dumbing Down: A Theology of Worship for This Urgent Time*, Grand Rapids: Wm. B. Eerdmans, 1995.

Delling, Gerhard, *Worship in the New Testament*, Philadelphia: Westminster Press, 1962.

Donaldson J and A. C. Coxe, *The Lord's Teaching through the Twelve Apostles to the Nations, The Ante-Nicene Fathers*, Vol 7, New York: Christian Literature Company.

Dunn, James D. G., *Romans 9-6*, Dallas: Word Publishing, 1988.

Dunn, James D. G., *The Epistles to the Colossians and to Philemon*, Grand Rapid: Wm. B. Eerdmans, 1996.

Ellingworth, Paul and Howard Hatton, *A Handbook on Paul's First Letter to the Corinthians*, New York: United Bible Societies, 1995.

Fair, Ian A., *The Theology of Wolfhart Pannenberg as a Reaction to Dialectical Theology*, PhD Dissertation, University of Natal, South Africa, 1974.

Fair, Ian A., *Conquering with Christ*, ACU Press, 2011.

Fee, Gordon D., *God's Empowering Presence*, Grand Rapids: Baker Academic, 1994.

Fee, Gordon D., *Paul, the Spirit, and the People of God*, Baker Publishing Group, 1994.

Fee, Gordon D., *The First Epistle to the Corinthians*, Eerdmans, 1987.

Ferguson, Everett, *A Cappella Music in the Public Worship of the Church*, Abilene: Biblical Research Press, 1972.

Ferguson, Everett, *Early Christians Speak*, Abilene: ACU Press, 3rd ed., 1999.

Ferguson, Everett, *Early Christians Speak*, Vols 1 and 2, Abilene: ACU Press, 1971, 2002.

Ferguson, Everett, Jack P. Lewis, and Earle West, *The Instrumental Music Issue*, Nashville: Gospel Advocate, 1987.

Ferguson, Everett, *The Church of Christ: A Biblical Ecclesiology for Today*, Grand Rapids: Wm. B. Eerdmans, 1996.

Ferguson, Everett, *The Church of Christ: A Biblical Theology for Today,* Grand Rapids: Wm. B. Eerdmans, 1996.

Ferguson, Everett, *The Early Church and Today*, Abilene: ACU Press, 2012.

Ferguson, Everett, *Baptism in the Early Church*, Grand Rapids: William B. Eerdmans, 2009.

Fitzmyer, Joseph, *1 Corinthians*, The Anchor Yale Bible Commentaries, New Haven: University Press, 2008.

Garland, David E., *1 Corinthians*, Grand Prairie: Baker Academic, 2003.

Grenz, Stanley J. and Roger E. Olson, *Who Needs Theology*, Downer Grove: InterVarsity Press, 1966.

Groeschel, Benedict J., and James Monti, *In the Presence of Our Lord*, Huntington: Our Sunday Visitor Publishing Division, 1997.

Grudem, Wayne, *Systematic Theology*, Grand Rapids: Zondervan, 2009.

Gundry, Robert H., *Matthew*, Grand Rapids: Wm. B. Eerdmans, 1982.

Guthrie, Donald, *New Testament Theology*, "Introduction," Downers Grove: InterVarsity Press, 1981.

Hagner, Donald A., *Mathew 1-13,* Word Biblical Commentary, Dallas: Word Books, 1993.

Hagner, Donald A., *Mathew 14-28,* Word Biblical Commentary, Dallas: Word Books, 1995.

Hartwell, Herbert, *The Theology of Karl Barth: An Introduction*, London: Duckworth, 1964.

Hicks, John Mark, *Come to the Table: Revisioning the Lord's Supper*, Abilene: Leafwood Press, 2002.

Hicks, John Mark, Johnny Melton, and Bobby Valentine, *A Gathered People, Revisioning the Assembly as Transforming Encounter*, Abilene: Leafwood, 2007.

Hicks John Mark & Greg Taylor, *Down to the River to Pray*, Siloam Springs: Leafwood Publishers, 2004.

Higgins, A. J. B., *The Lord's Supper in the New Testament*, SCM Press, 1952.

Hill, David, *The Gospel of Matthew*, Grand Rapids: Wm. B. Eerdmans, 1972.

Hoehner, Harold W., *Ephesians*, Grand Rapids: Baker Academic, 2002.

Holloway, Gary, Randall J. Harris, and Mark C. Black, *Theology Matters: Answers to the Church Today*, Joplin: College Press, 1998, 2000.

Holladay, Carl R., *Acts: A Commentary*, The New Testament Library, Louisville: Westminster John Knox Press, Kindle Edition, 2016.

Jones, Michael, *Theology of Worship*, Amazon Digital Services, 2014.

Keener, Craig S., *A Commentary on the Gospel of Matthew*, Grand Rapids: Wm. B. Eerdmans, 1999.

Kelly, J. N. D., *Early Christian Doctrines*, Adam & Charles Black, 1968.

Kitchen, Martin, *Ephesians*, London: Routledge, 1994.

Kostenberger, Andreas J. *A Theology of John's Gospel and Letters: The Word, the Christ, the Son of God* (Biblical Theology of the New Testament Series), Zondervan, Kindle Edition, 2009.

Kung, Hans, *The Church*, London: Burns and Oates, 1968.

Lea, Thomas D. and Hayne P. Griffin, *1, 2 Timothy and Titus*, New Century Commentaries, Broadman & Holman, 1992.

Lewis, C. S., *Essay Collection and Other Short Pieces*, ed. Lesley Walmsley, London: HarperCollins, 2000.

Lightfoot, Neil R., *How We Got the Bible*, Grand Rapids: Baker Books, 2003.

Lincoln, Andrew T., *Ephesians*, Word Biblical Commentary, Dallas: Word Books, 1990.
Lüdermann, Gerd, *The Acts of the Apostles*, New York: Prometheus Books, 2005.
Macarthur, John F., *John: Jesus? The Word, the Messiah, the Son of God*, Macarthur Bible Studies Book 6, Thomas Nelson, 2015.
Marshall, I. Howard, *New Testament Theology*, Downers Grove: InterVarsity Press, 2004.
Marshall, I. H. *Acts*, Downers Grove: Inter-Varsity Press, 1980.
Marshall, I. H., *The Gospel of Luke*, Grand Rapids: Wm. B. Eerdmans, 1978.
Marshall, I. H., *The Pastoral Epistles*, T. & T. Clark, 1999.
Marshall, I. Howard, *Last Supper and Lord's Supper*, Grand Rapids: Wm. B. Eerdmans, 1980.
Martin, Ralph P., *Worship in the Early Church*, Grand Rapids: Wm. B. Eerdmans, 1964, 2000.
Meade James K., *Biblical Theology*, Louisville: Westminster John Knox, 2007.
Murphey-O'Conner, Jerome, *Keys to First Corinthians*, Oxford England: Oxford University Press, 2009.
Metaxas, Eric, *Martin Luther*, New York: Viking, 2017.
Moloney, Francis J. *Sacra Pagina: The Gospel of John*, Liturgical Press, 2005.
Moltmann, Jürgen, *The Church in the Power of the Spirit: A Contribution to Messianic Ecclesiology*, New York: Harper and Row, 1977.
Mounce, William D., *Pastoral Epistles*, Word Biblical Commentary, Nashville: Thomas Nelson, 2,000.
Moo, Douglas J., *The Letters to the Colossians and to Philemon*, Pillar New Testament Commentary, Eerdmans Publishing, Kindle Edition, 2008.
Morris, Leon, *1 Corinthians*, InterVarsity Press, 1985.
Moule, C. F. D., *Worship in the New Testament*, Richmond: John Knox Press, 1967.
Mounce, Robert H., *Romans*, Nashville: Broadman & Hollman, 1995.
Mounce, William D., *Pastoral Epistles*, Word Books, 2000.

Naisbitt, John, *Megatrends: Ten Directions Transforming Our Lives*, Warner Books, 1982.

National Geographic: *Great Religions of the World,* 1971.

Noss, John B., *Man's Religions*, New York: Macmillan Publishing Co., 1974.

O'Brien, Peter, *The Letter to the Ephesians*, Grand Rapids: Wm. B, Eerdmans, Kindle Edition, 1999.

Pannenberg, Wolfhart, *Systematic Theology*, Vol. 1, Grand Rapids: Wm. B. Eerdmans, 1988.

Parrinder, Geoffrey, *Man and His Gods*, New York: Hamlyn Publishing Co., 1971.

Peterson, David, *Engaging with God, A Biblical Theology of Worship*, Downers Grove: IVP Academic, 1992.

Polhill, J. B., *Acts*, Nashville: Broadman & Holman Publishers, 1992.

Reiling, J. and J. L. Swellengrebel, *Translators Handbook of the Gospel of Luke*, United Bible Society, 1971.

Roberts, J. W., *Letters to Timothy*, R. B. Sweet, 1964.

Sayer, George, *Jack: A Life of C. S. Lewis*, Wheaten, Crossway Books. Lewis, 1988.

Segler, Franklin M. and Randall Bradley, *Christian Worship: Its Theology and Practice*, Nashville: Broadman and Holman, 2006.

Shelly, Rubel, *Sing His Praise! A Case for A Cappella Music as Worship Today*, Nashville: 20th Century Christian, 1987.

Smith, Ralph L., *Micah–Malachi*, Dallas: Word Incorporated, 1998.

Soulen, Richard N., and R. Kendall Soulen, *Handbook of Biblical Criticism*, Atlanta; John Knox Press, 1976, 2011.

Spence-Jones, H. D. M., ed., *Ephesians,* Pulpit Commentary, London; New York: Funk & Wagnall's Company, 1909.

Stone, Howard W. and James O. Duke, *How to Think Theologically*, Minneapolis: Fortress Press, 1996.

Swellengrebel, Reiling, *Translators Handbook of the Gospel of Luke*, New York: United Bible Society, 1971.

The Didache: The Lord's Teaching through the Twelve Apostles to the Nations. In the Anti-Nicene Fathers, (Vol. 7, pp. 379–380). Buffalo, NY: Christian Literature Company.

Thielman, Frank, *Ephesians*, Grand Rapids: Baker Academic, 2010.

Thiselton, Anthony C., *The First Epistle to the Corinthians*, Eerdmans, 2000.

Torrance, James B., *Worship, Community, and the Triune God of Grace*, Downers Grove: IVP Academic, 1996.

Towner, Philip, *The Letters to Timothy and Titus*, Eerdmans, 2006.

van Roo, William A., *The Christian Sacrament*, Roma: Pontificia Univ. Gregoriana. 1992.

Wagner, C. Peter, *The Book of Acts*, Grand Rapids: Baker Publishing Group, 2014

Wainwright, Geoffrey and Karen B. Westerfield Tucker, *The Oxford History of Christian Worship*, New York: The Oxford University Press, 2005.

Webber, Robert E., *Worship Old and New,* Grand Rapids: Zondervan, Kindle Edition, 1994.

Wells, David F., *The Courage to be Protestant: Reformation Faith in Today's World*, Grand Rapids: Wm. B. Eerdmans, 2017.

Wells, David, F., *No Place for Truth: or Whatever Happened to Evangelical Theology?* Grand Rapids: Wm. B. Eerdmans, 1994.

White, James T., *A Brief History of Christian Worship*, Nashville: Abingdon Press, 1993.

White, James T., *Introduction to Christian Worship*, Nashville: Abingdon Press, 1980, 2000.

Willimon, William H., *Word, Water, Wine and Bread*, Valley Ford: Judson Press, 1980.

Wilson, A. N., *C. S. Lewis*, New York: Fawcett Columbine, 1990.

Wright, N. T., *Paul and the Faithfulness of God,* Minneapolis: Fortress Press, 2013.

Wright, N. T., *Paul, A Biography*, Harper Collins, 2018.

Lexicons, Grammars, and Theological Dictionaries

Armentrout, Don S., *The Episcopal Dictionary of the Bible: A User-Friendly Reference for Episcopalians*, Church Publishing, 2000.

Bauer, Walter, *A Greek English Lexicon of the New Testament and Other Early Christian Literature*, revised by F. Wilber Gingrich and Frederick W. Danker, translated by William F. Arndt and F. Wilbur Gingrich, Cambridge: University of Chicago Press, 1957, 1979.

Blass, F., A. Debrunner, Robert Funk, *A Grammar of the New Testament*, 1961.

Bromiley, Geoffrey W., "Theology," *Baker's Dictionary of Theology*, Grand Rapids: Baker Book House, 1983.

Brown, Colin, Ed., *The New International Dictionary of New Testament Theology*, 3 vols, Zondervan, 1971.

Brown, Callum G., *What was the Religious Crisis of the 1960s?* Journal of Religious History Vol. 34, No. 4, December 2010. *Conclusion, secularism and religious decline*!

Brown, Callum G. *The Death of Christian Britain: Understanding Secularisation, 1800-2000*, N York: Routledge, 2009.

Dana, H. E. and Julius R. Mantey, *A Manual Grammar of the Greek New Testament*, 1957.

Foster, Douglas A., *et al*, eds., *Encyclopedia of the Stone-Campbell Movement*, Grand Rapids: Wm. B. Eerdmans, 2004.

Kittel, Gerhard, *Theological Dictionary of the New Testament*. Ed. G. W. Bromiley & G. Friedrich, electronic ed., Grand Rapids, MI: Eerdmans, 1964.

Richardson, Alan, *A Dictionary of Christian Theology*, London: SCM Press, 1969.

Scott, Liddell, *A Greek–English Dictionary*, Oxford: The Clarendon Press, 1958.

Swanson, James, *Dictionary of Biblical Languages with Semantic Domains: Greek New Testament,* electronic ed., Oak Harbor: Logos Research Systems, Inc., 1997.

The Anchor Bible Dictionary, Ed. David Noel Freedman, Doubleday, 1992.

The Shorter Oxford English Dictionary, Oxford: The Claredon Press, 3rd ed., 1972.

Zodhiates, Spiros, *The Complete Word Study Dictionary: New Testament*, Chattanooga: AMG Publishers, 1993.

Chapter 1: Some Initial Thoughts

Perhaps it might help those who do not know me, or the church in which I worship God, for me to introduce myself! I am a member of a fellowship of Christians who identify themselves as Churches of Christ in the heritage of the Stone-Campbell Restoration Movement which began in Scotland in the 18th century and took root in the early 19th century in the eastern regions of the United States of America. Similar Churches of Christ are found in almost every nation or world region.

Churches of Christ have no formal written creed and seek to find their faith-roots solely in Scripture. Churches of Christ identify themselves with the Restoration Movement that began in Scotland and Ireland which rejected being bound by synodal dogmatic religious creeds in favor of the freedom of individual conscience formed by biblical principles. Originally they were part of a 1733 Scottish Seceder church movement which withdrew from the Presbyterian General Assembly.[1] This movement was essentially a cry for religious freedom; freedom from religious domination by church structures such as the Roman Catholic Church, the Church of England, and other Protestant denominations which were rigidly controlled by their creeds and confessions of faith. In essence, the Restoration Movement was a "Back to the Bible movement" along the lines of Martin Luther's *Sola Scriptura* thinking.

Consequently, Churches of Christ today desire to model themselves on nothing other than Scriptural principles, the church promised by Jesus at Matt 16:18 and established by the Apostles' mission enterprise in response to Jesus' commission at Matt 28:18-20. The liturgy and practices of Churches of Christ are reflected in the book of Acts and the 1st century canonical "apostolic"[2] epistles and Gospels. Churches of Christ believe that this

---

[1] Keith B. Huey, "Seceders," *Encyclopedia of the Stone-Campbell Movement*, pp. 679f.
[2] By *apostolic* I infer epistles and Gospels written by the apostles of Jesus and disciples closely associated with those apostles, for example Luke, James, and Jude.

Scripturally based principle is the primary foundation and motivation of the faith, worship liturgy, and practical Christian life. We recognize that we have not always been faithful to this commitment, but humbly desire to be churches modelled on the biblical principles appropriately determined by sound exegetical study of the biblical text.

Churches of Christ are far from perfect and like all churches have in their history, even in their present religious practices, have too often drifted too far from their roots in Scripture. However, it is our prayer and desire to be biblically and theologically grounded with roots deeply embedded in Scripture. We believe in the priesthood of all believers, notably in the freedom to study and interpret Scripture without the control of the church or any synod of the church. We do believe that Scripture should be studied in a disciplined manner that honors the divinely inspired nature and purpose of Scripture (cf 2 Tim 3:14-17).

We also conduct several other kinds of meetings or gatherings during the week such as Bible classes, prayer groups, small study groups, and fellowship occasions. We aspire to be a *missional church*[3] deeply engaged in God's *Missio Dei*[4] through ministries that reach out beyond the confines of the local congregation, reaching out into all the world to those who do not know Christ.

In our congregational worship assemblies, we celebrate the Lord's Supper every Sunday, have prayers, Scripture readings, sermons, take up contributions, and sing "psalms, hymns, and spiritual songs" to the Lord. In most congregations of the Church of Christ world-wide the practice is to sing *acappella*,[5] which means without the accompaniment of musical instruments.

---

[3] *Missional* as I am using the term means being engaged in planting and establishing churches wherever the gospel of Christ needs proclaiming.

[4] The term *Missio Dei* is a Latin expression literally meaning the mission of God but in theological terms connotes taking up the mission of God of spreading his kingdom on earth as it is in heaven.

[5] The word *acappella* from *a cappella* literally means *as in the chapel* but by implication means singing in worship without the accompaniment of musical instruments. This point will be discussed in some detail in a later chapter titled Singing in the Worship Assembly. The term *acappella* is sometimes spelled *acapella* depending on individual preference.

Regarding our singing in the church's worship assemblies on Sunday, as mentioned above, most Churches of Christ sing unaccompanied by a musical instrument. Some of our members and congregations consider singing accompanied by an instrument or instruments to be a salvation issue. However, even in my personal commitment to singing *acappella* I make no judgment on others who sing accompanied by an instrument, and hopefully leave such decisions to Jesus to whom the church ultimately belongs. It will become apparent as the study progresses that singing accompanied by an instrument in my view cannot be sustained on biblical and theological principles and is driven more by sociological and cultural influences than by biblical teachings.

Most Churches of Christ in my acquaintance sing *acappella* because their understanding of the relevant Scriptures calls for rational instructional vocal singing, and according to our understanding of ecclesiastical history this is how churches of Christ in the first 700 years of Christianity sang in their assemblies. In a recent scholarly article in the *Restoration Quarterly* Professor Tom Olbricht has argued that:

> In most churches transplanted from Europe to America in the seventeenth and eighteenth centuries, the music of choice was acapella. Not until after 1800 did musical accompaniment enter the worship of these denominations … the preferred music in the majority of the American churches in 1800 was acapella.[6]

In keeping with the centuries old practice which was deeply grounded in biblical roots, most Churches of Christ world-wide have chosen to continue this biblical practice of singing *acappella* in Sunday, first day of the week (Acts 20:7) worship assemblies in which the Lord's Supper is celebrated.[7]

---

[6] Thomas H. Olbricht, "Acapella Singing in Early American Churches," *Restoration Quarterly*, vol. 57, # 2, 2015.

[7] To differentiate from other occasions of worship and devotion which might occur on any day of the week I will reference the formal worship of the church as the worship of a congregation of God in which singing, scripture reading, prayers, a sermon, and the celebration of the Lord's Supper or Eucharist are experienced.

Thus, in my understanding of formal worship singing *acappella* appears to be a ministry or practice set in deep biblical and theological reflection grounded in a sound biblical critical exegetical analysis of Scripture.

Although I include a chapter or two on singing in the worship assembly in this study, this book is not simply about singing in the worship assembly! I have mentioned the above few comments on singing in order to introduce the reader to where I stand regarding worship o*n the Lord's Day in congregational worship assemblies.*[8]

As stated in the previous paragraph, his book is not simply about singing in the worship assembly. It is about the very nature and theology of the worship assembly of which singing is only one aspect, although in my opinion an important one. I hope to establish the fact in this study that whereas *what* we do in worship is extremely important, *how* we do this and *why* we do this is of greater theological significance and forms the focus of this study.

Recently Dr. Douglas Foster, a professor of church history[9] and keynote speaker at a church elder and leadership seminar in Dallas, Texas, called Elderlink, was asked to address singing in the history of Churches of Christ in the USA. He introduced his discussion to the topic of church music *in the context of the worship assembly* with an insightful observation! He remarked that any discussion on church music and singing should flow out of, and be grounded in, a well-defined theology of worship. I hope in this study to flesh out such a theology of worship.

---

[8] I have emphasized this expression to draw attention to the fact that I am not discussing other forms of gatherings in which the church may engage even though I am of the guarded opinion regarding how far this singing practice should be taken. I recognize that religious concerts may be considered as worship occasions, but I find their dynamic to be different from the formal Lord's Day worship assembly *in which the Eucharist is celebrated* and God and Christ are the focus of the worship. I fully recognize that in the Christian life there are some grey areas in which charity and freedom are necessary.

[9] Dr. Foster is a professor of Restoration History and Director of the Center for Restoration Studies at the College of Biblical Studies, Abilene Christian University.

In keeping with this sentiment, it seems profoundly important to me that in the context of any discussion of worship, or any activity relating to the church worship assembly, whether it be the Lord's Supper, preaching, prayer, contributing, or singing, our thoughts should be grounded in a firm understanding and commitment to a biblically critical theology of worship and church. It is with this in mind that I have approached this study, seeking a theological foundation to worship.

I will repeatedly stress in this book that I am speaking of a *biblical* theology of worship in the church assembly and not of an *anthropological, sociological* or a *culturally driven* philosophy[10] of worship. Each of these terms needs clarification before I begin to unravel what I and others mean by a *theology of worship*.

By speaking of an *anthropological, sociological*, or *culturally driven* frame of worship I am addressing the *determining factors that drive or shape the worship*. In an *anthropological* approach to worship the *focus or concern is on the human side of the equation*; that is, *man and his needs and wishes are the focus* of the worship such as in an *evangelistic or seeker assembly*. The concern or driving factor of *anthropological seeker* services is decisively to attract and hold the attention of the persons attending the service *in an effort to reach out to them*. *The audience is the focus of the worship* while the human is the *practitioner* of the worship. Concern for the ones present is undoubtedly a noble concern! One certainly cannot criticize such a concern and I will say more to this point below! I am reminded of the anthropological concerns of David A. Wells' criticism of modern evangelical churches and theology, which I mentioned above in my Postscript, and share.

In a *theologically shaped or driven* worship service the aim is to *reach out toward God*, to hear God, and to "sing" praise *di-

---

[10] Rather than using the term *philosophy* one could use the term *theology* of worship here, but I believe that would be misleading since an anthropological or sociologically perceived theory or philosophy of worship is not strictly a theological approach to worship! Certainly, the worship of the people worshipping God needs to be *culturally and socially relevant*, but the direction of the worship is from theology to culture, not culture to theology.

rected to God hopefully to refocus the minds and lives of those attending the service on God. God is the focus of the worship and the human is the practitioner in the worship. Hang in with me as below we work through this understanding of worship!

While I certainly am not opposed to evangelistic outreach seeker services it will become apparent as I develop the thoughts of this study that since the focus of the evangelistic outreach assembly or seeker assembly is on attracting the attention of the *visitor* or *attendee* of the assembly, and grasping their mind, worship *toward* God obviously becomes a secondary or tertiary concern even though it is claimed that the service is a *worship* service! Here I mention the impact that Marva Dawn's *Reaching Out without Dumbing Down: A Theology of Worship for This Urgent Time.*

In contrast, a theology of worship's *aim* is primarily to focus attention on God and not man. I will stress that hopefully in a *theologically determined and driven worship assembly* the persons for whom we are concerned will be attracted by the heart and core of the worship assembly *toward the heart of God*, namely the God who loves them and seeks their redemption in Christ. One would hope that in such a worship service our visitors will hear the gospel of God and seek the higher heavenly calling *drawing self away from personal interests* toward a right relationship with God through Jesus Christ.

Consider for example the plea of the preacher behind the Epistle to the Hebrews, Heb 3:1; "Therefore, holy brethren, who share in a heavenly call, *consider Jesus*, the apostle and high priest of our confession." Worship should principally be to draw attention away from other interests to Jesus, not to self. Worship is intended to encourage and uplift the worshipper or guest by focusing on God and what he has done in and through Jesus. In Christian worship we *extol* and *praise* God for his majesty, holiness, greatness, and loving concern for his creation. *Our attention is focused on God* and not ourselves, or our fellow citizens who are caught up in a post-modern worldly mindset that proclaims that they are the center of everything! In worship we should encourage all to *consider Jesus first*!

As an example, drawn from Judaism and the missionary activity of the Apostle Paul we find Paul beginning his mission activity in the Greek communities of the *diaspora* by going first to the Jewish Synagogue *where YHWH was being worshipped* and, in that environment, proclaiming the saving gospel of YHWH in Christ. Although Paul obviously had an interest in reaching the Jewish people of the Synagogue community, he was well aware of the fact that in almost every Synagogue there would be a significant group of devout Gentile attendees. Nevertheless, Paul focused his attention on the YHWH of Scripture. Luke gave a technical term to these religiously minded Gentiles; he referred to them as a σεβομένη τὸν θεόν, *sebomenē ton theón, a worshipper* of God. The expression *worshipper of God* was used, notably in Acts, to refer to *devout Gentiles* who were attracted to Judaism and the Synagogue[11] *because of the monotheism of the Jewish faith, the Jewish high regard for the Law of Moses, and the religious devotion of the Jews*. The Synagogue liturgy was not focused on the Gentile worshippers of YHWH who were permitted to attend the Synagogue as "observers" or "worshippers." Worship in the Synagogue focused on YHWH and the *Torah*, the Law of Moses, and not on the Gentiles! In Paul's mind, any devout and theologically focused worship should focus on, and rejoice in what YHWH had done in Jesus. This was good news, the Gospel! Paul hoped that this would draw and encourage serious seekers of God to Jesus.

Thus, our purpose should be to introduce our visitors and ourselves to God and his glorious power and love, and not on ourselves or our guests to please them! I personally enjoy great singing in worship. I celebrate the great singing in our worship services not because I simply enjoy the singing but because it lifts me up and focuses my attention on God and his gracious love and saving work in Jesus.

The question to ask is *concerning who,* and *toward whom,* is the assembly directed; toward God to worship God, or toward man to attract man? Are we seeking to reach people by pleasing them, or to reach people by introducing them to God in all of his

---

[11] Cf. Acts 10:2; 13:50; 16:14; 17:4, 17; 18:7.

awesome glory, love, and power? I hope to clarify this distinction as we progress through this study.

As I have already mentioned, in a *sociological* or *culturally sensitive* service the focus is *primarily* on doing what will be attractive to ourselves and our visitors. I certainly am not opposed to being sensitive to cultural and sociological concerns and interests. How we dress, and being appropriately culturally sensitive, demonstrating appropriate behavior and respect for others. Sociological and culturally sensitive concerns do enter the equation. The apostles Paul and Peter each purposefully addressed the issues of appropriate adornment and behavior in the church service and Christian behavior (cf. 1 Cor 14: 23, 40; 1 Tim 2:9; 1 Pet 3:3). Although not necessarily exclusively to a worship service, but certainly not excluding such, they were both sensitive to appropriate culturally concerned mores. Paul and Peter exhort Christians to adorn themselves in a discreet manner that would not attract undue attention to themselves and away from Jesus and worshipping God.

What I have in mind here concerns not merely *how we dress in a culturally appropriate manner*, although that is important, but more so *what we do* in worship and *how and why we do what we do*! I have in mind *how we pray* 1 Tim 2:8, (the attitude involved in "lifting up holy hands toward God"), how we *speak* especially *in teaching* (1 Tim 2:8ff; 1 Cor 12, 14 both of which address inappropriate dress and behavior, and the use of appropriate speech in the worship assembly). I could add *appropriate singing* (1 Cor 14:13ff)! Which I did!

My point is that although cultural and sociological interests or sensitivities are important, they are not the *primary* or *definitive* factors in congregational worship settings even though Christians do need to be sensitive to appropriate cultural behavior.

There should be an attitude and behavior in worship which is in keeping with the concept of the divine presence, and worship directed toward the one holy and sovereign God. In particular I am always impressed by the sentiment expressed in Hosea 2:20, *"The LORD is in his holy temple; let all the earth keep silence before him"*! It might be helpful to introduce the topic of "silence in the Tabernacle or Temple" when the Christian priest[12] approaches God with thanksgiving! Perhaps we might learn something regarding worship by hearing the Old Testament![13]

At Exodus 3:2ff we have a fine example of the correct attitude in the presence of the Lord God. Moses was told by YHWH to remove his shoes from his feet for he was standing on holy ground!

> *² And the angel of the LORD appeared to him in a flame of fire out of the midst of a bush; and he looked, and lo, the bush was burning, yet it was not consumed. ³ And Moses said, "I will turn aside and see this great sight, why the bush is not burnt." ⁴ When the LORD saw that he turned aside to see, God called to him out of the bush, "Moses, Moses!" And he said, "Here am I." ⁵ Then he said, "<u>Do not come near; put off your shoes from your feet, for the place on which you are standing is holy ground.</u>" ⁶ And he said, "I am the God of your father, the God of Abraham, the God of Isaac, and the God of Jacob." <u>And Moses hid his face, for he was afraid to look at God</u>.*

Likewise, in the heavenly court worship scene of Rev 4:10 we read:

> *"the twenty-four elders <u>fall down before him</u> who is seated on the throne and worship him who lives for ever and ever; <u>they cast their crowns before the throne</u>, singing, ¹¹ "Worthy art thou, our Lord and God, to receive glory and honor and power, for thou didst create all things, and by thy will they existed and were created."*

Now that is a worshipful attitude!

---

[12] In the Christian era, Christ has become the High Priest, and every Christian is a priest who approaches God in worship.

[13] I refer here to an excellent study of parallel concepts in sacrifice in a thesis presented by Noah Osei to the faculty of Biblical Studies at Abilene Christian University in 2013. The thesis was accepted and approved in December 2013. Noah Osei, *Comparative Analysis of the Concept of Asham (reparation) Sacrifice in the Old Testament and Asante*. Osei's thesis is that when approaching other religious beliefs, it is helpful to set them in the context of Old Testament and New Testament concepts and principles.

What is important in these two texts is not simply the physical posture, but the spiritual attitudinal posture of worship. "God is in his holy temple,"[14] the assembled community of Christian believers, and we have come to worship him.

The Greek word προσκυνέω, *proskunéō* expresses this worship attitude well. It is found in many contexts but notably Rev 4:10. In the New Testament it is a common verb for worship essentially rendered *"to worship, to do obeisance, to show respect, to fall or prostrate oneself before another. Literally it means to kiss toward someone, to throw a kiss in token of respect or homage."*[15] This is the mindset and attitude that should shape our mind as we gather in the worship assembly to worship the almighty God!

In a genuine worship service offered to God in spirit and truth (John 4:24[16]) we do not pray to or venerate lesser beings, or even false gods, or anything other than the one true God. In our Christian faith even though we have "saintly mentors" we do not worship "saintly human beings," or an angel, even if this would be attractive and appeal to the sensitivities of our visitors! In certain Roman Catholic liturgies certain saints, or even Jesus' mother Mary are venerated. This practice is not followed in the Protestant heritage of Christian worship. In the Protestant tradition[17] Christians worship only the Trinitarian godhead, Father, Son, and Holy Spirit. Although members of Churches of Christ have high regard for the divine inspiration of Scripture we do not worship Scripture as in the Muslim faith regarding the Quran, nor do we venerate the human authors of Scripture as in "The Church

---

[14] I do not imply here that the church building is the temple of God, but the assembled body of people are the temple of God who dwells in this temple through his indwelling Holy Spirit (1 Cor 3:16, 17; 2 Cor 3:16).

[15] Zodhiates.

[16] Cf. my discussion in *Chapter 2: Some Thoughts from the Early Centuries of Christianity* on John 4:24.

[17] Although some members of Churches of Christ eschew any relationship with the Protestant tradition, Churches of Christ do fall within the broader sphere of Protestantism.

of Saint Peter." We worship only one triune[18] God in the tradition of the *Torah Shema*, Deut 6:4ff:

> [4] *"Hear, O Israel: The LORD our God is one LORD;* [5] *and you shall love the LORD your God with all your heart, and with all your soul, and with all your might.* [6] *And these words which I command you this day shall be upon your heart;* [7] *and you shall teach them diligently to your children, and shall talk of them when you sit in your house, and when you walk by the way, and when you lie down, and when you rise.* [8] *And you shall bind them as a sign upon your hand, and they shall be as frontlets between your eyes.* [9] *And you shall write them on the doorposts of your house and on your gates."*

In Revelation John was advised not to fall down in worship even before a mighty angel who spoke from God with a mighty message (Rev 19:10; 22:9)! Likewise, in Hebrews the preacher warns against venerating angels in place of Jesus (Heb 1:4-14).

In a theology of worship, the worshiper's attention and direction is toward the one holy Trinity[19] being worshipped. Christian worshippers place nothing, or no-one else, at the focal point of their worship!

Unfortunately, preachers, even Bible class teachers, and I am or have been both, sometimes are the focal point of the sermon or lesson! This is difficult to control for we are all inclined to be performers; this somehow is the nature of the beast! Preachers and teachers should be alert to the dangers of seeking to draw attention to themselves and away from God and his transcendent and powerful Word.

Paul instructed Christians with the tendency of self-aggrandizement in the use of spiritual giftedness in the Corinthian church to not speak in tongues in a worship assembly *in order to fulfill their personal spiritual and emotional needs and feelings,*

---

[18] This is not the place to discuss or enlarge on the Christian understanding of the Trinitarian godhead other than to state that the New Testament explains that the one God of the *Shema* is actually a triune God, God the Father, Son, and Holy Spirit.

[19] Although the term *trinity* is not found in the New Testament it is used as an abbreviation for "God, the Father, Jesus, the Son, and the Holy Spirit."

or to impress and please the visitors (1 Cor 12-14)! Such expressions should refer to speaking to God and not to themselves, or in a manner that is to impress others.

In our Christian assemblies Christians should pray and speak in a controlled rational manner that edifies[20] the hearer and focuses their attention on the one true God and Jesus Christ. Christians should be sensitive to not drawing attention to or focusing on their personal characteristics, personal spiritual giftedness, or the cultural preferences of the audience. Although it is difficult, worship leaders should be as restrained as possible so as not to draw the attention of the worshippers away from the worship and veneration of the one God who is at the center and focus of all worship!

I need to stress again that it is not simply *what* we are doing in worship, although I do have some appropriate concerns in this regard. What I am concerned with here is our *reason* for doing *what we do*, and *how* we express that. We need to determine whether the reason and focus of our worship activity is truly worshipping God; paying homage to God, or on pleasing our personal preferences or the persuasions of our neighbors?

I will develop the thought in this study that in the church worship assembly the focus is essentially on God and worshipping God, or worshipping toward God, and not toward the congregation or personal preferences. When we worship toward God appropriately the congregation is strengthened, encouraged, edified, and motivated.

A complex question arises in the statements made by Paul at Eph 5:19 that we should "address to one another in psalms, hymns and spiritual songs," and Col 3:16 that we should "teach and admonish one another in all wisdom and sing psalms and hymns and spiritual songs"![21] I will in due course draw attention in this study to the fact that there is inherent in worship directed toward God an element of horizontal edification and *speaking to*

---

[20] I will address the dynamic of edifying one another and speaking to one another at 1 Cor 14 and Eph 5:19 at a later point in this study.

[21] Refer to an exegetical study of Eph 5:19 and Col 3:16 in Addendum 4, Exegetical Studies, at the conclusion of this study on *A Biblical Theology of Worship*.

one another in psalms, hymns, and spiritual songs to edify one another as we worship God *and thus witness to our faith*. We will note that the vertical dynamic of worshipping *toward* God does have an edifying horizontal reciprocal dynamic to it for when one is worshipping God we are at the same time witnessing before one another through the words we sing and speak as we honor and praise God. There is thus both a *vertical* and a *horizontal* dynamic to worship, but *the vertical dynamic is primary*! Without the *vertical* dynamic the horizontal is emptied of its dynamic source of power!

Thus, we need to clarify in our minds whether our motivation in worship is *primarily* worshipping in a manner that is *directed toward God and to be pleasing to God, or alternately to be worshipping toward our friends in order to be pleasing to them!*

Such a decision is however not that difficult! We merely need to ask ourselves for what purpose are we worshipping! Is our intention to be worshipping God, or being *evangelistic* in order to reach our friends? Again, I need to mention for those who are already concerned about where this study is going, I am not in the least bit opposed to evangelistic seeker services! I would be in favor of such seeker services as long as they are not confused with a genuine Lord's Day worship service! It is my persuasion, however, that a genuine Lord's Day worship service should be directed toward God in worship of God, and not toward our friends in order to evangelize them. I am sure that some of you might ask why the genuine worship directed toward friends cannot achieve both goals. A genuine worship service directed toward God can be evangelistic and missional as we witness toward God, praise Him for his great love, mercy, salvation, and the secure future we have in Jesus Christ! But as we have already indicated, and will observe in this study, a seeker service, as well-intended as it may be, will focus on the human element in the service.

It was in this sense that many concerned Gentiles ca. the 1st century CE were attracted to the Jewish Synagogue because of its focus on one Lord, YHWH, Scripture, and a lifestyle that was lived in view of that God. The Jewish Synagogue, to its shame was not missional[22] toward the Gentiles as God had intended it to be. But the Gentiles were permitted to witness a worship service devoted to YHWH and not to them. The divine direction of the service, YHWH, shaped the dynamic of the service. My point is that a genuine worship of God that focuses on God and his *Torah/Word* will attract concerned people toward God. Genuine worship can be and should be evangelistic and missional in that it praises God for his great redemptive work in Christ and points unbelievers toward this great God of mercy and grace that wants all men to be saved!

I am reminded of the concerns of David Wells discussed in my earlier sections, Postscript and Preamble, where he expressed concerns over the general deconstruction of the worship of God toward an entrepreneurial program designed to attract the unchurched in a consumer market style. The result of this deconstruction results in a denigration of theology and the role of Scripture/Word.

We simply need to ask ourselves whether we have gathered to worship and praise God or to please ourselves or our friends. It is difficult to worship *toward God* and *toward our friends* at the same time just as Jesus once warned his disciples that one cannot serve God and *two masters* at the same time (Matt 6:24)! Paul likewise intoned that one cannot eat at a table with idols and the Lord at the same time (1 Cor 10:21) and thus "provoke the Lord to jealousy"! Likewise, Jesus expressed to the woman at the well in Samaria that true worship was not to be found in worshipping either toward Jerusalem or Mt Gerizim (John 4:21-24). One has to choose the "direction" of true worship. The choice for the Jew was either toward Jerusalem and the Temple or toward Jesus, or for the Samaritan toward Mt Gerizim and their Temple or toward Jesus. Apparently the woman chose toward Jesus!

One thought that triggers concerns for me is the repeated statement I hear from some that in a seeker style worship we should act in a *missional manner that will attract people in order*

---

[22]*Missional* as I am using the term means being engaged in planting and establishing new groups of believers, synagogues, or churches, wherever the *Torah* or the gospel of Christ was/is proclaimed.

to reach out and save more! Being motivated by the *Missio Dei* and seeking to save others is certainly to be praised as a noble intention, for the kingdom of God and the *Missio Dei* are certainly missional and concerned for the unchurched. The tricky question is determining *how* the worship of God in a formal setting can fit into the *Missio Dei*. We should ask, are worship and being missional equal overlapping ingredients in the *Missio Dei* or do they refer to different but vital functions of the *Missio Dei*? Are there specific instructions regarding worship that may not be applicable to other ministries such as benevolence or social justice in the *Missio Dei*? A related delicate question is determining what the worship of God in a formal setting looks like and how to achieve being missional in a formal worship setting! I will propose that they are not necessarily overlapping *foci* but are separate aspects of the *Missio Dei*! Hang in with me, for hopefully I will address this better in the following paragraph!

As we work through this paragraph, I hope I can clarify what I am stressing! When contemplating differences in the *direction* or *subject* of worship in the Lord's Day worship assembly, and the *direction* and *object* of a missional outreach we draw attention to the fact that these *are both separate foci* or aspects of the *Missio Dei*. In a *missional dynamic* of a congregational seeker service those attending the service are primarily the *subject, object*, and *direction* of the service which thus directs *the attention toward the attendees*. There is nothing wrong with that in a missional seeker assembly. However, in a Christian Lord's Day worship service of God the direction is reversed!

Several scholars speaking to the theology of worship refer to the Christian worship assembly embracing *only* God as *both* the *subject* and *object* of our worship. We are not the subject and we or the unchurched are not the object of the worship! It is profoundly important that we understand what is meant by God being the *subject* and *object* of our worship. I will explore this more fully later, but for the moment will draw attention to the Christian's Lord's Day *worship assembly—its dynamic and purpose*. According to Scripture, we do not decide to worship God; He has called us to worship! He is the *subject* calling us to worship! Since it is God who calls us to worship *him* and it is we who respond in our worship *of God*, it is God who becomes the *object* of our worship! Thus, God is both the *subject who calls us to worship, and he is the object of our worship!*

Rather than focusing on ourselves or our guests, thus becoming both the subject and object involved in worshipping in a manner that is pleasing to *us* or to our *guests* in a manner in which *we* and *they are the subject and object of our service*, we should remember that in *Christian worship assembly it is God who must always remain both the subject* and *object* of our actions. Since it is he who has called us to worship himself, *for our own good*, we must keep him as the focus and direction of our worship.

When we worship God in a genuine worshipful manner as the one calling us to worship being praised in our worship we are the ones who are enlightened and uplifted. I need to point out again that according to Jesus there is a worship that is not truly genuine spiritual worship (John 4:21-24).

Our guests in a Lord's Day worship service are certainly important, but our worship is *not about our guests*, it is about God and our relationship with him. In contrast to this in a seeker evangelistic or missional driven service our visitors or attendees *become the focus of attention.* We sing the songs that appeal to them and we structure the service in a manner that will appeal to them. They are both the subject and the object of concern. However, in a formal Lord's Day worship service in which we are called by God to worship him, *God is the driving force and target of worship*. Our motivation will be to please God in a theological and Scriptural manner, not in a manner that is culturally pleasing to those who might be our guests.

I will contend that in a genuine theology of worship the worship can be evangelistic, indrawing people to God, and the spiritual needs of our guests can and should be addressed, as should our own spiritual needs be addressed, but the *dynamic* of a Lord's Day worship service is different from the dynamic of an evangelistic seeker service. In a *genuine* Lord's Day worship of God (remember again Jesus' admonition to the Samaritan woman, John 4:21-24, those who worship God must do so in spirit and truth, that is, in a genuine spirit of worship) we can influence our guests *by demonstrating true spiritual humility and reverence before God and demonstrating how important our relationship with God is, and how deeply God is concerned about us and our guests.* We worship God and pray that our guests are drawn away from their own interests toward God and what God has been doing for them throughout the ages of history and specifically in the death and resurrection of Jesus.

Before you throw up your hands in horror or frustration let me again explain that I am not opposed to church assemblies whose focus is on seeking the lost or addressing the needs of the lost, or of building up fellowship relationships within the congregation. However, the dynamic of genuine theologically driven worship is radically different in focus and purpose, it is solely to worship God and sing his praise for his grace and magisterial redemptive work of all people in Jesus. *What I am concerned with is the erosion of sublime and holy worship in which the worship has shifted its focus and purpose from God to ourselves and/or our guests.*

Can we have both in one? Yes, for on the one hand when the focus is on God in genuine worship he is raised and we are edified and encouraged by his gospel Word. However, on the other hand, when the primary focus is on or driven by concerns for the unchurched guests, the focus on God is shifted to the periphery and the theological concerns of the Word are diminished or even lost.

As David Wells, Marva Dawn, and others have indicated, all one needs to do is attend a seeker driven service to notice that the central theological doctrine and power of the Word is hardly present other than for a mention of some Scripture alluded to in a "talk," mostly used out of scriptural and theological context, and has been replaced by some emotionally motivating story, secular themes, style, and influences. Worship has become a spiritual concert intended to please the visitors!

Evangelistic seeker services are, however, most appropriate if considered as evangelistic or "revival" meetings. I regret that in our contemporary culture we have jettisoned or diminished the importance of "revival" or "gospel meetings" as they were once practiced in a by-gone day. We have moved on from the likes of a past generation! I am keenly aware that we no longer live in a culture, both church and secular, that is interested in extended evening services whose design is reaching out to the lost or unchurched. That is where we are, and we must adjust to this increasingly secular and insular culture. However, we should not do this at the expense of worshipping God in formal worship assemblies on the Lord's Day in a genuine theology of worship. As Marva Dawn has so pointedly pointed out, we do not need to dumb down our worship service to reach out to and please our secular culture!

One possible reason among several for our lack of enthusiasm for "revival" or "gospel meetings" is that in an increasingly post-modern age[23] we no longer believe that those outside the church are lost! Being lost is an unpopular expression in our secular society. "Lost" is not "politically correct"! The "lost" in our contemporary secular culture are simply described as "unchurched"! In a 2015 Pew survey of religious and church preferences in the USA[24] the designation of preference in our secular culture is to identify oneself as a "None" indicating that one does not attend, belong to, or identify with any church or religious organization. A similar reflection on this phenomenon was discussed in a December 18, 2018 *Christian Chronical* article in which Christian Colleges in the USA reported on the decline of Church of Christ Freshman enrollment in Christian Colleges. Many Christian Freshman prefer some other term than Church of Christ in reporting their church or faith preference. Some call themselves simply Christians or some similar non-identifying term.[25]

---

[23] As some, including Wells have pointed out so clearly, we have already moved beyond the post-modern generation, passed the gen. X, gen. Y, and gen Z generation and are now seeking to identify our ever-changing cultural and social norms, whatever they might be or become!
[24] Pew Research Center, May 12, 2015, "America's Changing Religious Landscape."
[25] Christian Chronicle, www.christianchronicle.org, Dec. 2018, "*Number of freshmen who identify with Churches of Christ hits new low, annual survey finds.*"

How to reach the "none folk" and other persons who decline Christian terms of identity certainly is a challenge to concerned Christians, but I question whether what Marva Dawn[26] has termed "dumbing down" in worship, or ignoring or denying church "denomination" identity is the solution!

Another possible reason for reluctance to engage in active evangelism is that in our cocooning culture we are merely too busy to devote the time and energy to such efforts as additional church meetings which make inroads into our time, and consequently we build protective walls around our private time.

Another factor impacting our lack of interest in evangelistic gospel or seeker service meetings is that we are convinced that those outside of the church are merely not interested in traditional type churches and would rather join the modern wave of local community fellowship, non-traditional churches. This may be a real challenge that churches must face, but surely there are other ways of reaching them than through our seeker designed services.

One solution to this has been for a younger millennial and later generation to distance themselves from a "traditional church" model which in the mind of many has become outdated. In many cases this is unfortunately an accurate evaluation of some churches.

For many the disenchantment with traditional church results in a break away from their parents' church in an effort to exercise personal independence. Being contemporary, or possibly even politically correct is exercised by many by becoming a modern "community Bible fellowship church," thus buying into the "worship" mindset of our culturally inclined community church neighbors! This comment is not intended to denigrate the Christian contribution to our culture that many of the fine community churches provide. My purpose is merely to explain why many have turned away from traditional churches that have become locked into a past practice and an "old" world mindset characterized by a lifeless repetitive worship liturgy. The answer to this "old world" challenge for many has been to capitulate to the moods of a postmodern secular anti-traditional church culture.

---

[26] Dawn, *Reaching Out*.

However, there are more meaningful avenues of reaching out which lie in our sincere Christian witness and service in the community by addressing the real needs of our culture and by serving the needs of our community who are seeking help or hope in a culture that in itself offers little real hope. We just need to find more effective ways of doing evangelism!

My point is that one need not surrender a genuine theology of worship or doing church in favor of new secular shaped church experiences. Evangelism, the telling of the story of the victory of Jesus Christ needs to be more thoughtful and effective in reaching the needs and minds of a secular culture.

Whatever the reason for the apparent disinterest in traditional churches and evangelistic type "gospel meetings" may be, that is not the focus of this study. How to effectively reach out to and attract others is a much needed theological and evangelistic concern, and certainly one demanding of careful research and implementation, but that is not the essence of a theology of worship. Perhaps we need another book on the theology of evangelism!

However, combining a missional mindset or concern for the unchurched and a theology of worship into an evangelistic culturally oriented seeker service in my opinion is not the answer to reaching out to the non-churched or un-churched, as important as that may be. By doing so we diminish a genuine theology of worship in favor of a cultural anthropology of worship, adopting a program that is non-threatening and easy for our members.

One possible solution could be to have services on Sunday dedicated to worshipping God shaped by a genuine worship theology in which Scripture and doctrine define the theology, and another service shaped by the likes and wishes of a secular culture dedicated to reaching out to the un-churched, but that would place an imposition on our free Sunday time which might not be welcomed by many, especially those not interested in reaching out or having the church infringe on their private time! After all, in most churches today only about 50% of the members attend Sunday Bible classes. Asking them to attend an additional service would be too much! An additional service certainly may not be welcome especially when our favorite football or soccer team is playing on Sunday afternoon or evening! *Oops!* Unfortunately for too many Christians today going to a church service on Sunday is the extent of their involvement with "church". This misses completely what the kingdom of God and the *Missio Dei* involve. My intention here is not to be overly critical and judgmental, but only to demonstrate why we face the contemporary threat of secularism.

What has become popular in many cases is the combination of a doctrinally Scripturally driven theology of church and a contemporary relevant culturally driven and shaped church. As David Wells has argued this eventually deteriorates into a church service in which Scripture and doctrine focused on God are diminished and the worshipper or the unchurched have become the driving dynamic in the service. In some cases, Scripture reading has been supplanted by storytelling, videos, and sermons in which Bible translations and texts are chosen to suit the sermon rather than the text shaping the sermon.

In a 2016 discussion with a prominent preacher among churches of Christ I asked why he used so many different bible texts and translations in one sermon; some of the translations were questionable, not necessarily the product of a broad translation committee, but by one person or by one specific religious order.[27] His answer was that he searched for the translation that supported the point he wanted to make in his sermon. Surely that is getting things the wrong way. It is as though our theology and text have been shaped by our contemporary concerns and sermon rather than our theology and sermon being shaped by our text!

Years ago, a prominent Baptist preacher in Pietermaritzburg, South Africa,[28] tried to convince me that baptism was not *for* our salvation but *because of* our salvation. He quoted from a New Testament translation of Acts 2:38 that read something like this, "Repent and be baptized every one of you in the name of Jesus who was *anointed* (Christ, *christós*, *anointed*) *for* the remission of sins." However, Jesus was not simply *anointed* for the remission of sins! He *died* for the remission of sins! Under pressure I

---

[27] An example of this would be the Watchtower, Jehovah Witness translation of the Bible.
[28] He was a product of Baylor University theology school! Baylor University would certainly not endorse his choice of translation!

was able to determine that the translation he was citing was by the Jehovah Witnesses! Surely not a Baptist recommendation! This illustrates the problem of finding a translation that suits your theology rather than your theology being shaped by a true translation of the text. Surely there were better translations that treated the theology of Acts 2:38 more honestly and accurately than the JW translation!

Returning to my point on reaching out to the unchurched or lost, hopefully I will below address how a genuine worship service, directed to God, can be evangelistic without "dumbing down in order to reach out"!

In another chapter I will address the various fine congregational gatherings or meetings churches conduct in a worthy manner without considering them as theological worship services involving the Lord's Supper. We should recognize and emphasize the theological difference, purpose, and intention of such meetings. These meetings and gatherings are an addition to the regular Sunday congregational worship services in which the Lord's Supper is celebrated, the Word is read and explained, and God is worshipped. They are all vital to the health of a congregation. Possibly an aggressive seeker service could periodically be added to these fine church programs!

I am also keenly aware that *how* we do "church" today is considerably different from *how* "church" was done in the 1st century, and even more recently in the 20th century. The shift from small house churches or smaller "rural" churches to large auditorium based urban worship assemblies has out of necessity become the preferred manner of doing church today in our contemporary urban culture. Such urbanization of the church is a challenge and definitely part of our contemporary culture context, but the principles and theology of worship should remain firm regardless of culture and locality.

Over four decades ago we were introduced to the demographic shifts in our culture by John Naisbitt in his insightful book *Megatrends*.[29] Unfortunately, we heard Naisbitt but were slow or disinclined to take him seriously. We are now living in

---

[29] Naisbitt, *Megatrends*.

this demographic slide with its cultural shifts and have not been able to keep pace with the speed and impact of the shift.

As we progress in this study I will maintain that the worship theology of both the Old and New Testaments was concentrated on God and not the congregation, or the attendees, or the cultural changes. I will emphasize later that the New Testament does not set out a formal worship liturgy[30] but leaves that to the individual communities in a wide variety of cultural and ethnic contexts. Paul's concerns in his Corinthian correspondence were not to delineate a worship liturgy for all congregations, but were addressed to the selfish, self-serving, self-aggrandizing mindset and abuses of the Corinthian super-spirituals who were denigrating and demeaning the worship of God and Christ. He wrote at 1 Cor 11:27 that those who were worshipping in an unworthy manner were profaning the body and blood of the Lord! There are valuable principles and insights in what Paul wrote to the Corinthians.

We will note below and emphasize that the theological principles or themes of worshipping YHWH have not changed even though the context of the worship has changed from Old Testament Jewish Temple worship to Jewish Christian churches, and then under Paul to the multi-ethnic Jewish-Gentile churches. Culture does not change the theology of worship even though it challenges the worshippers to see beyond culture to God who is the purpose and focus of worship.

---

[30] I use liturgy here in the sense of *a formal order of worship*, not in the sense that we cannot identify what the early church did in its worship assemblies.

Chapter 2: Some Thoughts from the Early Centuries of Christianity

From what we can learn from the limited information gleaned from our New Testament studies, the literature of the early church such as the *Didache*,[1] ca 100-150 CE, and early church fathers such as Ignatius of Antioch ca 100 CE, Justin Martyr ca 150 CE, Tertullian ca 200 CE, Clement of Alexandria ca 175 CE, and Hippolytus ca 200 CE, the churches in the first two centuries of Christianity were singularly devoted in their worship assemblies to paying homage and veneration to God as the bestower of forgiveness through the atoning sacrifice of Jesus Christ. It appears that the Eucharist-Lord's Supper was the focal point of the worship service with attendant Scripture reading, homily, prayers and some singing of hymns. The focal point was not the personal interests, concerns, or passions of the worshipper or of the congregation, many of whom were drawn from a Gentile pagan background or had been Gentile "God-worshippers" associated with the Synagogue. The focus of the worship was decidedly on God, the Father, and His Son, Jesus Christ through whom God had redeemed man and brought about reconciliation between Himself and all people, Jew and Gentile.

It appears that the early church worship services were devoted to praising God for his majesty and holiness, and thanksgiving (*Eucharist*) for the atoning sacrifice of Jesus. There was encouragement and comfort in the very act of assembly for those facing persecution, *[23] Let us hold fast the confession of our hope without wavering, for he who promised is faithful; [24] and let us consider how to stir up one another to love and good works, [25] <u>not neglecting to meet together, as is the habit of some, but encouraging one another</u>, and all the more as you see the Day drawing near.* [2]

The phenomenal growth of the Christian faith was not attributed in the early centuries to dynamic worship services but to

---

[1] The *Didache* was an early second century document called *The Teachings of the Twelve Apostles*. The *Didache* gives us a picture of early church life beyond the writings of the New Testament.
[2] Heb 10:23–25.

the faithful preaching of the gospel regarding what God had done for all through the death and resurrection of Jesus. Hence the favored term for the Lord's Supper was *Eucharist*, Thanksgiving. Worship was focused on God in all of his majesty, sovereignty, holiness, and redeeming power, and the redemption in the cross of Christ.

As examples of the valuable early church writings regarding early Christian worship I am including two comments, one each from the *Didache* and Justin Martyr. They enrich our study of early church life and practice.

The Didache: "The Teaching of the Twelve Apostles"

The name Didache derives from the Greek *noun* ἡ διδαχή, *hē didachḗ, the teaching.* The term Didache is therefore the abbreviation of the full title, "*The Teaching of the Lord through the Twelve apostles.*" It was a church manual dating from somewhere between CE 70 and CE 150 although most scholars date it in the early 2nd century. Although most likely coming from a period after the death of the Apostles it was considered by the early church to represent the teaching of the Apostles. "It was highly prized as representing the church order of the early church dating from before the turn of the 1st century. It developed church orders relating to worship, baptism, the Eucharist, and the love feast."[3] Note for example the following citations from *The Didache*, Chapters 9 and 14:

> Now concerning the Thanksgiving (Eucharist), thus give thanks. First, concerning the cup: We thank thee, our Father, for the holy vine of David Thy servant, which Thou madest known to us through Jesus Thy Servant; to Thee be the glory forever. And concerning the broken *bread:* We thank Thee, our Father, for the life and knowledge which Thou madest known to us through Jesus Thy Servant; to Thee be the glory forever. Even as this broken *bread* was scattered over the hills, and was gathered together and became one, so let Thy Church be gath-

---

[3] Cf. *Encyclopedia of Early Christianity*, article on the *Didache* by Everett Ferguson.

ered together from the ends of the earth into Thy kingdom; for Thine is the glory and the power through Jesus Christ forever. But let no one eat or drink of your Thanksgiving (Eucharist) but they who have been baptized into the name of the Lord; for concerning this also the Lord hath said, Give not that which is holy to the dogs.[4] ...

But every Lord's day do ye gather yourselves together, and break bread, and give thanksgiving after having confessed your transgressions, that your sacrifice may be pure. But let no one that is at variance with his fellow come together with you, until they be reconciled, that your sacrifice may not be profaned. For this is that which was spoken by the Lord: In every place and time offer to me a pure sacrifice; for I am a great King, saith the Lord, and my name is wonderful among the nations.[5]

Notice the emphasis in the last paragraph on the weekly practice of celebrating the Eucharist on *"every Lord's day ..."*

Justin Martyr

Justin (100 – 165 CE) was an early Christian apologist. He passionately defended the morality of the Christian life and provided various ethical and philosophical arguments to convince the Roman emperor, Antoninus, to abandon the persecution of the fledgling church. Justin was martyred ca 165 CE.

As an example of the teaching on baptism ca CE 150 and church order, note Justin's comments from the mid-2nd century CE:

> I will also relate the manner in which we dedicated ourselves to God when we had been made new through Christ; lest, if we omit this, we seem to be unfair in the explanation we are making. As many as are persuaded and believe that what we teach and say is true, and undertake to be able to live accordingly, are instructed to pray and to entreat God with fasting for the remission of their

---

[4] *The Lord's Teaching through the Twelve Apostles to the Nations*. A. Roberts, J. Donaldson & A. C. Coxe, eds., *The Ante-Nicene Fathers*, Vol 7, pp. 379–380. New York: Christian Literature Company.
[5] Donaldson, *The Lord's Teaching through the Twelve Apostles*, p. 381.

sins that are past, praying and fasting with them. Then they are brought by us where there is water and are regenerated in the same manner in which we were ourselves regenerated. For, in the name of God, the Father and Lord of the universe, and of our Saviour Jesus Christ, and of the Holy Spirit, they then receive the washing with water. For Christ also said, "Except ye be born again, ye shall not enter into the kingdom of heaven. Now, that it is impossible for those who have once been born to enter into their mothers' wombs, is manifest to all. And how those who have sinned and repent shall escape their sins, is declared by Esaias the prophet, as I wrote above; he thus speaks: "Wash you, make you clean; put away the evil of your doings from your souls; learn to do well; judge the fatherless, and plead for the widow: and come and let us reason together, saith the Lord. And though your sins be as scarlet, I will make them white like wool; and though they be as crimson, I will make them white as snow. But if ye refuse and rebel, the sword shall devour you: for the mouth of the Lord hath spoken it."[6]

As further examples of early Christian practices and church order, notably regarding worship, we could include numerous comments by Tertullian ca 200 CE, Clement of Alexandria ca 175 CE, and Hippolytus ca 200 CE, *each of which emphasize the focus in worship and the Christian life as veneration and thanksgiving to God and Jesus Christ.* Their comments should enrich our understanding of early Christian worship and church order.

Jesus and the Samaritan Women at Sychar - John 4:24

Although dating before the establishment of the church, I find Jesus' discussion with the Samaritan woman at the well in Sychar/Shechem to be helpful in explaining any discussion on Christian worship. At the conclusion of his discussion with the Samaritan woman as described by John in his Gospel at John 4:19-24, Jesus made an interesting statement regarding the focus of attention in worship.

---

[6] Justin Martyr, *Apology 1*, ch 61.

After her disturbing encounter with Jesus regarding her past life, the Samaritan woman sought to shift attention away from her personal spiritual situation to the worship practices of her Samaritan community on Mount Gerizim. She even mentioned the Jewish practice of worshipping in Jerusalem rather than on Mt Gerizim. Jesus sidestepped the discussion of Mt Gerizim versus Jerusalem! In his discussion Jesus drew attention to the fact that the place, Jerusalem or Mt Gerizim, were not to be the place, center, or focus of attention in the eschatological kingdom regarding *genuine* worship. He explained that God seeks *a certain kind* of worshipper to worship him! His point was that God's new people of the kingdom of the eschatological age, that is the Christians,[7] *would not worship for their own pleasures or according to their own desires and concerns. True worshippers would worship God on his terms, not their own interests, cultural or ethnic! In the true or genuine worship of God the worshippers are the secondary partners in worship, God is the primary partner and the focus is on true genuine spiritual worship*! Notice Jesus' emphasis on genuine spiritual worship in this fascinating discourse:

> *[19] The woman said to him, "Sir, I perceive that you are a prophet. [20] Our fathers worshiped on this mountain; and you say that in Jerusalem is the place where men ought to worship." [21] Jesus said to her, "Woman, believe me, the hour is coming when neither on this mountain nor in Jerusalem will you worship the Father. [22] You worship what you do not know; we worship what we know, for salvation is from the Jews. [23] But the hour is coming, and now is, when the true worshipers will worship the Father in spirit and truth, <u>for such the Father seeks to worship him</u>. [24] God is spirit, and <u>those who worship him must worship in spirit and truth</u>."*

Clearly Jesus announced that God seeks genuine worshippers; that is, those who understand both the direction and nature of worshipping God *in a genuine spirit of devotion*. Contrary to

---

[7] In this discussion Jesus had reference to the new kingdom age. His comment *"the hour is coming, and now is ..."* refers to the last days, the eschatological age of Christianity.

both Samaritan and Jewish preferences the heart is the place and instrument of genuine spiritual worship.

Commenting on Jesus' discussion with the Samaritan woman, Andreas Kostenberger observes:

> But perhaps the climactic moment in the pericope, just preceding his (unusual) revelation of himself as the Messiah to the Samaritan in John 4: 26, *is Jesus' discussion of true spiritual worship—"worship in spirit and truth"* (not "in the Spirit and in the truth," as the TNIV has it)— in 4:21–24. This is part of the larger Johannine replacement theme, where Jesus is shown to be the new sanctuary in place of the old. Here Jesus is shown to take the opportunity, in dialogue with the Samaritan, to point out that worship is not a matter of geographical location of externals; *it is a spiritual matter, just as God is spirit(ual) and thus must be worshiped spiritually.*[8]

John Macarthur in similar vein writes:

> God-honoring worship doesn't merely conform to external religious rituals but must flow from hearts that are right with God and lives that are consistent with Scripture.[9]

In true or genuine worship in either Old or New Testament worship practices *the people are the worshippers, God is the only subject and object or direction of the worship.* We are not the focus or direction of genuine worship. The majestic, holy, sovereign, and powerful *God and Father is the only concentration or direction, or intent of our worship.*

Francis Maloney, like others when commenting on Jesus' discussion of the Samaritan woman at Sychar, points to the fact that God is not a place like Jerusalem or Mt Gerizim:

> What Jesus is about to announce as the new "place" for true worship is already present because Jesus is present. In this present time, when both Gerizim and Jerusalem are transcended, the true worshiper worships the Father in spirit and in truth, but it is the Father who seeks

---

[8] Kostenberger, *Theology of John's Gospel and Letters*, p. 203.
[9] Macarthur, *John: Jesus?*, Kindle location 588-589.

out such worshipers. The act of worshiping is described by the use of the verb *proskynein*. It implies the act of bending or prostrating oneself in the direction of the one worshiped. In this context, where holy mountains and their sanctuaries are being excluded, true worship is the orientation of oneself toward the Father in such a way that God becomes the imperative of one's life. The expression "in spirit and in truth" combines important Johannine terms (cf. already in the narrative, 1: 9, 14, 17; 3: 3-5, 21) to insist that Jesus reveals a God and Father who is to be worshiped with one's life. The Father seeks out (*zētei*) true worshipers (v. 23c) ... The hour has now come when the only acceptable act of worship (*dei proskynein*) is the total orientation of one's life and action toward the Father, sharing already in the gift of the Father (*en pneumati*), a gift that is all that it claims to be (*kai alētheia*).[10]

The little expression *worshipping the Father in spirit and truth* is an interesting construction which is in a form of *hendiadys*[11] in which *one thing* is stressed through *two things*. The first noun from *spirit*, πνεῦμα, *pneúma*, refers not to God the Holy Spirit but to the spiritual nature of man. The second noun form, *truth* (ἀληθινός *alēthinós*, *true, real, sincere, upright, genuine*), functions as an adjective to the first noun *spirit*, hence, *worshipping God in spirit and truth* means to worship God in *a genuine sincere spirit of worship*, or in *genuine spiritual worship*.

Where the Samaritans or Jews worship in the new age was not the point! It is *how* they worship the one and only true God. *The focus is not on the interests of the worshipper, it is on the God who seeks a certain kind of worshipper.*

Paul, at Rom 1:18ff in a striking pericope in his Epistle to the Romans bemoaned the shift in worship emphasis from God to the

---

[10] Moloney, *Sacra Pagina: The Gospel of John*, Kindle locations 3741-3753.
[11] Soulen, *Handbook of Biblical Criticism*, p. 72. Hendiadys is a syntactical form of grammar in which two words in the same case or tense are joined by the coordinating conjunction *kai, and*. The word *hendiadys* is a modification of the Greek phrase *hen dia dys*. Given that, *hen dia dys* literally means "one through two."

created beings which included man, a created being. In a scathing condemnation of such false worship Paul demonstrated that fallen man gave up worshipping the creator in favor of worshipping the created, even to worshipping his own passions or concerns. Cf. Rom 1:20-23!

> [20] *Ever since the creation of the world his invisible nature, namely, his eternal power and deity, has been clearly perceived in the things that have been made. So they are without excuse;* [21] *for although they knew God they did not honor him as God or give thanks to him, but they became futile in their thinking and their senseless minds were darkened.* [22] *Claiming to be wise, they became fools,* [23] *and exchanged the glory of the immortal God for images resembling mortal man or birds or animals or reptiles.*

It is an easy shift, and often an unrecognized one, to move God from the central concentration of our worship and substitute something else, even possibly our deep concerns for our neighbors, or our own interests and personal needs. It is most likely that such shifts are often made with good intentions without our realizing what is taking place!

We might not be ready to recognize this, and the following statement may be disturbing, but in the biblical story and the theology of worship, when God is shifted, even only slightly, out of the central focus of worship, monotheism is replaced by polytheism, and sadly even to the worship of false gods or concerns which control the direction of our worship! When human interests, or secular cultural interests become the focus or driving force in worship, *Sola Theou* has been replaced by *sola anthropos* or *sola cultura*. A subtle shift but nevertheless a shift away from God as the driving force or interest in worship!

Chapter 3: Introduction to Terminology

Some Useful Terminology

There are several terms that are rendered or translated as worship in our English and Greek Bibles. A brief study of four of these will help set the scene for what I am addressing in this study.

Worship. Our modern English term worship is derived from the Middle English noun worshipe, or worthssipe. The Old English worthscipe conveyed the thought of "reverent honor and homage paid to God or a sacred personage, or to any object regarded as sacred."[1]

The richness and several nuances in the general term worship are seen in the use of three Greek words commonly found in regard to the sense of worshipping God, *latreía, proskunéō, and sébomai* which we will shortly explore in greater detail.

Ralph P. Martin has observed, "to worship God is to ascribe to Him supreme worth, for He alone is worthy."[2]

As I am using the term worship in this study I am referring to the mindset, attitude, or spiritual dynamic experienced and expressed both *generally* in our Christian lifestyle in response to God's grace (Rom 12:1), and in this study more *specifically* to the worship service in a local congregation or church on Sunday, the first day of the week assembly in which the Lord's Supper or Eucharist is celebrated, prayers are said, Scripture is read and expounded in a sermon, and psalms, hymns, and spiritual songs are sung with reference to the Lord, cf. Acts 20:7; 1 Cor 11: 17-34; 1 Cor 14:1ff; Eph 5:19, Heb 10:25.

The term worship obviously has a sense encompassing more than the Lord's Supper Sunday assembly. As indicated above, worship also refers to a life of devoted service in which the committed Christian lives a daily life of devoted service offered to God in thanksgiving for his grace, mercy, and salvation. Paul expresses this worship as *presenting your bodies as a living sacrifice, holy and acceptable to God, which is your spiritual worship,*

---

[1] *Oxford English Dictionary*, 1971/2010
[2] Martin, *Worship*, Kindle location 88.

note Rom 12:1, 2. In this context, Rom 12:1, 2, Paul used a specific word for worship, stressing a meaningful facet in the richer meaning of worship. Here he used the term λατρεία, *latreía*, defining this as either *spiritual* or *reasonable* worship which we will discuss more fully below.

> *I appeal to you therefore, brethren, by the mercies of God, to present your bodies as a living sacrifice, holy and acceptable to God, which is your spiritual worship. ² Do not be conformed to this world but be transformed by the renewal of your mind, that you may prove what is the will of God, what is good and acceptable and perfect.*

Even in this daily context of spiritual worship we need to stress that the term worship expresses an attitude of committed living before God in homage, veneration, or spiritual service that is so well articulated by Paul as *spiritual worship*, τὴν λογικὴν λατρείαν[3], *tēn logikēn latreian*, Rom 12:1.

Paul obviously had in mind the daily transformed life of the Christian offered in worship and service to God and Christ in gratitude for God's grace and mercy. This may also be included in what Jesus had in mind when he explained to the Samaritan woman at Sychar (John 4:23, 24) that God seeks those who will *worship him in spirit and truth* in a daily *genuine life of spiritual worship or service, and in a formal worship service as expressed in the temple in Jerusalem*. However, since the discussion was introduced by the Samaritan woman in regard to worship in Jerusalem or on Mt Gerizim it is more likely that foremost in Jesus' mind was *genuine spiritual worship in the formal temple worship* which involved a shift in sacred space and time into the eschatological Christian worship experience. George Beasley-Murray

---

[3] Interestingly, the Greek rendered here as *spiritual worship* by the RSV is λογικὴν λατρείαν which derives from λογικός, *logikós* which in turn implies *logical, reasonable* but *spiritual* service since for the Greek *logikós* is where the deep spiritual thinking takes place. The following word, λατρεία, *latreía* is related to the cultic concept of *leitourgía*, from which our English word *liturgy* derives and which refers to *a public religious ministry or service*. Λατρεία, *latreía* involves a *religious dimension of worship*. Zodhiates, *The Complete Word Study Dictionary: New Testament*. The NIV aptly translates this expression as *"your spiritual act of worship."*

observes regarding Jesus' discussion with the woman at the well in Samaria:

> The woman's recognition of Jesus as a prophet leads her to raise the most burning issue between Samaritans and Jews, namely the place where God should be worshipped. The command in Deut 12:1–14 to worship God in the place that he will show follows the command to pronounce a blessing from Mt. Gerizim and a curse from Mt. Ebal (Deut 11:29). In the Samaritan Pentateuch of Deut 27:3 the place where an altar is to be built on arrival in the Promised Land is Gerizim, not Ebal as in the MT. That could conceivably be right, the text possibly having been changed through anti-Samaritan motives. References in the later books of the OT to worship in Jerusalem would not have been viewed by the Samaritans as authoritative, since the Pentateuch alone was binding for them. In the Persian period a temple was built on Gerizim; it was destroyed by John Hyrcanus in 128 B.C., but the Samaritans continued to worship on the sacred site.[4]

A former missionary and church leader in the mid-1960s created quite a stir when he published a series of articles in one of the Church of Christ's weekly religious journals, the *Firm Foundation*, stressing that the meaning of worship is not what is stressed in the text of 1 Cor 11:17-14:36. In the mind of the writer of these articles the implied context of such meetings was thus purely the edification of the congregation, and not necessarily formal worship. The thrust of the articles was to shift the focus of the Christian assembly from tired and worn out formal worship to edification. Obviously, he did not understand that what Paul was addressing in 1 Corinthians was abuses of the Lord's Day worship assembly which had degenerated into confusion and disarray in which little or no edification took place! We will note below that in a truly spiritual corporate worship assembly, when the worship is directed toward God and Christ, the worshipper should obviously be edified! Corporate worship of

---

[4] Beasley-Murray, *John*, pp. 61f.

God, in a genuine spirit of worship, and the edification of the worshipper of God, are bound together in the act of worshipping! Worship and edification in genuine worship are held together in a dynamic tension. The worshipper worships God and in doing so is edified and strengthened by being drawn into the presence of God in all of his glory.

Although the word worship is not always used in the New Testament as a term referring exclusively to the Lord's Day assembly[5] the expression Lord's Day worship obviously refers to an environment *in which worshippers are paying homage and reverent thanks to God and Christ*! One would hardly question the point that the central dynamic of worshipping God, especially when celebrating the Lord's Supper, involves a focused worshipful activity of paying homage to Jesus Christ and his Father for their gracious acts of salvation. Neither would one question the point that in doing this that one is involved in being edified and encouraged!

Thus, Paul critically addressed the failure of the Corinthian Church to celebrate the Lord's Super in a worshipful and respectful attitude at 1 Cor 11:17-34. Similarly, he criticized the Corinthians at 1 Cor 14:23-25 for abusing the spirit of worship in the worship assembly. They were using spiritual giftedness for personal aggrandizement by focusing on their individual charismatic gifts in the assembly. Note the underlined expressions in the following text from 1 Cor 14:23-25 emphasizing the nature of these assemblies as worship edifying occasions:

> *²³ If, therefore, <u>the whole church assembles,</u> and all speak in tongues, and outsiders or unbelievers enter, will they not say that you are mad? ²⁴ But if all prophesy, and an unbeliever or outsider enters, he is convicted by all, he is called to account by all, ²⁵ the secrets of his heart are disclosed; and so, falling on his face, <u>he will worship God</u> and declare that God is really among you.*

---

[5] In this study I will alternately use the terms Lord's Day celebratory worship meal, the Eucharist, Communion, and Lord's Supper to refer to the same worshipful experience and by doing so hopefully encourage the reader to explore the specific nuances of the different terms.

It is apparent that Paul expected all things in the Christian assembly in which the Eucharist or Communion was experienced to be done decently, respectfully, and in an orderly worshipful manner in which God and Christ would be honored and worshipped, and consequently the congregation would be edified by such worshipful activity (1 Cor 14:33, 40).

The Corinthian Christians were abusing the Lord's Supper or Eucharist by permitting the celebration to degenerate into common meal in which some were getting drunk, and the poor were abused or neglected (1 Cor 11:17ff). This certainly did not fit the definition of worship in any form, and neither was anyone edified by such action!

Even though the word worship is not used exclusively in the New Testament to refer to what the church does in celebrating the Lord's Supper when the whole church assembles together, the concept of worship surely is a theme Christians would appropriately use to describe what they did in the corporate gathering in a church assembly on the Lord's Day when the Lord's Supper or Eucharist was celebrated, prayers said, and hymns sung. Worship and edification are two aspects empowering the dynamic tension of praise-honor and edification. Simply put, genuine spiritual worship and edification are not an *either/or* dynamic, but a *both/and* dynamic.

As mentioned previously in this study I am focusing attention primarily on the Lord's Day assembly when the Lord's Supper is celebrated. Another book could be written on the Rom 12 dynamic of everyday worship.

Thus, Christians, when assembled in the Lord's Day worship assembly, pay homage and veneration to God in his full Trinitarian sense as the almighty creator, savior, redeemer, and sustainer of life, they consider this as worshipping God and use the term *proskunéō* to describe this.

The concept of *worship*, whether practiced in everyday life or corporately in the assembled body on the Lord's Day refers to *an attitude, a disposition, a direction, a focus, and a dynamic of paying respect and homage directed toward God.* God is both the subject and object of such worship and veneration. He is the one who calls us to worship and the one who is worshipped!

When we worship during the week by living lives of spiritual service to God, by loving our neighbor and helping the poor, God is also the focus and direction of this worshipful service through our everyday living for Christ. He calls us to a life of sacrificial living and is in that living the focus and object of our worship. Both corporate and personal living certainly are acts of *worship*. By paying homage and laying our lives down in service of God we worship in his holiness.

In the section that follows we will explore in greater detail the richer meaning of the three Greek words used to describe Christian worship. First, *latreía*, then *proskunéō*, then finally *sébomai*.

Latreía. Λατρεία, a noun, derives from the Greek verb λατρεύω, latreúō, which means to worship, or to offer divine service that conforms to reason. It can refer to religious or cultic[6] service, or to a life of service offered to God in general, based on a worshipful attitude. Cf. Rom 9:4, 12:1; Heb 9:1; Josh 22:27, Deut 4:28; Judg 2:11, 13.[7]

> Zodhiates adds regarding the origins of the verb latreúō:
> Allied to *látris*, a hired servant as opposed to *doúlos* ... a bond slave. Therefore, to serve or worship but not out of compulsion. *Latreúō* originally meant to work for reward, to serve. The meanings of service and worship are intertwined. It occurs some 90 times in the Septuagint and 21 times in the NT, 8 of which are in Luke and Acts with its syn. *douleúō* (1398), to work, serve.[8]

Hermann Strathmann in Kittel's *Theological Dictionary of the New Testament* makes several significant observations on *latreía*:

> *The Purely Religious Character of the word is Determined by the LXX.*

---

[6] By *cultic* we imply "a particular system of religious worship, especially with reference to its rites and ceremonies" or "a particular form of religious worship." *Collins English Dictionary, Oxford English Dictionary.*
[7] Zodhiates, Λατρεία.
[8] Zodhiates, Λατρεία.

> *The influence of the LXX may be seen in the fact that the word never refers to human relations, let alone to secular services. The ministry denoted by λατρεύειν is always offered to God (or to heathen gods: ἐλάτρευσαν τῇ κτίσει παρὰ τὸν κτίσαντα R. 1:25; τῇ στρατιᾷ τοῦ οὐρανοῦ, Ac. 7:42) ... According to LXX usage the primary reference of λατρεύειν is to the sacrificial ministry which is to be offered to Yahweh in contrast to other gods. This usage recurs in Ac. 7:7 (cf. Ex. 3:12); 7:42 (cf. Jer. 7:18 LXX); also R. 1:25 ... Of the five occurrences of this word in the NT, three refer to the sacrificial ministry ... The concrete idea of sacrifice seems always to cling to the noun no less than to the verb. This is also true in the last verse (Rom 12:1) ... The service which Christians are to offer consists in the fashioning of their inner lives and their outward physical conduct in a way which plainly distinguishes them from the world and which corresponds to the will of God. This is the living sacrifice which they have to offer. Using a term which was current in the philosophy of his day, Paul describes this sacrifice as a λογικὴ λατρεία, a service of God which corresponds to human reason, in which, however, divine reason is also at work. If man listens to the voice of reason, he must acknowledge that this is the true service of God.*[9]

Ralph P. Martin observes that *"to worship God is to ascribe to Him supreme worth for he alone is worthy."*[10] He adds that the Hebrew behind *latreía* is *abodah* which simply means *service* implying in the Old Testament *divine service* worthy of God's honor, a service by which God is glorified. *Latreía* in a religious or cultic sense, thus implies worshipping God in a manner that bestows honor on God.[11] In particular I find Martin's explanation of the Hebrew word *abodah, service,* helpful:

> *The second term is abodah, translated 'service'. It is from the same root that the term 'slave', 'servant' (ebed)*

---

[9] Hermann Strathmann in Kittel, *Theological Dictionary of the New Testament*, vol. 4, pp. 63ff. (Italicized text mine, IAF)
[10] Martin, *Worship,* Kindle location 86.
[11] Martin, *Worship,* Kindle location 108f.

> *is taken; and this is important. For the highest designation of the Hebrew in his engagement with the worship of God is just this word 'servant'. He delighted to call himself God's ebed (e.g. Psalm cxvi, 16); and expressed that joy in his private and corporate praise and prayer ... the Hebrew notion, implicit in the word ebed, expressed the relationship of servant and kindly master (Exodus xxi, 1-6) ... and when men called themselves the 'servants of God' in the cultic sense, they were paying tribute to the innate and honored relationship into which God had brought them ... The corresponding Greek term is latreía ('service'); and in the light of the background in the Old Testament, we should understand Paul's use of the same Greek word in Romans 1, 9; xii, 1; as well as his privilege and honor to be entrusted with the service of the Gospel. That service is his offering to God of that worth and honour by which he is glorified in the salvation of the Gentiles.*
>
> *From these two Bible terms we learn something of the worshipper's attitude to the command which God addresses to him. He is summoned into the presence of the Holy One of Israel; and he responds to this call with an appropriate sense of reverence ...* [12]

Zodhiates observes that when used in conjunction with the Greek with *logikḗ ... logical, latreía* is service which conforms to human reason.[13] However, since in the Greek mind, the concept of reason takes place in the spiritual realm of man this expression is correctly translated in the RSV and ESV as *spiritual worship*.[14] One needs to remember that Jesus in John 4:24 spoke of *genuine spiritual worship* in place of physical worship!

---

[12] Martin, *Worship*, Kindle location 108f.
[13] Zodhiates, λογικός *logikós* ... from *lógos* ... *reason*. Pertaining to reason and therefore reasonable, or pertaining to speech as reasonable expression. In Rom. 12:1, the "reasonable service" or worship is to be understood as that service to God which implies intelligent meditation or reflection without the kind of heathen practices intimated in 1 Cor. 12:2.
[14] Mounce, *Romans*, p. 231; Dunn, *Romans*, p. 711.

Proskuneō. This Greek verb "προσκυνέω, *proskuneō*, simply means to worship, do obeisance, show respect, fall or prostrate oneself before someone.

> Literally it means to *kiss toward* someone, to throw a kiss in token of respect or homage. It is spoken of those who pay reverence and homage to deity, to render divine honors, to worship, to adore, with the basic idea of prostration, which, however, is often dropped."[15]

A key text in which προσκυνέω, *proskuneō* is used would be John 4:20ff, notably John 4:24, "God is spirit, and those who worship (*προσκυνοῦντας* from *proskuneō*) him must worship (*προσκυνεῖν* also from *proskuneō*) in spirit and truth." *Genuine spiritual worship is spiritually bowing or prostrating oneself before God and paying him all of the homage he is due.*

Heinrich Greeven in Kittel likewise observes that the verb means "to bow toward, to kiss, to venerate in worship, to do obeisance."

> *In the NT, as in the world of Israelite-Jewish faith generally, the thought of God's transcendence closed the door on the kind of devaluation of προσκυνεῖν which may be seen in ... the Greek papyri ... The Fourth Evangelist joins hands with the divine of Rev, before whose eyes the worship of heaven involves constantly repeated proskynesis (falling down or toward in worship), Rev. 4:10; 5:14; 7:11; 11:16; 19:4. Here falling down is in each case specifically mentioned."*[16]

The Hebrew words behind *proskuneō* are *hishahawah* and *shahah*. They carry the same overtones of "submissive lowliness and deep respect including bowing down in lowly prostration before one in reverence for their majesty." Martin explains:

> *First, the Old Testament word hishahawah means literally 'a bowing down'; and emphasizes the way in which an Israelite fittingly thought of his approach to the holy presence of God. He bows himself down in lowly*

---

[15] Zodhiates, *προσκυνέω*.
[16] Heinrich Greeven in Kittel, *Theological Dictionary of the New Testament*, vol. 6, pp. 764f.

> *reverence and prostration. The term indeed is used of men's homage to their fellows who, as V. I. Ps, command respect (Genesis xxvii, 29; 1 Samuel xxv, 23; 2 Samuel xiv, 33; xxiv, 20); but the full significance is seen in the use of the word when it means the Hebrew's approach to God, the great King and sovereign Lord (Genesis xxiv, 52; 2 Chronicles vii, 3; xxix, 29). The Greek term used in the Septuagint to translate shahah, is proskunein, with the same overtones of submissive lowliness and deep respect.[17]*

Reference to any good Greek concordance of the New Testament will reveal that the word group προσκυνέω, *proskunéō* is found all over the Gospels in regard to worshipping God and Jesus, and also in the remainder of the New Testament in several places of worshipping God in some specific act of worship (Acts 24:11; Heb 1:6; 1 Cor 14:25).

Sébomai. Another Greek term that is sometimes used for worship is σέβομαι, *sébomai*. Zodhiates observes that this word means:

> *"... to worship, to reverence. In the NT, only in the mid. (Matt. 15:9; Mark 7:7 quoted from Is. 29:13; Acts 16:14; 18:7, 13; 19:27; Sept.: Josh. 4:24; Job 1:9). The participle form of the noun, sebómenos, refers to a worshiper of the true God (Acts 13:43, 50; 16:14; 17:4, 17). These worshippers of God were Gentile proselytes as expressed in Acts 13:43."[18]*

Foerster in Kittel, in an extended article on the cognate forms of *sébomai* observes, "Derivates of the stem σεβ- are used very commonly in Gk. and are a typical expression of Greek piety.[19]

> *In Acts the word is also used 6 times for the so-called God-fearers, i.e., σεβόμενοι with or without θεόν ... The first is the claim to worship the only true God ...*

---

[17] Martin, *Worship*, Kindle location 109.
[18] Zodhiates, *Sébomai*.
[19] Werner Foerster in Kittel, *Theological Dictionary of the New Testament*, vol. 7, p. 168.

> *Secondly, σεβόμενος with the accusative of the god denotes worship and not just reverence ... If, then, this formula is used for the God-fearers it means that they were not just impressed by, nor did they merely honour, the God of the OT. They also worshipped Him, and they did so in specific acts.*[20]

Although *sébomai* is not as common in the New Testament as *proskunéō* or *latreía* it carries the same sense of worshipping God by honoring, venerating, and paying reverence toward the divine.

Summary of Worship Terms

From this brief introduction to the meaning of the concept of worship we draw the following observations. Worship in the Old and New Testament involves:

a. Demonstrating the worth of God in a reverent attitude and behavior.
b. Offering divine service to God which is worthy of God.
c. Either literally or symbolically bowing in prostration before God in an attitude of submissive lowliness.
d. A recognition that God is the *subject* and *object* of the worship in the sense that worship *begins* with God and *ends* with God. The worshipper in this sense can also be the *subject* offering the worship. The worship flows from the worshipper toward God as the *object* of worship and not toward the worshipper or in the interests of the worshipper.

---

[20] Foerster, in Kittel, p. 172.

Chapter 4: What is a Theology of Worship?

Sigler and Bradley;
As we believe, so we worship ... Worship without theology is sentimental and weak; theology without worship is cold and dead. Worship and theology together combine to motivate a strong Christian faith and to empower a fruitful Christian life. Worship should be regulated and determined by doctrine.[1]

Since the title of this study is a Theology of Worship it might be appropriate to clarify at this point what is meant by Theology, Biblical Theology, and a Theology of Worship.

We might begin simply by asking "what is theology?" and "who needs theology?"[2] I have on several occasions fielded comments like "We don't need theology, just give us Jesus, or just give us the Bible!" Coming from a people deeply committed to Scripture that concern is perfectly natural, especially when the person making this charge does not understand what we mean by theology!

So, What is Theology?

The word theology derives from two Greek words, θεός, *theós* and λόγος, *lógos*. Without digging too deeply into the origins of the two Greek words the following simple definitions will help. *Theós* in Greek simply means *divine*, something *divine*, or *a god*, but when used in the Old and New Testaments is often used for the name of the Judeo-Christian deity, *God* or *Elohim*. Zodhiates observes, "In the NT and the Septuagint (Greek Old Testament) *Theós*, God, generally relates to the Old Testament plural word *Elohim* and can therefore denote God including the Trinity."[3]

Zodhiates observes regarding *lógos* that "*Lógos* is a masculine noun from *légō* ... to speak intelligently ... an intelligent

---

[1] Franklin M. Segler and Randall Bradley, *Christian Worship*, p. 49.
[2] Cf. Grenz & Olson, *Who Needs Theology?*
[3] Adapted from Zodhiates, *theós*.

word as the expression of that intelligence, discourse, saying something."[4]

Briefly defined, then, *theology refers to an intelligent discussion of matters relating to God.*

Michael Bird cites *The Compact Macquarie Dictionary* which defines theology as "The science which treats God, His attributes, and His relations to the universe."[5] Other than the confusion in the minds of some of equating theology with the term science,[6] we might think of theology as *a faith* which is a good definition of a system of logical belief, that is, a science, which is a system of knowledge and understanding. Charles Ryrie defines theology as "thinking about God and expressing those thoughts in some way."[7] Not bad other than theological thought comes down somewhere between the Macquarie definition as a *science* and Ryrie's broader comment on simply *thinking and expressing thoughts*! I prefer Robert Culver's definition of theology as "Christian theology is the study or organized treatment of the topic, God, from a standpoint of Christianity."[8] Bird summarizes several excellent comments intended to define theology as "the result of study, community reflection, and a dynamic interaction between God and his people ... Theology is the attempt to verbalize and to perform our relationship with God."[9]

There are different kinds of "theology" depending on the source or context of the discussion. One could speak of *social theology* in which the concept of God is discussed in relation to social interests of social justice and social concerns. There could

---

[4] Adapted from Zodhiates, *lógos*.
[5] Michael F. Bird, *Evangelical Theology*, Kindle location 472.
[6] Science is a broader term than often associated with it when restricted to the study of natural phenomena. *Science* (from Latin *scientia*, meaning "knowledge) is a systematic enterprise that builds and organizes knowledge and can refer to a way of pursuing knowledge. A branch of knowledge or study dealing with a body of facts or truths systematically arranged and showing the operation of general laws. *Dictionary.com*. Cf. also *Science, Oxford English Dictionary*.
[7] Charles Ryrie, *Basic Theology*, p. 9.
[8] Robert Culver, *Systematic Theology: Biblical and Historical*, p. 2.
[9] Michael F. Bird, *Evangelical Theology*, Kindle location 487; cf. also Grenz & Olson, *Who Needs theology*, pp. 36ff.

be *evangelistic theology* in which evangelism is discussed in the *mission* of God and what God is doing through Jesus Christ and the church. One could speak of *mission theology* in which one discusses God in the context of mission. One could speak of *kingdom theology* in which the kingdom of God is explored in the context of God's *Mission Dei*. *Islamic Theology* considers God in the context of the Koran. *Mormon Theology* is discussed in the context of the *Book of Mormon* and the *Pearl of Great Price*.

The discipline of *Systematic Christian Theology* examines what the Christian Scriptures say about God and topics related to God such as the Trinity, Jesus Christ, the Holy Spirit, the Atonement, and the Last Days. *Historical Theology* examines the development and flow of theological thought through the centuries of church history. Finally, one could speak of *Biblical Theology* in which one explores what God is doing as revealed in His Word in the context of the message of Old and New Testament stories.

In this book we are discussing *worship theology*. We will explore how worship and God interact, or what our action of worshipping says about God and what we say about God. In this book on the *theology of worship* we will also say something about the nature of *genuine worship* (*worshipping God in spirit and truth*, John 4:24), and the attitude and focus of the worshippers as they interact with God as revealed in his Word.

Prolegomena[10] to Theology

Michael Bird points to a profound aspect of doing theology. *Everyone has to begin somewhere*! He calls this beginning a *prolegomenon* to theology implying that one has to have a "word to say" or a viewpoint or presupposition regarding one's faith *before* one begins, or *as* one begins to think theologically. Prolegomenon derives from two Greek words, πρό, *pró* meaning *before* and λέγω, *légō* meaning *to speak* or *say*, hence having something to say *before*. I would prefer to call this a *presupposition*

---

[10] Prolegomena is the plural of prolegomenon which refers to *a critical or discursive introduction to something*. Miriam Webster Dictionary defines prolegomena as *a formal essay or critical discussion serving to introduce and interpret an extended work*.

regarding theology, but I do like Bird's use of the concept of prolegomenon, a word spoken in advance of beginning to do or speak of theology.

Let me illustrate this rather dramatically! A Muslim *begins* his theology with the prolegomena of the Koran and a view of his definition of God as Allah. A Jew would begin with the prolegomena of the Hebrew Bible (or as the Jew might define it as *Torah or Tanak*) and a view of God defined as a monolithic understanding of YHWH. Evangelical theology begins with the prolegomena of the Old and New Testaments in the Christian canon as the definitive understanding of inspired words providing authority to evangelism. For example, a prolegomena for evangelism or mission would include or begin with Jesus' Great Commission. The Christian prolegomena would also relate to a Trinitarian view of God, and a heavy emphasis on the gospel as the pivotal point of God's *Missio Dei*. A prolegomenon to traditional Evangelical theology would begin with the concept of the world *being lost in sin and needing to be "born again" through God's grace and the work of the Holy Spirit as the source of one's faith in the death of Jesus Christ. Traditional evangelical theology places a significant stress on the operation of the Holy Spirit in the origin of faith.*[11]

While not disagreeing with Bird's evangelical emphasis on the gospel I will propose that the presupposition or prolegomena of Christian theology must be *the revelation of God in his full Trinitarian form as revealed in the Christian canon of Scripture* which includes both Old and New Testaments. *The dynamic of Christian theology would be the discovery of who this God is as creator and savior and how he has gone about setting the world right again through his covenants with Abraham, Moses, and Jesus Christ.*[12] The central focus of Christian theology would be

---

[11] Cf. Michael Bird, *Evangelical Theology*, Kindle location 1720ff; Douglas A. Foster, *et al*, editors, *The Encyclopedia of the Stone-Campbell Movement*. In the strictest sense Evangelical churches should not be confused with other churches which stress atonement through God's grace and an obedient faith.
[12] Interestingly this became the prolegomena to N. T. Wright in his theological journey of justification in the Old and New Testaments.

the holiness of God and his almighty sovereign power and purpose as revealed in Scripture.

What this means for a Christian theology of worship is *that Christians speak of a biblical theology in which Scripture, not anthropology, sociology, or cultural concerns* become the defining prolegomena or presupposition leading up to a theology of worship. The focus of a theology of worship must be what Scripture says about God and not how anthropological interests define or see God.

Karl Barth in 1919 rejected the 19th century liberal anthropological approach to theology. He introduced a new radical direction to theology in what became known as neo-orthodox theology. In Barth's approach to theology God became the center or prolegomena of theology rather than man.[13] Herbert Hartwell made this insightful observation when introducing Karl Barth's theology:

> *We only need to compare Karl Barth's theocentric mode of thought with the anthropocentric theological writings of the nineteenth and the beginning of the twentieth century ... As far as Bart's theology is concerned, we must go even further. Though many theologies have been developed in the core of the history of Christianity, of only a few of them can it be said that they accomplished a real turning-point in man's theological thinking, let alone, to use another metaphor, have turned the helm through an angle of 180 degrees.*[14]

The core of Barth's theological reversal of 19th theology was to replace man and anthropology as the center or prolegomena of theology with a high view of God as the beginning point of all theological thinking.[15]

Perhaps we need to return to Barth's prolegomenon for theology when discussing a biblical theology, or a theology of worship! It will be my persuasion in this study that theology and worship should not be an anthropological centered dynamic

---

[13] Cf. Barth, *Protestant Theology in the Nineteenth Century*.
[14] Hartwell, *The Theology of Karl Barth: An Introduction*, p. 1f.
[15] Cf. Barth, *Protestant Theology in the Nineteenth Century*.

grounded in what man, culture, or sociology want or do. Our theology must center on God and not man; a theocentric center and driving force, and not an anthropocentric dynamic.

John Bowden noticed a clear distinction in Barth's theology between what Barth called *religion* as opposed to *theology*. Barth obviously rejected religion as the basis of his theological thinking since religion focused on what man does. Bowden observed regarding Barth:

> *Barth made a quite fundamental distinction between 'religion' and 'theology', and the two were not to be confused ... he regarded 'religion' as something entirely human. It was man's search for God, a search often so fruitless or perverted that it ended in a completely false god. Theology, on the other hand, was, and is, as its name signifies, 'God-talk': not talk about God, for God is not an object that can form the content of our discourse, but the human response to the word of God that has already been spoken to man before theology begins.*[16]

Two salient points stand out from Bowden's observation. 1) Barth's prolegomena or presupposition to theology was clearly *the word of God or the word spoken by God in Jesus Christ*, and 2) his radical rejection of an anthropological approach to theology influenced even his epistemology to the extent that he rejected any form of natural theology which involved man's rational dimension. Although Barth's definition of the *word of God* was unique for his day, referring to the message spoken by God in Jesus rather than words simply found in the written word. Barth affirmed that it is in the word of God, that is the message spoken by God in the life of Jesus, that is the prolegomena of theology:

> *The theology (think message, IAF) to be observed here is one which, nourished by the hidden sources of the documents of Israel's history, first achieved unambiguous expression in the writings of the New Testament evangelists, apostles, and prophets ..."*[17]

---

[16] Bowden, *Karl Barth*, p. 13.
[17] Barth, *Evangelical Theology*, p. 11.

My reason for drawing on Karl Barth's "radical"[18] approach to theology was his strident rejection of any anthropological or sociological approach to theology that focused more on man than on Jesus, the word of God. Nineteenth century theology was thoroughly anthropocentric and anthropological. It is this same anthropocentric tendency in some modern theologies of worship that concerns me. I see the same anthropological movement in some theologies today in which sociological and cultural concerns define theology and doctrine. Many evangelical theologians like Grudem and Bird are calling for a return to a theocentric approach, as seen in Barth's early 20th reactionary approach to theology. This does not mean that we refuse to admit that we are living in a post-modern anthropocentric culture that challenges any concept of ultimate external truth. It means only that we do not buy the mindset that ultimate truth lies in personal human or anthropocentric experience.

In keeping with many evangelicals who have a clear understanding of the challenges posed by post-modernism I maintain that the anthropological anthropocentric post-modern mindset has to be accepted as a current trend in our 21st century western culture, but rather than capitulating to this mindset we must address it sensitively albeit differently than out of a past or supposed dysfunctional rationalist approach that has been defined as an outdated *modernism*. Although accepting the fact that our apologetic to a post-modern culture will not be effective via a rationalist hermeneutic, we argue that theology must remain firmly grounded in a theocentric footing and not in a cultural or anthropocentric one. In theology we are not seeking to find what is pleasing to a contemporary culture. We are seeking to find a God who is speaking to a broken anthropocentric culture through his Christ-centered Word or message.

Adopting Barth's definition of religion, *religion* as the human practice of faith may tend toward an anthropocentric, cultur-

---

[18] By *radical* I infer that at the turn of the 20th century Barth's approach was *radical and countercultural*, it *landed in the playground of the theologians as a bomb*! That is radical!

ally oriented view of theology, but our *theology* as opposed to religion must remain theocentric not anthropocentric. Contrary to some tendencies, specifically in a theology of worship, we should hold that our *religion* is shaped by our *theology* and not our *theology* by our *religion*.

In this regard I have some difficulty accepting the model of biblical hermeneutic adopted by some contemporary preachers who in their sermons find the translation of a scriptural text that supports their theological point in a proof-text hermeneutic. I prefer an inductive approach to theology that begins with the text defining our theology or theological point! I see this as an anthropological approach to the text rather than a theological approach and use of Scripture. Dr. Phil Slate, former dean of the Harding Graduate School of Theology in Memphis, Tennessee, once observed in a dialogue on the use of music in worship that it is not the instrument that divides us but how we read and interpret Scripture. Likewise, how we do theology is grounded in how we read Scripture and not by what our contemporary culture believes. Regarding doing theology in the pulpit we can do so either anthropocentrically to suit our sermon point or audience, or theo-centrically to shape and define our homiletic point or theology from sound Scriptural hermeneutic. We do not define our theology and doctrine from our vantage point in a sermon but define our theology and doctrine from the theology of Scripture.

Since I have introduced the word doctrine above, and since doctrine is a concept that is not comfortably accepted in a postmodern culture, and in many church settings, I feel the need to address this in the context of doing theology!

Theology and Doctrine

So, what is doctrine? Many today do not like the word or the concept of doctrine because it speaks to them of church rules, dogmatism,[19] etc. However, doctrine is a healthy biblical term

---

[19] Dogmatism refers to the tendency to be dogmatic: the inclination to express strongly held opinions in a way that suggests they should be accepted without question. Dogma is a principle or set of principles laid down by an authority as incontrovertibly true, a formulated opinion that is authoritatively stated. *Oxford English Dictionary.*

and concept! In various forms, such as *doctrine, a different doctrine*, or *sound doctrine* the word is found 14 times in the New Testament Epistles and twice in the Gospels. The word in Greek is διδασκαλία, *didaskalía*, which primarily means "to teach. It basically means teaching or instruction … something taught, instruction."[20] In the New Testament it simply refers to the teaching of the apostolic church, which we today find in the New Testament as inspired and normative Scriptures regarding Jesus Christ (2 John 9, 10; Heb 6:1) and the Christian life (Rom 16:17; 1 Tim 4:6; Tit 1).

I have referenced the term *Didache* above in regard to the 2nd century work whose title is the *Didache*: "*The Teaching of the Twelve Apostles*" which was intended to draw attention to appropriate behavior in the new Christian churches springing up all over the Mediterranean *diaspora*. The young church found it necessary since not all Christians or churches had access to the apostolic writings, Gospels and Epistles, that were still in the form of being collected into some form of "library" codex. It was well intended but opened the door to formal credal works shaped by different sections of the church in support and defense of this religious opinion or behavior. It was against such eventual credal confessions that many in England, Scotland, and Holland eventually reformed or restored their Christian faith in restoration movements such as the British and Dutch Puritans, the Anabaptists, Amish, Mennonites, Churches of Christ, and other similar reformation movements.

When Scripture is taught from a dogmatic standpoint or a set list of church rules I can appreciate why some pull back, but when Scripture is taught from a mindset seeking to learn and understand God's will as revealed in Scripture it can be a positive experience. When doctrine is taught in what Barth calls *religion*, it refers to *a dogmatic binding set of church rules*. I can understand the reluctance of intelligent people to fall in line with human opinion, and much church doctrine as found in creeds is a little more than a compilation of human opinions suited to maintaining the nature or character of that church or religious group.

---

[20] Zodhiates, διδασκαλία.

However, when Scripture is taught and studied in a mindset of seeking God and His will as in a theocentric theology whose prolegomena is God and His word, doctrine can be a life shaping and enriching experience.

To express this simply, biblical doctrine is simply seeking to *understand* and *teach* about God and Jesus Christ *as taught in Scripture*. Doctrine refers to *teaching* and *learning* God's Word revealed in Scripture! Paul explained to his young mission associate Timothy that *Scripture inspired by the Holy Spirit is profitable for guidance, teaching, hence doctrine, in leading a Christian life, cf. 2 Tim 3:14-17.* In vs 3:16 Paul used the word διδασκαλία, *didaskalía*, which is interpreted in our New Testament as *teaching*. *Doctrine* is merely *Scriptural teaching* or the *teaching of Scripture*!

> *[14] But as for you, continue in what you have learned and have firmly believed, knowing from whom you learned it [15] and how from childhood you have been acquainted with the sacred writings which are able to instruct you for salvation through faith in Christ Jesus. [16] All scripture is inspired by God and profitable for teaching, for reproof, for correction, and for training in righteousness, [17] that the man of God may be complete, equipped for every good work.*

Who Does Theology?

In fact, all Christians do theology! Either positively or negatively! We do it with different degrees of intensity as we teach, deny, or explain in different ways what we believe about our view of ultimate reality, God, Jesus Christ, the Holy Spirit, the Church, Salvation, etc. In the Christian context whenever anyone tells the story of the Bible or explains what they believe about God they are doing theology.

Simply put, *theology,* derived from the Greek words *theologia,* or *theós* and λόγια, means *discussion about God and things related to God.*[21]

---

[21] Stone and Duke, *How to Think Theologically*; Geoffrey W. Bromiley, "Theology," *Baker's Dictionary of Theology*, pp. 518ff; Alan Richardson, "Theology,", pp. 335f.

Theology is done at different levels such as at the university or academy level which often results in publications; at the local church theology takes place in some form of faith statement either in a sermon from the pulpit or in the classroom. It may take place in the bible class level for "faith instruction" or edification; the home for faith instruction; or with one's neighbors and friends in an evangelistic outreach. In every case the terminology adopted, or degree of proficiency may differ, but we all do theology. We may do theology apologetically in defense of our faith; we may do theology dogmatically in defense of our opinion; we may do theology evangelistically when explaining the story and message of Jesus to others; we may do theology in the context of worship when defining the direction and content of worship; we do theology persuasively in sermons; we may do theology didactically when teaching a bible class, but we all in some fashion do theology![22]

The critical point in this discussion in this study as we discuss theology is determining our prolegomena[23] or presuppositions when doing theology.

Final Comments on the Method, Dynamic, and Source of Theology, and the Dynamic of a Theology of Worship

Since we all do theology, and how we do theology, is the point of this study, we will need to discuss briefly the method, driving force, and the primary concern for doing theology. Anselm, Archbishop of Canterbury in England, ca 1100 CE, explained theology as *faith seeking understanding*, the Latin being *Fides Quaerens Intellectum*. For Anselm, theology originates in one's faith seeking understanding or enlightenment in a philosophical model of thinking. We call his model of thinking scholasticism, a form of argumentation through debate at a highly scholarly academic level such as in a Middle Ages university academy. In many ways the pluralistic philosophy of postmodernism parallels Anselm's situation of a pluralistic society seeking to understand or define truth. In Anselm's model, theology was rooted in one's church-faith and then sought to identify

---

[22] Cf. Richardson, *Theology*.
[23] See the discussion of this term above.

and deepen that faith through careful contemplation and discussion on the divine. *Faith seeking understanding* is a reasonable method of doing theology. The critical point in this thinking is *the origin of that faith and the basis or prolegomena for doing that theological* search for meaning or understanding. However, in our study we are setting theology in the prolegomena of Scripture as the Word of God and not in church debates. So, in the sense that we are discussing a *theology* of worship, theology may be the church seeking to understand its worship enlightened by its biblical faith and not enlightened by its cultural or church surroundings.[24]

However, not all theologies begin with faith or a church faith! Noted Christian theologian and scholar, C. S. Lewis, began his search for meaning from within an agnostic view of reality and in the context of dialogue with J. R. R. Tolkien, noted Roman Catholic scholar, Hugo Dyson, and a small group of Oxford Academics known as the *Inklings*.[25] Wolfhart Pannenberg, noted Christian theologian of the 1960s, began his theological journey out of a position of agnosticism and through a careful examination of historical methodology. He redefined historical methodology, *and through an examination of the Gospel story of Jesus' resurrection came to a theology of faith in the story of Jesus' resurrection.* His theology was still faith, or a search for faith, seeking understanding. His prolegomena was a historical method and his source the Scriptural Gospel story of Jesus.[26]

Any Islamic thinker will follow a similar theological process of examining his/her religious views in the light of the resources at their disposal, most likely the Koran. Anselm's principle of *faith seeking understanding* would apply to the Muslim seeking to understand his/her faith in the light of the Koran.

In *Kingdom Theology* one seeks to understand what the sovereign God of all creation has been doing in his creation ever since the fall of man and through His covenant with Abraham.

---

[24] Charles, *Anselm of Canterbury, Proslogion*; Cf. also Grenz and Olson, *Who Needs Theology*, p. 13; Richardson, "Theology," p. 335, and Bromiley, "Theology."
[25] Cf. Sayer, *Jack: A Life of C. S. Lewis,. passim*; Wilson, *C. S. Lewis, passim*.
[26] Ian A. Fair, *The Theology of Wolfhart Pannenberg*.

Kingdom Theology follows the biblical story of God's working through Moses, Israel, and then in the eschatological (final) age through Jesus Christ. *Kingdom Theology* seeks to understand God's *Missio Dei* and intention for the church. *Kingdom Theology* is thus faith seeking understanding of the missional purpose of God in the history of the biblical story. *Kingdom Theology* is grounded in the biblical story as revealed in Scripture as it seeks to understand God's purpose.

Biblical Theology understands the prolegomena of biblical theology to be the *redemptive purpose* of the sovereign God *as revealed in and through Scripture*. The method of biblical theology is *faith seeking understanding* in the light of the Biblical story as revealed in Scripture with the intention of learning God's saving activity throughout the biblical account culminating in Jesus Christ and his mission in this world. *Biblical Theology* does not begin (its source) in the doctrine of the church or in one's personal doctrinal persuasion. It is firmly rooted in the story of God's eternal saving activity as revealed in Scripture. *Biblical Theology* is not grounded in an anthropocentric view of reality but seeks to address that post-modern anthropocentric mindset through solid Scriptural exegesis and theology.

When speaking of a *Christian Theology* obviously the process is to think carefully about one's faith in the context of Jesus Christ. The dynamic of *Christian Theology* will be *faith seeking understanding* in the light of the Scriptural story of Jesus Christ and the Christian life. The prolegomena would be a belief in the holiness and sovereignty of a Trinitarian God, and the source of that theology would be the Word of God as revealed in both the Old and New Testaments.

In a *Theology of Worship*, which is the theme of this book, the prolegomenon of worship theology is faith reflecting on the veneration and worship of the holy and sovereign Triune God who has in Christ Jesus redeemed man from a fallen world. In the Christian context worship is thus the expression of gratitude and reverence paid to our Father God in celebration of his saving activity in Jesus Christ. Neither the dynamic nor the prolegomenon of Christian worship are contemporary culture or contemporary sociological preferences. Neither are the dynamic or prolegomena of Christian worship the concern for reaching out to the lost, as important as that is in the *Missio Dei*. *Christian Worship* originates in reverence for and celebration of the redemptive activity of God as the *subject* and *object* of that worship.

In a Christian theology of worship, one seeks to examine Christian worship (not overlooking the foundational worship of Judaism) in the light of what the Holy Scriptures reveal about the nature and activity of God, and the nature of worship in the eschatological age of Christianity as reflected on in Scripture, notably the New Testament and early 1st century Christianity.

The foundation of a theology of worship is biblical doctrine appropriately understood and interpreted, and not culture. Thus, the method of doing a theology of worship is through careful examination of Scripture, the source of biblical theology, and not through the presuppositions of culture or contemporary society. One seeks to understand the focus and dynamic of Christian worship in the light of revealed Scripture.

A Christian theology of worship is *faith seeking to understand* the *nature and dynamic of worship* in the light of the Scriptural revelation of the nature and saving activity of God, and not in the light or preferences of secular culture. The prolegomenon of Christian worship is not culture or the sociological preferences of contemporary culture.

> *Christian theology is a reflection on the Triune God, seeking to determine what the Father, Son, and Holy Spirit have been working in history to bring about the redemption of man.*
>
> *Christian theology is grounded in the creative and redemptive teaching of God established and taught in Scripture, the Old and New Testaments, both understood as Scripture inspired by the Holy Spirit.*
>
> *Christian theology is grounded in what Scripture says about God and man and is addressed to culture and not shaped by culture or human interest. One cannot remove culture from the discipline of doing theology and faith seeking to understand God in any given culture, but*

Christian theology is not shaped by culture but is shaped by Scripture.

Theology takes place in culture but is not shaped by culture. Scripture is the prolegomenon of theology in culture; not culture the prolegomenon of theology. Theology takes place in culture but arises in faith seeking to understand God from Scripture.

A theology of worship is faith working with Scripture seeking to give honor, praise and veneration to the Triune God for their redemptive activity as reflected in Scripture.

A theology of worship is grounded in Scripture and sees Scripture as the prolegomenon of worship.

A theology of worship takes place within culture but is shaped by Scripture and not culture.

Chapter 5: The Prolegomena[1] Focus, and Essential Elements of Worship

The Prolegomena of Worship

As mentioned in the previous chapter Michael F. Bird discussed the role of prolegomena in his *Evangelical Theology: A Biblical and Systematic Introduction.* His thoughts resonate well with a study of the theology of worship.[2] His chapter title to his discussion on theology is "Prolegomena: Beginning to Talk about God." He opens the discussion as follows:

> *Prolegomena is where you clear the deck on preliminary issues and show how you intend to set up a system of theology. It is what you say before you say anything about theology – in other words, a type of pre-theology, giving a definition of the gospel ...*

In the similar manner to Bird's introduction to theology I plan in this chapter to make some preliminary observations about New Testament worship, to discuss various worship related concepts, and to provide what in Bird's definition we may term a *pre-worship* definition! Essentially the prolegomenon to worship must be a discussion of God, *who* he is and *what kind* of God he is. In other words, when thinking about worship we must first reflect deeply on the divine nature and activity of God, and then on our relationship with God.

Who is This God We Worship?

God is the only Lord of all, the most awesome holy creator and Lord of all creation! He is the savior of the world! He is the one to whom we owe our existence and our eternal destiny!

Reflect for a moment on Israel's well known *Shema*, the prolegomena and confession of Israel's faith and theology, Deut 6:4-9:

> [4] *Hear, O Israel: <u>The Lord our God is one Lord</u>;*
> [5] *and you shall love the Lord your God with all your*

---

[1] By the term *prolegomena* I imply the thoughts and principles that lie behind or in front of something. Prolegomena derives from two Greek words, *pro* which means *before* and *légō* which means *to speak or say*. A synonym for prolegomena could be a *presupposition*.

[2] Bird, *Evangelical Theology*, Kindle location 448.

> heart, and with all your soul, and with all your might. *⁶ And these words which I command you this day shall be upon your heart; ⁷ and you shall teach them diligently to your children, and shall talk of them when you sit in your house, and when you walk by the way, and when you lie down, and when you rise. ⁸ And you shall bind them as a sign upon your hand, and they shall be as frontlets between your eyes. ⁹ And you shall write them on the doorposts of your house and on your gates.*

Most men since prehistoric days have in some form worshipped a power greater than themselves. Consider the comment by John B. Moss in his highly accredited study, *Man's Religions*:

> All religions imply in one way or another that man does not, and cannot, stand alone, that he is vitally related with and even dependent on powers in nature and society external to himself. Dimly or clearly, he knows that he is not an independent center of force capable of standing apart from the world.[3]

The view that all men must worship is one that lies behind all worship concepts. Likewise, this view is a fundamental aspect of the Judeo-Christian view of man having been created inherently in the image of a God who has traditionally been understood as the highest being.[4]

Forms of religion and worship in general have varied widely through the centuries, but overall there is in man a sense of awe before a greater power that has some influence over life. Sometimes these powers were no more than the powers of nature themselves which were either naturalized, anthropomorphized, "creatureized," or "divinized"! The religions of Egypt and ancient

---

[3] John B. Moss, *Man's Religions*, p. 2.
[4] As a Christian who believes that God created man and everything in the beginning, understanding man to be a worshipping creature who by his created nature worships a higher being is not difficult. The view that all men must worship is not a major hurdle for me! I am fully aware of the fact that some anthropologists and psychologists question the concept that man is by nature a worshipping being but there is enough evidence to argue for the fact that man must worship some power or powers. Cf. National Geographic, *Great Religions of the World*; M. J. Charlesworth; Parrinder, *Man and His Gods*.

Hinduism reflect these tendencies to naturalize or divinize these powers. The apostle Paul reflects on these tendencies in religion, writing disparagingly from within his Jewish faith, regarding man's tendency to turn the divine into a creature. Rom 1:20-23:

> [20] *Ever since the creation of the world his invisible nature, namely, his eternal power and deity, has been clearly perceived in the things that have been made. So they are without excuse;* [21] *for although they knew God they did not honor him as God or give thanks to him, but they became futile in their thinking and their senseless minds were darkened.* [22] *Claiming to be wise, they became fools,* [23] *and exchanged the glory of the immortal God for images resembling mortal man or birds or animals or reptiles.*

What I find interesting as a student of world religions is that in almost every case worship in most religious forms was shaped by some presupposition regarding creation, man, and the powers of nature. Some prolegomenon lies behind the religion, the worship, and the worshipper! It is that something is greater than the individual and must be venerated! Sigmund Freud believed that God is an illusion based on the fear of a father figure and that it was man's insecurity that caused him to turn to religion! I would not question man's insecurity in the presence of higher powers but would not go as far as Freud in denying a divine power toward which man turns.[5] My point is that the form of any worship adopted by man is shaped by an awareness of higher powers and a recognition of one's weakness in the presence of such powers. In worship that awareness results in awe and reverence and veneration of that power. In that sense one of the Greek words for worship is *proskunéō*, to *fall down before* someone or something, to *prostrate oneself before a great power in reverent awestruck veneration*. It is no wonder that this word and concept is fundamental to the Judea-Christian faith.

In the Judeo-Christian faith the divine power is identified simply as God. In the Old Testament he was known as YHWH.

---

[5] Sigmund Freud, *The Future of an Illusion*, 1927.

He identified himself in the Book of Revelation as "I am the Alpha and the Omega who is and who was and who is to come, the Almighty."[6] He is also identified in the New Testament as the Father of all nations (Eph 3:14), and is worshipped in the heavenly throne room as the most holy and almighty God who created all things:

> "Holy, holy, holy, is the Lord God Almighty, who was and is and is to come!" [9] And whenever the living creatures give glory and honor and thanks to him who is seated on the throne, who lives for ever and ever, [10] the twenty-four elders fall down before him who is seated on the throne and worship him who lives for ever and ever; they cast their crowns before the throne, singing, [11] "Worthy art thou, our Lord and God, to receive glory and honor and power, for thou didst create all things, and by thy will they existed and were created." [7]

This worship and adoration is transferred in the next chapter of Revelation to Jesus, the Lion of the tribe of Judah, the Root of David[8] who is in every way equal to the one true God and Father. Paul argued that in Jesus all the fulness of divinity was pleased to dwell (Col 1:19; 2:9; Phil 2:6). The messianic being, Jesus the Lion of the tribe of Judah, is worshipped by all of the heavenly hosts:

> And when he had taken the scroll, the four living creatures and the twenty-four elders fell down before the Lamb, each holding a harp, and with golden bowls full of incense, which are the prayers of the saints; [9] and they sang a new song, saying, "Worthy art thou to take the scroll and to open its seals, for thou wast slain and by thy blood didst ransom men for God from every tribe and tongue and people and nation, [10] and hast made them a kingdom and priests to our God, and they shall reign on earth." [11] Then I looked, and I heard around the throne and the living creatures and the elders the voice of many

---

[6] Rev 1:8.
[7] Rev 4:8–11.
[8] Rev 4:5.

> *angels, numbering myriads of myriads and thousands of thousands, ¹² saying with a loud voice, "Worthy is the Lamb who was slain, to receive power and wealth and wisdom and might and honor and glory and blessing!" ¹³ And I heard every creature in heaven and on earth and under the earth and in the sea, and all therein, saying, "To him who sits upon the throne and to the Lamb be blessing and honor and glory and might for ever and ever!" ¹⁴ And the four living creatures said, "Amen!" and the elders fell down and worshiped.[9]*

So impressive is the vision of Jesus in Revelation that the Apostle John fell down before him in worship:

> *¹² Then I turned to see the voice that was speaking to me, and on turning I saw seven golden lampstands, ¹³ and in the midst of the lampstands one like a son of man, clothed with a long robe and with a golden girdle round his breast; ¹⁴ his head and his hair were white as white wool, white as snow; his eyes were like a flame of fire, ¹⁵ his feet were like burnished bronze, refined as in a furnace, and his voice was like the sound of many waters; ¹⁶ in his right hand he held seven stars, from his mouth issued a sharp two-edged sword, and his face was like the sun shining in full strength.*
> *¹⁷ When I saw him, <u>I fell at his feet as though dead</u>. But he laid his right hand upon me, saying, "Fear not, I am the first and the last, ¹⁸ and the living one; I died, and behold I am alive for evermore, and I have the keys of Death and Hades. ¹⁹ Now write what you see, what is and what is to take place hereafter. ²⁰ As for the mystery of the seven stars which you saw in my right hand, and the seven golden lampstands, the seven stars are the angels of the seven churches and the seven lampstands are the seven churches.[10]*

---

[9] Rev 5:8–14.
[10] Rev 1:12–20.

The Book of Revelation is in many senses a liturgy of worship of the Almighty God and the Savior Jesus Christ. Notice the hymn sung in Revelation 5 in worship of God, the creator and redeemer of mankind:

> *[8] And when he had taken the scroll, the four living creatures and the twenty-four elders fell down before the Lamb, each holding a harp, and with golden bowls full of incense, which are the prayers of the saints; [9] and they sang a new song, saying, "Worthy art thou to take the scroll and to open its seals, for thou wast slain and by thy blood didst ransom men for God from every tribe and tongue and people and nation, [10] and hast made them a kingdom and priests to our God, and they shall reign on earth"* [11]
>
> *... And they sing the song of Moses, the servant of God, and the song of the Lamb, saying,*
> *"Great and wonderful are thy deeds, O Lord God the Almighty! Just and true are thy ways, O King of the ages! [4] Who shall not fear and glorify thy name, O Lord? For thou alone art holy. All nations shall come and worship thee, for thy judgments have been revealed."* [12]

Worship in the Christian sense is therefore an act of reverence paid toward the Almighty God who either controls the past, present, and future, or at least is responsible for the quality of life we seek. Worship is an act in which the worshipper pays homage to his Almighty God and prostrates himself before the holiness, power, and majesty of that God. The direction of this act of reverential worship is always away from the worshipper toward the power or divine being. *Worship is religious devotion directed toward the Almighty God, creator and father of all mankind* and not toward man.

In the Christian faith worship must be directed in awe and reverence toward the one true God who by His grace has saved us, and toward His son, Jesus, the one who provided the atoning

---

[11] Rev 5:8–11.
[12] Rev 15:3–4.

sacrifice and power of God's redemptive act by laying down his life as an atoning sacrifice for man.

The Christian's prolegomena or presupposition for worship is his/her view of the glory, holiness, love, and omnipotence of the almighty God.

Worship in the Old Testament
Early Old Testament Worship

In an interesting incident I am opening this discussion with the early period of the Old Testament; the antediluvian period and the period that is commonly known as the Patriarchal age. Although we have little knowledge of instructions to worship during these early days of Israel's history there is clear evidence of the fact that God was aware of the worship of the antediluvian people as is seen in his apparent rejection of Cain's sacrifice for its lack of faith. Genesis records this interesting reflection on worship at Gen 4:1ff:

> *Now Adam knew Eve his wife, and she conceived and bore Cain, saying, "I have gotten a man with the help of the Lord." ²And again, she bore his brother Abel. Now Abel was a keeper of sheep, and Cain a tiller of the ground. ³In the course of time Cain brought to the Lord an offering of the fruit of the ground, ⁴and Abel brought of the firstlings of his flock and of their fat portions. And the Lord had regard for Abel and his offering, ⁵but for Cain and his offering he had no regard. So Cain was very angry, and his countenance fell. ⁶The Lord said to Cain, "Why are you angry, and why has your countenance fallen? ⁷If you do well, will you not be accepted? And if you do not do well, sin is couching at the door; its desire is for you, but you must master it."*

The Worship of the Patriarchs

For the purpose of this survey I am including here the times of Abraham, Isaac, Jacob, and Moses. Repeatedly during this period we find Abraham, Isaac, Jacob and Moses offering sacrifices and prayers to YHWH at altars erected for the purpose of worshipping YHWH.[13] This pattern was seen in the nation of Israel

---

[13] Gen 8:20, 12:7, 13:4, 22:9, 26:25.

under Moses[14] as they began their journey into the Promised Land. They and others worshipped God by offering sacrifices at altars erected for the very purpose of worshipping God. It is obvious that they and God were serious about worship!

Randall Bradley observes that worship permeates the whole of the Pentateuch. Even before the Leviticus ritual laws became part of Israel's religious life religious symbolism had been shaped and hallowed by centuries of patriarchal worship. In the beginning God had created humanity to commune with him. He took the initiative in seeking man and his worship. God knew that a sincere act of worship would be to man's advantage since it would draw man into community and discourse with him. The worship responses during these formative years included building altars and places of worship where sacrifices could be offered and ceremonies reenacted that would sustain a viable relationship between God and his creation.[15]

God called Abraham from the Chaldees and thus opened a relationship with Abraham and his family that would in time grow into a national religion and worship, and an international movement we know as Christianity. In these formative years God made a covenant with Abraham who in time was instructed by God to offer his son Isaac as a sacrifice to God (Gen 12 ff; Gen 22), thus testing Abraham's faith and establishing the degree and extent to which worship should be experienced. God repeated his covenant with Isaac and instructed Isaac in the nature of worship. Isaac built an altar to worship this God (Gen 26:24-25). Jacob had a dream of a ladder reaching up to heaven and subsequently erected a stone at a place which he called Bethel, *the house of God*, as a memorial to his experience. Notice God's and Jacob's comments:

> "*I am the* LORD, *the God of Abraham your father and the God of Isaac; the land on which you lie I will give to you and to your descendants;* [14] *and your descendants shall be like the dust of the earth, and you shall spread abroad to the west and to the east and to the north and to the south;*

---

[14] Exodus 20:24, 27:1 with strict instructions as to how to build the altar.
[15] Cf. the discussion of this in Segler and Bradley, *Christian Worship*, pp. 13f.

and by you and your descendants shall all the families of the earth bless themselves. [15] Behold, I am with you and will keep you wherever you go, and will bring you back to this land; for I will not leave you until I have done that of which I have spoken to you." [16] Then Jacob awoke from his sleep and said, "Surely the LORD is in this place; and I did not know it." [17] And he was afraid, and said, "How awesome is this place! This is none other than the house of God, and this is the gate of heaven."[16]

The practice of worshipping God became an integral part of Israel's life. Israel's worship in the centuries that followed consisted of the celebration and proclamation of the covenant that God had made with her ancestors, and a veneration of God for his faithfulness, majesty, holiness, and greatness. It was not by chance that God became known and worshipped in Israel's long history and tradition as *El Shaddai, the Almighty, the Lord of Hosts.*[17]

The patriarchal worship tradition and practice was expressed in reverence, awe, and veneration. The dynamic in this worship as in every sense falling down in worship[18] before an awesome God. Man's psychological or sociological preferences were not part of the scene!

Worship During the Wilderness Wondering of Israel in the Desert of Sinai, and in Judaism under the Law of Moses

It was during the early days of this period, prior to the Exodus, that God revealed himself to Moses and then Israel as a personal God, YHWH, or the "I AM WHO I AM" (*I am the one who is continually present and active*). It was in this context and experience that Moses was told to remove his shoes because he was

---

[16] Gen 28:13–17.
[17] Heb *šadday*, *ʾēl šadday*; Gk *pantokrator* (παντοκρατορ)]. *El Shaddai* was the general name given to the patriarchal family for god. *El Shaddai* was later identified with Yahweh. "*The Almighty*" translates the Hebrew *El Shaddai* of the pre-Mosaic tradition (Gen 17:1 …) and is identified with Yahweh in the Mosaic tradition (Exod 3:13–17; 6:2–3). Cf. "Almighty," *Anchor Bible Dictionary*, vol. 1, p. 160.
[18] It matters little whether we take this falling down in worship as a symbolic act of prostration before God or as it most likely was, a physical prostration before God in worship.

standing on holy ground, and that Moses hid his face because he was afraid to look at God! Moses' response was certainly a situation of intense fear, respect, awe, reverence and worship before this powerful experience with the divine!

Much of Israel's worship during the period of wandering in the desert of Sinai was impacted by two major factors: 1) the deliverance from Egypt by God's power and 2) the giving of the Law at Mount Sinai. The deliverance from Egypt would become a pivotal ingredient of, and incentive for centuries of worship, even down to the present day in Israel's history through the celebration of the Passover (Exod 12). In time the place of Israel's early worshipping grew from a tent experience into a more elaborate Tabernacle style of worship with a deliberate liturgy. Richard Freedman describes the Tabernacle as follows:

> *The (Tabernacle was the) Israelite tent sanctuary frequently referred to in the Hebrew Bible. It (was) also known as the tent of meeting ... and, occasionally, as the Tabernacle (or tent) of testimony ... It (was) the central place of worship, the shrine that housed the Ark of the Covenant, and frequently it was the location of revelation. It is presented in biblical narrative as the visible sign of Yahweh's presence among the people of Israel. More verses of the Pentateuch are devoted to it than to any other object. It contained the ark, an incense altar, a table, a seven-light candelabra, an eternal light, Aaron's staff that miraculously blossomed (Num 17:23–26), the vessels that were used by the priests, possibly a container of manna (Exod 16:33–34), and a scroll written by Moses ...*[19]

The liturgical laws given to Moses at Mt. Sinai became the codified regulations that even today are reverenced by Israel.

The point of significance regarding the wilderness wanderings and the Tabernacle was the principle that the Tabernacle represented the presence of God, and that the formal worship of Israel during this period was centered on the Tabernacle and that

---

[19] Adapted from Richard Elliott Friedman, "Tabernacle," *Anchor Yale Bible Dictionary,* 1992, vol. 6, p. 293.

worship was profoundly toward YHWH and not on the whims of the people. This was noteworthy in Moses' and God's rejection of the erection of a golden calf of worship at Mt. Sinai. No substitute gods, shrines, or worship not legislated by God during this period were tolerated.

Throughout these formative years of worship experience the direction of worship was always away from man and his culture toward God in his holiness and divine right and power. The cultural setting varied but the worship was shaped not by culture but by the will and direction of YHWH.

Worship During the Babylonian Captivity

The following material from the Jewish Encyclopedia describes in considerable detail the cultural and religious conditions under the Babylonian captivity when Judah was removed from Jerusalem, and the Temple of Solomon was destroyed and could therefore no longer function in the worship of God in Babylon. In this development we see the natural tendency to move away from the external cult practices of the Temple to a more personalized internalized emphasis on morality and personal spiritual expressions of faith.

> *The Israelites who were deported in 597 at first hoped for a speedy return to their homes. As they belonged without exception to the leading families, they had given credence to the sayings of the false prophets who had flattered them (Jer. xxvii.-xxix.; Ezek. xii. 21, xiii. 23); and in contradistinction to those who had remained at home, they came to regard themselves as the true Israel, although they themselves by no means conformed to the standard which the true prophets had pictured of an ideal Israel (Jer. xxiv.; Ezek. xi. 1-21), nor did they betray any evidence of a "new heart." When, therefore, contrary to their expectations, Jerusalem was destroyed in 586, they were, after all, compelled to follow the advice of Jeremiah (xxix. 4-9) and accommodate themselves to the conditions of a protracted exile.*
>
> *In consequence of the favorable external circumstances of the exiles, and particularly of such of them as*

were engaged in the diversified commerce in the Babylonian metropolis, the longing for home gradually disappeared, and they learned to content themselves with material prosperity. Most of these indifferent persons were lost to their people; for, in their anxiety to retain the wealth they had acquired, they learned to conform to the manners and customs of the country, thus sacrificing not only their national but also their religious independence and individuality. Hence the denunciation by the Prophets of the various forms of idolatry practiced among the people. Even if the description of the idolatry mentioned in Isa. lvi. 9-lvii. 13a belongs to pre-exilic times, many other passages so graphically describe the idolatrous practices of the exiles that the relation between these and the Babylonian cult cannot be mistaken ... Despite all this indifference and impiety on the part of the masses, there was nevertheless an element that remained true to the service of YHWH. These "servants of YHWH," who humbly submitted ... to His will, gathered about the few Prophets who remained faithful to the Lord, but whose voice and influence were lost amid the general depravity, and who, in addition to the pain caused by base ingratitude and faithlessness toward the God of their fathers, were also compelled to endure all the shafts of scorn and ridicule. While some, though without obeying the prophet's exhortations (Ezek. xxxiii. 31), listened to his words—either because they appreciated his eloquence, or because they were entertained and pleased by the holy enthusiasm of the man of God—others ridiculed this faith in the Lord and the fond hope of the devotees of YHWH of a future salvation and a redemption from pagan captivity ... The more the pious exiles felt themselves repelled by their pagan environment and their disloyal fellow-Israelites ... the closer became the union among themselves, and the stronger their allegiance to their Prophets and the Law.

What they had re-established almost immediately of the religion of their fathers was the sacred observances. True, a festive celebration of the high festivals was out of the question, in view of the unfavorable conditions and of the mood of the people. Such a celebration was, therefore, supplanted by solemn days of penance and prayer to commemorate the catastrophe which had befallen the people ... The fasts of the fathers were also observed, although in so superficial and thoughtless a manner that the prophet was compelled to condemn the mode of observance, and to censure fasting when accompanied by the ordinary business pursuits of every-day ...

As the faithful could not honor YHWH by sacrifices in a foreign land, nothing remained to them of all their ceremonial but the observance of the Sabbath (Hosea ix. 3-5) and such other customs as were connected with a certain independence of action. Such, for example, were the act of circumcision, which, together with the observance of the Sabbath, constituted a distinguishing mark of Israel; regular prayer, performed with the face turned toward Jerusalem (I Kings viii. 48); and fasting, already mentioned. When the Prophets of the Exile spoke of the conditions under which the divine prophecies would be fulfilled, they always emphasized the observance of the Sabbath as the foremost obligation, as the force which should unite and preserve the Jewish community ... On the other hand, it is evident from the demands and exhortations of the Prophets that they were now willing to dispense with the ceremonial, as the more external form of religious observance, in order to emphasize the exemplification of the essential religious spirit in works of morality and charity.

At the same time the idea found acceptance that the submission of the personal will to that of the Lord would prove the most acceptable sacrifice in His sight (Ezek. xi. 19, xviii. 31, xxxvi. 26; Isa. lxi. 1-3). Ezekiel also establishes the new principle that the essence of reli-

gion must be sought in individual morality: "The righteousness of the righteous shall be upon him, and the wickedness of the wicked shall be upon him" (Ezek. xviii. 20-32; compare Deut. xxiv. 16; Num. xxvi. 11); wherefore he, also, in contrast with the present disposition of the exiles, predicts a new heart and a new spirit (Ezek. xxxvi. 26).[20]

Second Temple Worship[21]

Attempting to present a summary of worship in Judaism in the Temple, especially the Second Temple, is perhaps a misguided attempt that does a disservice to Judaism at any single point in time since the Temple cult following the division of the Kingdom under Jeroboam and Rehoboam and the subsequent restoration under Ezra and Nehemiah presents a religion in considerable flux. Judaism during and following the restoration of Israel and the rebuilding of the Temple under Nehemiah reflected in many was a Jewish state and religion trying to reestablish itself under the Law/Torah which was for many an exercise in historical frustration since the temple cult was a mere hazy memory. For somewhere between 70 and 80 years there had been no temple, no sacrifices, and no religious festivals. From the first deportations of Judah ca 597 BCE to the rebuilding of Jerusalem and the Temple under Ezra/Nehemiah ca 516 BCE, a period of between 70 and 80 years, a new generation of Jews had been born to Israel. These new Israelites who had been raised in an age where there was no Temple and Temple cult now sought to restore the Temple cult to a temple that was not yet there!

The restoration of Israel as a nation and the Temple cult was a slow process faced by several serious challenges, the chief being the fact that there were few if any who had any experience in or memory of the daily religion of Israel outside of what they could read in their Scriptures and other religious writings, any of which were not readily available.

---

[20] Notes from JewishEncyclopedia.com, 1906. I have italicized certain comments for emphasis.

[21] Second Temple Judaism covers the period from the construction of the second Jewish temple in Jerusalem ca 515 BCE to its destruction by the Romans in 70 CE.

By the time that Herod rebuilt the Temple in Jerusalem the religious life of Israel had twice been decimated, first by Antiochus Epiphanes IV ca170 BCE, then by the Romans under Pompey in 63 BCE. Following the Maccabean Revolution under Mattathias ca 164 BCE the religious life of Israel and Jerusalem was dominated by religious strife among the major sects within Israel, primarily the Pharisees and Sadducees, with the temple cult being led by a succession of High Priests who were more political than religious leaders.

As early as 150 BCE a Jewish sectarian began to dominate Jewish life with three major sects emerging, the Pharisees, the Saducees, and the Essenes, each in contention for leadership around the Temple and in Jerusalem.

Josephus, 1st century CE historian, soldier and political figure, mentions the existence of the three sects in the middle of the second century BCE. His view was that sometime before the time of Christ, ca 1 BCE, some Essenes broke from the Temple religious leadership and established a restoration communal and religious center at Qumran which was possibly the foundation of the Dead Sea Community we speak of as the Dead Sea Covenanters.

This reaction to the religious life and leadership was a sign of the tumult and breakdown of the religious life and leadership of the Second Temple, which was condemned by Jesus (Matt 21:12f, and 241-44; John 2:13f), and consequently destroyed by the Romans ca 66-70 CE.

Although concerned and faithful Jews continued to celebrate the annual feasts of the Jews, notably The Feast of Unleavened Bread (Passover), the Feast of *Yom Kippur* (the Atonement), the Feast of Weeks (Pentecost), and the Feast of *Sukkoth* (Booths), the strict letter of the law of feasts was corrupted and turned more into a historical than a religious celebration.

It is apparent as we follow Jesus' confrontation with the Scribes and Pharisees and their opposition to his Kingdom message that all in the life of the second Temple was not right and, in many ways, corrupt. It was no accident that the religious life of the Second Temple did not form a pattern for Christian worship!

Synagogue Worship

As noted above, by the time of Jesus Christ the Second Temple which had been restored by Herod the Great was corrupt and in many ways dysfunctional. Under the influence of the Pharisean and Sadducean sects, who in many ways differed significantly with one another especially regarding the role of the Pentateuch, the Temple cult had fallen into decline. Two movements arose in reaction to this; the Qumran Covenanters and the Jesus movement in which Jesus took issue with both the Pharisees' and Sadducees' leadership in the Temple.

For this dysfunction and a number of other geographical reasons, alternate places of religious influence arose which we cover simply by referring to as the Synagogue as though Synagogues were an organized program.

Nevertheless, for a number of obvious reasons, the Synagogues did manifest remarkable uniformity. With roots in the Babylonian captivity in the absence of the Temple cult in Jerusalem meetings or gatherings of Jews in the "diaspora" developed in which prayer, readings of the Torah, and community "Jewish tribal" roots were cultivated. These places of gathering, eventually called Synagogues (from the Greek συναγωγή, *sunagōgē*, from *sunágō, to lead together, to assemble*[22]) developed to continue and strengthen the Jewish faith and commitment to YHWH. The Synagogue also functioned as a place of transmitting the Jewish traditions, and a cultural gathering point in the life of Jews spread throughout the Mediterranean world.

From our New Testament studies we understand that the Synagogue had already become a cultural and religious center in Palestine at the time of Christ, and as early as the second century CE had become a major opponent of the spread of Christianity.

As noted above in the comments from the Jewish Encyclopedia, the Synagogue cult was primarily focused on prayer and the reading of the *Torah*. The physical sacrifices were not permitted in the Synagogue cult since the offering of sacrifices away from the Tabernacle/Temple precincts and the Temple priests was not

---

[22] Zodhiates, συναγωγή.

permitted under the *Torah*. Note the following observation from Deut 12:5-10.

> *But you shall seek the place which the Lord your God will choose out of all your tribes to put his name and make his habitation there; thither you shall go, [6]and thither you shall bring your burnt offerings and your sacrifices, your tithes and the offering that you present, your votive offerings, your freewill offerings, and the firstlings of your herd and of your flock; [7]and there you shall eat before the Lord your God, and you shall rejoice, you and your households, in all that you undertake, in which the Lord your God has blessed you. [8]You shall not do according to all that we are doing here this day, every man doing whatever is right in his own eyes; [9]for you have not as yet come to the rest and to the inheritance which the Lord your God gives you.*

The Synagogue was not a replacement of the Temple cult but an alternative to the Temple within the religious and sacrificial boundaries permitted under the *Torah*. In the absence of a physical animal sacrificial element, the spiritual attitude of humility and submission toward the will of YHWH, in prayer, and a commitment to the *Torah* became the cultic practice of the Synagogue. We should note here that the religious cult and practices of the Temple were not transposed to the Synagogue as though the Synagogue became a miniature temple. The religious cult of the two places of worship was radically different.

The Sacrificial Element of the Temple Cult

At the heart of the Temple cult lay a humble and submissive attitude that recognized the glory and presence of YHWH in the Temple precincts. This was so because in the Holy of Holies was the Ark of the Covenant which was considered by Judaism to be the very seat and presence of the holy God and of his atonement. The Synagogue was never considered by the Jews to be a holy place in the sense that it represented the living presence of YHWH.

The rules of behavior in the Tabernacle/Temple were clearly established in the Sinai Wilderness shortly after YHWH had given instruction to Moses.

The tabernacle was the precursor of the temple during most of the period between the formation of Israel, at Sinai, and its final establishment in the Promised Land in the early period of the monarchy. A portable sanctuary in keeping with the demand for easy mobility, it was the symbol of God's presence with his people, and, therefore, of his availability, as well as a place where his will was communicated. At an early period it was anticipated that, when peace and security had been secured, a permanent national shrine would be established (Dt 12:10, 11). This was not realized until the time of Solomon, when the temple was erected (2 Sam 7:10–13; 1 Kgs 5:1–5). History, as well as the similarities in construction and underlying theology, illustrate the close connection between the tabernacle and temple.[23]

Clear instructions were given to Moses at Sinai (Ex 24-40) regarding the building of the Tabernacle, and the religious cult which controlled the behavior of the people, the priests, and the High Priest in their religious ceremonies and celebrations. This became the pattern carried over into the Temple.

Eventually the Temple precinct was composed of an "outer precinct" or area which was known as the Court of the Gentiles into which devout Gentiles could enter. Adjacent to the court of the Gentiles was the Court of Women into which devout Jewish women were permitted to enter. Within this Temple precinct was the Court of Israel into which only devout men could enter to pray and bring and offer their various animal sacrifices for burnt offerings. From the Court of Israel, through a gated entrance priests entered into the court of the Holy Place. Only priests could enter into the Holy Place. Located in this court were the Altar of Incense where burnt incense could be offered with prayers. Located in this Holy Place were the Seven Branched Candlestick or *Menorah* and the Table of Shewbread (Heb 9:1-6).

Within the innermost part of the Temple one found the Holy of Holies. Entrance into this Holy of Holies was through two large curtains. Only the High Priest could enter through these

---

[23] *Baker Encyclopedia of the Bible*, vol. 2, p. 2015.

curtains (Heb 9:7). Within the Holy of Holies were located the Ark of the Covenant, the Mercy Seat of God, Aaron's Rod and a Pot of Manna. On the Day of Atonement (Yom Kippur) the High Priest entered the Holy of Holies to offer the Sacrifice of Atonement for the sins of Israel.

Sacrifices were to be offered only in the Temple in Jerusalem as prescribed by the Law. These sacrifices could not by Law be offered in any other holy place, for instance in the Synagogue. Note God's instructions to Moses at Deut 12:1-14:

> *"These are the statutes and ordinances which you shall be careful to do in the land which the LORD, the God of your fathers, has given you to possess, all the days that you live upon the earth. [2] You shall surely destroy all the places where the nations whom you shall dispossess served their gods, upon the high mountains and upon the hills and under every green tree; [3] you shall tear down their altars, and dash in pieces their pillars, and burn their Asherim with fire; you shall hew down the graven images of their gods, and destroy their name out of that place. [4] You shall not do so to the LORD your God. [5] But you shall seek the place which the LORD your God will choose out of all your tribes to put his name and make his habitation there; thither you shall go, [6] and thither you shall bring your burnt offerings and your sacrifices, your tithes and the offering that you present, your votive offerings, your freewill offerings, and the firstlings of your herd and of your flock; [7] and there you shall eat before the LORD your God, and you shall rejoice, you and your households, in all that you undertake, in which the LORD your God has blessed you. [8] You shall not do according to all that we are doing here this day, every man doing whatever is right in his own eyes; [9] for you have not as yet come to the rest and to the inheritance which the LORD your God gives you. [10] <u>But when you go over the Jordan, and live in the land which the LORD your God gives you to inherit, and when he gives you rest from all your enemies round about, so that you live in safety,</u> [11] <u>then to the place which the LORD your God will choose, to make his name</u>*

> *dwell there, thither you shall bring all that I command you: your burnt offerings and your sacrifices, your tithes and the offering that you present, and all your votive offerings which you vow to the LORD.* ¹² *And you shall rejoice before the LORD your God, you and your sons and your daughters, your menservants and your maidservants, and the Levite that is within your towns, since he has no portion or inheritance with you.* ¹³ *Take heed that you do not offer your burnt offerings at every place that you see;* ¹⁴ *but at the place which the LORD will choose in one of your tribes, there you shall offer your burnt offerings, and there you shall do all that I am commanding you.*

The Second Temple at the time of the rise of Christianity, in addition to being the heart of Jewish worship, feasts, festivals, and sacrifices served several additional important functions. It was a place representing Jewish tradition, Jewish heritage, and Jewish identity. In addition, it functioned as a place of Jewish religious legal and political judgment.

Of importance to this study, the Temple was the place of Jewish religion, its many sacrifices including *Yom Kippur*, the Day of Atonement. Sacrifices were not be permitted in any other site than the Temple; not in Synagogues or any other religious shrine!

With the death of Christ God made a new covenant with his new covenant people, that is, the church as the body of Christ and the eschatological community of the kingdom. The previous covenant ensconced in the Law of Moses and established at Mount Sinai with Moses and Israel was annulled, cancelled, and replaced by the new covenant of Christ. This was in fulfilment of God's promises to Israel in Jer 31:31-34:

> *"Behold, the days are coming, says the LORD, when I will make a new covenant with the house of Israel and the house of Judah,* ³² *not like the covenant which I made with their fathers when I took them by the hand to bring them out of the land of Egypt, my covenant which they broke, though I was their husband, says the LORD.* ³³ *But this is the covenant which I will make with the house of Israel after those days, says the LORD: I will put my law within*

them, and I will write it upon their hearts; and I will be their God, and they shall be my people. [34] And no longer shall each man teach his neighbor and each his brother, saying, 'Know the LORD,' for they shall all know me, from the least of them to the greatest, says the LORD; for I will forgive their iniquity, and I will remember their sin no more."

The writer of the letter to the Hebrews argued that in Christ God was fulfilling the promise of that new covenant spoken of by Jeremiah. Note Heb 8:1-10:18, notably 8:13, "In speaking of a new covenant he treats the first as obsolete. And what is becoming obsolete and growing old is ready to vanish away," and 10:9, *"He abolishes the first in order to establish the second."*

The consequence of what God was doing in Christ in his new covenant and Christ's atoning sacrifice was that the sacred covenant and sacred places of the old covenant were being shifted to a new sacred place in Christ and not in any geographical location (Cf. John 4:21-26). In a remarkable explanation of this transfer Paul wrote in his Ephesian letter at Eph 2:11-22:

Therefore remember that at one time you Gentiles in the flesh, called the uncircumcision by what is called the circumcision, which is made in the flesh by hands— [12] remember that you were at that time separated from Christ, alienated from the commonwealth of Israel, and strangers to the covenants of promise, having no hope and without God in the world. [13] But now in Christ Jesus you who once were far off have been brought near in the blood of Christ. [14] For he is our peace, who has made us both one, and has broken down the dividing wall of hostility, [15] by abolishing in his flesh the law of commandments and ordinances, that he might create in himself one new man in place of the two, so making peace, [16] and might reconcile us both to God in one body through the cross, thereby bringing the hostility to an end. [17] And he came and preached peace to you who were far off and peace to those who were near; [18] for through him we both have access in one Spirit to the Father. [19] So then you are no

> *longer strangers and sojourners, but you are fellow citizens with the saints and members of the household of God, [20] built upon the foundation of the apostles and prophets, Christ Jesus himself being the cornerstone, [21] in whom the whole structure is joined together and grows into a holy temple in the Lord; [22] in whom you also are built into it for a dwelling place of God in the Spirit.*

In contrast to the Temple being the sacred dwelling space of God, the church[24] as the people and body of Christ now became that sacred dwelling space of God through Christ and the Holy Spirit.

Christian Worship in the New Testament and 2nd Century

As I will discuss later in another context, with its rich heritage in Judaism it is not surprising that the early Christian Church became a worshipping community! Although the forms of formal worship in the New Testament church soon became a major component of early church life, little is said expressly in the New Testament regarding the formal composition or structure of the liturgy of the early church. We have several texts which discuss Christians meeting together for a variety of reasons (Acts 1:15ff; 2:42-46[25]; 15:1ff; 20:7ff; 1 Cor 11:17f; 1 Cor 16:1f; Heb 10:25; et al) but little is said of the formal nature or structure of the worship gatherings. We know from New Testament references that Christians met together regularly to worship God, and from this evidence we conclude that they did this on the first day of every week which they called the Lord's Day (Rev 1:10) rather than the Sabbath. However, there is little evidence of a formal structure to these meetings reflected in the New Testament.

---

[24] In the New Testament the term church does not refer to a building but to the people called by God to live their lives and worship Him in and through Jesus Christ. The building itself is not a holy place but becomes holy only in the sense that it is there in the assembly of God's people that God meets with his people in worship.

[25] There is some discussion among scholars regarding the precise nature of these meetings of the early Jerusalem disciples relating to whether this text refers to a semi-formal or formal worship assembly in which a love feast or the Lord's Supper was celebrated. Reference to the studies by Fitzmyer, *The Acts of the Apostles*; Johnson, *The Act of the Apostles*; Bruce, *The Book of Acts*; Bock, *Acts*; Marshall, *Acts*; Lüdemann, *The Acts of the Apostles*.

Gerhard Delling aptly observes that we can only get a picture of an order of "primitive Christian Worship" from cautious inferences.[26] On the basis of Acts 20:7 (Delling cites Acts 20:36) "we may presume, perhaps, that the Pauline circle of Churches was accustomed to the sequence: address, prayer … the incorporation of the Lord's Supper into the preaching service […] no conclusions can be drawn from the report from Troas."[27]

David Aune in *The Anchor Bible Dictionary* makes a similar observation to that of Delling regarding the difficulty of identifying a worship structure for the early church from the New Testament Scriptures:

> *While many separate features of Christian worship, such as the celebration of the Lord's Supper, baptismal liturgies, hymns, doxologies, and creedal formulas, have been preserved in the NT and early Christian literature (particularly in letters), there is often little indication of the original liturgical setting within which such individual traditions were set. Thus while Paul preserves a short account of the Lord's Supper in 1 Cor 11:23–26, and later discusses many features of the Corinthian services of worship in 1 Corinthians 14, there is little indication of how these separate elements fit together as a whole. There have been a number of attempts to piece together the fragmentary evidence to reconstruct a liturgical setting for separate elements of worship services. Since Christian worship retained an elasticity and flexibility well into the 2^d century A.D., the structures of Christian worship described below exhibit little uniformity nor are they variants of a single order of worship.*[28]

In the few texts in the New Testament which are clearly worship assemblies one has to examine the context of the discussion to determinate the precise nature of the meeting. Invariably the discussion of the worship assembly is in a context not designed to define the formal liturgy of the worship. Take for instance, 1 Cor

---

[26] Delling, *Worship*, p. 42.
[27] Delling, *Worship*, p. 42.
[28] Aune, "Worship, Early Christian," *Anchor Yale Bible Dictionary*. p. 975.

11:17ff, the purpose of Paul's discussion of the Lord's Supper, which obviously took place in a formal gathering of the church to worship, was to discuss abuses of the Lord's Supper in the worship assembly. Likewise, Paul's discussion of the worship assembly in 1 Cor 14 addresses abuses of Spirit inspired activity, singing, praying, speaking in tongues, etc. in the worship assembly. It was not Paul's purpose to specify a liturgical structure of a worship assembly, only to address abuses in the worship assembly. Nevertheless, we can gather from Paul's discussion that the Corinthian church at least sang, prayed, spoke, and addressed one another in Spirit inspired tongues/dialects.

Acts 20:7 introduces an interesting point to the discussion of early church worship practices and occasions. Upon a careful exegesis of Acts 20:7 it appears that the occasion of the meeting of the church at Troas on the first day of the week was *the established regular practice* of celebrating the Lord's Supper on the first day of the week, at least at Troas.[29] In addition on this occasion Paul preached a sermon to the gathered church; possibly this was a final parting message to the church at Troas.

Howard Marshall observes regarding Acts 20:7 that
> "this passage is of particular interest in providing the first allusion to the Christian custom of meeting on the first day of the week for the purpose" of celebrating the Lord's Supper.[30]

John R. W. Stott likewise concurs with the view that Acts 20:7 implies a regular practice of at least the church at Troas to meet on the Lord's Day in a regular meeting to celebrate the Lord's Supper:

---

[29] The tense of the verbal participle συνηγμένων, *sunēgmenōn*, a perfect passive participle, can imply that this action reflects a regular habitual practice of gathering. Dana and Mantey, *A Manual Grammar of the Greek New Testament*, pp. 202f; Blass, Debrunner, and Funk, *A Grammar of the New Testament*, pp. 175f. Bruce along with others observes, "The reference to the meeting for the breaking of the bread on "the first day of the week" is the earliest text we have from which it may be inferred with reasonable certainty that Christians regularly came together for worship on that day." Bruce, *The Book of Acts,* Kindle Edition, p. 384.

[30] Marshall, *Acts*, p. 325.

> *First, the disciples met on the Lord's Day for the Lord's Supper. At least verse 7 sounds like a description of the normal, regular practice of the church in Troas. And the evidence is that the Eucharist, as a thankful celebration of the now risen Saviour's death, very early became the main Sunday service, in the context of an agapē, that is, a 'love feast' of fellowship meal.[31]*

Two other texts that address the worship assemblies of the early church are Col 3:16 and Eph 5:19.[32] Both of these texts mention the worship assembly but not in a manner that defines a precise liturgical structure. The emphasis of these two texts in their original contexts was to stress the importance of singing spiritual songs in worship as an appropriate expression of Christian living in contrast to a former pagan lifestyle of debauchery. Paul's purpose was to stress that singing toward God, and in regard to God and Christ in worship edified and built up the spiritual life of the worshipper as well as making a statement regarding the center of Christian spirituality. Paul made no effort to define a formal worship liturgy in these texts, but their mention in this discussion does touch tangentially on the liturgy of the early church. Singing obviously played a significant role in that worship!

It is not surprising that a formal worship assembly would play an important role in the spiritual life of the early church since the early converts obviously came from a rich heritage of formal worship in Judaism, in the Synagogue, and in the Temple cult. This is not to say that early Christian worship was a continuation of either the Temple or Synagogue cults, but certain features of their worship certainly did impact early Christian worship. The reading of Scripture, prayer, and singing had roots in both the Temple and Synagogue cult even if only as a reinterpretation of such.

Aune makes the following observation regarding the relationship of the Synagogue and early Christian worship:

---

[31] Stott, *The Message of Acts,* Kindle location 5894-5896.

[32] In view of the fact that some mistakenly deny that these two texts refer to a worship assembly I will address these two texts in a following chapter in regard to their referring to a worship assembly.

Christianity originated within Judaism and was considered a "sect" (hairesis) of Judaism (Acts 24:14), and according to Acts the spread of Christianity throughout the Roman world tended to begin with the evangelization of diaspora synagogues (Acts 13:5, 14; 14:1; 17:2, 10, 17; 18:4, 19; 19:8). There was therefore both contact and continuity between Christianity and synagogue Judaism. The Aramaic term for synagogue is by knyst', "place of assembly," while two widely used Greek terms are synagōgē (derived from the LXX), means "assembly," and proseuchē, "place of prayer," probably referring to a synagogue (Acts 16:13, 16). Synagogue worship was entirely verbal in character and was largely dependent on congregational participation. The essential features of synagogue worship were Scripture reading and prayer, neither of which was dominated by specialists. Synagogal prayers focused on praise and thanksgiving rather than on petition, and so were appropriate for a worship setting. While synagogue worship undoubtedly had a profound impact on early Christian worship, very little is known about the specific nature of Jewish worship and ritual before the codification of the Mishnah toward the end of the 2d century C.E. The recitations of the Shema, now consisting of three passages from the Torah (Deut 6:4–9; 11:13–21; Num 15:37–41), but probably much shorter originally (Dugmore, 1964:18–20), and of the Eighteen Benedictions go back at least to the 1st century A.D., though no corresponding statutory prayers were characteristic of early Christian worship. There is clear evidence that the Torah was read regularly on the Sabbath by the 1st century C.E. (Acts 13:15; 15:2 ...), and also strong evidence that the Torah reading was often followed by a homily. Exegetical preaching was practiced in synagogue Judaism before A.D. 70 (cf. Luke 4:16–30; Acts 13:15 ...)[33]

---

[33] Aune, "Worship, Early Christian," *Anchor Yale Bible Dictionary*, p. 978.

V. A. Matthews observes regarding the impact of the Synagogue on musical instruments in the New Testament:

> *It was in the synagogue, however, that music continued to flourish and serve as an emotional and didactic aid to the maintenance of Judaism. The Levitical guilds were now gone and instrumental music was forbidden in the synagogue, leaving vocal music to evolve in a new way. Thus the writers of the NT and the founders of the new Christian movement very likely adopted what they knew of synagogue music to their own worship. That would explain why Paul, who is familiar with musical instruments, considered them "lifeless" (1 Cor 14:7–8) and promoted worship in the form of "psalms and hymns and spiritual songs, singing and making melody to the Lord" (Eph 5:19).*
>
> *The borrowing from synagogue worship of both hymn and chorus singing added the emotional, communal feeling needed to help build the new movement. Instruction without the freedom to express joy and praise would have quickly become dull. In any case, many of these early Christian groups met in the local synagogue and they would have been familiar with the form of worship conducted there. It would have been only natural to employ the same hymns they already knew while adding new ones to reflect their new theological understanding. Among these may be the "Worthy art thou" hymnic fragments in Rev 4:11; 5:9–10, and the songs of victory and assurance in Rev 7:15–17; 11:17–18. Eventually, as the Christian movement became more international, Hellenistic musical influences were introduced, but antagonism to instrumental music, so closely associated with pagan religions and the spectacles of the Roman colosseum, continued for several centuries ...*[34]

What we can learn from the few texts that directly discuss the formal worship assembly of the New Testament church is that

---

[34] V. H. Matthews, "Music and Musical Instruments: Music in the Bible," *Anchor Yale Bible Dictionary*, p. 934.

this worship was addressed to or toward God and Christ in honor of their redemptive acts in Christ with the intention that this worship experience would be spiritually enriching and edifying to the congregation and all who may be in attendance. The incorporation of the Lord's Supper certainly introduced a sacramental[35] element into the worship and life of the congregation and participants in the worship which built on the sacramental element of baptism and baptismal creeds. These eventually found their way into the hymnody of the early church. I will say more on these sacramental and creedal elements in worship in the hymnody of the early church under the discussion of the *psalms*, *hymns*, and *spiritual songs* reflected in Col 3:16 and Eph 5:19.

Aune makes the following observations regarding the nature of early Christian worship as reflected in the New Testament:

> *Early Christian worship focused on God, but particularly upon the salvific benefits of what God had done for humanity through Jesus Christ. The focus of Christianity, both theologically and ritually, was therefore salvation. While salvation had been inaugurated in the past through the first coming of Christ (focusing on his incarnation, death, and resurrection), it had yet to be fully consummated in the future through the second coming of Christ, the Parousia. Many features of Christian worship, such as the celebration of the Eucharist ... and the singing of hymns, often combined historical features (aspects of the past mission and achievement of Jesus) with eschatological elements (centering on the future completion of eschatological salvation). For Christians God was present in worship in a variety of manifestations and degrees*

---

[35] *Sacrament* refers to those items in the Christian faith such as *baptism* which unite the believer with Christ and the *Lord's Supper* which reinforces that relationship. The English word "sacrament" is derived indirectly from the Ecclesiastical Latin *sacrāmentum*, from Latin *sacer* ("sacred, holy"). In Ancient Rome, the term meant a soldier's *oath of allegiance*, and also a sacred rite. Tertullian, a third-century Christian writer, suggested that just as the soldier's oath was a sign of the beginning of a new life, so too was initiation into the Christian community through baptism and Eucharist. William van Roo, *The Christian Sacrament*, p. 37.

> *... Though Christians worshipped the same God as Jews, the role of Christ in defining God is an essential and distinctive feature of Christian worship.*[36]

Worship in the Throne-Room of Revelation: God's Creative Power

The book of Revelation is in many ways liturgical in nature. Hymns of praise are raised to God as the omnipotent Almighty, Lord of Hosts, and to Jesus Christ as the one through whom God works in setting the world right again. Worship is exemplified in a majestic manner in the heavenly throne room scene of John's book of Apocalypse at Rev 4:8ff:

> *"Holy, holy, holy, is the Lord God Almighty, who was and is and is to come!"* [9] *And whenever the living creatures give glory and honor and thanks to him who is seated on the throne, who lives for ever and ever,* [10] *the twenty-four elders fall down before him who is seated on the throne and worship him who lives for ever and ever; they cast their crowns before the throne, singing,* [11] *"Worthy art thou, our Lord and God, to receive glory and honor and power, for thou didst create all things, and by thy will they existed and were created."*

The same reverence, awe, and worship is paid at Rev 5:9ff to Jesus, the Son of God for his redemptive role in God's eternal plan of redemption.

> *"Worthy art thou to take the scroll and to open its seals, for thou wast slain and by thy blood didst ransom men for God from every tribe and tongue and people and nation,* [10] *and hast made them a kingdom and priests to our God, and they shall reign on earth."* [11] *Then I looked, and I heard around the throne and the living creatures and the elders the voice of many angels, numbering myriads of myriads and thousands of thousands,* [12] *saying with a loud voice, "Worthy is the Lamb who was slain, to receive power and wealth and wisdom and might and honor and glory and blessing!"* [13] *And I heard every creature in heaven and on earth and under the earth and in the sea,*

---

[36] Aune, "Worship, Early Christian," *Anchor Yale Bible Dictionary*, p. 975.

and all therein, saying, "To him who sits upon the throne and to the Lamb be blessing and honor and glory and might for ever and ever!"

Ultimately, Hallelujah choruses are sung to God in praise of his judgment on the beast and the false prophet (Rev 19:1ff);

> [1] After this I heard what seemed to be the loud voice of a great multitude in heaven, crying,
>
> "Hallelujah! Salvation and glory and power belong to our God, [2] for his judgments are true and just;
> he has judged the great harlot who corrupted the earth with her fornication,
> and he has avenged on her the blood of his servants." [3] Once more they cried,
> "Hallelujah! The smoke from her goes up for ever and ever." [4] And the twenty-four elders and the four living creatures fell down and worshiped God who is seated on the throne, saying, "Amen. Hallelujah!" [5] And from the throne came a voice crying,
> "Praise our God, all you his servants,
> you who fear him, small and great." [6] Then I heard what seemed to be the voice of a great multitude, like the sound of many waters and like the sound of mighty thunderpeals, crying,
> "Hallelujah! For the Lord our God the Almighty reigns. [7] Let us rejoice and exult and give him the glory,
> for the marriage of the Lamb has come,
> and his Bride has made herself ready; [8] it was granted her to be clothed with fine linen, bright and pure"—for the fine linen is the righteous deeds of the saints.

My purpose in referring to these two passages from Revelation is to emphasize the direction and nature of the worship of the heavenly host, the angels and the four living creatures, was toward God and Jesus, not man or human interests, but solely toward God for his great power and redemptive actions. Surely nothing less should be expected from the saints!

We can conclude from this brief study of the worship of God from the earliest days of man even into the ultimate redemption of all men. Worship was and is the beginning and the end of the Christian Story. One can thus legitimately claim that from its early roots in Judaism and the Temple throughout the story of the Bible, worship was the heart and soul of the Jewish and Christian faiths!

Chapter 6: A Theology of Church

Introduction

We have become so familiar with the term church that we often forget that such a concept as a theology of church exists, and even when we admit to one we are not sure precisely what it should say to us!

One could ask why we need a theology of church. The answer is simple! The church is a theological entity built by Jesus, defined as the body of Jesus, and organized and grounded in God's *Missio Dei*[1] and Jesus' mission. The church separated from what God is doing in his kingdom and *Missio Dei* is nothing more than a society of likeminded friends who have fashioned some form of relationship with one another, and who meet together to share stories!

However, the church is far more than a social group of companionable people who gather together on a regular basis! Although relationships within the church are of profound significance the kingdom nature of the church is much deeper than relationships within the church. If the church is not understood as a function of the *Missio Dei* it is no more than any nice socially amenable group of people.

What I plan to do in this study is examine the church from six dimensions: 1) the meaning of the term church, 2) a theology of church, 3) the church in Jesus' ministry, 4) the church as a serving community, 5) the church as a worshipping community 6) the theology of worshipping God in spirit and truth. We will discover that the term church focuses on the *organization* of Jesus' people *to fulfill a divine purpose and mission*. The purpose and mission, we will emphasize, is to engage in God's *Missio Dei* and *to be a worshipping community* which reflects and proclaims God's majesty and redemptive nature. A brief look at Eph 1:3-11 will emphasize that God has called Christians to live their lives in such a manner that they bring glory to God for his atoning work

---

[1] *Missio Dei* is a Latin expression that speaks of God's mission and purpose on earth; what God is doing to redeem his creation.

in Jesus. We will notice that the church is pre-dominantly a *missional* and *worshipping* body of people.

Perhaps the term *missional* needs some clarification and definition, as the term is used in theological jargon. How I will be using it, refers to the missionary mindset of the church as it is committed to spreading the gospel of Jesus by planting new churches who in turn are missional in nature. A missional church is *centrifugal* (spreading outward) rather than *centripetal* (focused inward). The church should be *centripetal* only for the purpose of becoming *centrifugal*!

Jesus himself emphasized this in his great commission at Matt 28:16ff. Notice how Matthew sets the commission in the context of worshipping Jesus!

> [16] *Now the eleven disciples went to Galilee, to the mountain to which Jesus had directed them.* [17] *And <u>when they saw him they worshiped him</u>; but some doubted.* [18] *And Jesus came and said to them, "All authority in heaven and on earth has been given to me.* [19] <u>*Go therefore and make disciples of all nations*</u>, *baptizing them in the name of the Father and of the Son and of the Holy Spirit,* [20] *teaching them to observe all that I have commanded you; and lo, I am with you always, to the close of the age."*

The Term Church

The word *church* is used in common conversational language in English in a broader sense than it is used in the New Testament! In theological contexts the term church/*ekklēsía* is a *loaded concept tied closely to the kingdom of God.* Note the significance of church/kingdom in Jesus' promise to build his church/kingdom at Matt 16:18ff:

> [15] *He said to them, "But who do you say that I am?"* [16] *Simon Peter replied, "You are the Christ, the Son of the living God."* [17] *And Jesus answered him, "Blessed are you, Simon Bar-Jona! For flesh and blood has not revealed this to you, but my Father who is in heaven.* [18] *And I tell you, you are Peter, and on this rock I will build my church, and the powers of death shall not prevail against it.* [19] *I will give you the keys of the kingdom of heaven, and*

whatever you bind on earth shall be bound in heaven, and whatever you loose on earth shall be loosed in heaven."²⁰ Then he strictly charged the disciples to tell no one that he was the Christ.

In our study we will first engage in a brief *etymological* study of the word *church* and then proceed to examine the meaning of the word as it is used in the New Testament.

The Etymology of the English Word Church

I think it will prove helpful if we begin with an examination of the word groups surrounding the word *church* as it is used in the English New Testament, and then how the Greek ἐκκλησία, *ekklēsía* ended up being translated as *church* in our English Bibles. It is an interesting journey! We will note that strictly speaking the English word *church* does not derive directly from the Greek ἐκκλησία, *ekklēsía* but rather from another Greek word κυριακός, *kuriakós* which means *belonging to the Lord*. This is found in the German and Germanic languages as some form of *Kirche*. As we will notice in the next paragraph the word *church* arrived in our English language and use through the German word *Kirche*!

The German word *Kirche* does not derive from the Greek *ekklēsía* but from the Greek word κυριακός, *kuriakós* which primarily means "of a lord, or belonging to a lord;" in the Christian sense then *kuriakós* thus means "of or belonging to the Lord Christ." Certainly, the church belongs to the Lord, but this is not implied in the Greek *ekklēsía*!

There is some relationship between *Kirche* and the modern English word *church* which is more of a movement of thought than a factor of significance! Church derives from the Old English *cirice* and the Middle English *Chereche* which in turn was only remotely related to the Old German *kirika* from which the modern German *Kirche* derives.² As noted above, the Old German *kirika* had its roots in the Greek *kuriakón* which was read as

---

² The Scottish *kirk*, Swedish *kirk*, Danish *kirke*, and Afrikaans *kerk* are closely related to the German *Kirche* and not to the Old English *cirice*.

"the house of the Lord."[3] This progress in meaning is an example of the evolution across time and languages from Greek through the language of the Goths and Germans and Germanic languages into English!

So then, since we are moving toward a *theological* understanding of the English term *church* we begin our study of the church with the Greek κυριακός, *kuriakós* rather than the Greek ἐκκλησία, *ekklēsía,* which is the word used by Jesus and Paul in the New Testament! Note here that we are examining the German word Kirke, *kuriakós* as a *theological* understanding of the word church/*ekklēsía*!

Κυριακός, kuriakós. *In this brief discussion we will be exploring the theological meaning of the term* kuriakós *which the German language uses for* Kirche, *the* church.

We do this to notice how the German term *Kirche* explains the theological depth of the term *church* which might be missing in the Greek/English term *ekklēsía/church*!

Kuriakós is a Greek adjective derived from and related to the noun *kúrios*, meaning *lord or master*. The expression carries the sense of *belonging to a lord, master*, or *ruler*. We find *kuriakós* in our New Testament only in 1 Cor. 11:20 and Rev. 1:10 where it means *"belonging to Christ, or to the Lord."*

At Rev 1:10 we find the expression *"the day of the Lord or the Lord's Day."* The exact expression is κυριακῇ ἡμέρᾳ, *kuriaké hēméra*, means the *"day belonging to the Lord."* It is thus translated simply as *the Lord's Day*. In our western calendar we refer to *the day of the Lord*, κυριακῇ ἡμέρᾳ, simply as *Sunday*, the day Christians keep in commemoration of Christ's resurrection.[4]

---

[3] *Oxford English Dictionary*; Ferguson, *The Church of Christ*, pp. 129ff.; J. Y. Campbell, "The Origin and Meaning of the Christian Use of the Word EKKLESIA," *Journal of Theological Studies*, vol. 49, 1948, pp. 130-142; Roy Bowen Ward, "Ekklēsía: A Word Study," *Restoration Quarterly*, vol. 2, 1958, pp. 164-179; J. W. Roberts, "The Meaning of Ekklēsía in the New Testament," *Restoration Quarterly*, vol. 15, Number 1, 1972; K. L. Schmidt, "Ekklēsía," *Theological Dictionary of the New Testament*, vol. 3, pp. 501-536.

[4] Zodhiates, κυριακῇ; Fair, *Conquering with Christ*, p. 95, comments on Rev 1:10.

Theologically, then, Sunday in our English usage of *κυριακῇ ἡμέρᾳ, kuriakḗ hēméra, the day of the Lord* in the Greek refers to *the day belonging to and commemorating the resurrection of the Lord Christ.*

At 1 Cor 11:20 Paul spoke of the Lord's Supper that the Corinthian church was abusing. *"When you meet together, it is not the Lord's supper that you eat."* Here we find the Greek κυριακὸν δεῖπνον, *kuriakón deípnon*, implying *the supper that belongs to the Lord.*

It is not difficult to see how the term *κυριακῇ ἡμέρᾳ, kuriakḗ hēméra, the Lord's Day*, and Greek κυριακὸν δεῖπνον, *kuriakón deípnon, the Lord's Supper* could be superimposed in the Christian congregations' terminology referring to *the people who belong to the Lord Christ* who are gathered in a meeting on *the Lord's Day* in which *the Lord's Supper* is eaten and his resurrection celebrated.

The *theological* implications of referring to the church as *the people belonging to the Lord*, derived from *kuriakós*, is that the church is a body of people who are gathered together, ἐκκλησία, *ekklēsía*, who belong to the Lord Christ. All kinds of texts could impact this concept, such as 1 Cor 6:20; 7:23, *"You are not your own;* [20] *you were bought with a price. So glorify God in your body."*

Ἐκκλησία, ekklēsía. *We will note in this discussion that there are at least three ways in which the term* ekklēsía *is used in Scripture and specifically the New Testament: 1) an assembly of people called together for a purpose, 2) a congregation of people belonging to God and Christ, 3) a universal body of people belonging to God or Christ. As is usual in biblical interpretation, the context of the discussion determines the meaning of the term, not simply its etymology!*

The word *ekklēsía* which we find over 100 times in our New Testament has a wide range of meaning depending on context. The sense of *a called people* or *a people called for a purpose* is widely referenced and implied in the Greek *ekklēsía*. The simple meaning of the term *church/ekklēsía* as an *assembled* or *called people* is drawn from the noun *ekklēsía* which is simply built off a preposition ἐκ, *ek* primarily meaning *out of*,[5] and a verb καλέω, *to call*. But this simple meaning does not do justice to the syntax of two Greek words coupled together in one! The grammar of joining two or more Greek words into one is intended to intensify the meaning of the sum total of the word! Hence *ekklēsía called out* implies more than simply being called out and involves more than the meaning of being called out! We will see that it implies being *called or assembled for a purpose*!

It is not uncommon to hear in Christian sermons the word *ekklēsía* interpreted as a people *called out of darkness into light*. Theologically, there is no question that Christians are called out of darkness into the light of Christ and his kingdom (1 Pet 2:9; Col 1:13), but in the context of theology and Scripture this carries a theological interpretation drawn from Scripture rather than from the simple meaning of the Greek term *ekklēsía*! As stated above, in Greek when two Greek words such as ἐκ and *kaléō* are joined together the result is an *intensified refined meaning*, and not simply the sum of the two words.

As explained above although the word *ekklēsía* was comprised of two Greek words ἐκ, *out of, from, away from*, and καλέω, *kaléō to call*, in time and usage the emphasis on *out of* was diminished with the primary weight placed on *the calling*, hence, *a called people*, or *a people called for a purpose* and not simply a people *called out of* something. The meaning of *ekklēsía* became *a people called into* an assembly, or *an assembly called for a purpose*, and not simply a people *called out from* somewhere. In this sense in the New Testament and Christianity *ekklēsía* came to be used more as *an assembly of people*, or a *people congregated together* normally *with a purpose in mind*.[6]

Zodhiates observes that *ekklēsía* was used in the New Testament in both a *general* as well as a *specific* sense.

> ... Ἐκκλησία, *ekklēsía* ... *feminine noun from ékklētos* ... *called out, which is from ekkaléō* ... *to call out. It was a common term for a congregation of the*

---

[5] The primary meaning of ἐκ is *out of* or *from* but this small preposition has multiple meanings according to context. It can refer to origin, destination, place, etc. according to its association with surrounding nouns or verbs
[6] Arndt, *A Greek-English Lexicon of the New Testament*.

> *ekklētoí ... the called people, or those called out or assembled in the public affairs of a free state, the body of free citizens called together by a herald ... which constituted the ekklēsía. In the NT, the word is applied to the congregation of the people of Israel (Acts 7:38) 'The term ekklēsía denotes the NT community of the redeemed in its twofold aspect. First, all who were called by and to Christ in the fellowship of His salvation, the church worldwide of all times, and only secondarily to an individual church (Matt. 16:18; Acts 2:44, 47; 9:31; 1 Cor. 6:4; 12:28; 14:4, 5, 12; Phil. 3:6; Col. 1:18, 24). Designated as the church of God (1 Cor. 10:32; 11:22; 15:9; Gal. 1:13; 2 Tim. 3:5, 15); the body of Christ (Eph. 1:22; Col. 1:18); the church in Jesus Christ (Eph. 3:21); exclusively the entire church (Eph. 1:22; 3:10, 21; 5:23–25, 27, 29, 32; Heb. 12:23). Secondly, the NT churches, however, are also confined to particular places (Rom. 16:5; 1 Cor. 1:2; 16:19; 2 Cor. 1:1; Col. 4:15; 1 Thess. 2:14; Phile. 1:2); to individual local churches (Acts 8:1; 11:22; Rom. 16:1; 1 Thess. 1:1; 2 Thess. 1:1). Ekklēsía does not occur in the gospels of Mark, Luke, John, nor the epistles of 2 Timothy, Titus, 1 and 2 John, or Jude.*[7]

Zodhiates adds that *ekklēsía* was generally used:

> *Of persons legally called out or summoned (Acts 19:39, of the people); and hence also of a tumultuous assembly not necessarily legal (Acts 19:32, 41). In the Jewish sense, [it referred to] a congregation, [an]* <u>*assembly of the people for worship*</u>*, e.g., in a synagogue (Matt. 18:17) or generally (Acts 7:38; Heb. 2:12 quoted from Ps. 22:22; Septuagint; Deut. 18:16; and 2 Chr. 1:3, 5).*[8]

Karl Ludwig Schmidt in a significant and detailed discussion of *ekklēsía* in Kittel's *Theological Dictionary of the New Testament* observes that it is *a mistake to rely too deeply on the etymology of being a called out body* since in time the emphasis on *called out recedes into the background* with the emphasis being

---

[7] Zodhiates, "Ἐκκλησία."
[8] Zodhiates, "Ἐκκλησία."

on the use of the word group to refer to a _specific body of people gathered together for a specific purpose_.[9] Schmidt opens his discussion of the use of the term in the New Testament with these remarks:

> *A survey of the use of ἐκκλησία in the NT shows that it does not occur in Mk., Lk., Jn., 2 Tm., Tt., 1 Pt., 2 Pt., 1 Jn., 2 Jn. or Jude. No importance need be attached to its absence from 1 and 2 Jn., since it is found in 3 Jn. The same applies to 2 Tm. and Tt. in view of its use in 1 Tm. Jude is so short that we may discount its absence here as a matter of statistical probability. More surprising is its nonoccurrence in 1 and 2 Pt. 1 Pt. deals most emphatically with the nature and significance of the OT community and uses OT expressions, so that we may ask whether the matter is not present even though the term is missing. The same question arises in respect of the non-occurrence of the Word in the two Synoptists Mk. and Lk., and also in Jn.*[10]

Regarding the general use of the term in a broader context Schmidt adds:

> *General dictionaries ... give the two senses 1. "assembly" and 2. "church"; they call the former secular and the latter biblical or ecclesiastical. Following the general scheme, Liddell-Scott refers also to the LXX and gives us the following senses: 1. "assembly duly summoned, less general than σύλλογος," 2. a. in the LXX "the Jewish congregation," b. in the NT "the Church as a body of Christians."*
>
> *NT lexicons follow the same arrangement, but go on to make a distinction between the Church a. as the whole body of believers and b. as the individual congregation, e.g., the house church. This raises the question whether a. or b. comes first, i.e., in what sense we have a succession*

---

[9] Karl Ludwig Schmidt, Kittel's *Theological Dictionary of the New Testament*, vol. 3, p. 530.
[10] Schmidt, *Kittel.*, vol. 3, p. 504.

> *as well as co-existence of the two meanings. ... Bauer accepts the ... order: "The congregation as the gathering of Christians living in a given place, and universally the Church in which all those who are called are together"; he goes on to speak accordingly of the local and the universal ἐκκλησία. The dictionaries vary in their distinction between the congregation and the Church. In some passages it is hard to tell which is really meant according to our current use of the terms.*[11]

Everett Ferguson concludes his excellent discussion of the word *ekklēsía* in his definitive work, *The Church of Christ: A Biblical Theology for Today* with the following remarks:

> *The designation ekklēsía calls attention to the importance of meeting together for the nature of the church ... it may be affirmed now that the church by definition, is an assembly. It is the people who meet together on a regular basis. The word ekklēsía identifies the people of God assembled ... The meeting of the church occurs in the name of Jesus Christ.*[12]

Ferguson unfolds the meaning of the church as *ekklēsía*, notably in chapters 4 and 5, explaining that two of the primary purposes of referring to the people of Christ as *ekklēsía* is that they are gathered together *to worship* and *to minister*. Thus, inherent in the meaning of *ekklēsía* is the emphasis on the fact that as the gathered people of the Lord Jesus Christ they are *called for a purpose, to minister to the* Missio Dei *and to worship*.

As we will be referring to the term church as *ekklēsía* in this study we will have in mind *the local congregation assembling together* on a formal occasion *to worship* and celebrate the Lord's Supper, sing psalms, hymns, and spiritual songs to the Lord, read Scripture, pray, care for the needy in a benevolent contribution, and hear a sermon (homily) related to the biblical text. We will not lose sight of the vision of a universal church under the headship of Christ or the church's role of being called to fulfil the kingdom mission of the *Missio Dei* in the world, but our focus

---

[11] Schmidt, *Theological Dictionary of the New Testament*, vol. 3, p. 502.
[12] Ferguson, *The Church of Christ*, pp. 129-133.

will be primarily on the local congregation (*ekklēsía*) as a people called into assembly to worship God.

Although the *English* term *church* is found over 100 times in the New Testament it is found not once in the major Old Testament English translations! However, the Greek word *ekklēsía* is found many times in the Greek version of the Old Testament, the Septuagint.[13] A possible reason is that Israel was the congregation or ekklēsía of God!

Theologically (not historically) the first time we encounter the term *church* in a Christian context applied to a community of people called by God in Christ to be the *ekklēsía* of God is at Matt 16:17-19 when Jesus promised to establish a *new community* different from the *ekklēsía* of the Old Testament;

> '*And Jesus answered him, "Blessed are you, Simon Bar-Jona! For flesh and blood has not revealed this to you, but my Father who is in heaven. [18] And I tell you, you are Peter, and on this rock I will build my church, and the powers of death shall not prevail against it. [19] I will give you the keys of the kingdom of heaven, and whatever you bind on earth shall be bound in heaven, and whatever you loose on earth shall be loosed in heaven."*'

In this Matthean text the term *church* is used in conjunction with the term *kingdom*, not implying that they are simply synonymous. There is a connection between the two terms, with the kingdom implying God's sovereign reign over all creation, and his *Missio Dei* expansion of the kingdom into all the world. The church being the agent for conducting that *Missio Dei* through its various ministries. Jesus had in mind establishing a new community of believers, possibly a universal community, grounded on Peter's confession that Jesus is the Christ and foundation of this new community, with the purpose of carrying out the kingdom *Missio Dei* (cf Matt 28:18-20). This universal church is found in the New Testament in local congregations of "Jesus people" scattered geographically wherever people believe in Jesus' gospel and obey that gospel. Since these "Jesus people" are called by

---

[13] The term *ekklēsía* when found in the Old Testament is normally translated as *congregation* or *assembly*.

God and Christ *to assemble for worship and service they are called the church, ekklēsía* as in Paul's greeting to the Christians that assemble in Thessalonica, "Paul, Silvanus, and Timothy, To the church, *ekklēsía*, of the Thessalonians in God the Father and the Lord Jesus Christ: Grace to you and peace."

We find this also used in the church in Corinth, "*Paul, called by the will of God to be an apostle of Christ Jesus, and our brother Sosthenes, ² To the church of God which is at Corinth, to those sanctified in Christ Jesus, <u>called to be saints together</u> with all those who in every place call on the name of our Lord Jesus Christ, both their Lord and ours: ³ Grace to you and peace from God our Father and the Lord Jesus Christ.*"[14]

Thus, as the term ἐκκλησία, *ekklēsía* is used in the New Testament it refers most often to the community of believers, either universal or local, who saw Jesus as the Son of God who died and was raised from the dead, and who through their faith and obedience were brought into a broad fellowship of a *universal community* of believers who assembled together in *local* congregations *in order to worship God in Christ and to carry out the Messianic commission* Jesus had given to the Apostles and disciples of the early church (Matt 28:18-20; Mark 16:15, 16, Acts 1:6-8).

In summary, as I noted above, I understand the term *church, ekklēsía* used both for the *universal* community of believers, and local congregations of believers. Thus, the church is a *universal community* of believers in Christ which we call *Christianity* (Matt 16:17-19; Eph 5:21-32), but primarily for *local congregations* where Christians *gather*, or *assemble together*, *worship* together and *serve Christ in the Missio Dei* reaching out into all the world, in and from their local community (Matt 18:17; Acts 15:3, 4; Rom 16:1; Re 2:1).

The Church and the Term Synagogue. Although the term Συναγωγή, *sunagōgḗ* is not used often in the New Testament for the Christian community, it is in some senses a synonym for ekklēsía. The noun sunagōgḗ is related to the verb συνάγω, sunágō where the basic sense is "to lead, bring together, to

---

[14] 1 Thess 1:1; 1 Cor 1:1–3.

gather, a gathering, or a union."[15] Zodhiates explains that συναγωγή, *sunagōgḗ* refers to a gathering, a congregation, or a synagogue of persons. The congregation of Israel was designated by sunagōgḗ especially as they were gathered as a community in the Exodus wilderness. Sunagōgḗ as it is used in Scripture does not imply any community of people but refers to a community established in a special way and for a special purpose.

"The New Testament refers to a synagogue as the Sabbath assembly of the Jews (Acts 13:14, 15). In James 2:2 a synagogue is used to designate the worshiping assembly of the Jewish Christians. In most places in the NT, it is used as the assembly place of the Jews. As a Synagogue the term was used of a Jewish assembly or congregation, where congregational prayers were said, Scripture (the Torah) was read, where the Torah was explained. The Synagogue was a place for the gathering of the Jewish community for both social and religious purposes. It also held some judicial responsibilities (Matt. 10:17; 13:9; Luke 8:41; 12:11; 21:12; Acts 9:2; 13:42, 43; 22:19; 26:11)."[16]

Although the term συναγωγή, *sunagōgḗ*, could be used for a gathering of Christians for worship, the term was primarily used to refer to a gathered community of Jewish believers. In order to separate the two in their cultic and community responsibilities, and to delineate the differences in their foundation, the term preferred by the Christians was ἐκκλησία, *ekklēsía*; hence our English word *church*, rather than *sunagōgḗ* which referred primarily to a Jewish community or gathering of Jewish people.

---

[15] Wolfgang Schrage, Συναγωγή in Kittel, *Theological Dictionary of the New Testament*, vol. 7, pp. 798ff.
[16] Zodhiates, Συναγωγή, *sunagōgḗ, ibid.*

Chapter 7: A Theology of Church and Worship

In a postmodern generation the concept of church has often been either downplayed, disparaged, or even denigrated! This is understandable yet regrettable! For many the church has lost relevancy, has become focused on itself, often ignoring social injustice, the homeless, and the disenfranchised. Furthermore, I have noticed a growing tendency among university students where I have served for many years as a professor that a younger generation has become infatuated with the person of Jesus, and having a relationship with Jesus, but often not by being committed to a local church congregation. Many express the thought of being a disciple of Jesus without the trappings of church and religion. These young people are courageous and spiritually involved, but unfortunately, as I hope to demonstrate, biblically and theologically misguided. They unfortunately have a poor understanding of a theology of church and the kingdom.

The church was obviously important to Jesus; he founded it by dying for it (Matt 16:16-18; Eph 5:25). Paul obviously felt the church as a local congregation was important for he wrote several letters to local congregations and gave his life in ministry to both the church universal and local. Perhaps the importance of church has been lost today due to a poor understanding of the theology of the church in the ministry of Jesus and Paul.

In similar vein, in many regions of the western world traditional churches have lost numbers and charismatic Bible Fellowship churches have taken root in place of the traditional churches. This is an interesting development and to say the least, sometimes regrettable, but in many cases understandable! Some feel more attachment to a community church where fellowship is more generational and less traditional, and where the church serves its contemporary community rather than holding to a past tradition. Possibly because of exasperation with the apparent failure of traditional churches to address changing generational and demographic shifts many are calling for a new church or a new approach to church. Traditional church adherence in a modern fast-changing society has been surrendered in favor of contemporary church flexibility and relevance.

However, what is called for by many church leaders is not new churches but a spiritual and theological revival among churches in general, either traditional or contemporary. I am hoping that by outlining a theology of church and a theology of worship new energy will be found in existing churches where these churches are refreshed, rejuvenated, and revitalized!

A Preface to a Theology of Church and Worship

In preparation for developing a strong and vibrant theology of church and worship a preliminary statement regarding a theology of the church might be appropriate at this point of the study. I will flesh this out in later points in this chapter as we examine a worshipping and missional serving church.

> *The church is a community of people, both universal and local, who have been called by Jesus to be his disciples. They are called into a kinship, a gathered family of people who assemble together on the Lord's Day in order to worship God and Jesus Christ and to be edified and encouraged through their worship of God and Jesus. The focus of the worship is on God's redemptive activity in history. The thought direction in worship is to honor God, celebrate the death and resurrection of Jesus in a regular Lord's Day worship assembly, and to offer one's life to God in everyday life by living lives dedicated to God and Jesus in holy living, and by taking up Jesus' commission in the Missio Dei. Churches that worship God and Jesus in an appropriate genuine spiritual manner, that is in spirit and truth (John 4:24), will be restored and revived.*

The Church in Jesus' Ministry

As many have pointed out, of our four canonical New Testament Gospels only Matthew in three verses (Matt 16:18; 18:17) mentions the church! Mark, Luke, and John do not mention the church by referring to it by the term *ekklēsía*! However, we should not push this too far since the Gospels are replete with Jesus' teachings on the kingdom and after all the church must be a vital aspect of kingdom life and ministry! One simply cannot speak of the kingdom without speaking of the church since the church, especially the local church or congregation of disciples, is a vital agent of the kingdom through which God carries out his kingdom mission.

At Matt 16:18 we are introduced to what may be Jesus' first discussion of the church! In this case Jesus' discussion of the church was tied closely and related directly to the kingdom:

> *"And I tell you, you are Peter, and on this rock I will build my church, and the powers of death shall not prevail against it. [19] I will give you the keys of the kingdom of heaven, and whatever you bind on earth shall be bound in heaven ..."*

This text at Matt 16:13-20 is probably one of the best known and favored texts regarding the church. On this occasion Jesus was gathered with his disciples at Caesarea Philippi. His kingdom ministry had come to a critical point. He had repeatedly discussed the inauguration of his kingdom with his disciples and some of the Jewish leaders (Matt 12:28ff). Thus far in his preparation of the disciples for his kingdom ministry he had not personally referred to himself by the "magic" kingdom word, *Christ*, the *Messiah*, or *God's chosen king of the kingdom*. He had only referred to himself by the neutral term *Son of Man*. The disciples obviously did not yet have Jesus' vision of the kingdom and how it should function. Luke at Acts 1:6 indicates that the disciples had not yet grasped the full import of Jesus' kingdom message and ministry. Obviously, they still thought the kingdom would come about through Judaism and the nation of Israel being restored, a common messianic belief.

At Caesarea Philippi Jesus began to shift the focus from the *Son of Man* to the *Messiah*. He asked his disciples who the Jewish people thought he was. The answer is revealing! Note the text at Matt 16:13-20:

> *Now when Jesus came into the district of Caesarea Philippi, he asked his disciples, "Who do men say that the Son of man is?" [14] And they said, "Some say John the Baptist, others say Elijah, and others Jeremiah or one of the prophets." [15] He said to them, "But who do you say that I am?" [16] Simon Peter replied, "You are the Christ,*

the Son of the living God." ^{17} And Jesus answered him, "Blessed are you, Simon Bar-Jona! For flesh and blood has not revealed this to you, but my Father who is in heaven. ^{18} And I tell you, you are Peter, and on this rock I will build my church, and the powers of death shall not prevail against it. ^{19} I will give you the keys of the kingdom of heaven, and whatever you bind on earth shall be bound in heaven, and whatever you loose on earth shall be loosed in heaven." ^{20} Then he strictly charged the disciples to tell no one that he was the Christ.

Notice that immediately following Peter's amazing confession Jesus began to teach his disciples, preparing them for his passion and resurrection; Matt 16:21f. *"From that time Jesus began to show his disciples that he must go to Jerusalem and suffer many things from the elders and chief priests and scribes, and be killed, and on the third day be raised."*

This text has become foundational to Roman Catholic Papal claims. Roman Catholics argue that it was Peter who Jesus proclaimed would be the foundation and rock of the church. Many Protestants argue that the rock upon which the church was to be established was not Peter but Peter's confession that Jesus is the Christ, the son of God. The foundation being either the truth of Jesus' divinity confessed by Peter, or Jesus himself as the foundation. Some Protestant and Roman Catholics argue that Peter, from the Greek πέτρος, *pétros or* πέτρα, *pétra* meaning *stone* or *rock*, is part of the foundation along with other apostles who become the foundation of the church, cf. Eph 5: 20; Rev 21:14. This is not the place to argue the merits of the Protestant position, much of which I endorse. For such discussion I refer the reader to the many fine commentaries on Matthew's Gospel, or discussions on the Greek πέτρος.[1] The point to be considered here is that Jesus for the first time referred to future disciples as a *church*

---

[1] Hagner, *Matthew 1-13*; Hill, *Matthew*; Keener, *Matthew*; Gundry, *Matthew*; Davis and Allison, *Matthew*; Cullmann, πέτρος and πέτρα in Kittel, *Theological Dictionary of the New Testament*.

(an *ekklēsía*, referring to a community of people who would believe in him as the *Messiah*, the king of God's kingdom), and *that he would build this church,* and that it would be *his* church!

As noted above in the study of the term church, the term *ekklēsía* refers to *a community of people who gather together to carry out some function or purpose.* We have also noted that the term as it is used in the New Testament can refer to the universal church made up of many local congregations, or it can refer to a local congregation of people, a community gathered together to carry out God's *Missio Dei.*

At Matt 16:18 Jesus does not explain in detail what the function of *this new community of believers* would be but the disciples by this time were beginning to realize that being Jesus' disciples would involve a mission of taking his message out at least to the Jewish nation, cf. Matt 10:5ff, what we have come to call *the limited commission*;

> "Go nowhere among the Gentiles, and enter no town of the Samaritans, [6] but go rather to the lost sheep of the house of Israel. [7] And preach as you go, saying, 'The kingdom of heaven is at hand.'"

In time Jesus would explain his great commission to take that Gospel out into all the world to all nations (Matt 28:18-20, Mk 16:15). I particularly like the passage at Acts 2:6-8 where Jesus gave his final instructions to his apostles and the church:

> *And when they had come together, they asked him, "Lord, will you at this time restore the kingdom to Israel?" He said to them, "It is not for you to know times and seasons which the Father has fixed by his own authority. But you will receive power when the Holy Spirit has come upon you; and <u>you shall be my witnesses in Jerusalem, and in all Judea and Samaria and to the end of the earth</u>."*

As we build on Jesus' initial reference to building his church and his instruction to his disciples to go and preach his gospel to all nations we pick up the story of the church in the Book of Acts. Here we see the apostles and faithful Christians going everywhere preaching the Gospel of Jesus and establishing churches (congregations) wherever they went. Luke records that after Stephen's martyrdom and Saul of Tarsus' rampant persecution of the disciples in Jerusalem and Judea, the disciples scattered and went everywhere preaching the gospel. At Acts 8:4 Luke records:

"*⁴ Now those who were scattered went about preaching the word. ⁵ Philip went down to a city of Samaria, and proclaimed to them the Christ.*"

Following Jesus' commission in Acts 2:6-8 the initial ministry and impetus of the kingdom was to go everywhere planting churches which would in turn become church planting churches. That is the meaning of a kingdom *missional* mindset to doing church!

From the early days of the church Jesus built we learn that the church was an extended community of believers centered on faith in Jesus as the Son of God, the *Messiah*, and that this church had a mission: to further the *Missio Dei* of the kingdom of God through the preaching of the Gospel. The church was a missional community of believers who worshipped God for his holiness, sovereignty, great power and saving activity in Jesus, and engaged in extending the borders of God's kingdom into all the world. They became a new and vital witness to the world of God's eternal redemption through becoming a worshipping and missional kingdom seeking community who believed Jesus was the Christ who ruled in his kingdom mission.

We see emanating out of a community of disciples gathered in worship each Lord's Day a community of disciples dedicated to the missional mindset of the kingdom of Christ.

A Theology of Worship - The Church as a Worshipping Community.

Ralph P. Martin in his excellent study, *Worship in the Early Church* challenges our thoughts with the following astute and profound statement. He speaks of the primary role of worship in the Church's character:

> *... the church is a worshipping community, called into being by God Himself not as a social institution or a convenient meeting-place for whose individual interest and religious experience draw them together but as the body of Christ in the world. The Church of Jesus Christ is by definition the people of God called by Him to offer*

> *up spiritual sacrifices through Jesus Christ, and to proclaim the wonderful works of His grace (1 Pet ii, 5-9).*[2]

Martin draws our attention to the fact that the Church is a spiritual temple, erected to God's glory and his worship. "In time, the Church of Christ is summoned into being by God in order to be *a worshipping community*."

The Apostle Paul when writing to the Christians in Ephesus and Asia stressed in a long introduction the fact that Christians had been predestined by God to so live their lives that they would bring glory to God through Christ and in the church (Eph 1:3-12; 3:20, 21). I highlight below the worshipping theme in the theologically loaded passage at vs. 11 and close it with vss. 20 and 21:

> [11]In him, according to the purpose of him who accomplishes all things according to the counsel of his will, [12] we who first hoped in Christ have been destined and appointed to live for the praise of his glory ... [20] Now to him who by the power at work within us is able to do far more abundantly than all that we ask or think, [21] to him be glory in the church and in Christ Jesus to all generations, for ever and ever. Amen.[3]

In the parenetic body of this same epistle (Eph 3:13-21) Paul explained how with the strengthening power of the Holy Spirit the Christians and church would be empowered to so live their lives for the praise of God's glory. The whole epistle resonates with themes that demonstrate how Christians as God's called and predestined children empowered by the Holy Spirit would live lives worthy of their calling, and in worship bring glory to God.

Pointedly in the introduction to *Worship in the Early Church* Martin observes:

> *It is the excellent worthiness of God, therefore, which makes our worship possible; and when we offer Him our devotion, praise and prayer, this is to be the thought which is uppermost in our minds: He alone is*

---

[2] Martin, *Worship*, Kindle location 63.
[3] Eph 1:3-12; 3:20, 21.

> *worship-ful. We ascribe to him all that is in keeping with His nature and revealed person.*[4]

I gather from Paul in Ephesians and Martin's comments that the church is called by God to be a Holy Spirit empowered body of people in Christ whose purpose is to so live that they bring glory to God and worship him in a manner that reflects that glory.

The church is not a social gathering of people who assemble for the self-interest of the people. The church is the body of Christ whose worship is focused and directed to God in a manner that well reflects his glory.

Randall Bagley in his revised edition of Franklin M. Segler's excellent study of *Christian Worship* makes the following comment:

> *Worship is not an end in itself, not a means to something else. Karl Barth has appropriately declared that the "church's worship is the opus Dei, the work of God, which is carried out for its own sake." When we try to worship for the sake of certain benefits that we may receive, the act ceases to be worship; for then it attempts to use God as a means to something else. We worship God purely for the sake of worshipping God.*[5]

Both Barth's and Bradley's observations stress the point I made in the Preface to this study; when we turn the worship assembly in which we gather to praise God and Jesus through celebrating the Lord's Supper or Eucharist into a self-interest service which focuses on ourselves or the human dynamic, we shift the focus to the interest or the needs and desires of the participants rather than toward God. What I have in mind is the declared tendency in some worship services to conduct the service in a manner that will please us or appeal to our visitors. Again I stress, I am not opposed to seeker evangelistic services, but am concerned when the dynamic of a service whose purpose is to manifest worship directed to God in a holy and reverent manner has shifted its focus to either our own needs or preferences or to those of others.

---

[4] Martin, *Worship*, Kindle location 94.
[5] Segler and Bradley, *Christian Worship*, p. 3. (Italics mine, IAF).

Focusing on the needs or persuasions of others changes the dynamic of the service from worshipping God to pleasing ourselves or reaching our visitors. This is not to imply that visitors will be disinterested and will feel ignored when the focus is on God and Christ and not on the desires and interests of the worshippers! Nor is this to deny the importance of reaching out to those who do not know Jesus or even to downplaying the role that a seeker service might play. My point is not to confuse the dynamic and focus of the two profoundly significant ministries—worship and evangelism!

The best way to impress visitors and uplift ourselves is to draw attention to the solemn, awesome, redemptive power of God who loves us, members and visitors, to the extent that he came and died for us to bring us into a real genuine relationship with God as his children and missional kingdom.

Before I lose you on this point, let me stress again two qualifying points! *First*, I am not opposed to seeker-oriented services that seek to reach out intentionally to the visitors. Perhaps the following statement will date me somewhat, but in my early years of ministry as a missionary in South Africa I eagerly supported and engaged in what we called gospel meetings which were overtly evangelistic and seeker oriented. I recognize that today in our post-modern culture such meetings are not favored either by the church or our contemporary culture! In a culture in which the focus as a whole is entertainment oriented, or oriented toward self-interest, we will need to find new ways of reaching out to friends and those outside the body of Christ without diminishing the true value and focus of worshipping God. I do not have the solution to this need but do see in small group fellowship and Bible study group meetings such non-threatening opportunities to reach out beyond the confines of our "inner circle" of church believers.

Second, I do believe that when the church focuses its worship dynamic on God and his holiness in a deeply spiritual and reflective manner visitors will be impressed. Celebrating God's mighty deeds in creation, in retelling the history of his mighty saving acts and ultimate redemption in Christ, praising him for his glory and holiness, all in a genuine spiritual attitude (John

4:24, *worshipping God in spirit and truth*) will draw thoughtful visitors into a worshipful attitude directed toward God and not self. After all, that is what worship is intended to do! When true spiritual worship is engaged featuring the meaningful reading of Scripture, well-chosen songs sung in praise of God, a well-structured sermon, thoughtful prayers, and genuine celebration of the Lord's death and resurrection in the Eucharist, in a meaningful and clear purpose of praising God, visitors will be impressed and attracted.

In my many years of mission work, ministry, and church leadership I have yet to find visitors who were not impressed with our singing and celebration of the Lord's Supper when conducted in a spiritual manner. They might have had some questions regarding the liturgy of our worship but these in my experience have been serious questions regarding why we worship in the manner experienced. This has opened doors for meaningful discussion and study. I have not in my years of church experience found visitors who have been rebuffed by genuine spiritual worship, but then I readily admit that I am drawing here on my own happy ministry experience!

A vital question is, "How do we get our friends to visit with us in our genuine worship services which is focused on God and Jesus? I have already mentioned smaller Bible studies with friends or business associates, and small groups of disciples who meet regularly together for fellowship. But surely there must be some co-relationship between a life lived in respect and worship of God in our daily lives and friends with whom we related on a daily basis in a broken world. Do we not have some influence or opportunity in a world of broken homes and frayed relationships and people seeking help? Perhaps our personal failure to reach out personally in a fractured world has left an attitude of personal self interest in our personal work or play community experience.

My reason for embarking on this discussion, possibly even tirade, reflects our frustrating difficulty in getting people to visit with us in our Lord's Day worship experience. We should have learned by now that quick fixes are not often effective!

I believe it was Israel's commitment to the uniqueness of the monotheism and holiness of YHWH as the only God expressed through the reading and exposition of the *Torah* (Law of Moses) as God's inspired instruction for life, and their commitment to their faithful way of living a meaningful life that attracted serious Gentile seekers to Judaism and the Synagogue. The singular focus of the devoted prayers in the Synagogue impressed many thoughtful Gentiles and drew them to Judaism in contrast to the meaningless prayers of their pagan cults (cf. Jesus in the Sermon on the Mount, *"do not heap up empty phrases as the Gentiles do"* Mat 6:7). Follow Paul on his missionary journeys as he began in synagogues in which God-fearing Gentiles could be found and branched out into the Gentile world. Scripture describes these thoughtful Gentiles as worshippers of God. They were impressed and won over to worshipping the one true God by the genuine worship of faithful Jews. Consider Lydia, a Gentile from Thyatira, Acts 16:14, and Titius Justus, Acts 18:7, *a worshipper of God*, σεβομένη τὸν θεόν, *sebomenē ton theón* who were along with many other Gentiles drawn to Christ through the Synagogue and Judaism.

Marva Dawn summed up what I am saying about genuine worship and evangelism in a meaningful manner when she observed that a church does not need to dumb down its worship services in order to reach out. Dawn observes:

> *Many people advocate turning worship into "seekers' services" or "entertainment evangelism." These attempts to reach out to persons who do not know God are certainly laudable – one would hope that we all look for ways to share our faith – but it is a misnomer to call services "worship" if their purpose is to attract people rather than to adore God.*[6]

Dawn introduces the following perceptive plea and comments into our dialogue of enriching our worship services and reaching out to those who do not know Jesus:

> *Do pastors, musicians, worship participants, and parish leaders know when we are dumbing down the Church? ... I plead with you for careful theological reflection concerning the meaning and practice of worship.*

---

[6] Dawn, *Reaching Out,* p. 81.

Please forgive me and correct me if I err, but let my comments challenge us all to think more deeply about the issues at stake for the worship and life of the Church.

This book is written with these four goals: to reflect upon the culture for which we want to proclaim the gospel; to expose the subtle powers that beckon us into idolatries and that upset the necessary dialectical balances in the Church's life and worship; to stimulate better questions about if, why, and how we might be dumbing faith down in the ways we structure, plan, and participate in worship education and in worship itself; and to offer better means for reaching out to people outside the Church. It is my claim that we ought not to, and do not need to, conform to our culture's patterns, but that the Christian community must intentionally sustain its unique character and just as intentionally care about the culture around it in order to be able to introduce people genuinely to Christ and to nurture individuals to live faithfully.[7]

A Theology of Worship - The Church as a Missional Community

Our understanding of the church as a missional[8] community hinges on our understanding of the church as that agency responsible for the furthering of God's kingdom as a missional community. God and Jesus did not see the kingdom as something exclusively for Jerusalem and Israel! Just before his ascension to the father, Jesus' disciples asked him if he was ready to restore the kingdom to Israel, he mildly rebuked them, and charged them to wait for the outpouring of Holy Spirit from on high, and then to go out into all the world witnessing, preaching, and teaching the good news of the kingdom, Acts 1:6-8:

---

[7] Dawn, *Reaching Out*, p. 11.

[8] By *missional* I understand the kingdom and the church functioning as that body of God's people who are the *agents* responsible for planting new communities of believers, or churches, throughout the world. Being *missional* includes embracing the posture, thinking, behaviors, and practices of a missionary in order to reach others with the message of the gospel. Cf Ed Stetzer, *Planting Missional Churches*.

> *So when they had come together, they asked him, "Lord, will you at this time restore the kingdom to Israel?"* ^{7} *He said to them, "It is not for you to know times or seasons which the Father has fixed by his own authority.* ^{8} *But you shall receive power when the Holy Spirit has come upon you; and you shall be my witnesses in Jerusalem and in all Judea and Samaria and to the end of the earth."*

As we follow these disciples through the Book of Acts we find them and the early Christians doing exactly what Jesus instructed, they went everywhere preaching the gospel! In short order there were churches planted all over the Mediterranean world, churches in the diaspora, (1 Pet 1:1f), in Rome (Rom 1:1ff, 15:22-16:16), at Ephesus and all over Asia, in Colossae, Thessalonica, Corinth, *et al.*

The church as a worshipping community honors God and Jesus by executing the missional *Missio Dei* of the kingdom.

A Theology of Worship - The Church as a Serving Community

In the context which we have been exploring, the relationship between worshipping God, serving our neighbors, and the worshipful life we live every day two texts stand out in my mind, Matt 22:23ff and Rom 12:1.

First, which I believe stands at the threshold of our discussion of worshipping God, we explore briefly Matt 22:23ff;

> ^{34} *But when the Pharisees heard that he had silenced the Sadducees, they came together.* ^{35} *And one of them, a lawyer, asked him a question, to test him.* ^{36} *"Teacher, which is the great commandment in the law?"* ^{37} *And he said to him, "You shall love the Lord your God with all your heart, and with all your soul, and with all your mind.* ^{38} *This is the great and first commandment.* ^{39} *And a second is like it, You shall love your neighbor as yourself.* ^{40} *On these two commandments depend all the law and the prophets."*

This beloved text is one favored by Christians who are concerned that we do not pay enough attention to loving our neighbors. Certainly it is a great text and commandments, *but it is not the great commandment! The great commandment is that we should love the Lord our God with all our heart, soul, and mind!*

Loving and worshipping God with all our being is the foundation and even prolegomena of loving and serving our neighbors! Loving and serving our neighbors flows out of our love for God and certainly is extremely important to the Christian's faith.

Surely there is a foundation to the church as a serving community in loving God first and then as a result of this loving and serving our neighbors!

Second, Rom 12:1ff is a great text that likewise builds on loving God with all our being and fulfilling the great commandment. It is the command to love and serve our neighbors carried over into life and action. In a power packed text Paul stressed a profoundly important part of our worshipful life. He explains that our worship of God extends beyond our congregational worship on the Lord's Day into what we do every day in our lives of grateful worship/service. As a result of what God has done for us in Christ out of his love and grace we respond in worshipful living. Interestingly, this is the first paranetic or practical exhortation of Romans following the majestic theological arguments Paul presents of all people, both Jew and Gentile being justified by a righteous God through the faithfulness of Jesus and our faith in what God is doing in Jesus.

> *[1] I appeal to you therefore, brethren, by the mercies of God, to present your bodies as a living sacrifice, holy and acceptable to God, which is your spiritual worship. [2] Do not be conformed to this world but be transformed by the renewal of your mind, that you may prove what is the will of God, what is good and acceptable and perfect.*[9]

We observed in our discussion of worship terminology in Chapter 1 that the word used by Paul in Rom 12:2 was λατρείαν, *latreian*, and that he described this worship as λογικὴν λατρείαν, *logikēn latreian*, which is translated in our English translations as either <u>spiritual</u> worship, <u>reasonable</u> service, or <u>spiritual act</u> of worship. Zodhiates has noted that *latreía* "can refer to religious

---

[9] Rom 12:1, 2.

or cultic service, or a life of service offered to God in general based on a worshipful attitude."[10] It is in the sense of worship in a *life of holy service* that Paul uses the term here at Rom 12:2.

Strathmann in Kittel observed regarding *latreía*, "The influence of the LXX may be seen in the fact that the word never refers to human relations, let alone to secular services. *The ministry denoted by λατρεύειν is always offered to God.*"[11] Hence, our everyday living for God is a life *offered to God in worship*!

Paul's discussion of this spiritual worship/service in Romans 12 is interesting. In the opening verses he introduced himself to the saints in Rome as an apostle of Christ who was a servant (δοῦλος, *doúlos, slave or bond servant*) of Jesus Christ who was under obligation to preach the gospel to both Jews and Gentiles (Rom 1:14-17). He picks up this same theme at Rom 12:1, 2 calling on the saints to offer their lives in worshipful service to God by using the gifts that God in Christ has by grace given them. Worship *of* God translates into service *for* God and Christ! At Rom 12:6 he gets specific:

> *Having gifts that differ according to the grace given to us, let us use them: if prophecy, in proportion to our faith;* [7] *if service, in our serving; he who teaches, in his teaching;* [8] *he who exhorts, in his exhortation; he who contributes, in liberality; he who gives aid, with zeal; he who does acts of mercy, with cheerfulness.*

The Church is a body of redeemed serving saints who daily offer their spiritual giftedness in worship of God in their everyday life activities, and who are thus caught up in the ministry or service of the *Missio Dei*.

The Theology of Worshipping God in Spirit and Truth

Whether we begin with worship in general encompassing ancient pagan nature worship, polytheistic idolatry, the worship of monotheistic Israel, or the Trinitarian worship of Christianity, one principle surfaces; *worship flows from the worshipper toward*

---

[10] Zodhiates, λατρεία, *latreía*.
[11] Strathmann in Kittel, *Theological Dictionary of the New Testament*, vol. 4, pp. 63ff. (Italics mine, IAF)

the "deity" being worshipped. The deity or god is *the object toward which worship is directed.*

In the case of Judaism and Christianity one additional characteristic is evident; God is always *both* the *subject* and *object* being worshipped! He is the *object* of the worship since He is the one being worshipped! However, He is also the *subject* of worship since *He is the one who has called us to worship and who has laid down the fundamental principles of that worship.*

In the case of Judaism it was YHWH who called Israel to worship. Through the *Torah* He stipulated how and when the worship should take place; he established the High Priesthood and priesthood in general, the feast days, the Sabbath, the Tabernacle/Temple, and the type of sacrifices to be offered (cf. Exodus, Leviticus, etc.).

In the eschatological age of the church, in other words the age of the church as the body of Christ, the system was refocused; Jesus became the High Priest and every Christian became a priest to offer sacrifices. God had introduced a new covenant![12] Jesus became the atoning sacrifice offered once for all on a cross. The geographical location of the place of daily priestly sacrifices was changed; it was no longer Jerusalem or Mount Gerizim or the Tabernacle or Temple; it was in the lives of the Christians who as priests offer their lives in worshipful service of God.

From the Book of Hebrews we learn that Jesus entered once into the Holy of Holies in Heaven having made an eternal once for all time sacrifice of atonement. Note specifically Heb 3:1; 4:14f; 8:1ff;

> [3:1]*Therefore, holy brethren, who share in a heavenly call, consider Jesus, the apostle and high priest of our confession. 2 He was faithful to him who appointed him, just as Moses also was faithful in God's house.*
>
> [4:14] *Since then we have a great high priest who has passed through the heavens, Jesus, the Son of God, let us hold fast our confession. [15] For we have not a high priest who is unable to sympathize with our weaknesses, but one who in every respect has been tempted as we are, yet*

---

[12] Heb 8:1-13.

without sin. ⁱ⁶ Let us then with confidence draw near to the throne of grace, that we may receive mercy and find grace to help in time of need.

⁸:¹ Now the point in what we are saying is this: we have such a high priest, one who is seated at the right hand of the throne of the Majesty in heaven, ² a minister in the sanctuary and the true tent which is set up not by man but by the Lord. ³ For every high priest is appointed to offer gifts and sacrifices; hence it is necessary for this priest also to have something to offer. ⁴ Now if he were on earth, he would not be a priest at all, since there are priests who offer gifts according to the law. ⁵ They serve a copy and shadow of the heavenly sanctuary; for when Moses was about to erect the tent, he was instructed by God, saying, "See that you make everything according to the pattern which was shown you on the mountain." ⁶ But as it is, Christ has obtained a ministry which is as much more excellent than the old as the covenant he mediates is better, since it is enacted on better promises. ⁷ For if that first covenant had been faultless, there would have been no occasion for a second.

Jesus became the High Priest seated in the Heavens, the place of priestly sacrifice became the lives of the Christians themselves, and in the cultic worship became weekly Lord's Day gathering of Christians in corporate worship in whatever locality they may be gathered, anywhere on earth. *The eschatological community, the church, became the center of spiritual life and worship*!

In the eschatological age of the church the priesthood and sacrifices may have changed, *but the subject and object of the worship remained the same; the eternal God calls his people to worship him and he remains both the subject and the object of the worship.*

Given the diverse geographical, temporal, and cultural diversity of the church as a new worshipping community, many of the regulations regarding the worship which focused on Jerusalem and the Temple needed to change. For instance, the Jewish sacrifices, feasts, and festival dates were no longer relevant, and Jesus fulfilled the requirements of the Temple sacrifices. The Lord's Supper celebrated in local congregations became the new feast of the eschatological age. The Sabbath seventh day holy day of the week became the Christian first day of the week Lord's Day celebration. The exercises of the Temple in Jerusalem became the exercises of the local congregation. The daily sacrificial animal offerings became the lives of Christians which are offered daily in spiritual sacrifice. The Passover and *Yom Kippur* atoning sacrifice became Jesus' atoning sacrifice on the cross and the celebration of the Lord's Supper, the Eucharist replaced *Yom Kippur* and the Passover. Circumcision as a Jewish sacrament marking the Jews relationship with God became the Christian sacraments of faith, baptism, and the Lord's Supper. The Levitical nature of the Temple worship of Jewish life became the model of the Christian worship on the Lord's Day assembly and daily living for God.

As Delling and others have pointed out it is difficult to determine with certainty or precision the form of early Christian worship services.[13] Cullmann, in keeping with Delling's observation regarding there being no clear picture of New Testament worship, observes:

> *Our sources for the investigation of early Christian services of worship do not yield a perfectly clear picture of the outward development of the gatherings for worship; they do disclose, however, a fairly clear tendency in worship.*[14]

However, in some contrast to what might appear to be a negative critical evaluation of New Testament worship by Delling and Cullmann, from an examination of the few New Testament texts which describe the nature of the Christian assembly a few characteristics or "markers" can be identified which seem to be corroborated in the reflection of these texts in the early second century church literature and early discussions of Christian worship. These are 1) a weekly celebration of the Lord's Supper on

---

[13] Delling, *Worship*, p. 42; Aune, "Worship, Early Christian," *Anchor Yale Bible Dictionary*, p. 975.

[14] Cullmann, *Early Christian Worship*, p. 7.

the first day of the week, 2) praying, 3) singing, 4) the reading of Scripture and sermon or homily, and 5) a benevolent contribution. We will examine these in some detail below in chapters 6 - 10.

As we examine these "markers" of the Lord's Day Christian worship assemblies, one thing remains constant; *God is always both the subject and object of the worship!* The worshippers are never the focal point or direction of the worship, they are at best secondary participants in this worship experience.

Jesus' instruction to the woman of Samaria (John 4:24) stands out as a significant constant in worship; *we worship God in spirit and truth.* When Jesus discussed several issues with the Samaritan woman at the well at Sychar, among them being concerns regarding her married life and water that gives real eternal life, Jesus addressed the Jewish and Samaritan practice of worship in Jerusalem and on Mount Gerizim. Note the discussion as recorded by John at John 4:19-24:

> *[19] The woman said to him, "Sir, I perceive that you are a prophet. [20] Our fathers worshiped on this mountain; and you say that in Jerusalem is the place where men ought to worship." [21] Jesus said to her, "Woman, believe me, the hour is coming when neither on this mountain nor in Jerusalem will you worship the Father. [22] You worship what you do not know; we worship what we know, for salvation is from the Jews. [23] But the hour is coming, and now is, when the true worshipers will worship the Father in spirit and truth, for such the Father seeks to worship him.*

This is not the place to discuss why the Samaritans worshipped on Mt Gerizim other than to note that being "half-Jews" they were not permitted to worship in Jerusalem, so they substituted a temple on Mt Gerizim in place of the temple in Jerusalem. *Jesus was not interested in discussing the religious legality of this practice but wanted to stress that in the eschatological age already present in his ministry (cf. Matt 12:28; Acts 2:17 ff; Heb 1:1) God seeks a different kind of worship from the physical emphasis in the Jewish or Samaritan temples.* Contrary to the worship of the Jerusalem Temple which in Jesus' mind was corrupt, and the worship in the Samaritan temple which Jesus would likewise have held to be distorted, *Jesus stressed a new and different kind of worship, one in "spirit and truth."*

The little expression *"spirit and truth"* is in an interesting and powerful construction which is referred to technically in biblical interpretation as *hendiadys* in which one thing is said through two things.[15] With this in mind, since the word *truth* derives from the Greek ἀλήθεια, *alḗtheia* which means *real, valid, unconcealed, that which is genuine,*[16] *"spirit and truth"* carry the sense of *genuine real spiritual* worship. D. A. Carson[17] observes that spirit and truth do not imply two modes of worship but carry the sense of a God-centered worship. Genuine worship is not located in a place like Jerusalem or Mt. Gerizim but is focused on God as spirit, or toward God as spirit. Worship that is not focused, fixed on God, or toward God is simply not genuine spiritual worship. It is idolatry! If God as spirit and the giver of all spiritual gifts is not both the subject and object of worship in the kingdom eschatological age of the church,[18] then worship is not genuine spiritual worship!

We worship God in spirit and truth which is a genuine spiritual worship which arises from within our inner spiritual being! Worshipping God in an attitude of genuine spiritual worship becomes the spiritual dynamic and power of the life of the church! This thought addresses the question of *how* the church worships, speaking more of the *attitude* or *direction* involved in the worship. It does not simply speak of the *form* of *what* the church does do. *What* the church does is important, but the *why*, the *attitude*, or the *direction* of genuine spiritual worship is the overriding factor in worship.

---

[15] Technically, *hendiadys* is a form of parataxis in which two nouns or terms are coordinated by the use of the Greek coordinating conjunction *kai* most often translated as *and*. The second noun acts as an adjective for the first noun Cf. Richard N. Soulen, and R. Kendall Soulen, *Handbook of Biblical Criticism*, Atlanta; John Knox Press, 1976, 2011, p. 82.

[16] Zodhiates, ἀλήθεια.

[17] Carson, *John*, John 4:19-24.

[18] Cf. Heb 1:1, 2, and Acts 2:17, indicate that *the last days* or the eschatological age are the Christian age.

Simply put, when the church's focus, concern, or direction of worship is not solely on God or toward God that worship is not in *spirit and truth*, nor is it a *genuine spiritual worship*!

Summary

In this chapter we have examined what a theology of church and a theology of worship look like. The Church is a community of believers in Jesus which exists for worshipping God, serving God in their local community, and reaching out into all the earth. It is a community which honors God and Christ by serving in God's *Missio Dei.*

A *theology* of the church informs us that the church is a *divinely inspired and motivated worshipping community*. It was a fundamental part of God's eternal purpose in Jesus Christ. It was established in the ministry of Jesus with a divine commission to witness to the world through worshipping God in spirit and truth and taking the gospel and church into all the world.

Chapter 8: Types of Christian Assemblies in the 1st Century

That the early churches assembled on various occasions as communities of faith is well attested in the New Testament but not well defined as to what they did in these assemblies! We have noticed that the church gathered on the Lord's Day to celebrate the Lord's death and resurrection in the Lord's Supper, to pray, to sing, to read Scripture and hear a homily, and to make contributions for benevolent work. But in regard to other assemblies there is no clear instruction or inference. We can form some idea of these miscellaneous assemblies from remarks regarding them, or some correction relating to these assemblies. We see such comments reflected obliquely or tangentially in the Epistles, but in many cases, we have to resort to making some assumptions that are nothing more than assumptions.

In the very earliest days of the church, Christians gathered together on different occasions either unsure of what was happening, or as they gained a keener understanding of their role in the *Missio Dei* and then moving on into the greater world outside Judea.

Early Post-Resurrection Gatherings

Immediately following the resurrection of their Lord the disciples gathered together to come to some understanding of what had occurred and to await further instruction. Mark 16:9ff; Luke 24:36-49; and Matthew 28:16ff reflect on the gathering of the disciples shortly before Jesus' ascension when Jesus gave them what we commonly call "the great commission."

Luke 24:13 tells of two disciples on the road to Emmaus discussing the recent events after Jesus' crucifixion. Jesus appeared to them and set those events into the eschatological *Missio Dei* of the kingdom. He ate a meal with them, a significant "Jesus sign," and left them assured and encouraged.

At Acts 1:1-8 the disciples were gathered together and had questions regarding the kingdom. Jesus elaborated on this, setting their concern for the kingdom into the *Missio Dei*. Their great commission was explained in the more specific context of the outpouring of the Holy Spirit. Jesus had explained to them in his last meeting with them on the night of his betrayal that he would not leave them alone but would send to them the Holy Spirit, the παράκλητος *paráklētos*, to encourage and comfort them, John 14:1-20, and *passim* in this discussion.

> ¹ *"Let not your hearts be troubled; believe in God, believe also in me.* ² *In my Father's house are many rooms; if it were not so, would I have told you that I go to prepare a place for you?* ³ *And when I go and prepare a place for you, I will come again and will take you to myself, that where I am you may be also.* ⁴ *And you know the way where I am going."* ⁵ *Thomas said to him, "Lord, we do not know where you are going; how can we know the way?"* ⁶ *Jesus said to him, "I am the way, and the truth, and the life; no one comes to the Father, but by me.* ⁷ *If you had known me, you would have known my Father also; henceforth you know him and have seen him …*
>
> ¹⁶ *And I will pray the Father, and he will give you another Counselor* [paráklētos]*, to be with you forever,* ¹⁷ *even the Spirit of truth, whom the world cannot receive, because it neither sees him nor knows him; you know him, for he dwells with you, and will be in you.*
>
> ¹⁸ *"I will not leave you desolate; I will come to you.* ¹⁹ *Yet a little while, and the world will see me no more, but you will see me; because I live, you will live also.* ²⁰ *In that day you will know that I am in my Father, and you in me, and I in you.*

As they recalled this promise of Jesus they must have been deeply moved and encouraged. I can just imagine the mixed emotions this must have introduced with Jesus' new commission; the uncertainty, anticipation, encouragement and joy of this discussion!

This certainly was a profound meeting of the disciples gathered together in Jerusalem, seeking understanding of what had just occurred in their lives with Jesus' crucifixion and resurrection! To us today this is sort of "old hat" knowledge, for Christianity is now over 2019 years old. But to them this gathering had dynamic and cosmic *Missio Dei* implications.

Then again we read at Acts 1:14 how Luke describes the disciples gathered together with the women and brothers of Jesus, "with one accord devoting themselves to prayer." As we read about these several gatherings recorded at Luke 24, John 21, and Acts 1:1-8, and 1:14 we note that they certainly involved some uncertainty but also reverent awe and worship as the disciples began to grasp the full implication of their encounters with the resurrected Jesus. These meetings were not what we call a Sunday, 1st Day of the Week, Lord's Day Lord's Supper worship assemblies, but they were vital and significant to the life of the early church.

An interesting account of such an early gathering is recorded for us at Acts 2:41-47. There is considerable discussion as to whether part of this account, namely Acts 2:42, actually refers to a formal worship occasion or whether it was an attempt by Luke to strengthen his case of the formation of a new community grounded in the apostles' teaching and fellowship. Fitzmyer observes regarding this interesting text:

> *This statement is an idyllic description of the life of the primitive Christian community in Jerusalem, its spontaneity, harmony, and unity, its devotion to prayer and Temple worship ... it is composite as are the other two summaries in 4:32-37; 5:12-16 ... Four things are noted as characteristic of Jerusalem Christians: their adherence to the teachings of the apostles, a communal form of life, the breaking of bread, and prayers ... "The breaking of bread," known from Luke 24:30, 35, is the abstract formulation that becomes the way Luke refers to the Eucharistic celebration among Christians.*[1]

Fitzmyer continues by discussing the pros and cons of Acts 2:42 being a summary of a formal worship service in which the Lord's Supper or Eucharist was celebrated. He cites Jeremias who considered this text to be an account of an early worship service, and Haenchen who does not see this as the celebration of

---

[1] Fitzmyer, *Acts of the Apostles*, p. 268f. Cf. the excellent discussions of this text in Johnson, *Acts of the Apostles*, pp. 58ff; Lüdemann, *The Acts of the Apostles*, Kindle location 689ff; Bock, *Acts*, Kindle location 4043ff.

the Lord's Supper. Fitzmyer concludes his brief discussion of the pros and cons of this being a discussion of an early worship service by listing several scholars who like himself consider this text to be simply a summary of the early Jerusalem church's unity and fellowship.

F. F. Bruce, in agreement with most commentaries on this text, notes:

> *Luke presents in this paragraph an ideal picture of this new community, rejoicing in the forgiveness of sins and the gift of the Holy Spirit. The community, the apostolic fellowship, was constituted on the basis of the apostolic teaching. This teaching was authoritative because it was the teaching of the Lord communicated through the apostles ... The apostolic fellowship found expression in a number of ways, of which two are mentioned in verse 42 – the breaking of bread and prayers. The breaking of bread probably denotes more than the regular taking of food together: the regular observance of what came to be called the Lord's Supper seems to be in view.*[2]

This is not the place to debate the finer details of this interesting text. For deeper reflection the reader is encouraged to read Joachim Jeremias[3] and others who have given considerable detailed study to this. My point is that as the story of the kingdom and church unfolds *the disciples gathered together on several occasions in prayer and devotion illustrating a deep sense of community, fellowship, and benevolence, but to call most of these formal gatherings of the church to worship might be reaching beyond the text.*

The First Apostolic Decision Meeting.

Without a time-reference Luke records at Acts 1:15-26 the first recorded meeting of the "Twelve" Apostles. He writes, *"in those days Peter stood up among the brethren ..."*[4] The time had come for someone to be selected to fill Judas' role among the 12. The play on the number 12 in regard to the church in its early

---

[2] Bruce, *The Book of Acts*, p. 72f.
[3] Jeremias, *The Eucharistic Words*.
[4] Acts 1:15ff.

days is significant, demonstrating a continuation of the symbolism of the 12 tribes of Israel. Cf. Rev 7:4ff, the 12 thousand for each of the 12 tribes of Israel (the 12 tribes were obviously stylistically listed in this text) and the 12 angels at the 12 gates of the New Jerusalem representing the 12 tribes of Israel and the 12 foundations to the city representing the 12 apostles at Rev 21:9-14.

On this occasion, Acts 1:15ff, Luke records that there were 120 disciples gathered. They were involved in the process of the selection of Matthias as Judas' Apostolic replacement. Luke mentions that there was the reading or citing of Scripture, much prayer, and the involvement of the Holy Spirit. This certainly was a "highly religious" occasion. There was no mention of the celebration of the Lord's Supper so there was no indication that this was on the Lord's Day! We should remember that in the early days of the church in Jerusalem, as indicated later at Acts 2: 41-47, we learn that the disciples met in the Temple daily for prayers and the instructions of the Apostles. Acts 1:15ff is an excellent example of the several special gatherings that illustrate that early disciples gathered for special meetings, and that the gatherings were conducted in a "worshipful reverential" setting without the occasion being the church assembling on the Lord's Day for celebration and formal worship of, or toward God and Jesus, as seen in the Lord's Supper.

Without any indication that they were gathered together for specific Day of the Lord worship service, the disciples were gathered together when Peter and John were being tried by the Jewish leaders in the Sanhedrin, acts 4:5ff, Peter and John were released and joined the gathered disciples who had been praising God and praying for Peter and John. The impact of that gathering is well expressed by Luke at Acts 4:31-33.

> *³¹ And when they had prayed, the place in which they were gathered together was shaken; and they were all filled with the Holy Spirit and spoke the word of God with boldness.*
>
> *³² Now the company of those who believed were of one heart and soul, and no one said that any of the things which he possessed was his own, but they had everything*

> *in common. ³³ And with great power the apostles gave their testimony to the resurrection of the Lord Jesus, and great grace was upon them all.*

My point is that such deeply spiritual meetings or gatherings were significant and indicate great reverence and spiritual thanksgiving, but they should not be confused with the whole congregation gathering for formal worship on the Lord's Day, no matter how small the congregation.

I have already drawn attention above to the fact that although every day in the life of the Christian should be a day in which Christians worship God with their lives in a daily living sacrifice (Rom 12:1ff) this should not be equated with the gathering of the congregation for formal worship on the first day of the week (Acts 20:7) for a time of worship in which God and Jesus were worshipped in a celebration of the Lord's Supper, with prayer, Scripture reading, a homily,[5] and the singing of psalms, hymns, and spiritual songs.

Love Feasts

Little is said specifically by name in the New Testament regarding the so-called *agápē*[6] or *love feast* other than in Jude 12 and possible references to such feasts or meals at 2 Pet 2:13 and 1 Cor 11:17ff. However, we can safely conclude that the Jews and early Christians, as well as other religious groups such as the pagan worshippers of Dionysius, the god of the grape and wine, met regularly together in special feasts which had significant religious overtones.

Among the Jews, the Passover feast with its history of God's saving activity would begin in the Temple with the sacrifice of the Paschal Lamb but continue in the home around the family table. Such a meal would be intensely religious and worshipful. Israel celebrated several feasts with meals eaten around the family table. Such occasions would involve serious reflection on God's provision through the ages of Israel's history. From what

---

[5] Homily refers to a commentary or sermon based on Scripture.
[6] The Greek word *agápē* simply meant love but by association was used of the early fellowship meals shared by Christians.

we learn from the Old Testament the Jewish feasts served to bond the family and nation to its roots.

It was perfectly natural that especially the Jewish Christians would include similar feasts intended to bond themselves to one another, to demonstrate and enjoy care for one another, and to give thanks to God for his provision. Some of these meals developed into what became known in Christian circles as the *agápē* or *love* fellowship meal.

We have some idea from Acts 2:42-47 of the celebration of such meals among the Jewish Christians in Jerusalem.

> *[41] So those who received his word were baptized, and there were added that day about three thousand souls. [42] And they devoted themselves to the apostles' teaching and fellowship, to the breaking of bread and the prayers. [43] And fear came upon every soul; and many wonders and signs were done through the apostles. [44] And all who believed were together and had all things in common; [45] and they sold their possessions and goods and distributed them to all, as any had need. [46] And day by day, attending the temple together and breaking bread in their homes, they partook of food with glad and generous hearts, [47] praising God and having favor with all the people. And the Lord added to their number day by day those who were being saved.*[7]

Luke was not intending to lay out a program of formal worship when he recorded how the early Christians in Jerusalem were united together as a fellowship of believers in Christ, nor was he intending to establish a doctrine of the celebrating of the Lord's Supper! In this Acts text we find some indication of what developed later, possibly very early, into a formal worship service in which the Lord's Supper became a central emphasis, and Acts 2:42-47 may be the beginnings of what would later be called the *agápē* or love fellowship meal. Little is said beyond this text and 1 Cor 11:17ff in Scripture about the love feast other than Jude who touches it tangentially in his discussion of those who were corrupting the Christian faith.

---

[7] Acts 2:41-47.

Although Jude mentions the *agápē*, he does not say much of this love feast other than roundly condemning those who abused the spirit of the fellowship meal. A similar condemnation is found also in 2 Pet 2:13 which many scholars hold was Peter's adaptation of Jude 12. Jude wrote:

> [8] *Yet in like manner these men in their dreamings defile the flesh, reject authority, and revile the glorious ones.* [9] *But when the archangel Michael, contending with the devil, disputed about the body of Moses, he did not presume to pronounce a reviling judgment upon him, but said, "The Lord rebuke you."* [10] *But these men revile whatever they do not understand, and by those things that they know by instinct as irrational animals do, they are destroyed.* [11] *Woe to them! For they walk in the way of Cain, and abandon themselves for the sake of gain to Balaam's error, and perish in Korah's rebellion.* [12] <u>*These are blemishes on your love feasts*</u>, *as they boldly carouse together, looking after themselves; waterless clouds, carried along by winds; fruitless trees in late autumn, twice dead, uprooted;* [13] *wild waves of the sea, casting up the foam of their own shame; wandering stars for whom the nether gloom of darkness has been reserved for ever.*

It is interesting that whenever the *agápē* is spoken of, as at 2 Pet 2:13 and possibly 1 Cor 11:17ff it is in a negative context of abuse! I will comment on 1 Cor 11:17 under the next section on Formal Worship Assemblies.

The early church fathers spoke often regarding the holding of such *agápē* meals which became an almost official gathering that needed to be controlled carefully in a Christian spirit. Ignatius, ca 100 AD, in his letter to the *Smyrnaeans 8* wrote "It is not lawful to baptize or to have a love feast *apart from the bishop.*" Clement of Alexandria, ca 200 AD, also wrote of those who by their language abuse the "*sacred agápē*" indicating the high place such meals were held by the early church. Tertullian, *Apology* 39, 16-18, ca 200 AD, likewise spoke highly of the meal, "Our feast shows its motive by its name. It is called by the Greek word for love."

Everett Ferguson[8] observes that from what we can learn from the church fathers regarding the *agápē* love feast it certainly was early on held as a regular church activity that was under the supervision of a bishop. It was clearly associated in some fashion with the Lord's Supper indicating that the *agápē* love feast would on occasion be an appropriate time for celebrating the Lord's Supper, but it was also clearly understood that the two were separate functions in that when the abuses became excessive the love feast was discontinued while the Lord's Supper continued. 1 Cor 11:17-22 certainly indicates an early separation of the two meals:

> *[17] But in the following instructions I do not commend you, because when you come together it is not for the better but for the worse. [18] For, in the first place, when you assemble as a church, I hear that there are divisions among you; and I partly believe it, [19] for there must be factions among you in order that those who are genuine among you may be recognized. [20] <u>When you meet together, it is not the Lord's Supper that you eat. [21] For in eating, each one goes ahead with his own meal, and one is hungry and another is drunk. [22] What! Do you not have houses to eat and drink in? Or do you despise the church of God and humiliate those who have nothing? What shall I say to you? Shall I commend you in this? No, I will not</u>.*

Following his condemnation of the abuse of what was seemingly a love feast in the text above, in the following verses at 1 Cor 11:23-26 Paul enriched the Corinthians' understanding of what the Lord's Supper was all about; it related to something formal he had *received* and was now *delivering* to the Corinthians. The language *received* and *delivered* are somewhat technical[9] and imply that although the instruction for the Lord's Supper celebration had originated with Jesus at the Passover Last Supper with his disciples, further understanding and interpretation had been handed down to Paul in some fashion by apostolic church

---

[8] Ferguson, *Early Christians Speak*, pp. 129ff.
[9] For a biblical critical study of this expression and the pericope under discussion I refer you to Fee, *The First Epistle to the Corinthians*, pp. 531ff, Garland, *1 Corinthians*, 533ff, and other critical commentaries on 1 Corinthians.

practice in regard to the real meaning of the Lord's Supper.[10]
The Lord's Supper was intended to be more than a communal love feast. It was a memorial to Jesus' death and his institution of a new covenant. Paul wrote;

> *[23] For I received from the Lord what I also delivered to you, that the Lord Jesus on the night when he was betrayed took bread, [24] and when he had given thanks, he broke it, and said, "This is my body which is for you. Do this in remembrance of me." [25] In the same way also the cup, after supper, saying, "This cup is the new covenant in my blood. Do this, as often as you drink it, in remembrance of me." [26] For as often as you eat this bread and drink the cup, you proclaim the Lord's death until he comes.*

In the following verses (11:23-14) Paul again addressed the practice of confusing the *agápē* with the Lord's Supper and treating the Lord's Supper as a fellowship meal.

> *[27] Whoever, therefore, eats the bread or drinks the cup of the Lord in an unworthy manner will be guilty of profaning the body and blood of the Lord. [28] Let a man examine himself, and so eat of the bread and drink of the cup. [29] For anyone who eats and drinks without discerning the body eats and drinks judgment upon himself.*
> *[30] That is why many of you are weak and ill, and some have died. [31] But if we judged ourselves truly, we should not be judged. [32] But when we are judged by the Lord, we are chastened so that we may not be condemned along with the world.*

---

[10] Paul does not mention whether this tradition had been revealed to him by revelation of the Holy Spirit but this possibility should not be overlooked. It is quite possible that the tradition had been handed to Paul by one of the Apostles who had been present at the last Supper. Paul does argue that he had not received the gospel he preached from any human being but that he received his gospel message by a revelation of Jesus Christ (Gal 1:11ff). What this means is also debated but Paul is clear that his gospel message did not come from men. However, regarding the Lord's Supper message Paul is not discussing the gospel message but simply the celebration of the Lord's Supper and its meaning and significance.

> *³³ So then, my brethren, when you come together to eat, wait for one another— ³⁴ if anyone is hungry, let him eat at home—lest you come together to be condemned. About the other things I will give directions when I come.*

My main point in this discussion is to demonstrate that although the early Jewish Christians in the primitive Jerusalem church regularly enjoyed informal communal fellowship meals (Acts 2:44-47) these in time, by the second century, became a formal meal controlled by the church through the bishops, cf. Tertullian. The *agápē* most likely was not originally intended to be a formal worship service but became one with which the Lord's Supper was early associated. Possibly the Lord's Supper was celebrated within or as part of the love *agápē* feast. When the spirit of the Lord's Supper and the *agápē* were abused they were separated from the Lord's Supper as in 1 Cor 11:17-34. It appears that in time in other settings even the *agápē* when it was abused was discontinued, whereas the Lord's Supper was not.[11]

Formal Worship Assemblies

As I have indicated above, certain aspects of what I will call formal worship can be identified in the New Testament such as the Lord's Supper, prayer, benevolent giving, and Scripture reading and a sermon, the formal worship service is not clearly formalized in one text or location in the New Testament. Several fine scholars like Oscar Cullmann, Gerhard Delling, C. F. D. Moule, Ralph P. Martin, Franklin Segler and Randall Bradley observe that the sources we have at our disposal, chiefly the New Testament, "do not yield a *perfectly clear* picture of the outward development of the gathering for worship; they do disclose, however, a fairly clear tendency in worship."[12] However, they all conclude that we can identify early in the life of the Christian church a pattern developing around the worship of God and Jesus Christ, centered on the Lord's Supper. Consequently, the best we can do is draw on certain texts such as Acts 20:7; 1 Cor 11:17ff,

---

[11] Cf. an excellent discussion of the *agápē* in Ferguson, *Early Christians Speak*, pp. 129ff.
[12] Cf. Cullmann, *Early Christian Worship*; Moule, *Worship*; Delling, *Worship*; Martin, *Worship*; Segler and Bradley, *Christian Worship*.

1 Tim 2:8, 1 Cor 16:1, etc. to formulate some idea of how the early church in certain locations conducted its worship assemblies.

It is evident that there were clearly some models of worship assemblies that the early church drew on. The earliest Jewish Christians had been raised in a rich Jewish mindset of worship associated with the Temple cult. In regions distant from Jerusalem and the Temple Synagogues had early become the center for Jewish worship and community living. Worshipping in a formal mindset was not something new to the early Jewish Christians! They understood very clearly how to worship God! Furthermore, as the church moved out of the environs of Jerusalem into house churches throughout the world the Christians, both Jew and Gentile, were already familiar with the practice of gathering in Synagogues which like the Temple had a formal structure to them. The Synagogue cult in the absence of the Temple trappings was vastly different from the Temple cult and focused more on the reading and exposition of the *Torah*, prayer, and some vocal recitation and chanting of the Psalms.

The early form of congregational worship assemblies which began in the Temple surroundings, then became house churches, soon developed a formal approach which the Apostle Paul readily discussed when he saw worship degenerating into social functions in which self-aggrandizement surfaced and the focus of worship was on the individual rather than on or toward God (1 Cor 11:17ff; 1 Cor 14:1ff).

The Lord's Supper or Eucharistic[13] Assembly

From the minimal evidence we have in Scripture regarding the order that the early church may have placed on the different acts of worship in their formal worship assemblies, and from references to worship assemblies in the second and third centuries, it

---

[13] We learn from early 2nd century Christian literature, cf. Ferguson's carefully researched writings, *Early Christians Speak*, vols 1 and 2 that early on one of the favored terms used to describe the Lord's Supper was Eucharist. This is derived from the Greek εὐχαριστέω, *eucharistéō* which means to give *thanks*. The word appears in Lk 22:17 and 1 Cor 11:24 associated with Jesus giving thanks at the Passover meal.

is apparent that the Lord's Supper lay at the heart of the Christian assembly.[14]

That the manner in which the Lord's Supper was celebrated certainly weighed heavily on the mind of the Apostle Paul is reflected in 1 Cor 11-14. Immediately following a discussion of pagan worship assemblies or eating meats offered to idols, Paul opened his discussion of the Christian assembly by addressing the behavior of the women, commending them for upholding the teachings he had brought them (1 Cor 11:1-16), *"Be imitators of me, as I am of Christ. ² I commend you because you remember me in everything and maintain the traditions[15] even as I have delivered them to you."* Following his positive commendation regarding the behavior of the women he began serious critical comments regarding the Corinthian worship celebration, primarily relating to the Lord's Supper (1 Cor 11:17-22), and then on the worship assembly in general (1 Cor 14:1ff).

I like Thiselton's translation of 1 Cor 11:17, "Now in giving these directives I cannot continue my commendation because the meetings you hold *as a church* do more harm than good." [16] Thiselton's comment on the text emphasizes his concern:

> *The style of this section, together with Paul's redescription of what he understands to be taking place at the Lord's Supper, indicates that he is not responding to a question first raised by the addressees, but initiates the raising of an urgent matter for censure and re-education.* [17]

The RSV opens 1 Cor 11:17 with the negative particle "δὲ, *dé, but*" indicating negative comments to follow. Zodhiates ob-

---

[14] Cf. Ferguson, *Early Christians Speak, passim*; Kelly, *Early Christian Doctrines, passim*; Delling, *Worship*, pp. 128ff, *passim*; Cullmann, *Early Christian Worship*, pp. 1-36, *passim*; Jeremias, *The Eucharistic Words of Jesus, passim*; Willimon, *Word, Water, Wine, and Bread, passim*; Hicks, *Come to the Table: Revisioning the Lord's Supper, passim*.
[15] Referring again to the apostolic traditions that he received and in turn handed down to the churches.
[16] Thiselton, *Corinthians*, p. 848.
[17] Thiselton, *Corinthians,* p. 849.

serves regarding the negative particle δέ, *dé* that it is *strictly adversative*.[18] Since I have already discussed above Paul's discussion of the abuse of the Lord's Supper under the Love feast and *agápē* I will merely use this text at this point to demonstrate that the Lord's Supper and its appropriate celebration was integral to the liturgy of worship in the assembly of the early church, at least at Corinth, and as some have observed, at least within the circle of Pauline churches.

The seriousness of the Corinthian abuse of the Lord's Supper relates directly to the central role this worship celebration played in the worship assembly as a whole. Note Paul's observation at 1 Cor 11:18-22 which places the Lord's Supper central in the worship assembly:

> *For, in the first place, <u>when you assemble as a church</u>, I hear that there are divisions among you; and I partly believe it, [19] for there must be factions among you in order that those who are genuine among you may be recognized. [20] <u>When you meet together, it is not the Lord's supper that you eat</u>. [21] For in eating, each one goes ahead with his own meal, and one is hungry and another is drunk. [22] What! Do you not have houses to eat and drink in? Or do you despise the church of God and humiliate those who have nothing? What shall I say to you? Shall I commend you in this? No, I will not.*

Reinforcing the seriousness of the Lord's Supper as an act of worship to be celebrated in *the church assembly on the Lord's Day* Paul comments negatively on the issues of combining the *agápē* with the celebration of the Lord's Supper. The eating of meals can take place in homes, whereas the Lord's Supper should not be reduced simply to a meal, even an *agápē* meal, especially when it abuses the worship dynamic of the Lord's Supper. Note Paul's comments on this at 1 Cor 11:24-33:

> *Whoever, therefore, eats the bread or drinks the cup of the Lord <u>in an unworthy manner will be guilty of profaning the body and blood of the Lord</u>. [28] Let a man examine himself, and so eat of the bread and drink of the cup.*

---

[18] Zodhiates, δέ.

> *²⁹ For anyone who eats and drinks without discerning the body eats and drinks judgment upon himself. ³⁰ That is why many of you are weak and ill, and some have died. ³¹ But if we judged ourselves truly, we should not be judged. ³² But when we are judged by the Lord, we are chastened so that we may not be condemned along with the world.*
>
> *³³ So then, my brethren, when you come together to eat, wait for one another— ³⁴ if anyone is hungry, <u>let him eat at home</u>—lest you come together to be condemned. About the other things I will give directions when I come.*

Verses 18 and 33 of 1 Cor 11 serve as an *inclusio* to the discussion which implies that the *coming together to eat* in vs 33 is referring back to the issue of eating meals together as in the *agápē*. The wealthy should not abuse the poor in these meals and allow the Lord's Supper to degenerate to the level of an ordinary meal in which it seems that the needs of the poor were being neglected. The problem was conflating the *agápē* meal and the Lord's Supper into one event and experience.

The serious nature of the discussion of partaking of the Lord's Supper in the Corinthian assemblies, and the manner in which they partook of the meal, illustrates *the importance of celebrating the Lord's Supper in the assembly in an appropriate manner*. *First*, the Lord's Supper is celebrated in the church assembly, and *second*, it must be eaten in a manner appropriate to honoring the Lord's sacrifice.

A second text that reflects on the celebration of the Lord's Supper in a worship assembly is Acts 20:7. At Acts 20:6 Luke records, *"we sailed away from Philippi after the days of Unleavened Bread, and in five days we came to them at Troas, where we stayed for seven days."* Two interesting facts surface from this statement. The first is the mention of the days of Unleavened Bread, demonstrating that even to the early Jewish Christians these Jewish feasts were important to the psyche and spirit of the Jewish Christians, even though Luke was not Jewish and was not writing for a Jewish readership! The mention of the days of Unleavened Bread also says something about the Jewish calendar

Paul and his co-workers respected. Later at Acts 20:16 Luke indicates that Paul had planned to be in Jerusalem before Pentecost, another significant Jewish festival. Then Luke identified the significance of the gathering in Troas, *it was the first day of the week.* Later ca AD 96 in Rev 1:10 this is referred to as the Lord's Day, which honored the resurrection of Jesus. The Christians at Troas had gathered together or assembled as a church.

Acts 20:7ff reads:

> *On the first day of the week, when we were gathered together to break bread, Paul talked with them, intending to depart on the morrow; and he prolonged his speech until midnight. [8]There were many lights in the upper chamber where we were gathered. [9]And a young man named Eutychus was sitting in the window. He sank into a deep sleep as Paul talked still longer; and being overcome by sleep, he fell down from the third story and was taken up dead. [10] But Paul went down and bent over him, and embracing him said, "Do not be alarmed, for his life is in him." [11]And when Paul had gone up and had broken bread and eaten, he conversed with them a long while, until daybreak, and so departed. [12]And they took the lad away alive, and were not a little comforted.*

Most scholars are agreed that this breaking of bread is a reference to the Lord's Supper or the Eucharist. Fitzmyer is representative of this;

> *"when we gathered to break bread." This genitive absolute notes an early Christian liturgical gathering on a Sunday to celebrate the Eucharist or Lord's Supper. The purpose of the gathering is expressed by the infinitive klasai arton" (italicized text "to break bread" mine, IAF).*[19]

The point I am making, and which Fitzmyer emphasizes, is that this gathering seems to have been *a regular or habitual gathering on the first day of the week,* Sunday, in this case in the evening, to formally worship by participating in the Lord's Sup-

---

[19] Fitzmyer, *The Acts of the Apostles*, p. 669.

per. The perfect passive genitive participle συνηγμένων, *sunēgmenōn* implies *a habitual practice of gathering on the first day of the week*, a practice that had already begun in the past and was continuing in the present, thus a practice already habitual in the life of the early church, at least at Troas, and which was continuing in Paul's experience.[20]

On this occasion, Paul also delivered a sermon indicating that this may also have been a regular practice.

These two texts, 1 Cor 11:17-34 and Acts 2:7 indicate that it was early in the Christian life of the church and regular practice for Christians to gather in a worship assembly on the first day of the week, the Lord's Day, to celebrate the Lord's Supper. This emphasized their dedicated faith and the profound importance of celebrating the Lord's death and resurrection in a weekly cycle, illustrating its importance to Christian doctrine and faith, and the life of the early church. Along with baptism, the Lord's Supper forms two sacraments[21] or practices that proclaim the Christian's committed covenant relationship with Jesus.

Worship and Edification in the Assembly

There is some tension in this subheading in that ca 1960 a missionary/minister published a series of articles in a religious journal arguing that the gathering reflected in 1 Cor 12-14 was not for worship but for edification. His point was that a specific

---

[20] I have previously discussed this point regarding the perfect passive participle but since it is so important to the discussion I include the scholarly reference to this again. The tense of the verbal participle συνηγμένων, *sunēgmenōn*, a perfect passive participle, can imply that this action reflects a regular habitual practice of gathering. Dana and Mantey, *A Manual Grammar of the Greek New Testament*, pp. 202f; Blass, Debrunner, Funk, *A Grammar of the New Testament*, pp. 175f. Bruce along with others observes, "The reference to the meeting for the breaking of the bread on "the first day of the week" is the earliest text we have from which it may be inferred with reasonable certainty *that Christians regularly came together for worship on that day.*" Bruce, *The Book of Acts*, Kindle Edition, 1988, p. 384.

[21] As mentioned previously the term *sacrament* based on the Medieval Latin *sacramentum* implies some activity that ties the practitioner to the center of their faith. Sacrament is not a term regularly used in Churches of Christ but it does indicate the significance of baptism and the Lord's Supper. They identify the Christian believer with the source of their faith, Jesus Christ.

worship service was not on Paul's mind in these texts. The heavy emphasis on edification, instruction, and communicating in his mind seemed to set the environment on horizontal instruction and edification rather than on the vertical nature of worship. While his viewpoint was well made, however, he missed the point that Paul was making in these texts. Certainly, Paul argues at 1 Cor 14:26 that in these gatherings *all things should be done for edification*! The point our missionary friend missed was that worshipping God in spirit and truth is supposed to be edifying!

In general, in this first Corinthian letter Paul was addressing several abuses of fellowship that had crept into the church at Corinth. Word had come to him by letter and by visits from some of the members in Corinth regarding several problems. Primarily the Corinthian congregation was divided over several issues—the first related to who baptized whom (1 Cor 1:10-17).

Another issue was an immoral relationship one of the members had with his father's wife that had brought criticism from not only those within the church but also from some of the citizens of Corinth. A major concern was that the church leaders were ignoring the problem. Paul addressed this issue in 1 Cor 5:1-13.

One other major problem within the church was a spirit of superiority among many of the members who for a variety of reasons felt they were more important to the church than others. The wealthy were despising the poor and in this the spirit of the *agápē* love feast and Lord's Supper was being defiled (1 Cor 11:17-33).

However, major issues surfaced in particular in their public worship assemblies in which some women were speaking out in a manner that brought abuse on the worshipful spirit of their fellowship. Some of the members were misusing the gifts of the Holy Spirit such as speaking in tongues in a manner that brought attention to themselves. Others were praying and singing in a disorderly manner and thus debasing the spirit of worship especially at the Lord's Supper.

The focus of the discussion related clearly to the time when the Corinthian church *came together or assembled as a church* to worship (1 Cor 11:17, 18). Paul's charge was that the Corinthian

Christians should not abuse their giftedness in the worship assembly especially when visitors may be present. His charge was that they should conduct their worship in an orderly manner as in other churches of Christ (1 Cor 14:33), and if they were to exercise their giftedness it was to bring glory to God and Christ in order to edify one another, and not to aggrandize themselves and their giftedness.

Initially, in a disorganized worship assembly, appropriate worship of God could not take place, and the Lord's Supper was being abused. *Second*, when there was confusion in the assembly no one would be helped by the confusion and no one would be edified, encouraged, and drawn closer to God.

We learn four valuable lessons here. *First*, when worship is not conducted in a respectful manner and is conducted in a divisive manner that draws attention to themselves and away from God and Christ as the objects of the worship, neither the members nor their visitors would be edified. *Second*, visitors would be turned away by the disrespectful behavior of either the men or the women, and such disruptive behavior should be discontinued. *Third*, appropriate worship that focuses on God and Christ should be an edifying factor that draws people to God and his glory, grace, and love for all. *Fourth*, when the behavior of the congregation draws attention to the giftedness or preferences of the congregation the dynamic of the worship activity is in the wrong direction.

Edification can and does take place in a climate of worshipping God and Christ in an appropriate manner. In this the primary focal point of the worship is not simply edification but is God and Christ. Appropriate worship can and should be edifying as the participants encourage one another and teach one another by singing psalms, hymns, and spiritual songs from their hearts *to the Lord* (Eph 5:19). Praising God and Jesus lifts all out of their struggles. When God and Christ are praised in song for their majesty, sovereignty, and greatness, souls are lifted up toward God and Christ, and edified. However, when the worship is disorderly and focused on human giftedness, no one is edified and God and Christ are not honored and praised.

When worship is called by God as the subject of worship, and focused on God as the object or the direction of worship, Christians and their visitors are lifted up and encouraged, hopefully even evangelized, that is, taught the meaning of the Gospel and God's and Jesus' love for all!

Organizational Assemblies

What I imply by the term organizational assemblies is gatherings of Christians in order to organize their ministries and edification for the glory of God. As we work our way through Luke's book of Acts recounting the life of the early church we find the disciples gathering on several occasions for organizational purposes apart for the formal first day of the week worship assembly of the church to celebrate the Lord's Supper and worship God and Christ. They clearly understood the difference between the focus and purpose of the meetings.

As I have previously indicated in my discussion of Acts 1:1ff, Acts 1:15-26, Acts 2:1ff there are several organizational meetings recorded in Acts especially in the early years of the church.

The Jerusalem Meeting. I find the great Jerusalem meeting of Acts 15:1-35 particularly helpful. Early on in Paul's ministry of taking the gospel to the Gentiles, inter religious and ethnic problems had arisen between both the Jews and Jewish Christians regarding the need for all Christians, both Jews and Gentiles, to keep the Torah requirements of circumcision, as well as issues regarding ethnic and food restrictions as boundary markers regarding who was in a right relationship with God. Circumcision lay at the root of the issue. Paul had in Galatians argued firmly that to attach circumcision to the gospel of Christ resulted in a false gospel, which Paul firmly rejected. Note especially Gal 1:6-9, Gal 5:13, and acts 14:23.

> *Gal 1:6-9: I am astonished that you are so quickly deserting him who called you in the grace of Christ and turning to a different gospel— [7] not that there is another gospel, but there are some who trouble you and want to pervert the gospel of Christ. [8] But even if we, or an angel from heaven, should preach to you a gospel contrary to that which we preached to you, let him be accursed. [9] As*

we have said before, so now I say again, If any one is preaching to you a gospel contrary to that which you received, let him be accursed.

Gal 6:11-15: See with what large letters I am writing to you with my own hand. ¹² It is those who want to make a good showing in the flesh that would compel you to be circumcised, and only in order that they may not be persecuted for the cross of Christ. ¹³ For even those who receive circumcision do not themselves keep the law, but they desire to have you circumcised that they may glory in your flesh. ¹⁴ But far be it from me to glory except in the cross of our Lord Jesus Christ, by which the world has been crucified to me, and I to the world. ¹⁵ For neither circumcision counts for anything, nor uncircumcision, but a new creation.

Luke records an interesting but significant series of events at Acts 14:24-15:2 regarding Paul's missionary travels and ministry. Deep challenges were being raised by some Jews coming from Jerusalem regarding Paul's preaching to the Gentiles that circumcision was not a boundary marker for a relationship with God, and for salvation:

¹⁴:²⁴Then they passed through Pisidia, and came to Pamphylia. ²⁵ And when they had spoken the word in Perga, they went down to Attalia; ²⁶ and from there they sailed to Antioch, where they had been commended to the grace of God for the work which they had fulfilled. ²⁷ And when they arrived, they gathered the church together and declared all that God had done with them, and how he had opened a door of faith to the Gentiles. ²⁸ And they remained no little time with the disciples. ¹⁵:¹ <u>But some men came down from Judea and were teaching the brethren, "Unless you are circumcised according to the custom of Moses, you cannot be saved."</u> ² And when Paul and Barnabas had no small dissension and debate with them, Paul and Barnabas and some of the others were appointed to go up to Jerusalem to the apostles and the elders about this question.

How one fits Galatians into the chronology of Acts has for centuries been a problem for Lucan/Acts and Pauline scholars. The problem is that neither Luke nor Paul tell us everything that happened in the life of the early church and in Paul's ministry, chronologically or in detail. Whether Paul had written Galatians before the great Jerusalem meeting to discuss binding of circumcision on Gentiles, or after that meeting makes little difference, although I am of the persuasion that Galatians was written early and before the Acts 15 meeting. Whichever timing one chooses makes little difference, for Paul would have faced the issue of circumcision from the very beginning of his mission. Jews wherever he would have met in the synagogues would have challenged him on the Law, circumcision, ethnic, and food restrictions.

Obviously, the occasion for the Acts 15 Jerusalem meeting was that some from the Jerusalem church visited Antioch, the base for Paul's missionary activity (cf. Acts 13:1ff), and raised the issue of Paul's teaching on circumcision. Acts 15:3-5 specifies the reason for Paul's trip to Jerusalem and meeting with the church leaders; the church in Antioch had commissioned Paul, Barnabas, and "*some of the others*" to go to Jerusalem to resolve the issue:

> *³ So, being sent on their way by the church, they passed through both Phoenicia and Samaria, reporting the conversion of the Gentiles, and they gave great joy to all the brethren. ⁴ When they came to Jerusalem, they were welcomed by the church and the apostles and the elders, and they declared all that God had done with them. ⁵ But some believers who belonged to the party of the Pharisees rose up, and said, "It is necessary to circumcise them, and to charge them to keep the Law of Moses."*

According to Luke's account of the meeting the church in Jerusalem, together with whichever of the Apostles were present, met together to discuss the issue of circumcision and how to minister to both Jew and Gentiles. This certainly was a significant and pivotal meeting and discussion! It was a formal meeting called by the leaders of the Jerusalem church, but not a formal assembly of the church to worship and celebrate the Lord's Supper. It was an intensely religious and spiritual meeting.

The result of the meeting is summed up in Luke's account of speeches by James, the brother of the Lord, and the Apostle Peter. After the meeting the Jerusalem leaders asked Paul, Barnabas, and Silas to return to Antioch with a letter to the church in Antioch, indicating their conclusion to the discussion, Acts 15:22-29;

> *Then it seemed good to the apostles and the elders, with the whole church, to choose men from among them and send them to Antioch with Paul and Barnabas. They sent Judas called Barsabbas, and Silas, leading men among the brethren, [23] with the following letter: "The brethren, both the apostles and the elders, to the brethren who are of the Gentiles in Antioch and Syria and Cilicia, greeting. [24] Since we have heard that some persons from us have troubled you with words, unsettling your minds, although we gave them no instructions, [25] it has seemed good to us, having come to one accord, to choose men and send them to you with our beloved Barnabas and Paul, [26] men who have risked their lives for the sake of our Lord Jesus Christ. [27] We have therefore sent Judas and Silas, who themselves will tell you the same things by word of mouth. [28] For it has seemed good to the Holy Spirit and to us to lay upon you no greater burden than these necessary things: [29] that you abstain from what has been sacrificed to idols and from blood and from what is strangled and from unchastity. If you keep yourselves from these, you will do well. Farewell."*

We should not overlook the profound importance of this meeting in Jerusalem. It was not simply about food and ethnic preferences! It was significantly theological and reached deeply into the heart of the gospel of Christ, but it was not a congregational worship assembly.

Summary. My point in this discussion of organizational meetings of the church is that they were intensely religious and spiritual yet not formal worship assemblies on the first day of the week to celebrate the Lord's Supper and worship God and Christ. Several of them, if not all of them, were apparently *ad hoc* meetings to organize and generally discuss the Messianic ministry of the church; and the early church clearly understood the nature and importance of these occasional meetings!

Some of the meetings were for edification, some simply for organizational purposes, some to clarify doctrinal positions, and one in particular, Acts 2:1ff, held significant religious implications for the whole church, that is, involving the falling of the Holy Spirit on the disciples on the Day of Pentecost. But these occasional meetings, although of profound importance to the life of the church, were not formal assemblies of the church for the purpose of worshipping God and Jesus as in the Lord's Supper services.

Daily Worship of God

Although this pericope does not reflect any specific gathering or meeting, it does refer to the general notion of a worshipful attitude in the Christians living their devoted lives in daily worship of God.

Worship of God is not something reserved only for the formal Sunday worship assembly! The Christian's life in general should be devoted to God in daily worshipful living.

I remember well a Bible class being taught by a well-intended young Christian in South Africa who was concerned over Christians spending time, sometimes the whole day playing cricket,[22] or going fishing on Sunday. His argument was that Monday through Friday belonged to your employer, Saturday belonged to you and your family to use as you feel appropriate, but Sunday belonged to the Lord and should be reserved exclusively for Bible study and worship. In South Africa this would have been a reasonable argument in a Dutch Reformed culture which equated Sunday with the Christian version of the Jewish Sabbath! The young man's statement was well-intended but wrong for several reasons. *First*, Sunday is not the Christian equivalent of the Jewish Sabbath to be observed with all of the legal trappings of the Jewish Sabbath. *Second*, the whole week, not just one day,

---

[22] This was obviously in South Africa!

belongs to God. Christians worship God every day of the week with their lives whether at work, at home, at cricket, fishing, or in Bible study and worship on Sunday!

That was the point Paul was making at Rom 12:1-19! In response to God's amazing grace, mercy, love, forgiveness, redemption, and salvation in Christ Christians react every day at all times in a reverent worshipful life devoted to God. Paul emphasized this daily living worshipful response into a worshipful environment in the words he used:

> *I appeal to you therefore, brethren, by the mercies of God, to <u>present your bodies as a living sacrifice, holy and acceptable to God, which is your spiritual worship</u>. ² Do not be conformed to this world but be transformed by the renewal of your mind, that you may prove what is the will of God, what is good and acceptable and perfect.*
>
> *³ For by the grace given to me I bid every one among you not to think of himself more highly than he ought to think, but to think with sober judgment, each according to the measure of faith which God has assigned him ... 9 Let love be genuine; hate what is evil, hold fast to what is good; ¹⁰ love one another with brotherly affection; outdo one another in showing honor. ¹¹ Never flag in zeal, be aglow with the Spirit, serve the Lord. ¹² Rejoice in your hope, be patient in tribulation, be constant in prayer. ¹³ Contribute to the needs of the saints, practice hospitality. ¹⁴ Bless those who persecute you; bless and do not curse them. ¹⁵ Rejoice with those who rejoice, weep with those who weep. ¹⁶ Live in harmony with one another; do not be haughty, but associate with the lowly; never be conceited. ¹⁷ Repay no one evil for evil, but take thought for what is noble in the sight of all. ¹⁸ If possible, so far as it depends upon you, live peaceably with all. ¹⁹ Beloved, never avenge yourselves, but leave it to the wrath of God ...*

The expression which is "*your spiritual service*" (RSV) has been variously translated in our English translations but all with the same thought in mind. Our everyday lives are offered to God as a reasonable or spiritual service of worship. The NIV renders this as *"your spiritual act of worship."* The ESV reads *"your spiritual worship."* The KJV reads *"your reasonable service."* The Greek reads τὴν λογικὴν λατρείαν ὑμῶν, *tēn logikēn latreian humōn*. Literally this reads as *the logical service of yours*. However, the word λογικὴν, *logikēn* has a wider range of meaning than simply logical and can be more appropriately translated *spiritual* since this kind of service comes from one's deeper logical sense, hence, your *spiritual sense*. The word λατρείαν, *latreian* which can simply mean *service* but has a background in the Hebrew Bible and Jewish religious cult of *worship service*. So in this text, rich with liturgical meaning and implication, Paul stresses that Christians should *present*, παρίστημι, *paristēmi*, a sacrificial term,[23] their *bodies,* or lives, as *a living sacrifice* to God in a manner that is *holy and acceptable to God.*

With considerable care and detail Paul then follows up on his exhortation to offer one's daily life in worship to God with some specific ideas of worshipful service. Paul clarifies how this should be done specifically in relation to our attitude toward others since in Romans Paul was expressly concerned with how Jewish and Gentile Christians treated one another (cf. Rom 14, 15).

> *Rom 12:3-13: For by the grace given to me I bid every one among you not to think of himself more highly than he ought to think, but to think with sober judgment, each according to the measure of faith which God has assigned him. ⁴ For as in one body we have many members, and all the members do not have the same function, ⁵ so we, though many, are one body in Christ, and individually members one of another. ⁶ Having gifts that differ according to the grace given to us, let us use them: if prophecy, in proportion to our faith; ⁷ if service, in our serving; he who teaches, in his teaching; ⁸ he who exhorts, in his exhortation; he who contributes, in liberality; he who gives aid, with zeal; he who does acts of mercy, with cheerfulness.*

---

[23] Bo Reike, Kittel's *Theological Dictionary of the New Testament*. "Then there are verses in which the verb is linked to a particular theological mode of thinking … Rom 12:1. In religious connections, too, one may thus detect official and sacrificial modes of thought in the NT use of παριστάνω."

⁹ Let love be genuine; hate what is evil, hold fast to what is good; ¹⁰ love one another with brotherly affection; outdo one another in showing honor. ¹¹ Never flag in zeal, be aglow with the Spirit, serve the Lord. ¹² Rejoice in your hope, be patient in tribulation, be constant in prayer. ¹³ Contribute to the needs of the saints, practice hospitality.

Summary

We have drawn attention in this section to the fact that there are several different church assemblies or gatherings mentioned in the New Testament. Each had a unique purpose; some were for prayer or study, some for fellowship and benevolent service (Acts 2:43-47), some were for organizational purposes like selecting elders or an apostle (Acts 1:15-26), some were for discussing major doctrinal concerns (Acts 15), some were for fellowship meals (1 Cor 11), still others took place when Christians gathered together to worship God and celebrate the Lord's Supper (Acts 20:7; 1 Cor 11:17-34). These various gatherings were not all for the same purpose and different principles shaped them and provided the dynamic for their function.

Chapter 9: Discussion of The Lord's Supper, or the Eucharist[1]

Introduction

In the next few chapters, we will examine the different "components" that together shaped the worship assemblies in the early New Testament churches. We have already observed that the different acts of worship practiced in the early church were not all presented in detail in one place in the New Testament. From the discussion of each of these texts, which we will examine below, we learn that they related to the regular weekly assembly of the church in a meeting for worshipping God and Jesus and praising them for their redemptive work. However, such worship services were described in some detail in the literature of the second and third century churches.[2]

Several interesting factors contributed to the dynamic of these early worship assemblies. Two that grasp our attention from the early years of church life are referred to by some churches as the two Sacraments,[3] *Baptism* and the *Lord's Supper*. From what we learn from scripture and the practice of the early church, baptism was considered to be that point in which a person is united to Christ (Rom 6:1-11) and becomes a member of the

---

[1] Although the term Eucharist is not one commonly used in modern Churches of Christ it was the favored term for the Lord's Supper in the 1st and 2nd centuries of the early church. The term Eucharist derives from the Greek word εὐχαριστέω, *eucharistéō*; from *eucháristos, thankful, grateful, and well–pleasing. To show oneself grateful, to be thankful, and to give thanks*. Zodhiates.

[2] Cf. the excellent work by Everett Ferguson, *Early Christians Speak* as a valuable resource of early Christian writings.

[3] Churches of Christ do not often refer to sacraments preferring to call sacraments *important doctrines or practices*. Some churches refer to sacraments as *ordinances*. The term *sacrament* derives from the Latin *sacrāmentum*, meaning something that was holy, consecrated, and special. In Ancient Rome, the term meant a soldier's oath of allegiance, and also a sacred rite. Tertullian, a third-century Christian writer, suggested that just as the soldier's oath was a sign of the beginning of a new life, so too was initiation into the Christian community through baptism and Eucharist. Sacraments are therefore rites or practices considered by a Christian church to carry special significance and to either initiate the person into membership and to signify continued dedication. Cf. "Sacrament," *Oxford English Dictionary*.

body of Christ. The Lord's Supper signifies a participation in a continuing communion with Christ and the church as his body.

It is because of the dynamic relationship between baptism[4] and the Lord's Supper involving membership initiation and regular participation in the body of Christ, that I like to consider them as two bookends (*inclusios*) to fellowship with God and Christ.

In an interesting chapter on "Communion as Divine Intent" John Mark Hicks observes:

> *From beginning to end, from creation to eschaton, God desires a people for himself with whom he can share a loving fellowship ... In redemption God has called us into the "fellowship of his Son (1 Cor 1:9) to enjoy the "communion (koinōnía) of the Holy Spirit" (2 Cor 13:13) as we also experience the fellowship of the Father (1 John 1:3) ... Christians have been baptized into the fellowship of the Father, Son, and Holy Spirit (Matt 28:19) ... God intends to commune with a people he calls his own.*
>
> *At the center of that intent is the experience of communion at table. The altar, with its blood ritual, is God's act of atonement for the sake of reconciliation. God forgives through the cross. But the goal of atonement is koinōnía (fellowship). The goal of the cross is the table. The cross restores the communion that God created in the beginning; the altar enables the table. Just as God always intended communion, so he always intended the table. The table is the experience of communion.*[5]

Adopting Hick's terminology, baptism brings us into contact with the altar; the Lord's Supper brings us into communion with God and Christ. These two doctrines or sacraments define the sense of belonging to and continuing in fellowship with God and Christ.

---

[4] Although I will not in this study be reflecting deeply on the doctrine of baptism I refer the reader to three excellent studies on baptism, Beasley-Murray, *Baptism in the New Testament*; Ferguson, *Baptism in the Early Church*; Hicks & Greg Taylor, *Down to the River to Pray*.

[5] Hicks, *Come to the Table*, p. 23.

Gerhard Delling when discussing Ceremonial Acts in Christianity draws on what he considers to be the two main ceremonial acts that bind Christians to their faith, hence, Sacraments. He observes:

> *Baptism and the Lord's Supper can only be considered here in respect of the main features which are of importance for the understanding of primitive Christian worship ... The aim was to bring about a union with the divine powers and to mediate an imperishable life.*
>
> *According to the word used Christians also receive both of these things through Baptism and the Lord's Supper. Christianity also has holy ritual acts, a rite of initiation and frequently repeated celebration.*[6]

This chapter is not one devoted to studying the doctrine of Christian baptism but understanding the role of Christian baptism is essential to understanding the Lord's Supper and the Eucharist.

The Lord's Supper in Christian Churches

By Christian churches I mean churches across the broad field of Christian faith and practice. Primarily I will reference briefly the Roman Catholic Church, the Church of England (Episcopal Church), the Reformed Churches, the Lutheran Churches, the Baptist Churches, the Methodist Church, the Evangelical Bible/Fellowship Churches, and Churches within the Stone-Campbell Fellowship[7] (Churches of Christ, Christian Churches).[8] My purpose here is not in any sense critical but to demonstrate the breadth of the significance of the Lord's Supper to the Christian faith.

Some years ago, I was researching materials for a book on the Lord's Supper. One of my neighbors and her husband attended the Lutheran church in our small city. I asked her whether they used wine or red grape juice in their communion service.

---

[6] Delling, *Worship*, pp. 128f.

[7] The churches with which I am associated, Churches of Christ, fall within the Stone-Campbell Fellowship.

[8] I confess that this may be a truncated listing of Christian churches but for the purpose of our discussion at this point the listing is merely illustrative.

She replied that they used both since she and others were alcoholics and could not drink wine. I was impressed and enriched in my appreciation of the concern of their Lutheran church for their members! I picked up early in our discussion that she was a Christian Jew. I asked her what the key aspect of her conversion had been. She replied, "The communion service"! I asked what it was about the communion service that had got her attention. It turned out to be the seriousness of the Lutheran liturgy involving the communion.

On another occasion I had a discussion with an advanced scholar in New Testament with a PhD from an Ivy League university. He had converted from a church within the Stone-Campbell fellowship and became an ordained minister in the Lutheran church. He explained that it was the beautiful and theologically meaningful liturgy of the Lutheran ceremony of the Eucharist that had drawn his attention to worship. Being a member of a church within the Stone-Campbell Movement I had some difficulty appreciating some of the fundamental doctrinal issues this raised but could understand his desire for a more serious devotional dimension to the Lord's Supper.

I mention the above two instances to illustrate in a practical way the impact that a worshipful and theologically relevant understanding the Lord's Supper has had among Christian churches through the ages. To some degree, in some cases more than others, the Lord's Supper has been a defining factor in the practice of the Christian faith and worship and continues to be so today. For those interested in pursuing this line of thought regarding the impact of the Lord's Supper on churches I recommend the works listed as footnote to this point.[9]

---

[9] Cf. Marshall, *Last Supper and Lord's Supper*, pp. 57ff; Moule, *Worship*, p. 28; Jeremias, *Eucharistic Words Of Jesus, passim*; Higgins, *Lord's Supper in the New Testament*; Cullmann and Leenhardt, *Essays on the Lord's Supper*; Keener, *Matthew*, pp. 622ff; Hagner, *Matthew 14-28*, pp 771ff; Ciampa, *Corinthians*, 1 Cor 11:17ff; Blomberg, *1 Corinthians*, 1 Cor 11:23ff; Thiselton, *1 Corinthians*, 1 Cor 11:17ff.

As I was writing this piece I received an e-mail from a friend and fellow Christian which referenced an article by a lady member of one of the Christian churches mentioned above. She writes:

> Worship is one of the most powerful spiritual weapons God has given His people.
>
> True worship, as Jesus said, is in "spirit and in truth" and God is actively seeking people who are worshipping Him this way (John 4:23-24). You might assume that people who praise and worship the Lord are doing so without ulterior motives, but not always true.
>
> In fact, because of the tremendous spiritual power built into worship, it is often misused and abused by those who either miss the point entirely, lack understanding of Scripture, or are operating under the same influences that caused Satan to be thrown out of heaven like a flash of lightening (Luke 10:18).
>
> As Christians, it's hard to wrap our minds around the idea that not everyone who worships God is actually *worshipping* Him.[10]

Purdy continues by listing five wrong reasons why people worship. All are interesting and helpful, but one stood out for me, The Trap of Tradition. By this I understand worshipping because this is what we do by tradition or by habit. Carry that over to our discussion of the Lord's Supper. In Churches of Christ, where I find my home, celebrating the Lord's Supper regularly on Sunday is a mark of a faithful church. If our reason for worshipping goes only to that level, I agree with Alicia Purdy, and with those I have referenced above, we are missing it!

On another point, somewhat in opposition to Alicia Purdy's concern, Craig Blomberg observes regarding the tendency for some within the evangelical movement to shift their church allegiance:

> *Debates still rage as to whether the Lord's Supper should be called an ordinance or a sacrament. The latter historically has suggested the unbiblical notion of a*

---

[10] Alicia Purdy, www.*Crosswalk*.com, 15 July 2019.

> *quasi-mechanical "means of grace." The former seems to limit the ritual to an act of obedience to Christ. Our culture is one of the few in the history of the world that has lost respect for the immense value of tradition, ritual, symbolism, and religious drama. Not surprisingly, evangelical liturgical churches thus prove very appealing to many who are more and more frustrated with this loss. Some evangelicals, unable to find such churches within their own traditions have increasingly turned to Anglicanism, Catholicism, and even Greek Orthodoxy to recover those emphases. What we need are balances between liturgy and spontaneity in the Eucharist and in worship more generally.*[11]

Apparently, we find ourselves struggling to arrive at the right balance in the twin horns of the dilemma: free flowing experiences and the stiffness of tradition!

Regarding the diverse views and opinions regarding the importance of the Lord's Supper in Christian theology Craig Blomberg further commented;

> *THE LORD'S SUPPER, designed precisely to foster Christian unity, not only divided the Corinthians but has divided believers ever since. Early and medieval Roman Catholicism developed elaborate doctrines of transubstantiation (the bread and wine literally, though invisibly, turn into Christ's body and blood) and incomplete sacrifice (the Eucharist or mass completes the atoning work that Christ left incomplete), which went far beyond and even contradicted the explicit teaching of Scripture. Whereas the Protestant Reformers sharply broke with many Catholic practices, Lutheran and Anglican traditions at least remained quite similar with respect to Communion. Luther's doctrine of consubstantiation saw Christ's body and blood "really present in, with and under the wine." Zwingli and the so-called radical Reformers swung the pendulum to the opposite extreme, seeing*

---

[11] Blomberg, *1 Corinthians*, p. 205.

> *nothing but the memorializing aspect of the Lord's Supper. Calvinism and Methodism may have captured the best balance by perceiving a special spiritual presence evoked by the powerful symbolism of the elements, but even they often carried the debate far beyond terrain that the Scriptures clearly cover.*[12]

Later, commenting on a significant study of the Lord's Supper and the ecumenical movement, *Baptism, Eucharist and Ministry, Faith and Order Paper #111*,[13] Blomberg continued his discussion of the different approaches to the Lord's Supper by observing:

> *ONE OF THE ironies of the modern ecumenical movement is that many denominations or branches of the church have been willing to abandon fundamental doctrines of the faith (the deity of Christ, belief in the biblical miracles, the historical trustworthiness of Scripture, and so on) and hence achieve a measure of unity around liberal theological perspectives, while balking at agreement on issues that stem from purely human traditions that divide them. One of these divisive issues is the significance of the Lord's Supper and how it is to be celebrated. The most significant ecumenical document on the topic in recent years notes that areas of agreement have yet to be reached on the matters of the Eucharist as a sacrifice, the real presence of Christ in the elements, the epiklesis (calling upon the Lord to come and be present), the relation between communion and baptism, and whether or not the elements are changeable. Yet not one of these issues is demonstrably addressed in Scripture!*[14]

We should note that Blomberg is not criticizing the practice of the Lord's Supper in churches. Far from it! His concern is that churches have introduced too many human theories into the theology of *the Lord's Supper as discussed in Scripture*, thus diminishing its importance.

---

[12] Blomberg, *1 Corinthians*, p. 200.
[13] Geneva: World Council of Churches, 1982, pp. 10–17.
[14] Blomberg, *1 Corinthians*, pp. 204-205.

Christians Celebrate the Lord's Supper or Eucharist in the Worship Assembly

It is apparent from our study of the role of the Eucharist in the early centuries of Christian life that the Eucharist was the central point and driving dynamic of the worship assembly. Alongside the Eucharist celebration was the reading of the Apostles' words, or the Gospels, and prayer. Singing was a feature but certainly not a major one.

Although the term Eucharist is not common among Churches of Christ today, I like to think of the Lord's Supper as the Eucharist since it focuses attention on *thanksgiving* to God for his redemption in Christ and continuing fellowship with his people. The term Eucharist also addresses one of my regrets in my fellowship among Churches of Christ—our tendency to "diminish" the Lord's Supper into a 10 minute activity which in my opinion sets the Lord's Supper merely as the practice of a required doctrine to be done in order to be Scriptural, rather than a worshipful act to be celebrated as the central dynamic of our worship. You can usually determine the importance churches give to certain ministries by the time spent in worship celebrating a specific ministry, or the amount of money designated in the budget for specific ministries!

To determine whether this is the case, note how much time we spend in our worship assemblies singing, listening to a sermon, and making welcome and other announcements of all sorts! Most of these are important acts in the life of a congregation, but they are acts that have pushed the Eucharist into a corner. A necessary doctrinal feature that can be checked off on the list of being doctrinally sound, but not the principal act or central focus of worship! I am a "disciple" of C. S. Lewis who somewhere commented on this, I don't recall where and if it was more significant I would hunt it down![15] Lewis lamented and wished in his church that they would spend less time singing popular songs that appealed to the singer, and more time on the Eucharist! Spoken like a true rationalist! Don't get me wrong, I, like Lewis, enjoy

---

[15] I did track this down to Lewis' comments "On Church Music" in Lewis, *Essay Collection and Other Short Pieces*, pp. 40, *passim*.

singing hymns of praise to God and Christ but when we repeatedly sing songs which I refer to as 7/11 songs, that is 7 words sung 11 times, I could do with a little less singing and more meditation and prayer at the Lord's Table! Depending on how important the Lord's Supper is to the worship dynamic in your congregation you possibly will either agree with me or disagree! But I think I have made my point!

At its very heart the Eucharist in the very use of the term Eucharist draws attention to *giving thanks* to and praising God for our continuing communion with God and Christ and for his continued grace in our lives. Thanksgiving should lie at the very heart of the worship assembly in which the church gives thanks to God (*eucharistéō, to give thanks*) in worship and praise.

But back to the main point of this section of our study of the Lord's Supper! Christians all over the world in most main line churches in one manner or another to greater or lesser degree celebrate the Lord's Supper, the Eucharist, Communion, or Mass on the Lord's Day in worship. Central to this practice are the two Scriptures we alluded to in a previous section of this study, Acts 20:7 and 1 Cor 11:17-34. That is not to overlook the moving discussion of Jesus with his disciples at the Passover, which is often called the Last Supper, when he instituted what became known as the Lord's Supper, Matt 26:26ff; Mark 14:22ff; Luke 22:14f; and possibly John 13ff. We will shortly examine these in greater detail but at this point I merely refer to them as foundational reasons for practicing celebrating the Eucharist in the public worship of the church on the Lord's Day.

The Reason Christians Celebrate the Eucharist

I could begin this section by stating that we celebrate the Lord's Supper because it is Scriptural! That is one way of looking at this and in my opinion not a bad beginning point! However, by limiting the reason we participate in the Lord's Supper or Eucharist merely to a Scriptural or doctrinal purpose we bypass the main point of the theology of worship and the inner theology of the Lord's Supper.

Simply put, at his last supper with his chosen during the Passover or Feast of Unleavened Bread Jesus instructed his disciples to eat the bread and drink the cup as a reminder of his body/life (the bread) and cup (his blood) given for their sins. His intention was to set their thinking in a mode of remembering the Exodus and all that YHWH had done for them. Paul explained at 1 Cor 11:23ff that it had been Jesus' intention to institute a Passover-like celebration of YHWH's redemptive covenant. Paul explained that the disciples were *to do so in remembrance of Jesus* as a celebration of the new covenant of redemption and new exodus from sin and death found in his blood.

Matthew adds at Matt 26:26-29 that Jesus said, *do it*, which alone should be important enough for participation in the celebration of the Lord's Supper! Note Matt 26:26-29;

> *[26] Now as they were eating, Jesus took bread, and blessed, and broke it, and gave it to the disciples and said, "Take, eat; this is my body." [27] And he took a cup, and when he had given thanks he gave it to them, saying, "Drink of it, all of you; [28] for <u>this is my blood of the covenant, which is poured out for many for the forgiveness of sins</u>. [29] I tell you I shall not drink again of this fruit of the vine until that day when I drink it new with you in my Father's kingdom."*

We have Luke's version of this event at Luke 22:14-20:

> *[14] And when the hour came, he sat at table, and the apostles with him. [15] And he said to them, "I have earnestly desired to eat this Passover with you before I suffer; [16] for I tell you I shall not eat it until it is fulfilled in the kingdom of God." [17] And he took a cup, and when he had given thanks he said, "Take this, and divide it among yourselves; [18] for I tell you that from now on I shall not drink of the fruit of the vine until the kingdom of God comes." [19] And he took bread, and when he had given thanks he broke it and gave it to them, saying, "<u>This is my body which is given for you. Do this in remembrance of me</u>." [20] And likewise the cup after supper, saying, "<u>This cup which is poured out for you is the new covenant in my blood</u>.*

The theological implications of Jesus' instructions and the consequent Christian celebration of this new covenant and new exodus are enormous! Jesus' purpose in instituting the Eucharist became a rallying call to all Christians for over 2,000 years. While the heart and power of the Christian gospel remains the death burial and resurrection of Jesus as the Christ (1 Cor 15:1-5, Rom 1:15, 16), it is the remembrance of this at the Eucharist feast that is a constant reminder of our faith and roots.

However, when Paul discussed the abuses of the Lord's Supper at Corinth he lifted the celebration from a simple doctrinal observance to a major theological concern by adding the theological perspective of profaning the Lord's death during the Lord's Supper, cf. 1 Cor 11:17-33. Perceptively, Paul stressed the possibility of abusing not only the Lord's Supper in the worship assembly but also *profaning the body and blood of the Lord* (1 Cor 11:27)! Obviously, faithful remembrance of the Lord's life and death means the honoring and exultation of the Lord.

Furthermore, note that Paul did not simply refer to the Lord's Supper as something he had introduced to the Corinthians! He tied the practice of participating in the Lord's Supper directly to Jesus' institution of the meal by noting that his instruction was in accordance with the tradition that had been passed down from the Lord himself. Roy Ciampa and Brian Rosner observe;

> *Here again Paul makes it clear that his teaching is not idiosyncratic but reflects the standard and traditional teaching that had been passed down from the very beginning, from the Lord himself. The language of "receiving" and "passing on" was the standard language for the transmission of authoritative traditions. Paul's statement that he received it from the Lord did not suggest that Christ had revealed it to him in a vision, but that those who had passed this on to Paul had received it either directly from the Lord himself or from others who had.*[16]

Furthermore that Paul had duly delivered, or *handed down* this instruction to the Corinthian church was to be a major factor in their worship of God and Jesus Christ. The term *delivered*, παρέδωκα, *paradōka*,[17] implies a *formal handing down or over*;

---

[16] Ciampa, *1 Corinthians*, p. 548.
[17] Παραδίδωμι *paradídōmi* ...to deliver over or up to the power of someone. Zodhiates.

> *²³ For I received from the Lord what I also delivered to you, that the Lord Jesus on the night when he was betrayed took bread, ²⁴ and when he had given thanks, he broke it, and said, "This is my body which is for you. Do this in remembrance of me." ²⁵ In the same way also the cup, after supper, saying, "This cup is the new covenant in my blood. Do this, as often as you drink it, in remembrance of me." ²⁶ For as often as you eat this bread and drink the cup, you proclaim the Lord's death until he comes.*

Ciampa and Rosner observe regarding the handing over, deliverance, of the Lord's Supper tradition to the Corinthians:

> *Here again Paul makes it clear that his teaching is not idiosyncratic but reflects the standard and traditional teaching that had been passed down from the very beginning, from the Lord himself. The language of "receiving" and "passing on" was the standard language for the transmission of authoritative traditions. Paul's statement that he received it from the Lord did not suggest that Christ had revealed it to him in a vision, but that those who had passed this on to Paul had received it either directly from the Lord himself or from others who had. It was Paul himself who had brought the Corinthians into this stream of tradition that had come from the Lord, and now it was his responsibility to straighten out the abuses that had been introduced. The reminder that he was the one who had passed this on to the Corinthians also served rhetorically to reinforce his moral and spiritual authority in the community since it has to do with one of the most fundamental touch-points for their community experience and self-understanding.*[18]

We may challenge Ciampa and Rosner as to the meaning of how Paul received this tradition, but whichever way we go on this it remains that the tradition of maintaining the practice of celebrating the Eucharist goes directly back to the Lord himself.

---

[18] Ciampa, *1 Corinthians*, pp. 548-549, Kindle edition.

In the following discussion we will explore the meaning of celebrating the Lord's Supper as an act of worship and how this informs, edifies, and builds up the Christian faith and draws one closer to God, Christ, and to one another.

The Nature of the Lord's Supper as Eucharist

Referring to the Lord's Supper by the term Eucharist has profound implications in regard to how we approach the Lord's Supper. Some might object to this emphasis on the term Eucharist for Lord's Supper as this is not strictly a biblical term. I am not surrendering the term the *Lord's Supper* but am referring to it as the Eucharist since the purpose of the Lord's Supper was to *celebrate with thanksgiving* God's redemptive activity in Christ. The Greek word for *thanksgiving* is εὐχάριστος *eucháristos*. It is profoundly a biblical term, hence the Eucharistic expression for the Lord's Supper stresses and highlights the *thanksgiving involved in the feast or celebration*.

We do find the term eucharist used in regard to the Lord's Supper at 1 Cor 11:23; *"the Lord Jesus on the night when he was betrayed took bread, ^{24} and when he had <u>given thanks</u>, he broke it, and said, "This is my body which is for you. Do this in remembrance of me."* In fact, the only time the meal is referred to as the Lord's Supper (Greek κυριακὸν δεῖπνον, *kuriakón deípnon*) is in the New Testament in Paul's reference to the celebration in 1 Cor 11:20.

The background to the term *Eucharist* is found in Matt 26:26 where Jesus instituted the Lord's Supper on the evening of the Passover and just before this betrayal.

> ^{26} *Now as they were eating, Jesus took bread, and blessed, and broke it, and gave it to the disciples and said, "Take, eat; this is my body." ^{27} And he took a cup, and <u>when he had given thanks</u> he gave it to them, saying, "Drink of it, all of you; ^{28} for this is my blood of the covenant, which is poured out for many for the forgiveness of sins.*

In the 2nd century Christian literature, we find the term *Eucharist* favored when referring to the memorial of the Lord's Supper. The use of the term says much as to how the celebration was perceived in the early church. It was an occasion of *celebration* and *thanksgiving* for God's redemptive work in Christ.

Hans-Josef Klauck under the topic of "The Lord's Supper" in the *Anchor Bible Dictionary* observes:

> Among the early Christian writings outside of the NT the Didache, the letters of Ignatius of Antioch, and Justin Martyr's Apology deserve to be studied as witnesses to the Lord's Supper. In these writings the technical term for the Lord's Supper is eucharistia (cf. Did. 9:1; Ign. Smyrn. 8:1; Just. Apol. 66:1)—a word which took the lead in Christian tradition for a long time and which is still, as in the past, dominant in Catholic circles.[19]

Note in particular this comment in the *Didache*, an early 2nd century document. Observe also the connection of the Eucharist to baptism:

> *[1] Now concerning the Thanksgiving (Eucharist), thus give thanks. [2] First, concerning the cup: We thank thee, our Father, for the holy vine of David Thy servant, [2] which Thou madest known to us through Jesus Thy Servant; to Thee be the glory forever. [3] And concerning the broken bread: We thank Thee, our Father, for the life and knowledge which Thou madest known to us through Jesus Thy Servant; to Thee be the glory forever. [4] Even as this broken bread was scattered over the hills, and was gathered together and became one, so let Thy Church be gathered together from the ends of the earth into Thy kingdom;[5] for Thine is the glory and the power through Jesus Christ forever. [5] But let no one eat or drink of your Thanksgiving (Eucharist), but they who have been baptized into the name of the Lord; for concerning this also the Lord hath said, give not that which is holy to the dogs.[20]*

---

[19] Hans-Josef Klauck, "Lord's Supper," *Anchor Yale Bible Dictionary*, vol. 4, pp. 363ff.

[20] *The Didache: The Lord's Teaching through the Twelve Apostles to the Nations*. Italics mine, IAF.

Ignatius of Antioch, ca 100 CE, wrote to the church at Philadelphia; "Be careful therefore to employ one *eucharist*, for there is one flesh of our Lord Jesus Christ and one cup for unity with his blood ..."

Everett Ferguson in "Early Accounts of the Lord's Supper" in *Early Christians Speak* observes "the common name for second-century authors is *eucharist*."[21] In support of this statement Ferguson cites the *Acts of John* 86, 110 and the *Acts of Peter* 2, both by Leucius ca 150 CE.[22] In the *Acts of Peter* 2, we have this interesting reflection on Christian life in the mid-2nd century:

> *Now they brought unto Paul bread and water for the sacrifice, that he might make prayer and distribute it to everyone. Among whom it befell that a woman named Rufina desired, she also, to receive the Eucharist at the hands of Paul: to whom Paul, filled with the spirit of God, said as she drew near: Rufina, thou comest not worthily unto the altar of God, arising from beside one that is not thine husband but an adulterer, and assayest to receive the Eucharist of God. For behold Satan shall trouble thine heart and cast thee down in the sight of all them that believe in the Lord, that they which see and believe may know that they have believed in the living God, the searcher of hearts. But if thou repent of thine act, he is faithful that is able to blot out thy sin and set thee free from this sin: but if thou repent not, while thou art yet in the body, devouring fire and outer darkness shall receive thee forever. And immediately Rufina fell down, being stricken with palsy (?) from her head unto the nails of her feet, and she had no power to speak (given her) for her tongue was bound.*

The Eucharist and the Worship Assembly

The Eucharist should define the dynamic and the flow of worship in the assembly. It is obvious that the focus in the Eucharist is not on the participants unless their behavior was not reverent and in keeping with the theology of the Eucharist (cf. 1

---

[21] Ferguson, *Early Christians Speak*, vol. 1, pp. 95ff.
[22] Cf. *Anchor Bible Dictionary*, "The Acts of John and Peter."

Cor 11:17-34 where Paul charged that the Corinthians were *guilty of profaning the body and blood of the Lord*.) We can conclude from Paul's comment that should the celebration of the Eucharist be conducted in an unworthy manner in any form then the worship of God and Jesus would corrupt the whole worship experience which would then degenerate into an unworthy Worship service!

In support of the strict attitude of the 2nd century church regarding participating in the Eucharist in an unworthy manner we might refer again to the interesting account of Rufina in the pericope above from the *Acts of Peter 2*, "Rufina, thou comest not worthily unto the altar of God, arising from beside one that is not thine husband but an adulterer, and assayest to receive the Eucharist of God."

There can be little doubt that the meaning and celebration of the Eucharist in the early church shaped the worship dynamic of the worship assembly.

Ferguson observes that it is abundantly clear from the many resources available regarding the early Christian worship practices that the Lord's Supper was central to the worship and provided the dynamic of the worship in that it focused on God and Jesus:

> *The Lord's supper [sic] was a constant feature of the Sunday service. There is no second-century evidence for the celebration of a daily eucharist. The eucharist was the climax of the Christian worship service and that which distinguished it from the Jewish synagogue service ... The central place of the Lord's supper [sic] in early Christianity is abundantly indicated by all types of sources.*[23]

The Passover Institution of the Lord's Supper

The dynamic of the Lord's Supper as Eucharist hinges around the institution of the Lord's Supper by Jesus at the Passo-

---

[23] Ferguson, *Early Christians Speak*, vol. 1, p. 96.

ver celebrated with his disciples on the night before his betrayal.[24] The title to Jeremias' book on early Christian worship, *The Eucharistic Words of Jesus* expresses well the nature of the Lord's Supper and its institution by Jesus!

It was not by accident that Jesus chose the Jewish Passover festival as the occasion of his institution of the Eucharist. He could have chosen another significant festival for this occasion, for example, *Yom Kippur*, the *Day of Atonement*, when the minds of the people would be focused on the atoning sacrifice for the forgiveness of sins. But he chose the Passover! Why? It was not because he had no choice. He deliberately moved into Jerusalem during the Passover, possibly to draw significance from the Passover for what he was about to experience. He was about to begin a new Exodus, this time an exodus from the slavery to sin![25] It is also possible that Jesus wanted to distance his atoning sacrifice on the cross from the Jewish annual *Yom Kippur* animal sacrifice.

We can find several parallels between the Passover and Jesus' death! Both were a liberation from slavery, the Passover celebrating deliverance from Egyptian slavery and Jesus' sacrifice a deliverance from the slavery to sin. The Passover was a festival celebrating freedom from slavery; *Yom Kippur* was a yearly reminder of repentance and forgiveness of sin. However, Jesus' atoning sacrifice was *once for all time*, never needing to be repeated as were the *Yom Kippur* sacrifices. Cf. Heb 9:24-28:

---

[24] Cf. the excellent study of the Lord's Supper and the Passover by Jeremias, *The Eucharistic Words of Jesus*.
[25] Cf. Wright, *Paul and the Faithfulness of God, passim*.

> *For Christ has entered, not into a sanctuary made with hands, a copy of the true one, but into heaven itself, now to appear in the presence of God on our behalf.* <u>*25 Nor was it to offer himself repeatedly, as the high priest enters the Holy Place yearly with blood not his own;*</u> *26 for then he would have had to suffer repeatedly since the foundation of the world. But as it is, he has appeared* <u>*once for all at the end of the age*</u> *to put away sin by the sacrifice of himself. 27 And just as it is appointed for men to die once, and after that comes judgment, 28 so* <u>*Christ, having been offered once*</u> *to bear the sins of many, will appear a second time, not to deal with sin but to save those who are eagerly waiting for him.*

Not to diminish the significance of the atoning sacrifice of Jesus on the cross which stands foremost in the Christian psyche and was the fulfillment of *Yom Kippur*, it is striking that Jesus would choose the Passover festival for instituting the Lord's Super celebration! With its roots set in the Passover festival of celebrating freedom it is not surprising that the early church settled on the significance of *eucháristos* to describe the Lord's Supper celebration for it signified thanksgiving for the freedom from the slavery to sin. The early Christians thus called the celebration *Thanksgiving*, from εὐχαριστία, *eucharistía*.

There is considerable debate regarding the precise dating of the Last Supper and the Passover meal celebrated by Jesus with his disciples. Much of the difficulty relates to the apparent different chronologies followed by the Gospel of John and the Synoptic Gospels. This is not the place to debate such discussions in detail other than to refer the reader to the relevant resources for such a discussion.[26]

Joachim Jeremias' study, *The Eucharistic Words of Jesus* is widely considered to be definitive in regard to the dating and timing of the Passover meal. Jeremias accepted the fact that there are objections to the Synoptic Gospels setting the Last Supper at

---

[26] Marshall, *Last Supper and Lord's Supper*, pp. 57ff; Moule, *Worship,* p. 28; Jeremias, The *Eucharistic Words Of Jesus*, *passim*; Higgins, *Lord's Supper*; Cullmann and Leenhardt, *Essays on the Lord's Supper*; Keener, *Matthew*, pp. 622ff; Hagner, *Matthew 14-28*, pp. 771ff.

Jesus' last Passover meal, and considers them worthy of consideration. However, he nevertheless closes his detailed argument regarding the *pros* and *cons* to this discussion with the following observation:

> *The result of this investigation has been to show that none of the eleven objections are sufficient to refute the synoptic report that the Last Supper was a Passover meal.*[27]

As I have pointed out, and as Jeremias has so capably argued, the Passover was an ideal occasion for what Jesus had in mind when he instituted the Lord's Supper! *A remembrance of thanksgiving for God's gracious deliverance from sin.* Hence, εὐχαριστία, *eucharistía*!

What is relevant to the point I am making is that it was at the Passover Feast, loaded with all the theological significance of the exodus feast, that Jesus chose to institute the Lord's Supper.

Jesus did not do significant things of such import by accident!

So, in order to understand the Lord's Supper as *Eucháristos* we have to think Passover celebration, a celebration of freedom from slavery! It is my opinion that much of the dynamic in the experience of the Lord's Supper in Churches of Christ has focused on the cruel death and suffering of Jesus on the cross (*Yom Kippur*) in a mourning bench dynamic, *rather than a celebration of joy for what Jesus did*, setting us free from the slavery to sin. I do not intend that anyone should read into this statement any irreligious denigration of Jesus' suffering on the cross. Such suffering and the enormity of the price of the atonement Jesus paid must shape our love and appreciation for Jesus. However, it is my opinion that the setting of the Last Supper and institution of the Lord's Supper at the Passover festival should move our mindset and psyche from mourning to celebration and joy. Hence, εὐχαριστία, *eucharistía, eucharist, thanksgiving*!

---

[27] Jeremias, *Eucharistic Words of Jesus*, p. 85. His discussion of the topic is found on pp. 41-84.

Chapter 10: The Lord's Supper in Scripture

When seeking to unfold the theology of worship it is imperative that we set the discussion in the context of Scripture, and not church tradition! This is especially true regarding the Lord's Supper. In order to plumb the depths of what the Lord had in mind when instituting the Lord's Supper, Scripture must be the foundation of that theology. Once we have done this we can then notice how the early church in the first and second centuries understood and practiced the celebration of the Lord's Supper. Several texts address the Lord's Supper describing the significance of the celebration in different terminology according to their readership and the issue being developed. Each text discusses the importance of the celebration in a particular context, and then comments on its practice in the life of the church. Obviously the institution of the practice of the Lord's Supper was by Jesus, hence the Gospel textual sources must lie at the foundation of both the theology and practice of the Lord's Supper. The biblical texts we will reference to open our discussion will be the Synoptic Gospels' account at Matt 26:17-29, Luke 22:7-23, and Mark 12:23, and then consider Luke's account at Acts 20:7. We will spend some time working through Paul's teaching regarding the practice of the Lord's Supper in Corinth at 1 Cor 11:17-14. It will not be my intention in this study to offer a detailed exegesis of each of these texts. I will examine each text briefly and then reflect on some firm conclusions available in scholarly studies which will be referenced in relevant footnotes.

The Synoptic Reflection the Lord's Supper: Matt 26:17-29, Luke 22:7-23, Mark 12:23

The first thought that surfaces from the Lord's institution of the Lord's Supper was that he instituted this in the context of the Passover Feast and not the Day of Atonement.[1] But why choose

---

[1] For detailed discussion of the Passover Feast as the timing for the institution of the Lord's Supper cf. Joachim Jeremias, *The Eucharistic Words of Jesus*, London: SCM Press, 1966, and the major commentaries referenced in the footnotes of this chapter.

the Passover which celebrated the concept of the Exodus thanksgiving from the captivity or slavery rather than the Atoning celebration of the forgiveness for sin? There can be no question that the death of Jesus was the ultimate power or dynamic for the forgiveness of sin, but here the imagery celebrated in the Passover context was of the Exodus delivery from slavery and God's protection throughout the Exodus journey of the believer's life. Jesus could have chosen the celebration of *Yom Kippur*, the Day of Atonement, but he chose the Passover. We should remember that Jesus' journey to Jerusalem was not an accidental incident, nor was his selection of the day of his crucifixion an occurrence set by the Jewish powers, but one chosen intentionally by Jesus according to God's plan. Jesus knew what he was doing and why he would do so! Already in this choice one can see lurking behind the text the roots for the Lord's Supper being identified as *Eucharist*, Thanksgiving, for that was a major reason for the Passover celebration.

The Synoptics explain that Jesus took bread and wine to be the emblems for the memorial. The bread, Jesus explained, would represent his body or life given to provide the means of his sacrifice, and the wine to represent the new covenant opened in his blood shed for the redemption of all. Note Luke 22:19, 20:
*And he took bread, and when he had given thanks he broke it and gave it to them, saying, "**This is my body which is given for you**. Do this in remembrance of me."* [20] *And likewise the cup after supper, saying, "**This cup which is poured out for you is the new covenant in my blood**.*

Matthew's account at Matt 26:26 is very similar to that of Luke:
Now as they were eating, Jesus took bread, and blessed, and broke it, and gave it to the disciples and said, "Take, eat; ***this is my body***.*"* [27] *And he took a cup, and when he had given thanks he gave it to them, saying, "Drink of it, all of you;* [28] ***for this is my blood of the covenant***, *which is poured out for many for the forgiveness of sins.*

As I mentioned in the previous chapter, it does not take one long in a study such as this to notice that different denominations read The Lord's Supper or Mass differently according to their church tradition. The same is true in regard to Jesus' comment *"**this is** ..."* We will begin by merely mentioning the different ways in which this expression has been understood.

The Roman Catholic and Eastern Orthodox Churches read this as the bread *literally becoming, or being transformed,* into the body of Jesus, and the wine *literally becoming* the blood of Jesus. This doctrine is known as *Transubstantiation* which means that the bread and wine have *changed substance* from bread and wine into the body and blood of Jesus which are then eaten or drunk by the congregant or priest. Obviously this practice is a serious theological concept, and should not be demeaned or considered as cannibalism. However, the Greek expression τοῦτό ἐστιν, *touto estin, this is,* has a wide range of meanings which the Roman Catholics render as *this really is, or really has become,* while others understand this to mean *this represents or means.* I will elaborate on this shortly.

Martin Luther and other church leaders of the Protestant Reformation like Huldrych Zwingli (ca 1520 ff) rejected the concept of *Transubstantiation* and substituted the concept of *Consubstantiation* or *Impanation* which meant in differing degrees that the body and blood of Jesus were present *with or in* the emblems, either permanently or specifically during the prayers and participation of the eucharist. For Zwingli the Eucharist was a *memorial* of Christ's atoning death on the cross without any concept of the Eucharist in itself being an atoning sacrifice as in the Roman Catholic view. Different Synods of the Lutheran church today adopt the *Consubstantiation* or *Impanation* view.

Some Episcopal/Anglican, or Church of England churches, and to some degree various Methodist churches, adopt a *form* of the *real presence* of Jesus in the emblems. Fundamentally, the Anglican/Episcopal church rejects the Roman Catholic view of *Transubstantiation.* "But the concept of transubstantiation has generally been avoided and excluded from Anglican theologies of the Real Presence of Christ's body and blood in the eucharist."[2] Some Anglican/Episcopalians believe that the "Real Presence" of

---

[2] *The Episcopal Dictionary of the Bible.* www.episcopalchurch.org; www.answers.com/Q/Do_Episcopalians_believe_in_transubstantiation.

Christ is "in with and under" the elements of bread and wine which is similar to the understanding of *Consubstantiation*, but different in that Christ's presence remains among the consecrated elements permanently, even after the mass/eucharist ends, which is different from the Lutheran understanding. Essentially, the Episcopal Church has a wide range of Eucharistic theologies which all fall into the category of "Real Presence." The one thing they all have in common is that they all believe that when the priest or bishop consecrates the bread and wine somehow, and in some form, it is no longer just bread and wine, but it is also the Real Presence of Our Lord Jesus Christ.[3]

Most Evangelical churches like the Baptist church, the Churches of Christ, the Disciples of Christ, and several varieties of Open Community Bible Fellowship churches today understand the expression *this is* to mean *this represents* or *this means* the body and blood of Jesus. It is the view of most conservative Evangelical scholars that the expression τοῦτό ἐστιν τὸ σῶμά μου, *touto estin sōma mou, this is my body*, and ἐστιν τὸ αἷμά, *estin to haima*, this *is my blood*, of both Matthew and Luke were intended to say *this symbolizes* or *this represents* my body or my blood.[4]

Note how Matthew records the words of Jesus at Matt 26:26-28:

Now as they were eating, Jesus took bread, and blessed, and broke it, and gave it to the disciples and said, "Take, eat; <u>this is my body</u>." ²⁷ And he took a cup, and when he had given thanks he gave it to them, saying, "Drink of it, all of you; ²⁸ <u>for this is</u> my blood of the covenant, which is poured out for many for the forgiveness of sins.

²⁶ Ἐσθιόντων δὲ αὐτῶν λαβὼν ὁ Ἰησοῦς ἄρτον καὶ εὐλογήσας ἔκλασεν καὶ δοὺς τοῖς μαθηταῖς εἶπεν, Λάβετε φάγετε, τοῦτό ἐστιν τὸ σῶμά μου. ²⁷ καὶ λαβὼν ποτήριον καὶ εὐχαριστήσας

---

[3] Cf the discussion of transubstantiation, consubstantiation, *et al* in Alan Richardson, *A Dictionary of Christian Theology, passim*; Geoffrey W. Bromiley, "Transubstantiation," *Baker's Dictionary of Theology*, Grand Rapids: Baker Book House, 1960, p. 530; David E. Aune, "Early Christian Worship," *Anchor Bible Dictionary*, vol. 6: pp. 974ff.

[4] For scholarly discussion of this see the scholars referenced below.

ἔδωκεν αὐτοῖς λέγων, Πίετε ἐξ αὐτοῦ πάντες, ²⁸ <u>τοῦτο γάρ ἐστιν</u> τὸ αἷμά μου τῆς διαθήκης τὸ περὶ πολλῶν ἐκχυννόμενον εἰς ἄφεσιν ἁμαρτιῶν.

With one or two variations the words of Mark and Luke are much the same as Matthew's account.

What I intend to do now is demonstrate how several conservative scholars understand the words *touto estin, this is.*

Donald Hagner writes regarding this in his commentary on Matthew at Matt 26:26ff:

> The sense in which the bread and wine are the body and blood of Jesus in the Eucharist has been one of the notorious and divisive problems in the Christian church (for illuminating discussion of this along with other aspects, see Reumann; Cullmann and Leenhardt; Marshall). In the present note, only the following brief observations are possible. Jesus' use of the verb ἐστίν, "is" ("this is my body"; "this is my blood"), *can hardly be meant literally when Jesus is physically present with them at the meal*. The verb is to be taken seriously *but as involving a deep and important symbolism. As the Passover meal involved rich symbolism, so Jesus instills a new dynamic symbolism into these elements*. Christ *is* genuinely present in the elements, but without a change of these *into* his actual body and blood (as in transubstantiation). To eat of these elements is mysteriously to partake of Christ and his gifts, to enjoy the grace of the gospel (cf. John 6:56–57). Since the life of the Christian—the enjoyment of the gift of new life—depends so fundamentally upon the death of Jesus, the identification of the bread and wine of this supper as his body and blood is centrally significant. Yet although the eucharist points to the sacrifice of Jesus, it is not itself a sacrifice but a memorializing and contemporizing of the unique sacrifice accomplished by Jesus on the cross. *Understandably, this commemoration of the sacrifice of Jesus for the forgiveness of sins becomes the central component of Christian worship.*

... The bread symbolizes the body of Jesus, which is about to be given over to death on their behalf. The vicarious nature of this body (and its death) remains implicit here, but it becomes clear from the explanatory comments accompanying the reference to the blood in v. 28. The background is that of the sacrifice of the Paschal lamb (cf. Exod 12:21, 27). On the supper as a Passover meal, see esp. Jeremias, *The Eucharistic Words of Jesus*, 15–88; p 773 Higgins, *The Lord's Supper in the New Testament*; Marshall; Leaney; and Saldarini (to the contrary, Allen, Senn, Bokser).

... The symbolism of the bread and cup is only fulfilled in the participation of each individual disciple for whom Jesus' death was to be accomplished. In the parallel sentence to the saying of v. 26 concerning the body of Jesus, τοῦτο γάρ ἐστιν τὸ αἷμά μου, "for this is my blood," we have the same type of symbolism at work: *the wine symbolizes the blood of Jesus*, and to drink that wine is symbolically to partake of the blood and its atoning effect. [5]

Similarly, in his commentary on Luke, Earle Ellis observes that *this is my body* should be understood as *this means my body*: "This means..." (Moffatt). *The elements are representative and are he preached word made visible. The point is not the substance of the elements but their use as a proclamation of a past event and of the Lord present in the Body of believers.* "The Eucharist, therefore, is not a Passion play like the Mass; Christ's death is preached (1 Cor 11:26) not his dying re-enacted" M. Barth: cf. Higgins, *op. cit.*, p. 53).[6]

Hugh Anderson in his commentary on Mark, in similar fashion to Ellis, writes that in the statement *this is my body there was no intention on Jesus' part to identify or define the substance of the bread* [as in Transubstantiation, IAF], only to emphasize his

---

[5] Hagner, D. A. *Matthew 14–28,* pp. 772-773. Emphases mine, IAF.
[6] E. Earle Ellis, *The Gospel of Luke*, p. 256. Emphasis mine, IAF.

divine presence "within the disciple-community" when the Eucharist was celebrated.[7]

Craig Blomberg, in a detailed examination of the Lord's Supper, proclaims:

> Jesus now invests the bread with new meaning. It foreshadows his body figuratively broken and literally killed in his upcoming death. Jesus' words here have led to massive debates, intra-Christian persecution, and huge theological edifices, the weight of which they cannot bear. The doctrines of transubstantiation (the bread and wine become Christ's actual body and blood) or consubstantiation (Christ is really present "in, with, and under" the elements) make no sense of Jesus' words in their historical context. As Jesus holds up a loaf and declares, "This is my body," *no one listening will ever imagine that he is claiming the bread to be the literal extension of his flesh. Moreover, in Aramaic these sentences would have been spoken without a linking verb ("is"), as simply, this, my body and this, my blood. As frequently elsewhere, Jesus is creating a vivid object lesson. The bread symbolizes (represents, stands for, or points to) his crucifixion in some otherwise unspecified sense.* In vv. 27-28 Jesus turns from the bread to the cup. This is the third of four cups of wine drunk at various stages throughout the evening festivities. It was probably a common cup passed around for all to drink. "Offered" is the same verb as "gave" in v. 27 and does not imply that drinking was optional. Each of the four cups was linked to one line of Exod 6:6-7a. This one tied in with God's promise, "I will redeem you," in v. 6c and hence specifically to his original liberation of the Israelites from Egypt (m. Pesah. 10:6-7). But again Jesus adds new meaning. As they all drink (the "all" refers to all the disciples, not to all of the wine!), *he proclaims that the cup stands for his blood about to be shed in his death on the cross*. The "blood of the covenant" harks back to Exod 24:8. The use of "cup" rather than "wine" links this

---

[7] Anderson, *Mark*, p. 313.

passage with 20:22-23 and 26:39. "Fruit of the vine" (v. 29) was a stock phrase used in thanksgiving prayers for the wine (m. Ber. 6:1) and therefore does not refer to unfermented beverage, "though it was customary to cut the wine with a double or triple quantity of water."[8]

Finally, Craig Keener's detailed study of the Lord's Supper in comparison to the Jewish Passover and other ceremonial religious practices writes:

> That the bread "is" his body means that it "represents" it; we should interpret his words here no more literally than the disciples would have taken the normal words of the Passover liturgy, related to Deuteronomy 16:3 (cf. Stauffer 1960: 117): "This is the bread of affliction which our ancestors ate when they came from the land of Egypt." (By no stretch of the imagination did anyone suppose that they were re-eating the very bread the Israelites had eaten in the wilderness.) Those who ate of this bread participated by commemoration in Jesus' affliction in the same manner that those who ate the Passover commemorated in the deliverance of their ancestors. *The language of Passover celebration assumed the participation of current generations in the exodus event ... That Jesus was also in his body at the time he uttered the words further militates against interpreting the bread as literally equivalent to his body* (Moffatt 1938: 168).[9]

Many years ago as a graduate student in a Seminary in South Africa the topic of study in one course was the Eucharist. In the class were ministry students from the Church of England, the Baptist Church, the Methodist Church, the Lutheran Church, and me, from the Churches of Christ. We even had a lady who was Jewish but who was taking the class to understand what Christians taught about the Worship of Jesus. At the close of the lectures, the question was raised as to what the different churches

---

[8]Blomberg, Craig L. *Matthew*, pp. 390, 391.
[9] Keener, Craig S. *Matthew*, Kindle locations 17709-17720.

did with the elements that remained after the service. The occasion although serious was a fun time all in good spirit but decidedly critical! One response by a Methodist scholar was that the breadcrumbs were fed to the birds, and the wine drunk by the minister. The response to the wine comment brought some laughter and the comment, "not a bad idea." The Church of England ministers and the Lutheran ministers said they ate or drank the emblems since it would be blasphemous to throw them away in the trash can, after they had been sanctified in prayer. The Baptist minister and I said that we simply threw the remaining emblems away, or placed them in the refrigerator to be used the following week, since they were merely bread and wine and symbols of Jesus' presence which had not been changed into the body and blood of Jesus. Obviously, the Baptists and I, being teetotaling Christians could not drink the wine! In my case we had recently at that time viewed one of the children, the son of the Texan missionary, sneaking up to the Lord's Table and eating and drinking the emblems. Jokingly, in a spirit of ecumenism, we all agreed that this should not be considered an unforgivable sin, but nevertheless should not be recommended!

My point in this little story is to illustrate how different theological persuasions interpret the Eucharistic emblems within church traditions in their celebration of the Lord's Supper! My concern is that church tradition should not be the basis for defining the celebration and emblems used in the ceremony. Scripture alone should be the foundation for such discussion, recognizing the difficulty of not permitting ecclesiological presuppositions to become the foundation of theology.

From my somewhat lighthearted comments it should not be implied that the Baptist minister or I were trivializing the celebration or the "safeguarding" of the emblems. The context of the discussion was a lighthearted group occasion. We understood the use of the emblems in the different religious traditions, and the consequent discarding of the unused emblems in the ceremony. We also each understood the seriousness with which the emblems were taken since they do represent in some form the presence of the Lord in the ceremony, and the intention for participants to focus on Jesus' crucified body and atoning blood shed on the cross.

Young theological students in their comradery can lose their brains!

Paul, Corinth, and the Lord's Supper at 1 Cor 11:17-33

We turn now to possibly the first theological discussion we know of concerning the celebration of the Lord's Supper, 1 Cor 11-13. In his extensive discourse on problems in the Corinthian church worship service, specifically in regard to the participation in the Lord's Supper and the use of charismatic gifts, Paul illuminates our understanding of how the Lord's Supper was celebrated in the early church ca CE 55, specifically in Corinth. In his study of the abuse of the Lord's Supper, Paul cautioned against defaming the Lord's Supper by denigrating the eating of the emblems and reducing the Lord's Supper to the level of an ordinary meal.

The expression *Lord's Supper* as a reference to the Eucharist appears only once in Scripture, in Paul's first letter to the Corinthians at 1 Cor 11:20. The celebratory observance of this "Supper" is described in the New Testament by different descriptive terms. The *Baker Encyclopedia of the Bible* has this observation regarding the Lord's Supper. It refers to:

> The supper Jesus shared with his disciples a few hours before he was arrested and taken to his trial and death; [it refers to] the ceremony of the bread and wine that Christians have come to call the Lord's Supper (1 Cor 11:20), the breaking of bread (Acts 2:42, 46; 20:7), Holy Communion (from the expression of 1 Cor 10:16), the Eucharist (the Greek word for "thanksgiving," see Mk 14:23), or the Mass. The apostle Paul speaks of handing on what he had "received from the Lord" concerning the institution of this supper "on the night when he was betrayed." Like Luke, Paul gives the Lord's command to his disciples, "Do this in remembrance of me" (1 Cor 11:24, 25). According to Acts 2, the early Christians from the beginning of the life of the church met regularly for "the breaking of bread."[10]

---

[10] "The Lord's Supper," *Baker Encyclopedia of the Bible*, vol 2, p. 1352.

At this point some discussion of the Love Feast might be helpful! In another chapter in this study of a theology of worship, we note that there is some evidence of some churches combing a normal Love Feast with the celebration of the Lord's Supper, as in Corinth. We have no hard evidence of how widespread this practice was but note that later in the early life of the church this practice was discontinued. Obviously, Paul's instruction to the Corinthians must have stimulated a deeper study of the Lord's Supper resulting in the discontinuation of this practice.

However, we should be cautious of simply conflating early Christian practices into our modern Christian thought! For the European and Western world today Sunday has in large measure become a public holiday day, even in some circles a holy-day, or a religious day of rest. In the ancient world such "religious days off" were not universally enjoyed by the Christians. We have some reliable information describing the early Sunday worship service.

Many of the Christians were slaves and not freedmen. They fellowshipped and worshipped either early in the morning before daybreak, and then went to work, or they celebrated later in the evening. In addition, the communal sharing of a fellowship meal was a customary practice among both the Jewish and Christian communities, cf. Acts 2:42ff.

As we will note below it was the habit of people in the 1st century, Jews and Gentiles, to eat the main meal of the day in the evenings, and on occasion they may also have celebrated the Lord's Supper at the same gathering. The fellowship gathering for an evening meal was called by the early Christians a *Love Feast* (*agape*, Jude 12). This should not be taken as an argument for the Lord's Supper being a Love Feast, only that the occasion provided a good opportunity to celebrate the Eucharist on a Sunday evening. It is easy to conflate these two celebrations into one "ceremony" as the Corinthians did to their disgrace.

Consider Acts 20:7 and the church service in Troas, *it was celebrated late at night on the first day of the week*. My purpose here is merely to point to the fact that for some cultural reason the church service in Troas was held at night. We will study this text later in greater detail below.

In comments regarding early Christian church services, note Everett Ferguson's extended discussion of this, noting his comments on a letter from Pliny to Trajan, the Roman Emperor, in *Early Christians Speak*.[11] Ferguson observed there was scant external evidence discussing early worship services:

> Our earliest description of Christian worship outside the New Testament comes from a non-Christian source. Pliny in reporting to the emperor Trajan on his investigations of Christians, spoke of their assemblies … The value of this early testimony is offset by its limitations. Pliny's information comes largely from Christians who have apostatized or have lapsed back into the world …

Regarding Pliny's observations, Ferguson summarizes the comments made by Pliny in a letter to Trajan:

> … they [the Christians] were of the habit of meeting *on a fixed day before it was light*,[12] when they sang alternate verses of a hymn to Christ, as to a god, and bound themselves by a solemn oath, not to any wicked deeds … after which it was their custom to separate and then reassemble to partake of food – but food of an ordinary and innocent kind.

In addition, Ferguson enlarges on Pliny's descriptions of the early Christian worship services:

The "fixed" or stated day for the common assembly would have been Sunday … *The pre-dawn gathering* would have been necessitated by the social circumstances of the Christians: as slaves and workmen they could get away for their meetings only at such times … The gathering later in the day, presumably in the evening, was for dinner. The meal was the "love feast" (or agape, Jude 12) which was observed in the evening at the time of the main meal of the day.

Finally, commenting further on early Christian evidence of Christian worship Ferguson writes:

> Nearly a century later Tertullian [a Christian theologian and apologist, ca 200 CE] listed among the Christian

---

[11] Everett Ferguson, *Early Christians Speak*, 3rd ed., pp. 81ff.
[12] The emphases in some places of the following citations are mine, IAF.

customs: "We take the sacrament of the eucharist, which was commanded by the Lord at meal time and for all alike, in congregations *before day break* and from the hand of none but the presidents [elders]."

In time, as Christianity spread and grew in popularity under the Constantine Roman conversion to Christianity, and the establishment of the Roman church, ca 303 CE, Christian freedom saw the rise of the Christian Sunday and a holy day of rest (as in the Jewish Sabbath day of rest), the spread of localized Christian assemblies as houses of assembly, the building of church buildings.

Cathedrals became the popular or authorized places of assembly with set times established that were convenient for Christian services. My point in mentioning this growth in Christian practice is merely intended to demonstrate that times for extended Christian services were not universally available in the early churches of the 1st and 2nd centuries CE. Not many of the 1st century churches were large. They were mainly smaller house churches. Obviously, the church in Corinth could have enjoyed a centralized house church service, but this would not have been the universal practice as would be seen in the many small house churches in Rome. Jerome Murphy-O'Conner, in his magisterial work *Keys to First Corinthians*, has argued that the early house churches of the 1st and 2nd centuries were small in size, and most likely not as large as we today might assume the churches to have been.[13]

Christians gathered for worship services on the Lord's Day, the Day of the Resurrection, Sunday, or as it was described by Luke, *the first day of the week*. The services were held at a time when it was convenient, often late in the evening. We will note in a later discussion below in the Acts 20:7 study, that the church in Troas (Acts 20:7) gathered for the celebration of the bread and wine in the evening on Sunday, the first day of the week at which time Paul preached to the gathering. The Christians in Troas, most likely a Gentile community of believers, may have used the

---

[13] Murphey-O'Conner, *Keys to First Corinthians*.

occasion of a fellowship meal for sharing with Paul and his companions, including a Eucharist celebration which may also have been the occasion of a Love Feast with Paul. At this gathering it would have been a convenient occasion for their partaking of the Eucharist. The point we will make was that it was on *the first day of the week* when this Christian service of the Eucharist was held.

Now back to 1 Cor 11:17ff! The text is long, but since it is so important to our discussion of the Eucharist and the Love Feast, I will include the whole text with some sections underlined for emphasis. Most scholars agree that this gathering in Corinth was on the first day of the week, and that Paul's outpouring of indignation arose out of his concern regarding the behavior of the Corinthian church in their assemblies that triggered the next three chapters following his 1 Cor 11:17 outburst. At 1 Cor 10 Paul had warned about Christians being involved with pagan feasts and idolatry. At 1 Cor 11:7ff he turned to the appropriate behavior of the Corinthians in Christian worship.

> [17] *But in the following instructions I do not commend you, because <u>when you come together</u> it is <u>not for the better but for the worse</u>.* [18] *For, in the first place, when you <u>assemble as a church</u>, I hear that there are <u>divisions among you</u>; and I partly believe it,* [19] *for there must be factions among you in order that those who are genuine among you may be recognized.* [20] *When you <u>meet together, it is not the Lord's supper that you eat</u>.* [21] *For in eating, each one goes ahead <u>with his own meal</u>, and one is hungry and another is drunk.* [22] *<u>What! Do you not have houses to eat and drink in? Or do you despise the church of God and humiliate those who have nothing</u>? What shall I say to you? Shall I commend you in this? <u>No, I will not</u>.*
> [23] *For <u>I received from the Lord what I also delivered to you</u>, that the Lord Jesus <u>on the night when he was betrayed took bread</u>,* [24] *and when he had given thanks, he broke it, and said, "<u>This is my body which is for you. Do this in remembrance of me</u>."* [25] *In the same way also the cup, after supper, saying, "<u>This cup is the new covenant in my blood. Do this, as often as you drink it, in remembrance of me</u>."* [26] *<u>For as often</u> as you eat this bread and*

drink the cup, <u>you proclaim the Lord's death until he comes</u>.
²⁷ Whoever, therefore, <u>eats the bread or drinks the cup of the Lord in an unworthy manner will be guilty of profaning the body and blood of the Lord</u>. ²⁸ Let a man examine himself, and so eat of the bread and drink of the cup. ²⁹ <u>For anyone who eats and drinks without discerning the body eats and drinks judgment upon himself.</u> ³⁰ That is why many of you are weak and ill, and some have died. ³¹ But if we judged ourselves truly, we should not be judged. ³² But when we are judged by the Lord, we are chastened so that we may not be condemned along with the world.
³³ So then, my brethren, <u>when you come together to eat, wait for one another</u>— ³⁴ <u>if anyone is hungry, let him eat at home</u>—lest you come together to be condemned. About the other things I will give directions when I come.
[14]

First, it seems obvious in the paragraph above that Paul was discussing a special gathering of the local congregation in Corinth. The words *come together* are from the Greek, συνέρχομαι *sunérchomai … to go or come with someone, to meet together*. The point being that the people had gathered together at some place *for a purpose* and that purpose was to worship God and Jesus.[15]

Second, Paul observes that they had *assembled as a church*, γὰρ συνερχομένων ὑμῶν ἐν ἐκκλησίᾳ. The word *συνερχομένων, gathered together,* explains that they had *come together as a church* with the noun *church* being a translation of the Greek noun ἐκκλησία, *ekklēsía,* meaning *a called out group,* which in turn derived from the verb *ekkaléō … to call out. Ekklēsía* was a

---

[14] 1 Cor 11:17–34.
[15] Zodhiates, συνέρχομαι *sunérchomai …* from *sún …* together with or together, and *érchomai …* to come. To go or come with someone, to meet together. … With the dative. of person… to come together with someone … Generally and usually, to come together, convene, assemble… As marking result (1 Cor. 11:17, 34); with *eis …* unto, with the accusative of place … (1 Cor. 11:18); *epí tó autó …* at the same place (1 Cor. 11:20; 14:23)

common term for a congregation of the *ekklētoí ... the called people, or those called out or assembled in the public affairs of a free state, the body of free citizens* called together by a herald ... which constituted the *ekklēsía*. In the New Testament the word is also applied to *the congregation of the people of Israel* (Acts 7:38).[16] The point being that *the Corinthian Christians had gathered together in an assembly of the church with a purpose in mind*.

Third, the expression when you meet together, it is not the Lord's supper that you eat. For in eating, each one goes ahead with his own meal, and one is hungry and another is drunk. This clearly indicates that Paul had in mind their turning the Lord's Supper into a common meal, or perhaps a Love Feast. It was obvious that the church was abusing the Eucharist by turning it into a Love Feast or common meal in which they ate their full and got drunk! For this Paul was not commending them but judging them! In such a meal the poor were being humiliated by the rich! This was hardly a Eucharist in which the Lord was being praised! The point is that the church in Corinth was denigrating the Lord's Supper by permitting it to be confused with a common meal, albeit a supposed Love Feast. Their Eucharist was more like a pagan wine drunken feast in honor of Dionisius the god of wine than a feast of purity to the Lord.

Fourth, Paul in 1 Cor 11:23 turns more serious, connecting his discussion of the Lord's Supper to *the tradition or inspired instruction* he had received from the Lord. This comment has given rise to several theological interpretations regarding the expression or concept introduced by Paul with the words παρέλαβον ἀπὸ τοῦ κυρίου, which *I received from the Lord*. The word παρέλαβον, *parelabon* is a technical word which in the Jewish tradition often implied *accepted instruction* or *the instruction received by authoritative teaching according to a tradition*.

The point at this stage of Paul's argument is that Paul referred to a tried and accepted tradition which he *had received*

---

[16] Zodhiates, Kittel, Balz and Schneider, Exegetical Dictionary of the New Testament, ἐκκλησία, *ekklēsía*.

from the Lord, Ἐγὼ γὰρ παρέλαβον ἀπὸ τοῦ κυρίου, *ego yar parelabon apo tou kúriou.* The words *from the Lord* in the RSV and ESV, and other translations, has opened the door to a host of extremely scholarly viewpoints, all containing some varied validity! This expression could mean that Paul had personally received the tradition from the Lord, or that it was according to the instruction of the Lord that had been handed down from the apostles and had become a standard tradition which was later written into the Gospels, or that Paul had received the tradition handed down to him in some fashion. We should remember that 1 Corinthians was written some 20 to 30 years before the writing of our Synoptic Gospels, so Paul could not have read about this in the Gospels! What was written in our Gospels was certainly what the early apostolic church taught, handed down, and subsequently was recorded by Matthew, Mark, and Luke!

Ellingworth covers in brief the various approaches to this verse. He observes:

> The verbs translated *I received* (compare 15:1, 3) and *I also delivered* (see 11:2) were commonly used among Jewish and other teachers when speaking about traditional teaching. In the ancient world and in many places in the modern world, a personal relationship with a teacher counted at least as much in education as the reading of books.
>
> The word translated *from* is not the preposition commonly used in speaking of direct personal communication found, for example, in Gal 1:12; 1 Thes 2:13; 4:1; 2 Thes 3:6. Some scholars believe that Paul's choice of a less common preposition indicates that he is thinking of Jesus as beginning a tradition that Paul received indirectly, not directly, from Jesus. Others believe that he received this "teaching" directly from Jesus in some supernatural way. Others, though, take the view that the story of the founding of the Lord's Supper may have come to Paul through human channels, but that this tradition came to life for him through communion with the risen Lord. It is the context, particularly the close similarity between the accounts given here and in the synoptic Gospels (especially Luke),

which suggests that Paul is relying on a tradition already being handed on within the church.[17]

Ciampa and Rosner observe:

> Here again Paul makes it clear that his teaching is not idiosyncratic but reflects the standard and traditional teaching that had been passed down from the very beginning, from the Lord himself. The language of "receiving" and "passing on" was the standard language for the transmission of authoritative traditions. Paul's statement that he received it from the Lord did not suggest that Christ had revealed it to him in a vision, but that those who had passed this on to Paul had received it either directly from the Lord himself or from others who had. It was Paul himself who had brought the Corinthians into this stream of tradition that had come from the Lord, and now it was his responsibility to straighten out the abuses that had been introduced. The reminder that he was the one who had passed this on to the Corinthians also served rhetorically to reinforce his moral and spiritual authority in the community since it has to do with one of the most fundamental touch-points for their community experience and self-understanding. It reinforces the Corinthians' awareness that Paul plays the role of the spiritual father of this community, the one who established the original connection between the Corinthians and the Lord who redeemed them. The language of the passing on of traditions also ties this passage to the beginning of the chapter, where Paul referred to the keeping of the traditions he had passed on to them.[18]

However, although this view has appeal to some scholars and is within the boundaries of exegetical concerns, not all scholars agree with the view that Paul received this "tradition" from

---

[17] Ellingworth, *First Letter to the Corinthians*, pp. 259–260. Cf also Fitzmyer, *First Corinthians*, pp. 435f; Garland, *1 Corinthians*, pp. 544ff; Thiselton, *The First Epistle to the Corinthians*, pp 867ff; Fee, *The First Epistle to the Corinthians*, pp. 546ff.

[18] Ciampa, *First Letter to the Corinthians*, pp. 548-549.

others in the Christian faith. Leon Morris provides a traditional conservative alternate discussion on the topic and its various possibilities. Morris favors the view that Paul received the tradition directly from Jesus in a supernatural revelation in the same manner that he also had received the mystery of the gospel by revelation. Morris' comments on *the tradition* having come directly from the Lord agree with the more conservative mindset of many scholars and are quite within the concept of a tradition being received from the Lord:

> The verbs *received* and *passed on* (*paralambánō* and *paradídōmi*) are almost technical terms for receiving and passing on traditions (cf. v.2). This, taken with the general probability, leads most commentators to view what Paul means "received a tradition which goes back to the Lord". *Against this is the emphatic I (egō); why should Paul say "I received of the Lord" if he meant "I received from other men a tradition that derives ultimately from the Lord"? Revelations were made directly to Paul (Acts 18:9f; 22:18; 23:11; 27:23-25; 2 Cor 12:7; Gal 1:12; 2:2). The use of apo rather than para for from does not necessarily indicate an indirect report (although it would be consistent with it), for it sometimes refers to direct communication (Col 1:7; 3:24; 1 Jn 1:5). Paul seems to be referring to a direct revelation (cf.* Craig, Paul may still be asserting that his interpretation of the Lord's Supper was received by him from the risen Lord') ... Paul brings out the poignant truth that that feast of love that was to bring such strength and consolation to Christians was instituted at the very same time when human malignancy was engaged in betraying the Saviour to his enemies.[19]

We are fully aware of the several possibilities proposed by Ellingworth, Davids, Ellingworth, Thiselton, Fitzmyer, Fee, and Morris. Here we are confronted with a complicated textual hermeneutic issue which from the information we have available may not be finalized with certainty. I am of the view that either

---

[19] Leon Morris, *1 Corinthians*, pp. 157f. Emphasis mine, IAF.

way this is held, Paul had in mind a dominical[20] tradition he had received, either directly or indirectly from Jesus, and either way the tradition had its origin with the Lord himself. It is a tradition that therefore carries with it the full authority of Jesus himself. In Paul's mind the instruction and tradition regarding the celebration of the Lord's Supper is thus an authoritarian, dominical, and apostolically accepted tradition regarding how the Lord's Supper should be celebrated.

It is clear from the seriousness of the discussion, depicted by Paul's clear condemnation of the Corinthians' debauchery, and his charge that they were despising the church or the body of Christ in their practice, that Paul was referring to a dominical tradition with roots in Jesus' institution of the Eucharist. Careful reading of the text in the context of Paul's condemnation of the Corinthian behavior does fit well with an instruction that originated with Jesus. Careful reading of the texts sets the tradition of the Eucharist firmly within the context of Jesus' institution of the Lord's Supper during the Passover Feast which was a "dominical" type of feast of remembrance instituted by YHWH through Moses at Ex 12:11ff, OT *passim*. The regular practice of the church in the 1st century, in the context of the meaning of *eucháristos, thanksgiving,* speaks of *remembrance in the tradition of the Passover*!

A side issue here is that the Passover Feast was not optional, to be celebrated if Israel thought it a good idea! In similar vein, neither was the Eucharist an option to the Christians to celebrate if they felt it a good idea, hence Paul's sharp condemnation of the Corinthian corruption.

The major issue in the Corinthian correspondence was their disloyalty to the principles of Christ, hence his sharp rebuke at 1 Cor 5:6f over a brother living in open adultery:

> *⁶ Your boasting is not good. Do you not know that a little leaven leavens the whole lump? ⁷ Cleanse out the old leaven that you may be a new lump, as you really are un-*

---

[20] Dominical, a saying or tradition relating to or from Jesus Christ as Lord. Cf. Oxford English Dictionary.

leavened. For Christ, our paschal lamb, has been sacrificed. [8] Let us, therefore, celebrate the festival, not with the old leaven, the leaven of malice and evil, but with the unleavened bread of sincerity and truth.

It is in the same disloyalty to Christ that the church in Corinth was denigrating the Eucharist by treating it simply either as a Love Feast, or an ordinary meal. Thus Paul took the celebration of the Lord's Supper back to the original purpose of Jesus, the institution and remembrance theme of the Lord's death.

Referring back to Jesus' instruction regarding the Lord's Supper, at 1 Cor 11:25ff Paul clarified Jesus' instruction:

and when he [Jesus] had given thanks, he broke it, and said, "This is my body which is for you. <u>Do this in remembrance of me</u>." [25] In the same way also the cup, after supper, saying, "This cup is the new covenant in my blood. Do this, <u>as often as you drink it</u>, in remembrance of me." [26] For as often as you eat this bread and drink the cup, <u>you proclaim the Lord's death until he comes</u>.

From the above discussions on the significance of the term *tradition* it seems obvious that both Jesus and Paul saw the purpose of the tradition regarding the Lord's Supper as an *act of remembering* all that Jesus' death meant to the Christian faith. *The ceremony was one of remembrance* and not an atoning repetition of Jesus' sacrifice as is held by those who interpret the feast under the term Transubstantiation in which it is believed that the one *eating the body and drinking the blood* was literally eating Jesus' body and drinking his shed blood, thus substantive real participation in Jesus' atoning sacrifice. The Eucharist was not a repetitive sacrifice for the remission of sins, but *a celebration of remembering Jesus' atoning death* and all that Jesus had accomplished on the cross.

Thiselton draws attention to the point that remembering does not simply mean calling to mind, but involves a participation in what is being remembered:

When we place *this kind of reflection* alongside the *biblical* traditions concerning **remembrance, do this in remembrance of me** takes on a fuller and more accurate meaning than the inadequate notions that have beset the dated "subjective" versus "objective" debates of the past. **Remembrance** of Christ and of Christ's death (i) retains the biblical aspect of a *self-involving remembering in gratitude, worship, trust, acknowledgment, and obedience* (see biblical examples above). (ii) It also carries with it the experience of *being "there" in identification with the crucified Christ who is also "here" in his raised presence*. However, still further, it embraces (iii) a *self-transforming retrieval of the founding event of the personal identity of the believer (as a believer) and the corporate identity of the church (as the Christian church of God)* as well as (iv) a *looking forward to the new "possibility" for transformed identity opened up by the eschatological consummation* (v. 25). All of this is gathered together in Paul's point that such **remembrance** constitutes a self-involving *proclamation of Christ's death* through a life and a lifestyle which derives from understanding our identity as Christians in terms of sharing the identity of Christ who is **for** the "other."[21]

In a later comment Thiselton observes:

> The repetition of **do this in remembrance of me** in conjunction with ὁσάκις ἐὰν πίνητε underlines the four self-involving aspects which we described in connection with the bread: (1) trust and grateful acknowledgment; (2) identification with Christ and his death as those who were "there"; (3) allowing a reshaping of narrative identity in accordance with the founding event which defines the Christian story; and (4) looking ahead to projected eschatological worlds which give meaning to present identity and to present endeavor ..."[22]

Zodhiates discusses the Greek word ἀνάμνησις *anámnēsis* translated as *remembering* in both Old and New Testament contexts:

---

[21] Thiselton, *First Corinthians,*. p. 880. Cf. also Fee, *1 Corinthians*, p. 552ff; Fitzmyer, *First Corinthians*, pp. 440ff.
[22] Thiselton, *First Corinthians* pp. 885–886.

ἀνάμνησις *anámnēsis* ... to remind. Remembrance. A commemoration (Heb. 10:3). A memorial (Luke 22:19; 1 Cor. 11:24, 25), as applied to the Lord's Supper. "In remembrance of me" means that the participant should remember Christ and the expiatory sacrifice of His death. The memory of the greatness of the sacrifice should cause the believer to abstain from sin. See Septuagint.: Num. 10:10; Ps. 38:1.[23]

The point Jesus, Paul, and others made by using the word ἀνάμνησις *anámnēsis* was that this act of *remembering* was not simply a cognitive recalling but a *dynamic life involving action* in which what Jesus did on the cross and implied in the institution was *a constant life changing experience* and encounter with Jesus' death and resurrection.

Blomberg elaborates on this:
> Each time the Corinthians ate the bread of the Lord's Supper, they should have recalled this death and acted in ways consistent with Christ's immeasurable self-giving and grace on their behalf. The last line of verse 24 (and v. 25) is probably best translated, "Do this as my memorial."[24]

Fitzmyer and others have pointed to the fact that the *verb* in the expression "this *do*," τοῦτο ποιεῖτε, *touto poiēte,* is a present imperative plural verb from ποιέω, *poiéō,* which implies that the Corinthians *must keep on remembering,* or *continue remembering* Jesus' body and blood in the Lord's Supper. Fitzmyer expresses this well, *"Keep doing this ... Keep performing the same action over* [the} *bread ... "*[25]

This comment does not seem to imply that *whenever the church might decide to* gather and *remember* to celebrate the Lord's Supper they should do this by remembering Jesus' death! There is imbedded in this prefect tense verb a sense of *constant regular repetition!*

---

[23] Zodhiates, ἀνάμνησις *anámnēsis*.
[24] Blomberg, *1 Corinthians*, p. 790.
[25] Fitzmyer, *First Corinthians*, p. 440.

Zodhiates observes that the Greek word ὁσάκις, *hosákis* which might be translated simply as *whenever* does not necessarily imply an occasional remembering. He comments on the combination of *hosákis* with the particle *án,* a particle denoting supposition or possibility:

The two words together*, hosákis án*, mean however often, or as often as you do this (1 Cor. 11:25, 26). This means "each time that you do so" … it rather means that each and every time you do so, no matter whether frequently or otherwise, the Lord's table must be a reminder of Christ's death until He comes back. With eán, a conditional particle, *hosákis eán* reads as in Rev. 11:6, "*every time* they will".[26]

Fee at 1 Cor 11:26 explains in theological and Christological terms why Paul had focused on the abuse of the Lord's Supper which he had begun at 1 Cor 11:1 by commending the Corinthians for remembering him and the traditions he had delivered to them, obviously referring to the *traditions* he had received and had passed on to the Corinthians. At this point we will not engage the challenging interpretation of women wearing a head covering in the assembly but refer to it only as a point of Paul's commendation to the church. At 1 Cor 11:17 Paul's tone changed from commendation to condemnation! Note the opening word *but* at v. 17. *But* from the Greek δὲ is an adversative conjunction[27] in this context meaning *to the contrary.* He continues, *but,* [to the contrary] *in the following instructions I do not commend you, because when you come together it is not for the better but for the worse!*

At 1 Cor 11:26 Paul becomes more specific, *For as often as you eat this bread and drink the cup, you proclaim the Lord's death until he comes*. Fee picks up the discussion here by pointing to the opening word of 1 Cor 11:26, *for*, γάρ, *gár*; which Zodhiates describes as "a causative particle standing always after

---

[26] Zodhiates, ὁσάκις, *hosákis*. Emphasis mine, IAF.
[27] Zodhiates, δέ *dé*; a particle standing after one or two words in a clause, strictly adversative, but more frequently denoting transition or conversion, and serving to introduce something else, whether opposed to what precedes or simply continuative or explanatory. Generally it has the meaning of *but, and,* or *also, namely.*

one or more words in a clause *and expressing the reason for what has been before*, affirmed or implied ..."[28] Fee adds:

> The explanatory "for" suggests that he is now giving this reason for repeating the tradition at this point of the argument. It is not because they have forgotten the words, nor because they had abandoned the Lord's Supper. Rather, it is because their version of the Supper gives the lie to its original intent ... The bread and the cup of this meal together *signify the death* of the Lord; "For," he now explains, "as often as we do this, in *his* remembrance, we are to be reminded through proclamation of the salvation that was effected for us through that death."[29]

Paul's point was when they gathered together for the Lord's Supper, it was not to enjoy a meal or feast, but to remember what the Supper really signified; Jesus' atoning death, and by remembering they would proclaim his death until he returns.

There is no reason that the expression *whenever* in the context of either Jesus' or Paul's instruction should be understood to mean *whenever you decide to celebrate* the Lord's Supper, whether once a month, or once a year, or on any occasion you decide to do so, as is the practice of some churches. Paul's instruction is quite clear, *whenever* you gather together in the assembly, *you must do so in remembrance of Jesus' death*, and not simply for a meal or some corrupt form of Love Feast. We will note shortly that the early apostolic church was of the habit of gathering together on the first day of each week to celebrate the Lord's death, and by so doing they proclaimed the Lord's death, and would do so until he returned. Their gathering was not simply to engage in some form of Love Feast, for in doing so the Corinthian congregation had desecrated the holy feast into a common meal where people ate and drank wine as in an ordinary meal. Paul instructed them that *whenever* they gathered together there was to be nothing ordinary or mundane about the Eucharist! In the act of remembering they should be pulling the past actions of Jesus, his death, *into their lives*, and would be proclaiming and

---

[28] Zodhiates, *γάρ, gár*.
[29] Fee, *First Corinthians*, p. 556. Cf. also Fitzmyer, *First Corinthians.*, pp. 444f.

celebrating the center of their faith until Jesus returned. Theologically, the appropriate practice of the Lord's Supper pulled the past, present, and future into a magnificent proclamation of their faith.

Thus, in explaining Jesus' *instructions* and referring to them as *traditions*, Paul stressed that the celebration of the Lord's Supper should not degenerate into a common meal, but should be experienced and enjoyed *as often as they eat or drink it,* that is, as *often* as the church gathered together in worship, in a manner that both recalled and embodied the full meaning of the purpose of Jesus' death and institution of the Lord's Supper. As Paul indicates in his discussion of the Lord's Supper in 1 Cor 11 the celebration was not to be a haphazard, careless, simply emotional experience but one guided by serious theological thought and vigilant adherence to a tradition that had its roots in Jesus' own instruction, and one carefully followed by the early apostolic church.

As we will shortly observe while exploring Paul's visit to Troas, Acts 20:5-12, churches in the context of Acts 20:7,1 Cor 16:2, in the 1st and 2nd centuries, gathered to worship on the first day of the week (Acts 20:7), or the first day of *every* week (1 Cor 16:2)! We have previously examined the several gatherings of the early church, gatherings for a variety of reasons, one of which was the celebration of the Lord's Supper.

Paul, Troas, and Acts 20:7

Luke has presented us with a fairly descriptive pericope at Acts 20:1-16 of Paul's journey on his way to Jerusalem to present the gracious gift of the Gentile churches to the Jerusalem church. Earlier, Luke had indicated that he had approached his task of writing with careful attention to details:

> ^{1} *Inasmuch as many have undertaken to compile a narrative of the things which have been accomplished among us,* ^{2} just as they were delivered to us by those who from the beginning were eyewitnesses and ministers of the word, ^{3} *it seemed good to me also,* having followed all things closely *for some time past, to* write an orderly account for you, *most excellent The-ophilus,* ^{4} that you may

know the truth concerning the things of which you have been informed.[30]

Since Luke-Acts were originally one book (narrative) in two volumes (scrolls) we have every reason to believe Luke approached his writing of Acts with the same attitude of careful examination of the details involved!

In Acts 20:7 we learn that it was on the first day of the week that Paul and the Christians gathered and partook of the Lord's Supper. Luke indicates in v. 6, *et al,* that he was with the group in Troas so he had first-hand experience of this gathering:

> *¹ After the uproar ceased, Paul sent for the disciples and having exhorted them took leave of them and departed for Macedonia. ² When he had gone through these parts and had given them much encouragement, he came to Greece. ³ There he spent three months, and when a plot was made against him by the Jews as he was about to set sail for Syria, he determined to return through Macedonia. ⁴ Sopater of Beroea, the son of Pyrrhus, accompanied him; and of the Thessalonians, Aristarchus and Secundus; and Gaius of Derbe, and Timothy; and the Asians, Tychicus and Trophimus. ⁵ These went on and were waiting for us at Troas, ⁶ but we sailed away from Philippi after the days of Unleavened Bread, and in five days we came to them at Troas, where we stayed for seven days.*
>
> *⁷ On the first day of the week, when we were gathered together to break bread, Paul talked with them, intending to depart on the morrow; and he prolonged his speech until midnight. ⁸ There were many lights in the upper chamber where we were gathered. ⁹ And a young man named Eutychus was sitting in the window. He sank into a deep sleep as Paul talked still longer; and being overcome by sleep, he fell down from the third story and was taken up dead. ¹⁰ But Paul went down and bent over him, and embracing him said, "Do not be alarmed, for his life is in him." ¹¹ And when Paul had gone up and had broken bread and eaten, he conversed with them a long while,*

---

[30] Luke 1:1-4.

until daybreak, and so departed. ⁻¹² And they took the lad away alive, and were not a little comforted.

¹³ <u>But going ahead to the ship, we set sail for Assos</u>, intending to take Paul aboard there; for so he had arranged, intending himself to go by land. ¹⁴ And when he met us at Assos, we took him on board and came to Mitylene. ¹⁵ And sailing from there we came the following day opposite Chios; the next day we touched at Samos; and the day after that we came to Miletus. ¹⁶ For Paul had decided to sail past Ephesus, so that he might not have to spend time in Asia; for he was hastening to be at Jerusalem, if possible, on the day of Pentecost.

Of particular relevance to our study, note that at v. 7 Luke stresses that it was *on the first day of the week* that the disciples were gathered *for the breaking of bread*. During the gathering Paul preached a sermon to the gathered group.

Several issues of interest to our study surface in Luke's account. *First*, there is the mention of the *first day* of the week and the discussion as to whether this was Saturday evening or Sunday evening is addressed. *Then* there is the discussion of the gathering to break bread, whether this was an ordinary meal or a sacred meal as in the Lord's Supper or both, and *finally*, what is implied in the meaning of the expression *when we were gathered* together.

First, we have this interesting and perplexing question: was this reference to the first day of the week, that is the day following the Sabbath day! On the Jewish calendar the Sabbath day concluded at sunset on the Sabbath, or the seventh day, and the first day of the week began on the evening of the Sabbath *after* sunset. This raises the question of whether Luke was referencing the Jewish calendar, or the Gentile Julian Roman calendar introduced by Julius Caesar ca 46 BCE. We will note that the opinions of the scholars vary indicating that there are several challenging issues relating to addressing this question. At the same time there is the meaning or the purpose of the breaking of the bread. Each of these questions are covered well in the following scholarly citations:

F. F. Bruce in his commentary on Acts suggests that this *gathering* was the *first day of the week, Sunday, according to the Gentile, Roman Julian calendar*, with Paul departing on the next day, Monday, the second day of the week:

> The reference to the meeting for the breaking of the bread on "the first day of the week" is the earliest text we have from which *it may be inferred with reasonable certainty that Christians regularly came together for worship on that day. The breaking of the bread was probably a fellowship meal in the course of which the Eucharist was celebrated (cf. 2:42).* It is plain from the narrative that members of the church at Troas ("they") were present as well as the travelers of Paul's company ("we"); the occasion was probably the church's weekly meeting for worship. Paul's ministry in Troas a year or two previously had evidently been more fruitful than he realized at the time (2 Cor. 2:12–13). This Sunday (perhaps April 24, A.D.) was the travelers' last full day at Troas; they were to continue their journey the next day. The meeting was held in the evening *(Bruce footnote: On Sunday evening, not Saturday evening. Luke is not using the Jewish reckoning from sunset to sunset but the reckoning from midnight to midnight: although it was apparently after sunset when they met, their departure in the morning was "the next day.")—a convenient time for many members of the Gentile churches*, who were not their own masters and were not free in the daytime—and Paul conversed with them. Church meetings were not regulated by the clock in those days, and the opportunity of listening to Paul was not one to be cut short; what did it matter if his conversation went on until midnight?[31]

John Polhill in his commentary on Acts adopts a similar view to that of Bruce:

> 20:7 Paul and his traveling companions spent a week in Troas (20:6), evidently awaiting the departure of their

---

[31] Bruce, *Acts* (revised), 1988, Kindle locations 12293-13315.

ship. *On their last day there, which happened to be a Sunday, Paul met with the Christians for worship. This is one of the earliest references to Christians meeting for worship on Sunday, the first day of the week.* Christians may have continued to observe the Jewish Sabbath as well, but eventually the Lord's resurrection day became the sole day of worship for Christians.

At Troas, aware of his intended departure the next day, Paul hung on to every minute with the Christians there and spoke well into the night, even until midnight. There is some question whether this was Saturday night or Sunday night. If Luke's reckoning was the normal Jewish method, it would have been Saturday night, since the days were reckoned as beginning at sunset and running until the following sunset. *If Luke was following Roman reckoning, and this seems to have been the case, days were reckoned from midnight to midnight, as is our own procedure.* It thus would have been Sunday night, and Paul's projected departure was Monday morning. In any event, at Troas we are given a glimpse into the main elements of an early Christian worship service. It was observed on the first day of the week and consisted of the breaking of bread (the Lord's Supper) and preaching. That the Lord's Supper was accompanied by a larger fellowship meal may be indicated by the reference to their "eating" in v. 11 (cf. 1 Cor 11:20f.).[32]

Peter Wagner seems open to the Julian calendar, but appears to be ambivalent on this:

> Many of the commentators who write about this passage draw the conclusion from the phrase "the first day of the week, when the disciples came together to break bread" that by this time in A.D. 57, Sunday worship had become normal for Christians. The traditional worship day for the Jews, of course, was Saturday—the Sabbath or the last day of the week. Although … most Christians conduct their primary worship services on Sunday. The

---

[32] Polhill, *Acts*, p. 418.

roots of Sunday worship, interestingly enough, go back largely to custom and consensus rather than to explicit biblical mandate. *In the particular case of Troas, it could be argued at least as strongly that the only reason the Christians met on the first day of the week was that Paul's ship was scheduled to sail the second day of the week.* It could well have been a farewell party, highlighted perhaps by the Lord's Supper ...*In any case, it is known that Christians eventually decided that they should worship on Sunday to honor the Lord's resurrection on the first day of the week.* It is also true that this occurred in a Roman social setting where Sunday, not Saturday, was the day off each week. In any event, by the end of the first century, Sunday was being called the "Lord's Day," according to The Didache, an ancient record of the apostles' teachings (Didache 14:1). Whether this was the practice at the time of the meeting in Troas, however, is questionable.[33]

Carl Holladay's comments on Acts 20:7f are in two forms, first a list of footnotes and then a brief running commentary. I have listed the running commentary first followed by the footnotes in which much of the weight of the commentary depends. Holladay's view is similar to that of Bruce and Polhill, favoring the Sunday evening meeting and the Julian Gentile calendar:

> This episode presupposes a community of believers in Troas although one has not been reported previously (cf. 16:8, 11). The "we" passage from 20:5– 6 continues, but the "we" in verses 7– 15 now includes the seven Pauline coworkers (v. 4) who have traveled to Troas. "Common meal" renders *klasai arton*, "to break bread," which ordinarily means "to eat" or "have a meal," usually together (cf. 2:42, 46; 27:35), but since the phrase is used of the Eucharist in Luke 22:19 || Mark 14:22 || Matt 26:26, here it may have the sense of "sacred meal" (similarly, 1 Cor 10:16– 17; 11:23– 26). "Engaged in a discussion" (*dielegeto*, v. 7; also v. 9, dialegomenou) suggests give-

---

[33] Wagner, *Acts*, Kindle locations 8617-8631.

and-take dialogue with an argumentative edge. "Upstairs room" (*en tō hyperōō*, v. 8) probably implies a private home ... "Talking for a long time until daybreak" ... does not suggest an all-night monologue since *homileō* is a Lukan term for dialogue, thus conversing ... For all of its brevity and lively humor, this story provides a capsule description of an early Christian meeting, with distinctive features or activities that one might encounter as part of such a group: *a Sunday night meeting in a private home, thus as a house church; a communal meal, "breaking bread," that easily acquires a eucharistic character*; extended discussion, conversation, and discourse led by Paul or some other prominent teacher; a miracle or some other dramatic display of power ....

Holladay's footnotes:

a. Lit., "on the first of the Sabbath(s)" (*en tē mia tōn sabbatōn*). The singular *sabbaton* typically refers to the seventh day of the week, the Jewish Sabbath, which begins at sunset on Friday and concludes at sunset on Saturday. Sometimes the singular form refers to a period of seven days (Luke 18:12; Mark 16:9; 1 Cor 16:2). The pl. sabbata (or genitive *sabbatōn*) can refer to a period of seven days. The phrase used here is a shortened form of *hē mia hēmera tōn sabbatōn*, i.e., the first day of the week. This latter phrase is used of Easter morning in Luke 24:1 || Mark 16:2 || Matt 28:1 || John 20:1 (cf. 19:31; 20:19); cf. 1 Cor 16:2 (*kata mian sabbatou*). Since Jewish chronology reckons the day from sunset to sunset, the main interpretive question here is whether the gathering is envisioned as occurring on Saturday or Sunday evening, probably the latter.

b. Lit., "we having gathered together to break bread" (*synēgmenōn hēmōn klasai arton*).

c. Instead of lampades, "lamps," the D-text reads *hypolampades*, possibly "small windows" or "lookout holes," thereby anticipating the mention of a window in v. 9. Metzger 1998, 422; BDAG 1038 s.v. hypolampas.

d. Lit., "while Paul was discussing at length" (*dialegomenou tou Paulou epi pleion*).

e. Lit., "being overwhelmed by the sleep" (*katenechtheis apo tou hypnou*).

f. Lit., "he was taken up dead" (*ērthē nekros*).

g. Lit., "both having broken the bread and having eaten" (*kai klasas ton arton kai geusamenos*).

h. Lit., "and they led [brought] the boy alive" (*ēgagon de ton paida zōnta*).

i. Lit., "they were encouraged not moderately" (*pareklēthēsan ou metriōs*).[34]

I. Howard Marshall adopts the same viewpoint as Bruce, Polhill, Wagner, and Holladay regarding Luke's use of the Julian Roman calendar rather than the Jewish Calendar:

> The disciples in Troas gathered together on the first day of the week (Luke 24:1) to break bread and to have a last opportunity of listening to Paul. The breaking of bread is the term used especially in Acts for the celebration of the Lord's Supper (2:42; cf. 1 Cor. 10:16), and this passage is of particular interest in providing the first allusion to the Christian custom of meeting on the first day of the week for the purpose. It is not altogether clear what method of time reckoning Luke is employing. According to the Jewish method of calculating the new day from sunset, Paul would have met with the Christians on what was Saturday evening by our reckoning and would thus have resumed his journey on Sunday morning. According to the Roman method of reckoning the new day as beginning at dawn, the Christians would have met in the evening of either Sunday (the first day of the Jewish week) or Saturday (the first day of the Roman week). Since elsewhere Luke reckons the hours of the day from dawn (3:1), he appears to follow the Roman method of time reckoning and the Jewish calendar (cf. Luke 24:1). Bruce (Book, p. 408 n.25) argues that he regards the following morning,

---

[34] Holladay, *Acts*, pp. 390-391.

on which Paul intended to depart as the morrow, and that 'daybreak' in verse 11 signifies the beginning of the new day; hence the meeting was on Sunday evening and Paul departed on Monday morning. Paul's address to the church lasted until midnight. This may seem a long time by modern Western standards (cf. also 28:23), but in some countries, especially in the Third World, services lasting for several hours with correspondingly long sermons are quite common. Added to this fact, which could have wearied some of the congregation, the upper room (1:13; 9:37) where the disciples were gathered was lit by oil lamps. The simplest explanation of the motive for mentioning these is that they emitted an odour which helped to send Eutychus off to sleep. Haenchen (p. 585 n.2.) comments that if Eutychus, seated by a window, fell asleep, how much more must the other people in the room away from ventilation have felt sleepy; he evidently forgets that some people become sleepy more quickly than others. Surely here we have a piece of eyewitness information.[35]

From the above references it seems reasonable to conclude that this visit and gathering was on Sunday evening, the first day of the week, during which the Pauline group shared a meal with the congregation at Troas, and during which at some point the Lord's Supper was celebrated. As mentioned by several scholars this is the earliest reference in Scripture of Christians gathering together for a meal during which the Lord's Supper was celebrated on the first day of the week.

C. F. D. Moule, the dean of British New Testament Scholars in his *magnus opus* on worship in the New Testament concurs with the above statement and concludes his discussion of Acts 20:7 with this remark:

> Almost all we have to go by, therefore … is the fact that in Acts 20:7 coming together on the first day of the week to break bread is mentioned as though it were a matter of course. But a weekly "coming together" is further

---

[35]Marshall, *Acts*, pp. 344, 345.

suggested by the fact that in 1 Cor 16:1f. St Paul instructs the Corinthians to make an allocation of money ... In Didache14:1 the injunction to come together every "Lord's day" ... to break bread is explicit the term "the Lord's day" ... suggests that it was a day for worship ...

To Sum up thus far, there appears to be sufficient evidence for believing that, from the earliest days, a sacrament such as came to be called Holy Communion or Eucharist was celebrated, probably weekly, and usually in the context of a communal meal.[36]

Before we close this section regarding the weekly Eucharist or Lord's Supper there is one more item of interest! It relates to the Greek expression *when we were gathered together*, which is wrapped up in the Greek verbal preposition συνηγμένων, *sunēgmenōn*. *First*, the verbal preposition derives from the verb συνάγω, *sunágō* which Zodhiates describes as *to lead, assemble, gather together*.[37] *Second*, being a verbal participle of a perfect tense verb implies *a continuous activity with its root in the past*, that is, the activity was begun in the past and continues in the present. This speaks to a *habitual practice that began at some time in the past*.[38] In regard to Acts 20:7 the tense and mood of the verb and the nature of the participle functioning as a modal participle imply that the disciples were *of the habit of gathering on the first day of the week*. Furthermore, this implies that the gathering on the first day of the week was for a reason other than simply for a common evening meal. They may very well have eaten an evening meal, but the emphasis was on the established habit of gathering for the Lord's Supper, not just eating a common meal which they most likely did every day of the week!

---

[36] Moule, *Worship*, pp. 28ff.
[37] Zodhiates, συνάγω, *sunágō*.
[38] Cf. Dana and Mantey, *A Manual Grammar of the Greek New Testament*, pp. 203f.

Chapter 11: Prayer

It should not come as a surprise that prayer, along with baptism and the Lord's Supper, forms the heart of the Christian *sacraments*,[1] or defining acts of worship! If we are permitted to use the term sacrament without incorporating a Roman Catholic doctrine!

Prayer is pivotal to Christian worship, personal and corporate in the Sunday worship assembly and in the Christian's private daily worship!

Prayer was critical and central in Jesus' relationship with his Father and his disciples. Jesus prayed often and taught his disciples to pray by example and personal instruction. Watch Jesus praying to his Father in the garden of Gethsemane shortly before his betrayal, Matt 26:36ff, and then in private on the mountain, Matt 14:23, *"And after he had dismissed the crowds, he went up on the mountain by himself to pray."* Luke informs us that the disciples of Jesus were aware of John the Baptist teaching his disciples to pray, and asked Jesus to teach them to pray, consequently we have that magnificent model prayer of Jesus as recorded at Luke 11:1-13, and at Matt 6:9ff when Jesus was instructing his disciples of the danger of hypocritical prayer as exampled by the Gentiles. We will return to that model prayer shortly. But Jesus also taught his disciples by example to pray by praying with them as on the night before his betrayal, and in John 17:1ff.

> [1] *When Jesus had spoken these words, he lifted up his eyes to heaven and said, "Father, the hour has come; glorify thy Son that the Son may glorify thee,* [2] *since thou hast given him power over all flesh, to give eternal life to all whom thou hast given him.* [3] *And this is eternal life, that they know thee the only true God, and Jesus Christ whom thou hast sent.* [4] *I glorified thee on earth, having accomplished the work which thou gavest me to do;* [5] *and now,*

---

[1] *Sacrament*, a Christian rite such as baptism, the Eucharist, and prayer that are believed to have been ordained by Christ and are a sign or symbol of corporate membership in the church.

> *Father, glorify thou me in thy own presence with the glory which I had with thee before the world was made.*

Neither should it come as a surprise that prayer would feature prominently in the worship liturgy of the early Jerusalem church, and then in churches down through the centuries.

Previously to the Christian era, prayer played a prominent role in the liturgy surrounding the Second Temple, and in the Synagogue. Times of trouble, both political and religious uncertainty, not to mention deep spiritual concern, formed a nucleus for spiritual and faith formation.

The interaction of the individual and the "temple," whether it be the Hindu shrine, the Jewish Temple, the Islamic Mosque, or the Christian Congregation, has been an integral part of the richness of life enjoyed by the individual since time immemorable.

David Wells, in a remarkable analysis of the present day postmodern autonomous individual in comparison to the individual of Martin Luther's 16th century, has argued that what made Luther's Reformation so effective was his ability to see himself and all others in a relationship with God and His Word and grace through faith in Christ. Personal fulfillment in isolation from an external truth leads only to frustration and hopelessness. There must be an external truth by which one measures oneself for personal value, and that truth is found in a deep relationship with God through a deep community worship of Jesus Christ.[2]

Now you may ask, what has that to do with prayer and congregational communal prayer? The same thought is true in regard to worship. I have heard it said on too many occasions in the church that personal private worship is more important than congregational Sunday worship services. The Scripture reference cited is Rom 12:1ff. Usually, this comes from those who have not experienced a full life of fellowship and praise in a church worship service, and who have not spent enough time really reading the Scriptures both in private and in the worship assembly. I will address this last point in the next chapters.

---

[2] Wells, *The Courage to Be Protestant Reformation Faith in Today's World*, pp. 38ff.

As I have on occasion been prone to note, there are those who claim that the importance of communal worship in the assembly far exceeds the value of personal worship, citing the role of worship in the Temple, the Synagogue in Judaism, and the Church in Christianity. There is much to be said for this, as I will shortly reference, but the whole dynamic is in error! Private worship in the absence of community worship in the church assembly is in one sense bankrupt, or at least seriously impoverished! Likewise, Community worship in the absence of private worship is simply not scriptural!

Community worship and prayer enrich private worship and prayer, while private worship and prayer plays out in life the dynamic learned from community worship and prayer.

What we are examining here is the role of prayer in community Sunday worship services. For an examination of personal prayer, I recommend Tony Ash, *Pray Always*, Leafwood Publishers, 2008.

Paul Helm in the *Baker Encyclopedia of the Bible* has written regarding prayer in the "temple" context:

> Prayer is both a private and a congregational activity. It is an integral part of church worship for the essence of worship—God being addressed as "Thou"—cannot be conceived apart from prayer. So, worship cannot be scriptural unless prayer is included.
>
> This does not mean simply that prayer ought to be an ingredient in worship, but that the structure which the Christian gospel gives to services of worship is impossible to achieve without prayer. This structure might be expressed as: Sin—Grace—Faith. Worship starts from the recognition of sin and need (hence, prayers of confession of sin), proceeding to an awareness of God's provision of forgiveness, righteousness, and new life in Christ, in turn leading to the response of faith (prayer and praise for pardon, thanksgiving to God for his "unspeakable gift," and intercession to God for that grace for others). So not only

is prayer an element in gospel-worship, that worship is shapeless without prayer.³

Luke mentioned at Luke 2:36-38 the deep devotion of Anna whose deep personal devotion and expectation of God's fulfillment of his promises was so deep that she spent the closing years of her life in the Temple;

> *And there was a prophetess, Anna, the daughter of Phanuel-el, of the tribe of Asher; she was of a great age, having lived with her husband seven years from her virginity, ³⁷ and as a widow till she was eighty-four. She did not depart from the temple, <u>worshiping with fasting and prayer night and day</u>. ³⁸ And coming up at that very hour she gave thanks to God, and spoke of him to all who were looking for the redemption of Jerusalem.*

We learn of the practice of the disciples praying in the Temple also from Acts 2:41ff;

> *So those who received his word were baptized, and there were added that day about three thousand souls.*
> *⁴² And they devoted themselves to the apostles' teaching and fellowship, to the breaking of bread and the prayers.*
> *⁴³ And fear came upon every soul; and many wonders and signs were done through the apostles. ⁴⁴ And all who believed were together and had all things in common; ⁴⁵ and they sold their possessions and goods and distributed them to all, as any had need. ⁴⁶ <u>And day by day, attending the temple together and breaking bread in their homes</u>, they partook of food with glad and generous hearts, ⁴⁷ praising God and having favor with all the people. And the Lord added to their number day by day those who were being saved.*

I have already commented above about the profound role the Synagogue played in the pattern of worship adopted by the early church. In the absence of the sacrificial cult, in the Synagogue the reading of the Law as *Torah* and prayer formed the heart of Synagogue worship. A sermon or homily was included in the

---

³ Helm, *Baker Encyclopedia of the Bible*, p. 1749.

Synagogue liturgy when one was present who was capable of delivering such. Paul's experience in Synagogues throughout the diaspora bears testimony to his being invited to preach in the Synagogue.

Eric Meyers in *The Anchor Bible Dictionary* observes regarding the Synagogue;

> *The meeting place and prayer hall of the Jewish people since antiquity. During Second Temple times the term "synagogue" referred both to a group of people and/or a building or institution. Although these notions are not mutually exclusive, it is quite probable that at its inception the synagogue did not refer to an actual building but to a group or community of individuals who met together for worship and religious purposes.*[4]

David A. Fiensy draws attention to the standard form of prayer one would expect to find in a diaspora Synagogue, illustrating that prayer played a prominent role in the Synagogue liturgy. His opening comments reinforce this view. His point is that there appears to have been a standard form of prayer in diaspora Hellenistic Synagogues;

> *The title "Hellenistic Synagogal Prayers" (Hel. Syn. Pr.) summarizes what scholars such as K. Kohler, W. Bousset, and E. R. Goodenough have concluded regarding certain prayers in the Greek language scattered throughout the Christian Apostolic Constitutions (Apos. Con.).*[5]

Turning now to early Christian comments regarding the role that prayer played in the early Christian's life Everett Ferguson references several resources documenting prayers in the early Christian experience. There is little specific reference in the early Christian literature to prayer in the worship assembly, but there are numerous references to prayer in the daily life of Christians. Ferguson observes;

---

[4] Meyers, "Synagogue," *Anchor Yale Bible Dictionary*, Vol. 6, p. 262.
[5] Fiensy, "Prayers, Hellenistic Synagogal," *Anchor Yale Bible Dictionary*, Vol. 5, p. 450.

> *Prayer occupied an important place in the daily life of Christians. The Didache provided that one pray three times a day ... In addition, provision was made at certain places for daily meetings at the beginning of the day for communal prayer and instruction ... The pervasiveness of prayer in the lives of the Christians may be seen in the number of prayers written on potsherds and scraps of papyrus or inscribed on tombstones, houses, and churches ... Morning prayers were made facing the east ...* [6]

The emphasis on prayers on every day of the week and the many instructions regarding the need for regular prayer certainly infer that prayer was a regular part of their weekly worship services. Ferguson observes that it was not the practice of the early church to recite the Lord's Prayer in communal prayer service but he observes that this prayer formed the structure around which prayers were uttered. [7]

It is not surprising that the theology of daily prayer would flow naturally in, and out of, the Sunday worship service! The influence of the Psalms of the Old Testament in both Jewish and Christian life and worship would naturally have an impact on the structure and practice of worship in the early church. Several theologians discussing the importance of daily prayer in daily worship of God have commented meaningfully on the importance of prayer as a component of the weekly Sunday worship service that brings *balance* to one's daily prayers. The dynamic of public worship, which essentially focuses the attention of congregational worship on God, brings direction and balance to our daily prayer and worship of God.

Robert Webber observes in regard to this balance:

> Finally, an important Hebrew word associated with worship is *hodah*, "to give thanks." Several times the Psalms invite us to "give thanks to the LORD, for he is good" (Ps. 136:1). This word conveyed more than what we understand by gratitude. It meant "to make confes-

---

[6] Ferguson, *Early Christians Speak*, vol. 1, pp. 140.
[7] Ferguson, *Early Christians Speak*.

sion," in the sense of affirming the Lord as God. For biblical worshipers, giving thanks was directly related to covenantal worship, Israel's pledge of loyalty to the Great King. The comparable Greek word is *exomologeo* (sic), the verb used by Paul when he declared "that at the name of Jesus every knee should bow … and every tongue confess that Jesus Christ is Lord, to the glory of God the Father" (Phil. 2:10–11). Paul's image is a powerful picture of the purpose of Christian worship.[8]

An important point that Walker draws attention to is the *covenantal* role that worship and prayer play in the Christian's life. Worship and corporate prayer emphasize the covenantal relationship Christians enjoy with God. God has called us and saved us and in Christ has expressed a covenant between himself and the believer; Christians in worship and prayer express and acknowledge that covenantal relationship in thanksgiving and faithfulness.

James White likewise emphasizes the balance that communal prayer in the worship service brings to private daily prayer.

> When one reviews the dynamics of other forms of Christian worship one is struck by the degree to which they predominantly express God's gracious self-giving to people. The normal Sunday service of the word is oriented around the proclamation of God's word through readings, a sermon, music, and other arts. The eucharist, too, largely focuses on God's self-giving through actions with bread and wine. It is true that such services do include elements of hymnody, psalmody, and prayer, but their emphasis is elsewhere. Daily public prayer has a different and more personal focus: our response in praise to God in the midst of daily life. It is a response not just to word and sacraments but to the totality of daily experience—the sun coming up, the squabbles in the family, the tedium of work. Thus it is a sharing of our words to God in a corporate fashion. Even though common forms must

---

[8] Webber, *Worship Old and New,* Kindle location 447-452.

be used to make it fully communal, each of us supplies the gifts for which we give thanks, the complaints that we express, the joys for which we give praise. This ability to express ourselves in the setting of daily life makes daily public prayer distinctive. Much of the importance of this kind of worship is in giving balance. This operates on several levels. There is a need to balance daily public prayer with the weekly rhythm of Sunday (or Sabbath) worship. We have previously mentioned the differing dynamics of the Sunday service of the word and the eucharist. It is, of course, possible to have daily sermons as Zwingli did in Zurich or a daily eucharist as some Roman Catholics and Anglicans do. But these have dynamics that services focusing on prayer and praise do not, and the more intimate quality of prayers provides a desirable balance to services better seen as weekly than as daily. There is also the matter of balance between public prayer and private prayer. We have not mentioned the latter, but it is assumed that public prayer is usually accompanied by prayer in private at other occasions during the day. Neither replaces the other; each strengthens its companion. We must, then, see private prayer as the other end of the same pole, not as a distinct object. Private prayer brings energy and focus to public prayer. But public prayer provides a good balance for private prayer in relating it to the whole of praying Christianity.[9]

Segler and Bradley discuss the importance of the Lord's model prayer and the role it should play in our corporate worship services:

> The prayer begins in adoration, as God's name is hallowed, and concludes in doxology, as all things are committed to God's purpose and glory. One dynamic characteristic of the early congregation of Christians in Jerusalem was its practice of continuing steadfastly in prayers (Acts 2:42). The Christians may have prayed at stated hours replacing the Jewish synagogue tradition. Their

---

[9] White, *Introduction to Christian Worship*, Kindle location 2410-2435.

prayers may have included both new and old elements as seen in Ephesians 5:19; Colossians 3:16; and James 5:13. The story of the church in Acts indicates that the people joined as a congregation in the practice of common prayer. When Peter and John returned from prison, the congregation lifted up their voices together to God and said: "'Sovereign Lord, who made the heaven and the earth, the sea, and everything in them, it is you who said by the Holy Spirit through our ancestor David, your servant: "Why did the Gentiles rage, and the peoples imagine vain things?" ... When they had prayed, the place in which they were gathered together was shaken; and they were all filled with the Holy Spirit and spoke the word of God with boldness'" (Acts 4:24–25, 31). Prayer is the heart of corporate worship.[10]

One focal comment on the balance brought to daily prayers by corporate worship prayer is that corporate prayer in the worship assembly brings direction, focus, and enrichment to our daily prayers and Christian life.

Since our focus on prayer in this study is prayer as an aspect of the Sunday worship assembly, we will explore the role the Lord's Prayer should play in our prayer liturgy.

If we take Jesus' model prayer at Matt 6:9ff seriously, we learn several salient principles that should characterize and drive both private and communal prayer. Jesus said:

Pray then like this:
Our Father who art in heaven,
   Hallowed be thy name.
   Thy kingdom come.
   Thy will be done,
      On earth as it is in heaven.
   Give us this day our daily bread;
And forgive us our debts,
   As we also have forgiven our debtors;
And lead us not into temptation,
   But deliver us from evil.

---

[10] Segler, *Christian Worship: Its Theology and Practice*, p. 121.

We note the structure of this prayer. It has five component parts:
1. Worship and adoration of God, vs 9b.
2. Prayer for God's sustenance, physical and spiritual, vs 11.
3. Prayer for forgiveness, vs 12.
4. Prayer for spiritual direction, vs 13a
5. Prayer for spiritual protection from evil, vs 13b.

Each of these components should feature prominently in our congregational prayers as we lead the congregation in reverent praise and worship.

Prominent in these prayer statements are the three imperatival phrases following the address to the Father, *Our Father who is in heaven:*
1. *Let your name*, (the person, who you are) *be sanctified*, (held holy on earth and in our lives) *just as it is in heaven.*
2. *Let your kingdom reign be seen on earth*, (and experienced in our lives) *just as it is in heaven.*
3. *Let you will be done* on earth, (and in our lives, on earth just) *as it is experienced in heaven.*

Then follow prayers relating our personal life, physical and spiritual:
4. *Give us this day our daily bread*, both physical and spiritual, or, as one translation expresses it, *give us today our needs for today*!

Christians who bow before the holy God recognize their failures and sins, and acknowledge this before God:
5. *Forgive us our debts, sins*, as we have forgiven those who have sinned against us.

One major reason Christians have assembled is the recognition of their need to be instructed, encouraged, and even chastised by our father.
6. *Lead us not into temptation* and *protect us from Satan and evil influences.*

From Jesus' prayers, and the prayers of Scripture, we learn that our prayers should involve every aspect of our life, and also our congregation's life. Our prayers should not be careless, haphazard, and meaningless, as Jesus warned his disciples at Matt

6:9 in his model prayer. Our prayers must occupy our minds, be carefully thought out; occupy our spirits, reflect the deepest aspects of our lives and relationship with God and others. Our prayers should include our needs and concerns for others, help for healing, sustenance, and strength, and focus and our commitment to others, both congregational and global.

In this regard, I am reminded of Paul's instruction to Timothy and the congregation at Ephesus, 1 Tim 2:1ff:

> *First of all,[11] then, I urge that <u>supplications, prayers, intercessions, and thanksgivings be made for all men</u>, ² for kings and all who are in high positions, that we may lead a quiet and peaceable life, godly and respectful in every way. ³ This is good, and it is acceptable in the sight of <u>God our Savior, ⁴ who desires all men to be saved and to come to the knowledge of the truth.</u> ⁵ For there is one God, and there is one mediator between God and men, the man Christ Jesus, ⁶ who gave himself as a ransom for all, the testimony to which was borne at the proper time. ⁷ For this I was appointed a preacher and apostle (I am telling the truth, I am not lying), a teacher of the Gentiles in faith and truth.*

Finally, there are several kinds of prayers illustrated in Scripture that express our need for God to be present and active in our lives, both as individuals and congregations.

Our prayer should include prayers of *praise*, Ps 31; of *thanksgiving*, Ps 34 of *confession* of sin, Ps 51, Ps 26; of *petition* for help; and of *intercession*.

---

[11] *First of all,* πρῶτος, *prōtos,* meaning *of primary importance.* Mounce, *Pastoral Epistles,* 1 Tim 2:1, p. 78, "Therefore, *above everything else,* I urge [you] to make requests, prayers, petitions, [and expressions of] thanksgiving on behalf of all people."

Chapter 12: Scripture

Conservative Christians understand Scripture to refer to the canonical books of the Old and New Testaments. They hold them to be the inspired, authoritative, and normative foundation to faith and practice in Christian churches.[1] This study lies deeply within that mindset.

In one sense this chapter on Scripture and the following on Preaching could be considered as one chapter but I have chosen to separate them for emphasis or focus. It is my view that Scripture is the foundation of all preaching and that the sermon or preaching alienated from Scripture fails to meet a defining category of preaching as is seen in both the Old and New Testaments. One can make announcements without bedding such in Scripture, but any reasonable person will be able to differentiate an announcement from the preaching of a sermon! Announcements are rooted in the needs of the community; a sermon is rooted in the message of Scripture!

A key Greek term that sets the scene for this brief discussion on the role of Scripture in a formal worship service is ἀναγινώσκω, *anaginóskō, public reading*. Zodhiates suggests that ἀναγινώσκω, *anaginóskō* has a fairly wide range of meanings, but essentially it carries the sense of *knowing by public reading*:

> ἀναγινώσκω, *anaginóskō. Knowing. To perceive accurately. Later it came to mean to recognize. In Attic Gr., it usually meant to read and always so in the NT and the Sept. The consequential meaning is to know by reading (Matt. 12:3, 5; 19:4; 21:16, 42; 22:31; 24:15; Mark 2:25; 12:10, 26; 13:14; Luke 6:3; 10:26; John 19:20; Acts 8:28, 30, 32; 15:31; 23:34; 2 Cor. 1:13; Eph. 3:4; Rev. 1:3; 5:4; Sept.: Deut. 17:19; 2 Kgs. 5:7; Is. 29:11, 12). To read aloud before others (Luke 4:16; Acts 13:27;*

---

[1] Cf. Bruce, *The New Testament Documents, Are They Reliable?*; Lightfoot, *How We Got the Bible*; Marshall, *New Testament Theology*; Wells, *The Courage to be Protestant;* Wells, *No Place for Truth.*

15:21; 2 Cor. 3:15; Col. 4:16; 1 Thess. 5:27; Sept.: Deut. 31:11; 2 Kgs. 22:11; Neh. 13:1).[2]

Rudolf Bultmann in Kittel's *Theological Dictionary of the New Testament* makes similar comments:

> *ἀναγινώσκω in Greek means "to know exactly" or "to recognize," and for the most part it is used with the sense of reading or public reading (cf. both older usage and the pap.). In this sense it is by no means uncommon in the LXX ... In the NT ἀναγινώσκειν is used of the reading of a letter (Ac. 15:31; 23:34; 2 C. 1:13; 3:2; Eph. 3:4) and esp. of public reading in the congregation (1 Th. 5:27; Col. 4:16).*[3]

When we today speak of reading Scripture we think of taking up our Bibles and reading some text either from the Old Testament or the New Testament. We overlook the fact that neither the Jew during the Second Temple era, nor the Christian in the first century CE, had their sacred writings as we now have Bibles in book or codex form!

In fact, it took centuries before our Bibles were printed in a book or codex form. The Old Testament books existed in scroll form and the New Testament for many years existed in individual letters, Gospels, or documents that were circulated among the Christian churches. Even within the Synagogues the Old Testament existed in scrolls either in Hebrew or Greek. If the congregations, either Jewish or Christian, were to hear their Scriptures it would be *read aloud*, ἀναγινώσκω, to them in their assemblies.

Several interesting texts refer to the regular public reading of the Old Testament or apostolic letters in either the Synagogue or the church. Cf. Luke 4:16; Acts 13:27; Acts 15:21; Col 4:16; 1 Thess 5:27; Rev 1:3.

Of particular interest to our study at this point is Paul's admonition to Timothy, a young co-worker and missionary who he had left in Ephesus to set certain things in order.

---

[2] Zodhiates, ἀναγινώσκω, anaginóskō.
[3] Kittel, *Theological Dictionary of the New Testament*, vol. 1, p. 343. I have adapted the English spelling used by English translation of Kittel to the American spelling!

> *¹¹ Command and teach these things. ¹² Let no one despise your youth, but set the believers an example in speech and conduct, in love, in faith, in purity. ¹³ Till I come, <u>attend to the public reading of scripture, to preaching, to teaching</u>. ¹⁴ Do not neglect the gift you have, which was given you by prophetic utterance when the council of elders laid their hands upon you. ¹⁵ Practice these duties, devote yourself to them, so that all may see your progress. ¹⁶ Take heed to yourself and to your teaching; hold to that, for by so doing you will save both yourself and your hearers.* [4]

In a different comment in his second letter to Timothy Paul instructed Timothy to approach his preaching and ministry with all diligence for not everyone would take Scripture seriously. He reminded Timothy that the Scriptures he had learned from his mother and grandmother had come by inspiration of the Holy Spirit and were intended to teach Christians how to live for Christ:

> *¹⁵ Do your best to present yourself to God as one approved, a workman who has no need to be ashamed, rightly handling the word of truth.* [5]

> *¹⁴ But as for you, continue in what you have learned and have firmly believed, knowing from whom you learned it ¹⁵ and how from childhood you have been acquainted with the sacred writings which are able to instruct you for salvation through faith in Christ Jesus. ¹⁶ All scripture is inspired by God and profitable for teaching, for reproof, for correction, and for training in righteousness, ¹⁷ that the man of God may be complete, equipped for every good work.* [6]

> *¹ I charge you in the presence of God and of Christ Jesus who is to judge the living and the dead, and by his appearing and his kingdom: ² <u>preach the word</u>, be urgent*

---

[4] 1 Tim 4:11–16.
[5] 2 Tim 2:15.
[6] 2 Tim 3:14–17.

in season and out of season, convince, rebuke, and exhort, be unfailing in patience and in teaching. ³ For the time is coming when people will not endure sound teaching, but having itching ears they will accumulate for themselves teachers to suit their own likings, ⁴ and will turn away from listening to the truth and wander into myths. ⁵ As for you, always be steady, endure suffering, do the work of an evangelist, fulfil your ministry.[7]

In a real life situation, not every Synagogue or Christian church would have someone capable of preaching a sermon, cf. Lk 4:16ff, and Acts 20:7:

> Luke 4:16 *And he came to Nazareth, where he had been brought up; and <u>he went to the synagogue, as his custom was, on the sabbath day. And he stood up to read</u>;* ¹⁷ *and there was given to him the book of the prophet Isaiah. He opened the book and found the place where it was written,*
> ¹⁸ *"The Spirit of the Lord is upon me,*
> *because he has anointed me to preach good news to the poor.*
> *He has sent me to proclaim release to the captives and recovering of sight to the blind,*
> *to set at liberty those who are oppressed …*
> Acts 20:7f *On the first day of the week, when we were gathered together to break bread, Paul talked with them, intending to depart on the morrow; and he prolonged his speech until midnight.*

It is a matter of regret that today in many churches little attention is given to the reading of Scripture aloud to the congregation. In most cases the public reading of Scripture is not an integral part of the worship liturgy, it is referenced, or quoted by the preacher during the sermon, if necessary! Much time is given to congregational singing and the sermon, but little attention is devoted to reading the Scripture together as a congregation. The impact of hearing the Word of God has been replaced by hearing the preacher's interpretation of that Word. Now before you jump

---

[7] 2 Tim 4:1–5.

out of your skin in indignation, I am not against hearing good sermons in which serious attention is given to the application of the Word in our everyday lives! But I am concerned that we are more committed to hearing our interpretation of the Word in song and sermon than we do in listening to the Word carefully read as a congregation! Nothing makes a statement more effectively to the fact that we are a people of "the book" than spending meaningful time reading that book together in our assemblies. We could not impress our visitors more regarding the importance of Scripture to our faith than by meaningful, careful reading and listening to Scripture together in our assemblies. Admittedly, Scripture should be read aloud by people who can read well and who can articulate that Scripture well in words that can be heard!

It should not matter today if, as in most congregations, we read from a variety of translations. That is if they are sound translations edited by a committee of scholars rather than simply translated by a preacher. What matters is that we are focused on reading and hearing the Word of God as a significant dynamic of our worship assembly. This point speaks directly to what I am addressing in this study of a theology of worship.

A Theology of Worship is attention focused on God, "bowing" in reverence before God, and hearing God in both Scripture reading and the sermon, as he speaks through the text and in the message of Scripture in the sermon.

It would add much to the public reading of Scripture if the reader would begin with a statement like this, "*Hear the Word of God!*" And close the reading with a statement like "*May God bless the reading and hearing of His Word!*"

Robert Webber has some interesting comments on the reading of Scripture in the assembly of the saints:

> The public reading of Scripture goes all the way back to Mount Sinai. It was the emphasis of Ezra the scribe that made the Scripture central to Jewish worship, especially in the synagogue. Ezra was a Babylonian Jew who led the second wave of immigrants to Palestine. Upon discovering the weak spiritual condition of the people of Jerusalem, he rent his garments, fasted, and prayed for renewal.

Ezra instituted extensive reforms, including the renewal of worship.

> Ezra opened the book. All the people could see him because he was standing above them; and as he opened it, the people all stood up. Ezra praised the LORD, the great God; and all the people lifted their hands and responded, "Amen! Amen!" Then they bowed down and worshiped the LORD with their faces to the ground. The Levites . . . instructed the people in the Law while the people were standing there. They read from the Book of the Law of God, making it clear and giving the meaning so that the people could understand what was being read. Nehemiah 8:5–8

It is interesting to note all that is going on in this incident: the reader standing in a place where he can be seen; the people standing as the book was opened, lifting their hands, saying "Amen," and bowing to the ground; the Levites reading, making it clear, giving the meaning; the people understanding. This was no passive mumbling of Scripture, no mere preliminary to the sermon! This strong emphasis on Scripture was carried directly from the temple to the synagogue and on into Christian worship.

There is little direct evidence prior to Justin Martyr (A.D. 150) concerning the methods of reading Scripture in Christian worship. Nevertheless, the allusion to the reading and use of Scripture in the New Testament literature (see Acts 2:42; 13:5; Col. 4:16; 2 Tim. 3:16) and in early Fathers (1 Clement 13:1; 14:2; Epistle of Barnabas 21:1, 6) leaves little doubt that the description of Christian worship in Justin Martyr refers to a well-established tradition.

> And on the day called Sunday there is a meeting in one place of those who live in cities or the country, and the memoirs of the Apostles or the writings of the prophets are read, as long as time permits; then when the reader has finished, the president in a discourse urges and invites [us] to the imitation of these noble things.

By the third century the liturgy of the Word included readings from the Law, Prophets, Epistles, Acts, and Gospels, with Psalms sung by cantors between the lections. Reading was characterized by an active involvement on the part of the people. Special attention was given to the reading of the Gospel as indicated by the canons of Addai: "At the conclusion of all the scriptures let the gospel be read, as the seal of all the scriptures; and let the people listen standing up on their feet, because it is the glad tidings of the salvation of all men (emphasis added).

The people responded by singing psalms between Scripture readings. There is abundant evidence of the use of the psalms in the records of the third century.3 Eusebius (260–340), bishop of Caesarea and author of the classic Ecclesiastical History, wrote, "The command to sing psalms in the name of the Lord was obeyed by everyone in every place: for the command to sing is in force in all the churches which exist among the nations. [8]

From Webber's comments we surface an interesting suggestion—the reading of Scripture should focus on God's redeeming activity notably as recorded in the Gospels!

We have noted above that reaching back even to the life of Israel, the reading of Scripture was a central feature of the life of Israel and the early Christians. The example of Ezra reading the Law to Israel after the restoration ca 445 BCE became an integral ingredient in Israel's return to faith. From Luke 4:16 we learn that it was part of Jesus' and the Synagogue's practice on the Sabbath Day. Paul instructed Timothy to remember the atoning role of Scripture at 2 Tim 3:14-17, and his instruction to the young preacher to pay attention to the public reading of Scripture, 1 Tim 4:13 again stresses the urgent need for the reading of Scripture in facing the inroads of false teaching (1 Tim 4:1ff).

The many examples of the second and third century weekly assemblies builds on the emphasis of Scripture reading in the life of the early church.

---

[8] Webber, *Worship Old and New*, Kindle locations 2987-3011.

In an era of religious fragmentation among Christian churches today in which many churches are becoming sectarian or culturally driven, concerns for the future of the church in a secular society are raised in an almost regular cycle. A survey of religious literature and religious surveys addressing this concern reveals that churches of all denominations are concerned with the global decline of religious faith.

Casey Leins, Staff Writer, US News, April 11, 2017,

> The world's religious landscape is undergoing a major restructuring, as the population becomes increasingly religious and Muslim, according to recent studies.
>
> The percentage of people who identify as non-religious is expected to fall from 16 percent in 2015 to 13 percent in 2060, the Pew Research Center reports. These "religious nones," which include atheists, agnostics and those who do not identify with any particular religion, tend to be older and have fewer children than those who are religious. As a result, their death rates will begin to exceed their birth rates, the study explains ... In the U.S. alone, the Christian population decreased by nearly 8 percent between 2007 and 2014. Over that same time period, the Muslim population showed a slight increase.
>
> But unlike the global projections, the U.S. has seen, and will continue to see, a rise of the "religious none." A larger portion of the nation's population describes themselves as religiously unaffiliated, jumping up 7 percent from 2007 to 2014. And unlike other countries, religiously unaffiliated people in the U.S. tend to be younger than those who belong to a religious group.[9]

Understanding the history and dynamic of faith-failure, or corruption of faith among believers, Jewish and Christian throughout the ages, becomes essential to the future life of any restoration of the Christian faith. Many are seeking such restoration through the establishment of new culturally aligned

---

[9] Cf. Callum Brown, *What was the Religious Crisis of the 1960s*? Cf. also Callum Brown, *The Death of Christian Britain: Understanding Secularisation*.

churches, or as Marva Dawn expresses it, seeking to keep the church relevant through dumbing the faith down in order to reach our secular neighbors.

Unfortunately, we have observed that the decline of Scripture concern among Christian churches runs concurrently with the secularization of the Christian faith. We will notice in the next chapter that too often when story telling becomes the springboard and attraction of a sermon rather than biblical reference and interpretation, the emphasis on Scripture reading, the public reading of Scripture, is either on the decline or seriously absent. Before you get too negatively excited about this statement, it should not be read to mean that story telling should have no place in preaching, that is not my point. When Scripture is introduced to ground the story, we decline into proof texting and deductive reading of Scripture rather than deductive exegesis and interpretative understanding of Scripture. There are also many great stories in Scripture that rise out of an inductive approach to the text rather than stories being read into the text!

Chapter 13: Preaching and Homily

In this chapter we will examine the content and style of the preaching we find described in Scripture and the life of the early church. I will reflect somewhat in passing on some of the so-called preaching we hear today from some pulpits.

I have on occasion used the term *inductive* referring to how we do theology or read Scripture. I will below also be speaking of *deductive* use of Scripture. Both are useful ways of using Scripture. As I will be using these terms, we have as a background the concept of *inductive and deductive thinking*, which can be useful. But this will need some explanation since I will be speaking of *biblical interpretation* and not simply *thought processes*.

Inductive Preaching in Jesus' Ministry

Simply put, *inductive* preaching is the result of an *exegetical* approach to reading Scripture, which likewise refers to how we use or interpret Scripture. *Exegesis* refers to letting the Scripture define itself, or speak to us, getting the meaning of the text out of the text itself in its appropriate context.

In contrast to this we have *deductive* preaching that begins with a topic and then reads our understanding into the text. This is *eisegesis* which means or implies reading into the text a preconceived meaning. The preaching looks biblical in that it uses Scripture, but the preacher is reading his meaning into the text.

Inductive preaching involves beginning with a text, interpreting the text within its context, that is exegetically, and letting the text speak to us and explain its theological principles. *Inductive* preaching begins with a text and lets the meaning of the sermon flow out of the text and its contexts. This involves an *exegetical* approach to the text. The preacher looks for *theological principles within the text and its context* and then seeks to find ways in which the theological principle can impact our lives in our context.

Deductive preaching begins with an idea and then finds a text that develops the point that the preacher is wanting to make. In preaching on a topic the preaching begins with a topic and moves to the text. All preachers will need to preach topically to some degree, but still move from the meaning of the text in its context. The difference is where and how the preacher begins, with the text or with the topic. Any topic can be found covered somewhere in Scripture! That is, it is covered somewhere in Scripture. The preacher through exegesis should know how to find such texts! The danger is that we fall too easily into the trap of proof-texting in which we look for a text that we believe develops our topic. We face the problem of reading our interpretation into the text.

An example of the difference in inductive and deductive preaching is seen Jesus' deductive use of Luke 4:16ff, and how some have shifted Jesus' use of citing Isa 61:1, 2 out of its original kingdom theological intention. Inductive preaching seeks to determine the theological principle ensconced in the root text, Isa 61:1, 2, and then asks what the theological intention of the text was. Jesus was obviously referring to the root meaning of the Isaiah text. Some find the theological principle to be the benevolent feature of the general *Missio Dei* without seeking to determine what Isaiah was addressing in his suffering servant kingdom theology. Isaiah's concern was Israel's difficulty at being the suffering servant who would carry God's kingdom message to the world. A messianic servant certainly would be interested in the suffering of the lost as part of his ministry, but benevolence was not the theological principle or theme of Isaiah's message! Kingdom proclamation and expansion were his concern. Certainly, concern for the poor and social injustice would be a concern for a future king of Israel. However, in a kingdom theology, and the Messianic concern of the kingdom of God, especially in Isaiah's servant songs, would be a centrifugal missional outreach to the Gentiles. The coming Messiah would be concerned for this centrifugal *evangelistic* aspect of the kingdom message. The inductive context and messianic theological principle of Isaiah's message must determine any future application of the text.

I find in Jesus' use of Luke 4:16 a classical example of some reading into Jesus' use of this text a meaning not intended by either Isaiah or Jesus.

Jesus was about to inaugurate his messianic kingdom activity and in order to demonstrate that he was the Messiah he picked up that theme from Isaiah 61 and referred to the fact that he was in fact healing the sick and ministering to the poor.

Luke 4:16-30 began with Jesus entering the Synagogue in Nazareth, his hometown, on the Sabbath, and standing up to read from Isa 61:1ff. This is a classic example of Jesus using an inductive reading of Isaiah.

> *¹ The Spirit of the Lord GOD is upon me,*
> *because the Lord has anointed me*
> *to bring good tidings to the afflicted;*
> *he has sent me to bind up the brokenhearted,*
> *to proclaim liberty to the captives,*
> *and the opening of the prison to those who are bound;*
> *² to proclaim the year of the Lord's favor,*
> *and the day of vengeance of our God;*
> *to comfort all who mourn;*
> *³ to grant to those who mourn in Zion—*
> *to give them a garland instead of ashes,*
> *the oil of gladness instead of mourning,*
> *the mantle of praise instead of a faint spirit;*
> *that they may be called oaks of righteousness,*
> *the planting of the Lord,*
> *that he may be glorified.*

Luke records that after he finished reading this text from Isaiah he closed the book (NIV *rolled up the scroll*), gave it back to the Synagogue attendant, the *Hazzan*, sat down, and *began to say* to them[1], "*today this scripture has been fulfilled in your hear-*

---

[1] This is the first passage in the Gospel where Luke records a public speech of Jesus. Reiling Swellengrebel, *Translators Handbook of the Gospel of Luke*. Regarding the meaning of Hazzan and the use of ὑπηρέτης, *hupērétēs*, servant, at Luke 4:20 Marshall has the following comment, "after the reading, Jesus rolls up the scroll and hands it back to the synagogue attendant. ὑπηρέτης is generally regarded as the equivalent of *ḥazzān*, Marshall, *Luke*. Karl Rengstorf observes, "In the depiction of Jesus at worship in the synagogue at Nazareth (Lk. 4:16ff.) the ὑπηρέτης is the one who takes from Him the scroll of Isaiah which he has just used (v. 20), namely, the "assistant" of the presi-

ing." What Scripture? Isaiah 61:1, 2 with its contextual theological implications. Thus, we have Jesus using an inductive interpretation of Isaiah to reference and inaugurate his kingdom ministry!

This is not the place to engage the profound Messianic kingdom suffering servant ministry, or the *Missio Dei* aspects with its benevolent ministry implications of the text. This would be a worthwhile discussion if we were examining a theology of benevolent ministry, but I must resist that temptation here, and focus on why this "Jesus" occasion gets my attention in this chapter on inductive preaching in the worship assembly.

Jesus' use of Isaiah was not simply that kingdom ministry is benevolent! His purpose was to announce that he was inaugurating his Messianic kingdom ministry which involved much more than benevolence, as important as that is! Jesus was announcing that he was about to begin God's appointed kingdom message and age that would unite all men in the kingdom of God, both Jew and Gentile. This was not to be a political "get rid of the Romans" ministry. This was not to be an emphasis on benevolence in which Christians should take care of the indigent, as important as that is. *This was the beginning of a full-blown ministry of divine atonement and reconciliation which was not on the Law of Moses, but on an obedient faith in Jesus as the suffering Messiah.*

Regarding the expression *he began to speak,* I. Howard Marshall observes:

> ἤρξατο *(he began) may be simply a case of Semitic redundant usage, [emphasizing the beginning of hi preaching, IAF] especially if what follows is to be regarded as a summary of the sermon rather than its opening words. It could simply refer to the transition from reading to preaching (cf. Plummer and B. Reicke). But surely what follows is the arresting opening of a [kingdom IAF] sermon, so that the use of the verb is justified.*

---

dent of the synagogue who has certain functions to perform, especially in worship, at the latter's direction. Karl Rengstorf in Kittel, *Theological Dictionary of the New Testament*, vol. 8, p. 540ff.

> *Perhaps Luke wishes to stress that these are the opening words of Jesus' public ministry.* [2]

Obviously, the occasion was a formal service in the Synagogue. Jesus' style of behavior and the attention given to his discussion/homily by the gathered group reinforces this. Jesus was using the Isaiah text inductively to explain that his homily was the outgrowth of the full kingdom theology of Isaiah's messianic message. Every action drawn from Jesus' ministry indicates that he saw himself as the fulfillment and proclaimer of God's prophetic *kingdom* word.

Jesus *came preaching the gospel of the kingdom.* Mark 1:14 draws attention to the profound significance of Jesus' message.

> *"Now after John was arrested, Jesus came into Galilee, preaching the gospel of God,* [15] *and saying, "The time is fulfilled, and the kingdom of God is at hand; repent, and believe in the gospel."*

Mark perceptively refers to Jesus' action as *preaching* (κηρύσσω, *kērússō*; meaning *to preach, to herald,* or *to proclaim*)[3] the kingdom ministry, adding that the time was fulfilled for the inauguration of the messianic kingdom. The call to *repent* gave a sense of urgency to Jesus' kingdom message. Mark fixes Jesus' preaching to the gospel of God regarding the coming kingdom. Preaching the good news of God's kingdom message, or as it is referred to on many occasions in Scripture, simply *the gospel* (εὐαγγέλιον, *euaggélion, to bring good news*[4]) carried a sense of urgency and every Jew would have understood this. In the context of Jesus' ministry and preaching in the New Testament and early church it is only with some difficulty that one can separate Jesus' preaching from proclaiming the good news of the kingdom.

Preaching the gospel message of the kingdom obviously featured prominently as a central point of Jesus' ministry, and Jesus focused his preaching *inductively* on the Messianic component of Scripture!

---

[2] Marshall, *The Gospel of Luke,* pp. 184–185.
[3] Zodhiates, κηρύσσω, *kērússō*.
[4] Zodhiates, εὐαγγέλιον, *euaggélion*.

Preaching in the Early Church

We learn early from Luke's account of the inauguration of the church's kingdom ministry that preaching inductively from the theological center of Jesus' life, death, and resurrection was a pivotal component of the life of the church's theology and eventually in the formal worship assembly of the early church.

Acts 2:14-40 records what was possibly the first sermon preached by an Apostle in the new *Messianic* kingdom church age! Peter's great Pentecost sermon in many ways is the epitome of Christian preaching. Notice the *inductive* nature of Peter's sermon. *It began with a firm footing in Scripture, followed by an exposition of the text, a theological conclusion, and a response.* The focus of the sermon was fixed on what God had done in Jesus Christ to set things of the kingdom in action and to redeem mankind.

> *14But Peter, standing with the eleven, lifted up his voice and addressed them, "Men of Judea and all who dwell in Jerusalem, let this be known to you, and give ear to my words. 15 For these men are not drunk, as you suppose, since it is only the third hour of the day; 16 <u>but this is what was spoken by the prophet Joel</u>:*
>
> *17 'And in the last days it shall be, God declares, that I will pour out my Spirit upon all flesh, and your sons and your daughters shall prophesy, and your young men shall see visions, and your old men shall dream dreams;*
> *18 yea, and on my menservants and my maidservants in those days*
> *I will pour out my Spirit; and they shall prophesy.*
> ...
> *22 "Men of Israel, hear these words: Jesus of Nazareth, a man attested to you by God with mighty works and wonders and signs which God did through him in your midst, as you yourselves know— 23 this Jesus, <u>delivered up according to the definite plan and foreknowledge of God, you crucified and killed by the hands of lawless men</u>.*
> *24 But God raised him up, having loosed the pangs of death, because it was not possible for him to be held by it.*

> ²⁵ For <u>David says concerning him</u>,
>   'I saw the Lord always before me,
>   for he is at my right hand that I may not be shaken;
> ²⁶ therefore my heart was glad, and my tongue rejoiced;
>   moreover my flesh will dwell in hope.
> ²⁷ For thou wilt not abandon my soul to Hades,
>   nor let thy Holy One see corruption.
> ²⁸ Thou hast made known to me the ways of life;
>   thou wilt make me full of gladness with thy presence.'
> ²⁹ "Brethren, I may say to you confidently of the patriarch David that he both died and was buried, and his tomb is with us to this day. ³⁰ Being therefore a prophet, and knowing that God had sworn with an oath to him that he would set one of his descendants upon his throne, ³¹ <u>he foresaw and spoke of the resurrection of the Christ, that he was not abandoned to Hades, nor did his flesh see corruption</u>. ³² This Jesus God raised up, and of that we all are witnesses. ³³ Being therefore exalted at the right hand of God, and having received from the Father the promise of the Holy Spirit, he has poured out this which you see and hear. ³⁴ For David did not ascend into the heavens; but he himself says,
>   'The Lord said to my Lord, Sit at my right hand,
> ³⁵ till I make thy enemies a stool for thy feet.'
> ³⁶ <u>Let all the house of Israel therefore know assuredly that God has made him both Lord and Christ, this Jesus whom you crucified</u>."
> ³⁷ Now when they heard this they were cut to the heart, and said to Peter and the rest of the apostles, "Brethren, what shall we do?"

Acts 20:7ff also surges to mind as an early example of preaching in a worship assembly. Here we see Paul gathered with the church in Troas to celebrate the Lord's Supper on the first day of the week and preaching a prolonged speech until midnight. Ignoring for emphasis the fascinating event of Eutychus falling asleep during Paul's sermon (how could he dare fall asleep during the great Paul's sermon!) and falling out of the window to his demise, and Paul raising him from the dead, we return to the occasion and Paul's preaching. Luke explains that Paul was *speaking* (διαλέγομαι, *dialégomai, speaking to present intelligent discourse, to teach publicly, to discourse, to present intelligent arguments*[5]) during a Lord's Supper assembly. We have no indication as to the content of Paul's sermon or lesson, but this text supports the inclusion of a sermon during a formal worship assembly.

The historical testimony of the early church to the practice of preaching in the assembly establishes this practice firmly in the life of the early church.

Everett Ferguson demonstrates that from its earliest days preaching and the Lord's Supper were integral components celebrated in the church worship assemblies of 1st and 2nd church life.[6]

From the many references to the life of the early church I have chosen one from Justin Martyr, a Christian apologist ca 150 CE. Justin documents the worship activity on a Sunday worship service. Note the emphasis on reading Scripture (the memoirs of the apostles or the writings of the prophets), the president verbally instructing the assembly, prayer being said, and the Lord's Supper being celebrated in the partaking of the bread and the wine, and the contribution for benevolence gifts being gathered.

> And we afterwards continually remind each other of these things. And the wealthy among us help the needy; and we always keep together; and for all things wherewith we are supplied, we bless the Maker of all through His Son Jesus Christ, and through the Holy Ghost. And on the day called Sunday, all who live in cities or in the country gather together to one place, and the memoirs of the apostles or the writings of the prophets are read, as long as time permits; then, when the reader has ceased, the president verbally instructs, and exhorts to

---

[5] Zodhiates, διαλέγομαι, *dialégomai*.
[6] Ferguson, *Early Christians Speak*, pp. 65ff; Ferguson, *The Church of Christ,* pp. 207ff.

the imitation of these good things. Then we all rise together and pray, and, as we before said, when our prayer is ended, bread and wine and water are brought, and the president in like manner offers prayers and thanksgivings, according to his ability, [2] and the people assent, saying Amen; and there is a distribution to each, and a participation of that over which thanks have been given, and to those who are absent a portion is sent by the deacons. And they who are well to do, and willing, give what each thinks fit; and what is collected is deposited with the president, who succours the orphans and widows, and those who, through sickness or any other cause, are in want, and those who are in bonds, and the strangers sojourning among us, and in a word takes care of all who are in need. But Sunday is the day on which we all hold our common assembly, because it is the first day on which God, having wrought a change in the darkness and matter, made the world; and Jesus Christ our Saviour on the same day rose from the dead. For He was crucified on the day before that of Saturn (Saturday); and on the day after that of Saturn, which is the day of the Sun, having appeared to His apostles and disciples, He taught them these things, which we have submitted to you also for your consideration.[7]

In the following brief analysis of preaching in the early church I have adapted and refer to an excellent article in the *Anchor Bible Dictionary* by Fred B. Craddock, professor of preaching and homiletics at the Candler School of Theology, Emory University, in Atlanta, Georgia.[8]

> "A cursory study of preaching in the life of Israel and the early church engages the very heart of the Judeao-Christian faith. Reflection on the life of Israel without considering the great prophets of Israel, and a study of

---

[7] "Justin Martyr", in Donaldson, *The Apostolic Fathers with Justin Martyr and Irenaeus,* vol. 1, pp. 185–186.
[8] Cf Craddock, "Preaching," *The Anchor Yale Bible Dictionary,* vol. 5, pp. 451–454.

Christianity without reflection on the ministries of John the Baptist, Jesus, the Apostles, not to overlook other evangelists, prophets, and teachers in the New Testament would reduce the canon of Scripture to some fascinating stories, mostly without meaning! Preaching in the New Testament church defined the very heart of the Christian faith."

Simply put, preaching is the proclamation, announcing, declaration of a message from God, with the intention to present publicly the good news, to deliver a religious discourse related directly or indirectly to a text of Scripture. Even though preaching has long been significantly linked to the life and activity of both Jewish and Christian communities, it is so varied in content, mode, audience, and purpose that it resists the constraints of a dictionary, even a Bible dictionary.

Preaching as a Mode of Communication

In the histories of both the synagogue and the church, preaching as a mode of communication has ranged from an informal discussion called a homily (from *homilein*, translated in the RSV as "talking," Luke 24:14, 15, and as "conversing," Acts 20:11) to a carefully constructed speech following the dimensions of ancient rhetoric. Both types of communication hold a rightful place in the church assembly in communicating the message of God's will to the congregation.

Preaching in the Hebrew Scriptures

The Hebrew Scriptures contain few clear references to that which we term "preaching." However, two activities seem clearly to fall in this category: prophetic proclamation and the teaching of the *Torah*. The word *bašēr*, containing "joy" in its stem, refers to bringing or announcing good news or a message of joy, as in 2 Sam 4:10; Ps 40:9; Isa 40:9; 61:1. The other term meaning "to proclaim or to call," *qĕrā'* (Jer 11:6; Mic 3:5; Jonah 1:2; 3:2), can also be translated "to read aloud," as in the public reading of the *Torah* in Neh 8:8–9.

In the Greek translation of the Hebrew Bible these two words were rendered most often by *euangelizō*, to evangelize, and *kērussō*, to announce or proclaim. These two meanings are the most common terms for preaching in the New Testament.

Finally, the New Testament refers to certain persons in the Hebrew Scriptures as preachers: Jonah (Luke 11:32), Noah (2 Pet 2:5), and Enoch (Jude 14, 15).

Words in the New Testament Which Refer to Preaching

There are primarily two terms *kērussō*, meaning, "to announce or to proclaim publicly," a word used approximately sixty times (Mark 1:14; 1 Cor 1:23; Acts 10:42), and *euangelizō*, meaning "to announce good news" (Acts 5:42). The stem word *angellō*, from which we get "angel" or "messenger," appears in the New Testament with a variety of prefixes and in the RSV is variously translated: "to proclaim" (Acts 17:23); "to declare" (1 Pet 2:9); "to command" (Acts 17:30); "to preach" (Acts 5:42). There are terms which by context refer to preaching. These are words which do not intrinsically specify such activity but which by reason of context clearly indicate a public telling of the Christian message. There are many such terms. The more common among them are: "to cry out" (Acts 23:6; Rom 9:7); "to speak" (Rom 15:19; 2 Cor 2:12); "to talk" (Mark 2:2); "to make known" (Eph 6:19); "to prophesy" (1 Cor 14:1–4; 1 Pet 1:10); "to speak boldly" (Acts 13:46; 18:26); "to exhort" (Acts 2:40; 15:32); "to bear witness, to testify" (Acts 2:40; 20:24; John 1:15).

Preaching in the Early Church

Preaching and evangelizing by proclaiming the word or gospel became a major ministry of the early church. The tradition of preaching from the prophets as seen in Jesus' ministry was continued by the preaching ministry of the apostles. In addition, other persons shared in gospel proclamation, for example, Philip, Acts 21:8 (εὐαγγελίζω, *euaggelízō*) and Eph 4:11, which refers to Christ's gifts to the church, *And his gifts were that some should be apostles, some prophets, <u>some evangelists</u>, some pastors and teachers.* In fact, the whole church at times became involved in forms of preaching—Acts 8:4, "*Now those* (Christians) *who were scattered went about preaching* (εὐαγγελίζω, *euaggelízō*) *the word.*"

In its preaching the early church understood itself as continuing the message of Jesus, but there was one major difference: Jesus, the messenger of the kingdom was now the central feature of the message itself. Note 1 Cor 1:17ff, *For Christ did not send me to baptize but to preach the gospel, and not with eloquent wisdom, lest the cross of Christ be emptied of its power.*
[18] For the word of the cross is folly to those who are perishing, but to us who are being saved it is the power of God. Paul continued with this emphasis at 1 Cor 2:1ff, *When I came to you, brethren, I did not come proclaiming to you the testimony of God in lofty words or wisdom. [2] For I decided to know nothing among you except Jesus Christ and him crucified.* At Col 1:27ff Paul again stressed the content of his preaching, *To them God chose to make known how great among the Gentiles are the riches of the glory of this mystery, which is Christ in you, the hope of glory.*
[28] Him we proclaim, warning every man and teaching every man in all wisdom, that we may present every man mature in Christ.
[29] For this I toil, striving with all the energy which he mightily inspires within me.

From the beginning, preaching style seems to have been varied. The Epistle to the Hebrews, for example, is a sermon (Heb 13:22), representing a style of preaching (citing, interpreting, and applying a text) which later became popular and widespread. But it does not stand alone in the New Testament.

Acts contains a number of sermons and portions of sermons (2:14–36; 3:12–26; 13:16–41; 17:22–31), most of them delivered by Peter and Paul. One should keep in mind that all the preaching reported in Acts comes to us from Luke, whose own fingerprints are on the reports. In fact, Luke had earlier stated the content of the proclamation as "repentance and forgiveness of sins" (Luke 24:47), and the sermons in Acts regularly convey those two themes. While it may remain an open question as to how broadly representative of the whole church Luke's sermon reports are, it has long been the practice of historians to draw upon Acts to provide summary sketches of early Christian preaching.

The most influential of these opinions is that of C. H. Dodd (1937), whose reading of Acts (and Paul, but sermons are fragmentary in the letters) extracted the following: prophecies are fulfilled and the new age is launched by the coming of Christ; Christ was born of the seed of David, died according to the Scriptures to deliver us from this present evil age, was buried, and rose on the third day according to the Scriptures; Christ is exalted at the right hand of God as Son of God and Lord of all; Christ will come again as Judge and Savior. In short, God has in Jesus Christ done the promised work of salvation and all persons are now invited to turn from their former ways and believe the good news.

The reader of Acts should be aware of the clear differences in the preaching of the church to those who knew and believed the Hebrew Scriptures, Jews and those attached to the Synagogue, "*So Paul stood up, and motioning with his hand said: "Men of Israel, and you that fear God, listen,*" (Acts 2:16–36; Acts 3:12–26; Acts 13:16–41), and the messages to Gentile audiences totally unfamiliar with the Scriptures, (Acts 14:8–17), Paul in Lystra, *When an attempt was made by both Gentiles and Jews, with their rulers, to molest them and to stone them, ⁶ they learned of it and fled to Lystra and Derbe, cities of Lycaonia, and to the surrounding country; ⁷ and there they preached the gospel. ⁸ Now at Lystra there was a man sitting, who could not use his feet; he was a cripple from birth, who had never walked.* Likewise, at Acts 17:22–31, Paul was in Athens "*So Paul, standing in the middle of the Areopagus, said: "Men of Athens, I perceive that in every way you are very religious* ...)." The points of contact with the listeners are quite different. To the Jews Paul would begin with the Scriptures, but to the Gentiles he began with a relevant Gentile view and then moved on to demonstrate that Jesus fulfilled all their hopes.

Before moving to preaching as reflected in Paul's letters, it should be remembered that quite a number of New Testament scholars believe that the four Gospels are our primary sources for getting at the content of early Christian preaching. That these narratives represent Christian preaching is not in direct conflict with the preaching reflected in Acts. There is a difference in form, to be sure, but it is hardly reasonable to suppose that the church's preaching would be silent about "all that Jesus began to do and teach until the day when he was taken up" (Acts 1:1–2).

That Paul understood his mission to be that of a preacher is quite clear from Paul himself: "For Christ did not send me to baptize but to preach the gospel" (1 Cor 1:17); "Woe to me if I do not preach the gospel!" (1 Cor 9:16). However, his letters, usually occupied with issues within the young congregations, do not offer the reader samples of his preaching. Instead there are reminders to the churches of what he preached when he was present with them. "Now I would remind you, brethren, in what terms I preached to you the gospel" (1 Cor 15:1). This statement is followed by a summary: Jesus died for our sins according to the Scriptures, was buried, was raised on the third day according to the Scriptures, and has appeared to his followers, including Paul (1 Cor 15:3–8). Sometimes Paul was briefer: he preached Christ was crucified (Gal 3:1). What is of special importance, however, is that Paul says his message was what he received, the tradition which had been given to him and which he passed along to the churches (1 Cor 15:3; 11:23). This says not only that Paul had predecessors but that there was strong continuity between his preaching and that done by others. Whatever the distances he experienced, and at other times helped create between himself and other apostles, Paul did not preach a new or different gospel. So strongly did Paul feel about his message that he called it a revelation of Jesus Christ (Gal 1:12) and pronounced anathema upon anyone offering a different gospel (Gal 1:8–9).

Preaching as Distinguished From Teaching

Some early scholars, following the study of preaching and teaching by Dodd, C. H., *The Apostolic Preaching and Its Development*, 1937, tended to separate *kērygma* (preaching) and *didachḗ* (teaching) into two different categories of communication. However, such a sharp distinction cannot be maintained on the basis of either biblical texts or careful thought. For example, the Sermon on the Mount (Matthew 5–7) is a body of *teaching* (5:2; 7:29) about life and relationships in the kingdom, and yet the audience consisted not only of Jesus' disciples but also "the crowds" (5:1; 7:28). Was Jesus *preaching or teaching*? That depends on how you imagine the setting, *more formal or more casual*.

Documents describing synagogue activity in the Second Temple era refer to preaching and teaching interchangeably. Israel gathered on occasions to be renewed and reconstituted by the recital of the Exodus, the narrative which created the community. Preaching was not differentiated in the Synagogue from teaching.

It seems unreasonable to suppose that the early Christian church, created by the proclamation of the gospel, did not gather again and again only to be renewed and reconstituted by *the preaching by which it was first called into being*. The early church gathered repeatedly to be *taught or instructed* in the faith. In fact, many of the words cited above in some contexts clearly refer to preaching. They are the same words as "to speak," "to say," "to exhort," "to state boldly," etc. which elsewhere indicate the teaching and instruction of Christians.

Modes of communication do not always distinguish preaching and teaching, and neither does the nature of the audience. As to content, preaching without *instruction* lacks substance; teaching without *kērygma* lacks identity.[9]

Conclusion

It is obvious from the relevant documents and resources that the role of formal teaching either defined as preaching or teaching in a carefully constructed sermon, or a more freely flowing homily, played a significant role in the life of the early church.

One other important point that we learn from both the preaching of Jesus and the Apostle Paul was that their message, teaching, sermon, or preaching, was firmly grounded in the exposition of the prophetic writings of Scripture.

An unfortunate tendency in the modern church is to preach topical sermons. There is nothing wrong with this as long as the sermon is based on an *inductive* study of Scripture related to that topic. Unfortunately, this is often not the case! Topical preaching easily degenerates into proof texting in which the text is taken out of context to suit the purpose of the preacher.

---

[9] Cf Craddock, "Preaching," *The Anchor Yale Bible Dictionary,* vol. 5, pp. 451–454.

Chapter 14: Singing in the Worship Assembly

Introduction

If participating in the Lord's Supper could be in an unworthy manner (1 Cor 11:27), having profound implications for worshipping God in spirit and truth, how would singing and praying in an unworthy manner impact worshipping God? And what would singing in an unworthy manner look like?

The words *sing* and *singing* appear 11 times in the New Testament, 4 times in Revelation, 2 times in 1 Corinthians, and once each in Romans, James, Ephesians and Colossians. *Hymns* being *sung* appear 6 times in the New Testament, most in association with 1 Corinthians, Ephesians, and Colossians. Surprisingly, although *singing* does not appear often in the New Testament in regard to Christian practice, singing has played a major role in the celebration of the Christian faith down through the centuries of Christianity.

Of the 11 times *sing* or *singing* appear in the New Testament (in 10 verses), 7 in particular are clearly relevant to our study regarding Christians singing in the early church era, Acts 16:25; Rom 15:7-15; 1 Cor 14:14 (twice); Eph 5:19; Col 3:16; and James 5:13. The other 4 are in Revelation and are not relevant to singing in the early Christian church era as reflected in the 1st century. Revelation speaks of worshipping in the celestial church or singing in the heavenly throne room. Furthermore, much of the symbolism in Revelation draws on the Old Testament and Jewish Mysticism which is highly symbolic. We will briefly examine Rom 15:9 and James 5:13 as they may not specifically be in reference to the church worshipping in any worship assembly as on the Lord's Day. There are some (possibly Ralph P. Martin) who feel that James 5:13 may have a church assembly in mind but this is not convincing. Nevertheless, both Rom 15:9 and James 5:13 do have reference to Christians singing in some community form.

One other text sometimes surfaces in this discussion. That is 1 Cor 14:26 where Paul writes; *"When you come together, each one has a hymn, a lesson, a revelation, a tongue, or an interpretation. Let all things be done for edification."* The word *hymn*, ψαλμὸν, *psalmón*, is derived from the Greek ψαλμό, *psalmós* which primarily means a *psalm*, a hymn or *song of praise*. There is some debate among scholars as to whether this is a recognized Psalm drawn from the Old Testament, or any spiritual song of praise. Some feel that it may refer to a psalm/song well known in 1st century church circles. Most see this hymn singing to be spontaneous because of the *charismatic* context of the text, implying that the hymn refers to a Holy Spirit inspired song. Obviously from the context of Paul's argument in 1 Corinthians a Christian in the 1st century church may well have sung or *chanted* such a Holy Spirit inspired hymn or spiritual song in the assembly. The point is that Paul was simply not commanding, condoning, or condemning the chanting of a hymn or singing a hymn, or that one simply has permission to sing or chant a hymn which one would assume to be permissible under the appropriate circumstances. *Paul's point in 1 Cor 14:26 is that hymns sung as a solo indiscriminately in the assembly were not behaving in an orderly or edifying manner (1 Cor 14:26, 40), and should therefore be controlled.*

What we are examining in this and the following chapter is the role singing played in the theology of worship which worship in the assembly in the New Testament and early church was directed *toward* God and Christ. We will notice in this discussion of singing in the worship liturgy of the assembled church that singing had a *horizontal corporate dimension* in which the congregants were to be addressed and edified, but that such singing should *primarily be vertical* in *honor and worship of God* for his atoning and redemptive activity in Jesus. In both Eph 5:19 and Col 3:16 Paul mentions as a leading factor that this singing was *to the Lord* and *to God* implying that the direction of the singing was worship primarily directed *toward* God.

In this chapter we will examine scholarly opinion regarding whether the singing referenced in 1 Cor 14:15; 26; Eph 5:19; Col 3:16 was in fact reference to the *assembled* congregational worship service on the Lord's Day in which the Lord's Supper was celebrated.

We will in the next chapter briefly examine the question whether the major texts in our New Testament which refer to singing in the worship assembly of the early church (1 Cor 14:15; 26; Eph 5:19; Col 3:16) implies *acappella* vocal singing or whether these texts may include singing accompanied by one or more musical instruments.[1]

My major concern at this point, however, is to demonstrate *how* singing related to and impacted the *theology of the worship* of God *in the public worship assembly of the church* as reflected in the New Testament. In due course we will briefly consider *why* singing was included in the theology and practice of worship in the early church as reflected in the New Testament. There is obviously some relationship in meaning and significance between *how* a church sings and worships, and *why* it does so!

In this study of the *theology of worship* in the New Testament we will primarily *not* be developing a full *theology of singing* in the assembly which would involve a fuller and more detailed biblical critical exegetical examination of the texts which lie beyond the purpose or provenance of this study of a *theology of worship*. Such an exegetical study can be found in Addendum 4 at the close of this study. We will however in a following chapter pay some passing attention to some *brief* exegetical comments on the relevant texts.

Since it is the consensus of much scholarly opinion that Eph 5:19 and Col 3:16 are parallel passages and relate to the worshipful singing of Christians in the public worship assembly of the church I will begin examining Eph 5:19, then turn to Col 3:16, and finally examine 1 Cor 14:13-33. 1 Cor 14:13-33 is slightly different from Eph 5:19 in that Paul in the Corinthian correspondence, notably 1 Cor 12-14, was addressing *abuses* he detected in the worship assembly. In doing so he reflected on the *speaking*,

---

[1] Naturally, since I have already observed above that I am of the persuasion that singing in the church's formal worship assembly in which the Lord's Supper was celebrated in the New Testament church was acappella, it is obvious that my understanding of the words and expressions ᾄδοντες καὶ ψάλλοντες (*adontes kai psallontes*, ᾄδω, *ádō*, and ψάλλω, *psállō*), as they are used in regard to Christian worship in the New Testament, refer to *vocal, rational singing from the heart toward God,* and that *the heart was the instrument* referenced by Paul in these texts.

prophesying, singing and *praying* in the public worship assembly in the context of a church blessed with Holy Spirit inspired members, some of whom were using their giftedness for personal self-satisfaction and self-aggrandizement.

There are some who hold that Ephesians 5:19 and possibly Col 3:16 were not in the context of the public worship assembly of the church on the Lord's Day but refer to singing praises on other occasions. It is also claimed by some that the only text referring to singing in the assembly, 1 Cor 14:26, addressed only singing solos in the assembly. This view lifts the text and the singing right out of the context of Paul's discussion and miss-applies it. Nevertheless, it is obvious that some singing took place in the assembly on the Lord's Day with the proviso that it was done appropriately, decently, and in order and for the worship of God and the edification of the congregation, and not simply experienced for the pleasure of the singer.

Other than these three texts that refer to congregational singing in the assembly (1 Cor 14:15, 26, Eph 5:19, and Col 3:16) I find no mention in the New Testament of Christians *gathering together* on other occasions merely to sing psalms, hymn, and spiritual songs. Christians might have done so, but we have no reference supporting this other than Paul and Silas in the Philippian jail, and that occasion certainly was not a gathering of Christians, even a small gathering of two, assembled together outside of the Lord's Day worship assembly to edify one another in psalms, hymns, and spiritual songs!

A Brief Glimpse at Acts 16:25

In this fascinating story Paul and Silas were in prison in Philippi for preaching Jesus and "disturbing" the peace. *"But about midnight Paul and Silas were praying and singing hymns to God, and the prisoners were listening to them ..."* They were singing and praying to God! It is obvious that they were not in a church worship service but were exercising their Christian freedom and right to sing hymns of praise to God, and to pray to God. Were they worshipping God? Certainly, but the occasion was their worship of God in their daily life, and not in a worship assembly.

Their singing and praying obviously had an impact on the occasion, for when the prison was destroyed by an earthquake none of the prisoners escaped!

A Brief Glimpse at James 5:13

At James 5:13 James encouraged Christians struggling with various difficulties to pray and sing. Regarding the Greek word for *singing* in James 5:13, *psállō*, there is some discussion regarding whether this is in the context of a worship service or merely a personal private activity. I am of the opinion that James is addressing the Christian community, drawing on the dynamic of congregational worship practices but also stressing the importance of the Christians individually praying and singing praise to God. *Singing* is one of the fundamental backgrounds to *psállō* in the New Testament regardless of where the singing takes place. Normally, context will define where this takes place as in 1 Cor 14:15-26.

Ralph P. Martin, when commenting on James 5:13, connects 1 Cor 14:15, Col 3:16, and Eph 5:19 as all three set in the worship of the church. Martin leaves the context of James 5:13 open, but does find the practice proposed in James 5:13 to take place in the worship communal liturgy of the church, albeit in his observation he recognizes the possible difference between a Jacobean church and a Pauline church. He observes:

> The call in v 13 also speaks to those who are in good spirits (εὐθυμεῖν); they are to "sing a song [to God]" (ψάλλειν). Verse 13b repeats the (quasiconditional) question [regarding] imperative pattern of v 13a. To be in "good spirits" is more than to be outwardly happy, an emotion that is dependent on circumstances (see *Comment* on 5:11). The cheerfulness described here is that of the heart (Moo, 175) and is independent of prevailing conditions. A believer can be in good spirits even if the situation is bad (see, for instance, Acts 16:25; 27:22, 25 …), and as an evidence of inner joy one should sing to God. ψάλλειν, appearing almost sixty times in the LXX, can mean either praise by means of a harp or a song sung to God with (Pss 33:2, 3; 98:4–5; 147:7; 149:3) or without (Pss 7:17; 9:2, 11) the accompaniment of an instrument (Ropes, 303). It may also be that

James is reminding his readers that they must not forget God in the good times (a lapse exemplified in the merchant traders, 4:13–16). As Davids (192) writes: "Turning to God in need is half the truth; turning to him in praise *either in the church or alone* when one is cheerful (whatever the situation) is the other half." <u>Praying and singing are also related in the practice of worship in the Pauline churches (1 Cor 14:15; Col 3:16–17; Eph 5:19–20: see Martin, Worship in the Early Church, 2d ed. [Grand Rapids: Eerdmans, 1974] 43–48).</u> *It may be then that this pericope in 5:13–16 was formed in a context of communal liturgy in the Jacobean congregation.*[2]

Douglas Moo likewise references James' instruction for the need of the Christian community to be praying and singing:

James specifically exhorts the community to sing songs of praise. The Greek verb here is *psallo*, from which we get the word "psalm." While the verb means simply "sing," all three of its other NT occurrences connote a song of praise to God (Rom. 15:9; 1 Cor. 14:15; Eph. 5:19; see the cognate noun in 1 Cor. 14:26; Eph. 5:19; Col. 3:16). So, especially coming from one who is doing well, the song here is almost certainly a song of praise to the Lord; see NLT, "continually sing praises to the Lord." The "continually" in the NLT rendering reflects the present tense of the verb *psalleto*, which often adds the nuance of a continual or repeated action. Giving praise to God, like our petitions for sustenance in times of trouble (*proseuchestho*, "pray," is also present tense), should be a regular part of our lifestyle.[3]

However, the verbs pray προσευχέσθω, *proseuchesthō* and sing ψαλλέτω, *psalletō* are in the present tense *third person singular* which seems to me to imply individual activity, thus not necessarily stressing congregational worship service activity but Christian personal activity.

---

[2] Martin, *Worship*, Underlining emphasis mine, IAF.
[3] Moo, *Colossians*, Kindle locations 3605-3610.

However, that James 5:13 may have reference to personal praying and singing says absolutely nothing about Eph 5:19 and Col 3:16 addressing congregational worship services.

A Brief Glimpse at Rom 15:9

In the one reference to singing in Rom 15:9 Paul is simply quoting an Old Testament Psalm (Psalm 18:49) among other Old Testament texts to encourage the saints in Rome to so welcome those with whom they disagree that God would be glorified among the Gentiles.

> *[7] Welcome one another, therefore, as Christ has welcomed you, for the glory of God. [8] For I tell you that Christ became a servant to the circumcised to show God's truthfulness, in order to confirm the promises given to the patriarchs, [9] and in order that the Gentiles might glorify God for his mercy. <u>As it is written, "Therefore I will praise thee among the Gentiles, and sing to thy name</u>"; [10] and again it is said, "Rejoice, O Gentiles, with his people"; [11] and again, "Praise the Lord, all Gentiles, and let all the peoples praise him"; [12] and further Isaiah says, "The root of Jesse shall come, he who rises to rule the Gentiles; in him shall the Gentiles hope." [13] May the God of hope fill you with all joy and peace in believing, so that by the power of the Holy Spirit you may abound in hope.*

A Brief Glimpse at Love Feasts

Some suggest that the singing referenced in Eph 5:19 and Col 3:16 might have been during one of the love or *agápē* feasts and not in a church assembly for worship, but the minimal evidence we have for love feasts indicates that these were associated with the Lord's Supper on the Lord's Day which seems to imply a congregational worship service. The only "direct" reference to a love feast in the New Testament is Jude 12 and this only in passing with no mention of singing. Carousing is mentioned but in a negative implication. Most scholars see in 1 Cor 11:17-34 a possible end of any practice of celebrating the Lord's Supper in a meal, at least in Corinth and the Pauline churches, although we do find mention of love feasts in the 2nd century in the *Didache*. Some find a mention of a love feast indicated at Acts 2:46f, but this is debated, and Luke does not identify this as a love feast. Most scholars see Acts 2:42-47 as a summary of early Christian fellowship.

Summary Observations

There is scant evidence in scholarly publications that Eph 5:19 and Col 3:16 refer to singing outside of the assembled worship service of the church. Certainly, worship in general takes place in the Christian's life walk every day of the week, but there is no evidence at all that *singing to one another* should be a daily experience.

However, there is an overabundance of evidence in scholarly circles that Eph 5:19 and Col 3:16 along with 1 Cor 14:15-26 refer to the gathered assembly of the church on the Lord's Day for worship and edification.

I will below cite a good number of scholarly commentaries, monographs, and journal articles which bear testimony to these texts referring to a formal worship service.

The evidence is that there are numerous scholars, in fact, the majority of modern internationally recognized scholars, who clearly consider Eph 5:19, Col 3:16 and 1 Cor 14:15, 26 as asserting that these scriptures are in reference to worship in the congregational worship assembly on the Lord's Day.

I readily confess that there may be other scholars whom I have not cited, but the following should be adequate to make my point that scholarship in general sees Eph 5:9, Cor 3:16, and 1 Cor 14:15, 26 referring to the pubic worship assembly of the church.

I will later follow this view up with a detailed exegetical examination of Eph 5:15ff.

I have not considered publications by those who are not considered New Testament scholars but who are ministry practitioners rather than textual scholars. While I respect the views of ministers and other ministry leaders, scholarly research and publication are not their field of expertise. This may sound academically elitist, but then, we are engaged in precise scholarly research of the biblical text in search of a theology of worship!

Eph 5:15-20 and Col 3:16-17

Eph 5:15-20 Look carefully then how you walk, not as unwise men but as wise, [16] making the most of the time, because the days are evil. [17] Therefore do not be foolish, but understand what the will of the Lord is. [18] And do not get drunk with wine, for that is debauchery; but be filled with the Spirit, [19] addressing one another in psalms and hymns and spiritual songs, singing and making melody to the Lord with all your heart, [20] always and for everything giving thanks in the name of our Lord Jesus Christ to God the Father.

Col 3:16, 17 Let the word of Christ dwell in you richly, teach and admonish one another in all wisdom, and sing psalms and hymns and spiritual songs with thankfulness in your hearts to God. [17] And whatever you do, in word or deed, do everything in the name of the Lord Jesus, giving thanks to God the Father through him.

The question we are pursuing with these two texts at this point is determining whether the singing occasion referred to is a formal worship assembly or merely Christian singing in general other than in the formal worship assembly.

As mentioned above there are some who hold to the view that Eph 5:19 and Col 3:16 are not in the context of a public worship assembly. It is my opinion, however, from the overwhelming opinion of New Testament scholarship that both Eph 5:19 and Col 3:16 refer to the formal worship service assembly of the church.

I will first document one, W. G. Blaikie, who questions or implies that Eph 5:19ff and Col 3:16 *do not* to refer to a worship assembly but refer to a general occasion in which Christians might gather. One would be hard pressed to hold that Blaikie's view is representative of modern scholarship![4]

---

[4] The large number of Greek manuscripts, most related to biblical studies that have been discovered over the last 100 years, the *Dead Sea Scrolls*, the *Nag Hammadi Tractates, et al*, have added many valuable insights into the biblical texts not available to good scholars such as Blaikie and others of the 19th century. All scholars owe them a deep debt of gratitude for their foundation to biblical scholarship.

I will then list the many fine scholars who believe the context of the discussion is a formal worship assembly of the church.

In the following list of *internationally* recognized scholars[5] I will first list those scholars who have written major commentaries on the New Testament related studies. Following this, I will list *recognized scholars* within the Stone-Campbell movement of Churches of Christ who have *published works* related to the topic under discussion.

W. G. Blaikie in *The Pulpit Commentary* Edited by H. D. M. Spence (1880-1897)

Blaikie feels that the meeting of Eph 5:19 was one for social Christian enjoyment rather than for worship, but then adds that Col 3:16 refers to public worship. He concludes that Eph 5:19 *could* in some measure refer to public worship. He writes:

> **Speaking to one another**. *Literally, this would denote antiphonal singing, but this is rather an artificial idea for so simple times. It seems here to denote one person singing one hymn, then another, and so on; and the meetings would seem to have been for social Christian enjoyment rather than for the public worship of God. In the Epistle to the Colossians it is "teaching and admonishing one another with psalms," and this has more of the idea of public worship; and if it be proper to express joyful feelings in the comparatively private social gatherings of Christians, it is proper to do the same in united public worship.*[6]

Oscar Cullmann, *Early Christian Worship*, 1953

In his ground-breaking study of early Christian worship, which along with Gerhard Delling is cited in almost every study

---

[5] By the term *internationally recognized scholars* I intend those who have published major refereed commentaries or journal articles. I do not include those who are not recognized as scholars but who have written church related journal articles. Forgive the academic definition of scholar! Unfortunately, some not proficiently trained in biblical hermeneutic and theology have written church related journal articles which have not been broadly refereed and are consequently received as pseudo-scholarly works!

[6] Blaikie in Spence-Jones, *Ephesians,* Pulpit Commentary, pp. 210, 211.

of a theology of worship, Cullmann observes that the singing of psalms and hymns as an aspect of the Christian worship was not necessarily taken over from Judaism. However, psalms and hymns were fundamental to the worship of the early developing church. Cullmann suggests that in regard to 1 Cor 14:26, Col 3:16, and Eph 5:19 the use of psalms and hymns was most likely an overflow of Spirit inspired worship. The point is that Cullmann considered singing psalms and hymns to be part of the early Christian worship. Cullmann cites Col 3:16 and Eph 5:19 in support of such singing. Note Cullmann's comments:

> *1. The Sources.*
>
> *Our sources for the investigation of the early Christian service of worship do not yield a perfectly clear picture of the outward development of the gatherings for worship; they do disclose, however, a fairly clear tendency to worship ... We know now the basis of early Christian Worship; sermon, prayer, and supper (the Lord's Supper) ... We learn further, however, from the Pauline Epistles that already in the very earliest period the worship life of the community ... Paul mentions in 1 Cor 14:26 the Psalms, revelation, speaking with tongues and the interpretation of tongues ... We see how perfectly free and unrestricted spiritual utterances have their place alongside fixed liturgical forms. The frequent mention of Psalms and Hymns (apart from 1 Cor 14:26 especially Col. 3:16 and Eph. 5:19), the use of which in the service was taken over from Judaism ... are likewise to be thought of, on the one hand, as free compositions and on the other hand as repeated pieces of a liturgy.*[7]

In summary, then, what Cullmann was arguing was that in the early Christian worship services psalms and hymns were sung, not necessarily because they were sung in Jewish worship, but as an outpouring of Spirit-filled worship.

---

[7] Cullmann, *Early Christian Worship*, pp. 7, 20ff.

Gerhard Delling, *Worship in the New Testament*, 1952

It is not scholarly responsible to engage any discussion of singing and worship in the New Testament without citing Gerhard Delling! Delling is unquestionably the "father" of modern discussions of the theology of worship in the New Testament. With this in mind, I have referenced several comments regarding singing in the worship assemblies in Delling's foundational work on worship in the church. In his chapter of Creed and Hymn Delling observes:

> *There are, however, many hymn-like passages in primitive Christian literature, which have the character of a confession of faith, and the use of these in Worship may be inferred ... Maurer rightly stresses that the credal declaration in primitive Christianity was inseparable (at least as an outward action) from the sacraments. The ceremony is nothing without the attesting Word ... Philo's picture [of the Therapeutes, IAF] clearly provides several points of comparison with Worship in the New Testament ... In the services in the Pauline area, at least, it is plain that alongside kerugma and doctrine and 'spiritual' utterances in the narrower sense, a not insignificant place is given to praising, glorifying and giving thanks to God, in exalted language and fixed forms, in the presence of the congregation. Three concepts are used for these activities; psalmois (psalms), humnois (hymns), and ōdai (songs); it is scarcely possible to distinguish them absolutely from each other.*[8]

A careful reading of Delling's chapter on Creed and Hymn reveals that Delling has in mind Eph 5:19 and Col 3:16 and the singing of psalms, hymns, and songs in the church worship assemblies. Although he does not often cite Eph 5:19 or Col 3:16 it is obvious from the terminology he uses that he has these texts in mind.

C. F. D. Moule, *Worship in the New Testament*, 1961

Interestingly, Moule on several occasions cites the work of Oscar Cullmann on early Christian worship. When discussing

---

[8] Delling, *Worship in the New Testament*, pp. 42 ff; 82 ff.

whether the singing of psalms and hymns in the worship service were primarily eucharistic observes:

> *So again there are Christian hymns in the Apocalypse; but there is nothing to prove them eucharistic ... which may, as has been argued by professor W. C. van Unnik, only be an echo of the "eschatological" consciousness of all Christian worship, despite its particular association in later times with the Eucharist. "Psalms and hymns and spiritual songs" (Eph 5:19; Col 3:16) must have been heard on many occasions – and incidentally, they were probably unaccompanied ... If stringed music is referred to, it is "in the heart" only (Eph 5:19, Col 3:16).*[9]

Andrew Lincoln, *Ephesians*, 1990

I have italicized certain of the following quotes from Lincoln for emphasis.

> *Although the first participial clause mentions hymns, its focus in fact is not on praise of God. The psalms, hymns, and spiritual songs are part of believers' addressing of one another in the assembly, serving as a means of edification, instruction, and exhortation (cf. also Col 3:16, "teaching and admonishing one another"). In this regard, it is significant that much of what is taken to be hymnic in the Pauline corpus has a didactic and paraenetic function in its present form and context (e.g., Phil 2:6–11; Col 1:15–20; 1 Tim 3:16). As most scholars hold, it is difficult to draw any hard and fast distinctions among the three categories of psalms, hymns, and spiritual songs mentioned both here and in the material in Col 3:16 from which this writer draws ...*[10]
>
> *The second participial clause builds up the sentence in the writer's characteristic style by employing the verbal forms of two of the previous nouns—ᾠδή, "song,"*

---

[9] Moule, *Worship in the New Testament, passim.* Italics in quote, IAF. In most of the following citations I have italicized certain expressions for emphasis.

[10] Lincoln, *Ephesians*, p. 345.

and ψαλμός, "psalm." Although its original meaning involved plucking a stringed instrument, ψάλλω here means to make music by singing (cf. also 1 Cor 14:15; Jas 5:13), so that there is no reference in this verse to instrumental accompaniment (cf. the discussion in BAGD 891; pace Barth, 584). If the singing involved in the first participial clause has a horizontal and corporate dimension, that of the second clause has a more vertical and individual focus. The singing is now directed to the Lord, who, as in v 17, is Christ (a change from Col 3:16 where the singing had been addressed to God). Pliny's account (Epistles 10.96.7) of Christians who "recited to one another in turns a hymn to Christ as to God" is often cited in connection with these songs directed to Christ. Believers who are filled with the Spirit delight to sing the praise of Christ, and such praise comes not just from the lips but from the individual's innermost being, from the heart, where the Spirit himself resides (cf. 3:16, 17, where the Spirit in the inner person is equivalent to Christ in the heart) ... [11]

Whereas the previous section had carried this out in terms of sexual morality and the antithesis between light and darkness, 5:15–20 begins with the contrast between wisdom and folly. Wise living is then shown to be Spirit-filled living, which is described primarily in terms of its consequences for the community's corporate worship. [12]

Robert G. Bratcher, *A Handbook of Paul's Letter to the Ephesians*, 1993

Bratcher observes regarding Eph 5:19:

The readers are told to Speak to one another with the words of psalms, etc. (literally "speaking among yourselves with psalms" etc.). It is impossible to differentiate precisely among psalms, hymns, and sacred songs. Psalms are Old Testament psalms, used also by Chris-

---

[11] Lincoln, *Ephesians*, p. 346.
[12] Lincoln, *Ephesians*, p. 347.

tians in their corporate worship; hymns could be specifically Christian compositions in honor of Jesus as Lord and Savior; and "spiritual songs" (RSV) could be spontaneous outbursts of inspired singing, prompted by the Spirit. It is quite possible that hymns and sacred songs are synonymous, referring to Christian compositions generally, so that in translation only one word is needed ... [13]

What follows in Greek is simply "in your heart," which TEV understands to mean with praise in your hearts. But some translate "in your hearts" (NEB, TNT, NIV, JB), which can only mean inaudible singing; so Westcott: "the outward music was to be accompanied by the inner music of the heart." But it seems difficult to believe that the writer was telling them to have the strains and choruses of songs and psalms running through their minds. Others translate "from the heart," "heartily," "with all your hearts" ... Abbott, however, notes that the normal way to say this is "from the heart" (see the synonymous "from the soul" in verse 6:6). TEV understands the Greek phrase here to mean "with praise in your heart," but it may be preferable to take the phrase to mean "with all your heart" (RSV), that is, heartily, enthusiastically. [14]

Ralph P. Martin, *Ephesians, Colossians, and Philemon*, 1991
Careful reading of Martin's discussion of this Eph 5:19 reveals that he has in mind the *public worship service* which "spills over" into public life.
On Ephesians 5:19. The cameo of 5:19-20 is again of interest in allowing us to take a peep at the early churches in their worship practices ... Our use of "words sung to music" in modern worship should make room for the third type of public worship utterance ... and once we compare the wording of verse 20 with parallels in Col 3:17, 23 we can see how much gratitude spills over to

---

[13] Bratcher, *Handbook on Paul's Letter to the Ephesians*, p. 135.
[14] Bratcher *Handbook*, p. 136.

the whole of life's activity and turns worship into an everyday activity[15] ... The test of such an experience follows 19-20, which have the worship of the Christian assembly in view.[16]

On Colossians 3:16, 17. Christ's "word" ... has its setting in a worship setting that opens with the all to thanksgiving (v. 15c). As the letter is read out in a public gathering in some congregation (Nympha's at Laodicea, 4:15-16, as well as in Colossae, Phil 2), these exhortations will take on special significance, urging the people to encourage one another by words of (true) wisdom, that is, Pauline teaching as well as vocal praises. Early hymn-singing activities evidently covered a wide range of material drawn from the Old Testament Psalter, Christ songs like the one in 1:15-20, baptismal chants as in Eph 5:14, and ecstatic/charismatic hymnody (1 Cor 14:15, 26). The ministry of teaching and instruction was now set in this liturgical framework; it was by such poetic creations, inspired by the Spirit, that believers were consolidated and given weapons to defend the faith. The idea of hymns as teaching vehicles in early Christianity is a recent one ... with topical relevance; it puts a question mark against such "free" worship with pitiably weak, sentimental, and introspective chorus/song singing in some churches today.[17]

Frank Thielman, *Ephesians*, 2010

In an excellent discussion of the contrast of singing in a drunken orgy and singing under the influence of the Holy Spirit Thielman observes:

> *One result of being filled in the Spirit is speaking to one another in the form of ... (psalms, hymns, and spiritual songs). Paul may have intended to contrast the crude singing typical of Greco-Roman feasting ... with the Spirit-inspired singing of corporate Christian worship (e.g., Eadie, 1883; 399; Swete 1909; 241) ... All three kinds of singing are forms of "speaking" to one another within the worshipping community.*[18]

---

[15] Martin, *Ephesians, Colossians, and Philemon: Interpretation*, p. 64.
[16] Martin, *Ephesians.*, p. 67.
[17] Martin, *Ephesians*, pp. 125f.
[18] Thielman, *Ephesians*.

Clinton E. Arnold, *Ephesians*, 2010

Arnold opens his discussion of Eph 5:15-21 by setting it in the context of the corporate community gathering for worship.

> *In a continuation of his language related to the temple, Paul speaks of believers "be[ing] filled" with the Spirit. He associates this infilling with the corporate community of believers coming together for worship. As they sing, worship, and give thanks, God responds with his empowering touch.*[19]

Arnold cites several scholars who propose a Dionysian cult as the setting for the drunkenness discussed at Eph 5:18 but observes that although such contexts are possible, perhaps a broader setting of pagan Roman drunkenness may be more fitting to the setting. Regarding Eph 5:19a which is seen in contrast to being filled with wine in drunkenness Arnold offers several translations or interpretations and concludes:

> *The regular act of gathering together with other believers to worship God and sing praise to his name is one of the means by which believers are filled with the Spirit ...The translation would be something like, "be filled with the Spirit as you worship ... (NRSV) ... another would be "be filled by the Spirit by means of worshipping..." Rather the text is simply asserting a connection between being filled with the Spirit and the church gathering together for corporate worship."*[20]

Arnold continues with an exegesis of the text, commenting on the singing and the songs sung and emphasizing that *the singing and edification is in the context of the corporate worship assembly* when by being gathered together under the influence of the Spirit the believers in the corporate worship assembly sing songs directed to God and Jesus Christ.

Peter T. O'Brien, *Ephesians*, 1999, *Colossians*, 1982

O'Brien addresses the two texts, Col 3:16 and Eph 5:19, which he sees as parallel, in considerable detail in his two commentaries. Since his commentary on Colossians is earlier I will

---

[19] Arnold, *Ephesians*, Kindle location 9430.
[20] Arnold, *Ephesians*, Kindle location 9692ff.

begin by noting several significant observations O'Brien makes regarding *singing in the worship community service* in Colossians. On several occasions he cross references his comments with Eph 5:19, and on occasion with 1 Cor 14:15, 26.

Colossians 3:16. O'Brien's comments in his study of Colossians are detailed, technical, and compacted with references to many scholarly works. With this in mind, I have selected certain comments germane to this study that relate to the occasion of addressing one another in psalms, hymns, and spiritual songs. It is apparent from the flow of his discussion that O'Brien understands the addressing of one another to primarily be in a formal worship assembly. It is also apparent that O'Brien also understands that what takes place in the assembly can also take place in other settings:

> *As the Colossians were exhorted to let the peace of Christ rule their lives (v 15), so now they are admonished to let the Word of Christ (ὁ λόγος τοῦ Χριστοῦ is parallel to ἡ εἰρηνη τοῦ Χριστοῦ, "the peace of Christ") dwell richly among them ...*
>
> *That Word is to dwell richly in their midst. ἐνοικέω ... "live in," "dwell in," "indwell"; appears only in a metaphorical sense in the New Testament (all six occurrences are in the Pauline corpus). So God himself will dwell among his people (2 Cor 6:16 citing Lev 26:11, 12), and the Holy Spirit dwells in believers (Rom 8:11 [cf. v 9]; 2 Tim 1:14; cf. 1 Cor 3:16). Not only the Word of Christ but also faith (2 Tim 1:5) may be said to dwell among God's own ... ἐν ὑμῖν has been taken to mean "in your hearts" ... "among you" ... or "in you," that is, "in your church ... Bruce [F. F. Bruce] ... claims that Paul would not have wished to be pinned down too firmly to the alternatives of either "within you" (as individual Christians) or "among you" (as a Christian community). He does add, however, that "if one of the two had to be accepted, the collective sense might be preferred in view of the context." ... If the double reference of ἐν ὑμῖν ("within you" and "among you") is in view then this rich*

indwelling would occur when they came together, listened to the Word of Christ as it was preached and expounded to them ... and bowed to its authority ...

ἐν πάσῃ σοφίᾳ διδάσκοντες καὶ νουθετοῦντες ἑαυτούς κτλ. As the word of Christ richly indwells the Colossians, so by means of its operation they will "teach and admonish one another in all wisdom by means of psalms, hymns and spiritual songs" (this lengthy clause gives a modal definition of the preceding ... "Teaching and admonishing" (διδάσκονρες καὶ νουθετοῦντες; some exegetes consider that these dependent participles occur with an imperatival force, ... either way the teaching and admonition in all wisdom arise from the indwelling of the word, cf. Delling, TDNT 8, 498, Ernst, 229, and Dunn, Jesus, 237) were previously mentioned as activities of Paul and his co-workers, for it was by such instruction and admonition that the public proclamation of Christ as Lord was effected (see on 1:28). Here, however, it is the members of the congregation ... who teach and admonish one another (ἑαυτούς, "yourselves," which does not really differ from ἀλλήλους, "one another," being reflexive in a reciprocal sense ...bind the two participles together ...

... ψαλμοῖς, ὕμνοις, ᾠδαῖς πνευματικαῖς. This mutual instruction and warning are to take place "by means of psalms, hymns and spiritual songs." ... The parallel passage in Ephesians 5:19 (which interestingly enough the RSV *renders as "addressing [λαλοῦντες)] one another in psalms and hymns and spiritual songs, singing and making melody to the Lord with all your heart") gives the same general sense as our interpretation ... The objection that mutual teaching and admonition would not take place in such psalms, hymns and spiritual songs is not valid. If the apostle had in mind antiphonal praise or solo singing for mutual edification in church meetings ... then mutual instruction and exhortation could well have been possible ... It is not possible to distinguish sharply between each of the three terms "psalms," "hymns" and "songs" ... and Worship in the New Testament ... 86, 87,*

> *and Martin ... 116) taken together these three words "psalms," "hymns" and "songs" describe "the full range of singing which the Spirit prompts" ... As the word of Christ indwells the members of the community and controls them so they teach and admonish one another in Spirit-inspired psalms, hymns and songs ...* [21]

Ephesians 5:19. O'Brien's comments on this text in his commentary on Ephesians are more readable than his work on Colossians. *We will note again that O'Brien considers this text to be parallel with the Col 3:16 text and message*:

> *In the Colossian parallel the singing is addressed to God (Col 3:16). Here in Ephesians praise is offered to the Lord, which, in the light of this chapter (vv.8, 10, 17, 20) as well as the rest of the letter, refers to 'Christ'.* [22]

O'Brien is not convinced that Eph 5:18 is in reference to the drunken orgies of the Dionysian cult, but does not rule this out. He prefers a reference to the Graeco-Roman pagan worldly practice of drunken orgies, or mere drunkenness which would not be an appropriate expression of wise living (Eph 5:15ff)![23] He does comment, as do some others that this drunkenness may refer to what had taken place in some of the Christian love feasts or *agápē* as in 1 Cor 11:17ff. O'Brien's comments indicate that wise living (Eph 5:15ff) *in contrast to pagan drunkenness is expressed in Spirit-filled worship of God and Jesus Christ* both corporately and individually. *It is apparent that O'Brien sets this worship in the corporate worship assembly in which the body is mutually edified by singing psalms and Spirit-filled hymns directed to the Lord Jesus and to one another in a vertical and horizontal dimension.* O'Brien's purpose is not simply to address what takes place in the corporate worship assembly but to demonstrate the wisdom and meaning of a Spirit-filled life in contrast to a life of drunkenness. Nevertheless, O'Brien makes the strong point that psalms sung in a *horizontal and corporate worship* setting are

---

[21] O'Brien, *Colossians, Philemon*, pp. 206-210.
[22] O'Brien, *Ephesians*, pp. 395f.
[23] O'Brien, *Ephesians*, pp. 393f.

spiritually edifying and uplifting in contrast to a drunken experience as in the pagan culture.

O'Brien observes that in the two expressions at Eph 5:19, *"addressing one another in psalms and hymns and spiritual songs, singing and making melody to the Lord with all your heart,"* although two clauses are to be understood as "describing the same activity from different perspectives."[24]

> *"The first from a horizontal and corporate dimension with its reference to believers addressing one another, presumably in formal worship but also on other occasions, in Spirit-inspired psalms, hymns, and songs. This is akin to Colossians 3:16, which may be based on Ephesians 5:19, where members of the congregation are to teach and admonish one another in psalms and hymns ... the Apostle has in view mutual instruction, edification, and exhortation which take place in a range of songs prompted by the Spirit ... through these songs members of the community who are continually filled by the Spirit will instruct, edify, and exhort one another...*
>
> *According to v. 19a, believers speak in psalms, hymns, and songs to one another, reminding each other of what God has done in the Lord Jesus Christ. A further distinction is the purpose of this singing, namely, to instruct and edify members of the body. In a sense, this singing has a horizontal and corporate focus to it. In v. 19b the singing and making music are directed to the Lord Jesus. This activity has a vertical focus and a personal dimension, for believers praise the Lord Jesus 'with their whole being'. It is in and through singing and making music, by which other members of the body are instructed and edified, that praise is offered to the Lord Jesus. The same singing has a twofold function and purpose."*[25]

---

[24] O'Brien, *Ephesians*, p. 394.
[25] O'Brien, *Ephesians*, pp. 394ff..

Klyne Snodgrass, *Ephesians*, 1996

Snodgrass emphasizes what several other scholars have identified in this pericope the role of the Holy Spirit. For several reasons most see this as an indication of the function of the Holy Spirit in the gathered community in worship. Snodgrass cites the significant study of Gordon D. Fee, *God's Empowering Presence*, "Furthermore, Fee is correct to emphasize the communal focus of this text: *The whole church is instructed to be filled with the Spirit*." We will shortly note that Fee connects Eph 5:19 with Col 3:16 which he sees as parallel texts which address *the corporate worship of the church.*[26]

Careful reading of Snodgrass reveals that he, along with most New Testament scholars, sees this text in Eph 5:19 being parallel to Col 3:16,[27] and that Eph 5:19, the instruction to be filled with the Holy Spirit, singing psalms, hymns and songs, instructing one another are *to be a function of the early church meeting in worship of the Triune God.*

Gordon D. Fee, *1 Corinthians*, 1987, *God's Empowering Presence*, 1994

I have already cited Fee above under Snodgrass' observations where Fee holds that Eph 5:19 and Col 3:16 are both parallel texts mentioning that the indwelling and operation of the Holy Spirit and *the congregational singing of hymns which took place in the early church in their regular gathering to worship God and Christ.*[28]

In a detailed discussion of behavior in the worship assembly in Corinth Paul addressed primarily three problems, 1) abuse of the Lord's Supper (11:17-34); 2) abuses of Holy Spirit giftedness (12-14); and the behavior of certain women in the worship assembly (14:33f). In the context of this discussion *which is clearly in the congregational worship assembly* as we note in the following quote from our text "*when you come together* it is not for the better but for the worse. [18] For, in the first place, *when you*

---

[26] Fee, *God's Empowering Presence*, pp. 648, 722.
[27] Snodgrass, *Ephesians*, pp. 290f.
[28] Fee, *God's Empowering Presence*, pp. 648, 722.

assemble as a church, I hear that there are divisions among you; and I partly believe it ..." (11:17, 18) Fee makes this observation:

> To *"praying"* Paul adds *"singing with the Spirit"* and *"with the understanding."* Singing was a common part of worship in Judaism and was carried over as an integral part of early Christian worship as well, as v. 26 and Col 3:16/Eph 5:19 illustrate.[29] The evidence from Colossians and Ephesians suggests that some of the singing was corporate; the language of these passages further indicate that besides being addressed as praise to God, such hymns served as vehicles of instruction in the gathered community ... in which spontaneous hymns of praise were offered to God in the congregation.

F. F. Bruce, *Ephesians*, 2012, *Colossians*, 2010
On Ephesians

Bruce does not discuss the text in great detail but does set it in the same context and discussion as 1 Cor 14:15 and Col 3:16. He references scholars as well as Pliny who observe that this type of singing to one another *took place in the early Christian worship assemblies.* Bruce explicitly considers this text in Eph 5:19 to be parallel with Col 3:16.[30]

On Colossians

> *Whatever view is taken of the punctuation or construction of the sentence, the collocation of the two participial clauses (as they are in the Greek text), "teaching and instructing . . ." and "singing . . .," suggests that the singing might be a means of mutual edification as well as a vehicle of praise to God. In 1 Cor. 14:26 Paul insists that, when Christians come to their meetings prepared with a psalm or any other spiritual exercise, they must have regard to the essential requirements of general helpfulness and good order. In our present passage, as in the closely similar Eph. 5:19, antiphonal praise or solo singing at church meetings is probably recommended.*

---

[29] Fee cites G. Delling, K. H. Bartels, R. P. Martin, and J. G. D. Dunn in support of this claim.
[30] Bruce, *Ephesians*, Kindle location 1848-1958.

> We recall the younger Pliny's report to the Emperor Trajan (A.D. 111-112) of the way in which Christians in Bithynia met on a fixed day before dawn and "recited an antiphonal hymn to Christ as God";153, or Tertullian's description eighty or ninety years later of the Christian love-feast at which, "after water for the hands and lights have been brought in, each is invited to sing to God in the presence of the others from what he knows of the holy scriptures or from his own heart."
>
> It has been asked sometimes if a strict threefold classification of praise is signified in the mention of "psalms, hymns, and spiritual songs." It is unlikely that any sharply demarcated division is intended, although the "psalms" might be drawn from the OT Psalter (which has supplied a chief vehicle for Christian praise from primitive times), the "hymns" might be Christian canticles (some of which are reproduced, in whole or in part, in the NT text), and the "spiritual songs" might be unpremeditated words sung "in the Spirit," voicing holy aspirations. Plainly, when early Christians came together for worship, they not only realized the presence of Christ in the breaking of the bread but also addressed prayers and praises to him in a manner which tacitly, and at times expressly, acknowledged him to be no less than God. If here the Colossian Christians are encouraged to sing in their hearts to God, the parallel Ephesians passage speaks of "singing and making melody in your hearts to the Lord" (meaning, presumably, Christ). The voice must express the praise of the heart if the singing is to be really addressed to God. Again, the necessity of a thankful spirit is emphasized, although the phrase rendered "with thanksgiving" might mean "with grace" or "in a state of grace."[31]

---

[31] Bruce, *Colossians,* Kindle Edition, Kindle locations 2572-2591.

Harold W. Hoehner, *Ephesians*, 2002

To say that Hoehner's commentary on Ephesians is exhaustive (930 pages) is not an overstatement! That it was published by Baker Academic, however, speaks highly of it!

Hoehner considers Eph 5:19 to be parallel to Col 3:17. He observes that being filled with the Spirit is not the believer's action but that of the indwelling Holy Spirit and that this continuous filling refers not only to the church in a worship assembly, but that it certainly includes such a function.[32]

After a detailed discussion of the syntactical relation of the words related to singing, addressing, psalms, hymns, and songs *Hoehner maintains first that there is no intentional emphasis on an instrument in the singing, that it was most likely verbal unaccompanied by any instrument other than that motivated by the Spirit and that in the case of both Eph 5:19 and Col 3:16* this mutual edification would have taken place in the church worship assembly. His closing comments on this discussion are as follows:

> *Were these psalms, hymns, and spiritual songs a reflection of the worship of the early church? ... Certainly at the end of the first century and the beginning of the second century ... Admittedly, early in the church's life there was singing, as seen in 1 Cor 14:26 where, when the church assembled, believers were to have, among other things, a psalm. Consequently, as singing had been important for the worship of Israel, so, too, was it important to the early church and the life of the church throughout the centuries ... The singing of praises is part of the believer's individual and corporate worship. Music is the means by which believers minister to each other and worship the Lord.*[33]

Markus Barth, *Ephesians*, 1974, and *Colossians*, 1994

Barth observes that in the Ephesian letter, being filled with the Spirit, however it is interpreted, and singing in order to praise God and edify one another, are to be seen in conjunction with one another. *Eph 5:19 and Col 3:16 are parallel texts addressing*

---

[32] Hoehner, *Ephesians*, pp. 704ff.
[33] Hoehner, *Ephesians*, pp. 710ff.

congregational involvement in the worship assembly. He observes that "early Christian congregations were singing, jubilant exulting assemblies."[34] In line with several scholars he sees parallels to the singing referenced by Pliny in regard to the Therapeutes. Singing in a manner in which the congregants edify one another had a special place in the Christian worship assemblies. Barth observes:

> ... *"singing" is part of the mutual edification of the saints. An intramural rather than a missionary purpose is to be fulfilled by singing. This means not only that its special place is in common worship (not excluding the family), but also that it has to be so qualified that the faith, obedience, love, and joy of fellow Christians is stimulated and increased. The singer's private pleasure alone, not to speak of ancient or modern exhibits, cannot be its primary purpose.*

Barth cites others who maintain that the "cultic" worship significance of the singing and assembly cannot be overstated, citing Gaugler and Schlier (two German scholars) in support of this.[35]

In his Colossian commentary of Col 3:16, which Barth sees as parallel to Eph 5:19, he observes that the singing that is meant here "*should have a central position in the worship service of the Colossian community*, but v 16 does not need to be limited to the setting of the worship service." His point is that the quality of singing referenced here does refer to the congregational "worship service of the Colossian community" but is not limited only to that service.[36]

Douglas Moo, *Colossians*, 1998

I have cited a long section from Moo as he engages the text critically in a sound biblical critical exegetical style. Moo considers Col 3:16 and Eph 5:19 to be parallel references.

> No conjunction or particle links v. 16 to v. 15, perhaps as a way of enhancing the obvious parallelism between the two: "let the peace of Christ rule in (*en*) your hearts"

---

[34] Barth, *Ephesians*, p. 582f.
[35] Barth, *Ephesians*, p. 583.
[36] Barth and Blanke, *Colossians,* p. 428.

parallels let the message of Christ dwell among (*en*) you (the Greek word order is even the same) ... Probably Paul means not "the word, or message, that Christ proclaimed" but "the message that proclaims Christ," "the message about the Messiah" ... Paul uses the phrase to summarize the authentic teaching about Christ and his significance, an immediately relevant example of which we have in the first two chapters of Colossians. ... TNIV's *among you* translates a phrase that could also be translated "in [each of] you." (The "in you" found in many versions would most naturally suggest this concept.) Some interpreters argue for this individualized application based on the parallelism with v. 15 ("in your hearts"). *But the rest of this verse, with its focus on the worship of the collective body, suggests rather that Paul is urging the community as a whole to put the message about Christ at the center of its corporate experience.* Specifically, Paul urges them to let it dwell richly among them. The message about Christ should take up permanent residence among the Colossians (NJB: "find a home with you"); *it should be constantly at the center of the community's activities and worship.* "Richly" suggests that this constant reference to the word of Christ should not be superficial or passing but that it should be a deep and penetrating contemplation that enables the message to have transforming power in the life of the community. The rest of v. 16 is governed by three participles (in the Greek text), the first two of which are clearly coordinate: "teaching and admonishing"; "singing." But their relationship to one another and, especially, the relationship of the various modifying phrases to them, are debated. These relationships should be clarified before we look at the details. The three main options are reflected, respectively, in the TNIV, ESV, and HCSB: TNIV: "as you teach and admonish one another with all wisdom through psalms, hymns and songs from the Spirit, singing to God with gratitude in your hearts"

… But the former option (followed in the TNIV) is perhaps the better. As O'Brien points out, it has three things in its favor: (1) it provides a better balance between the two clauses; (2) it deals seriously with the lack of an "and" (*kai*) before "singing"; and (3) *it matches the structure of the parallel in Ephesians 5:19: "speaking to one another with psalms, hymns and songs from the Spirit. Sing and make music from your heart to the Lord." … in which case "teaching and admonishing" and "singing" are parallel ways in which the "message of Christ" dwells richly in the community. …* We conclude, then, that the TNIV has the basic structure of the verse right: *Paul wants the community to teach and admonish each other by means of various kinds of songs, and he wants them to do this singing to God with hearts full of gratitude.* If this is the basic structure of the verse, then it falls into three parts, each of which is slightly subordinate to the part before it: "Let the message of Christ dwell among you richly as you teach and admonish one another . . . singing to God with gratitude in your hearts." The question then arises as to just how each clause modifies the one before it. As we noted, the Greek equivalents to "teach" and "admonish" are in the form of participles. It would make some sense to identify them as instrumental, in which case the "teaching and admonishing" would be the means by which the word would dwell richly in the community. *… The best option, then, is to see them as loosely connected to the preceding imperative, indicating two of the modes in which the word of Christ establishes its central place in the community.* The "as you teach and admonish" construction in the TNIV brings this out quite well, as does the "teaching and admonishing" construction chosen in many other translations. *… And, of course, in contrast to the previous text, this text gives to each member of the congregation the responsibility to teach and admonish other members.* Our text, as we

have argued, without limiting the means to these activities, identifies "psalms, hymns and songs from the Spirit" as the way in which believers teach and admonish each other. Whether we can distinguish the meanings of these three terms is questionable. ... *This verse is one of the very few that provide us with any window at all into the worship of the earliest Christians.* It is, of course, too brief, and its specific contours too uncertain, to give us much specific information. But it does make three points that are worth emphasizing. *First*, the "message about Christ," or, more broadly, we could say, "the word of God," was central to the experience of worship. *Second, various forms of music were integral to the experience.* And, *third*, teaching and admonishing, while undoubtedly often the responsibility of particular gifted individuals within the congregation (such as Paul [Col. 1:28] or Epaphras [Col. 2:7]) or elders (1 Tim. 3:2; 5:17; see also, e.g., 1 Cor. 12:28; 2 Tim. 2:2), were also engaged in by every member of the congregation.[37]

David Garland, *Colossians*, 1998

Garland considers Col 3:16 to be parallel to Eph 5:19, relating the content of these texts to the worship assembly of the congregation. In his opening comments on Col 3:16 Garland clearly sets the discussion in the context of congregational worship in his heading *Christian worship.*[38]

> *Worship is our response to what Christ has done and continues to do. It shapes our faith and makes it meaningful for our daily lives as we respond to the God who has saved us and calls us to be his people. The presence of Christ and our joining together in offering up prayers and songs to God establishes and strengthens our mutual bonds. Our worship provides guidance for our lives in our hearing the Word applied, brings to our awareness*

---

[37] Moo, *Colossians and Philemon*, Kindle locations 5315-5319. Moo footnotes extensively. I have not included the many footnote references provided by Moo. The interested reader should refer to Moo's commentary.

[38] Garland, *Colossians, Philemon*, Kindle location 5305ff.

> *the needs of others in our intercessory prayers, and presents the opportunity for expressing our repentance. It prepares us for spiritual battles we must often face alone during the week.*[39]

This certainly sounds like Garland considers Colossians 3:16 to refer to the regular Christian assembly for worship! He leads into his discussion of Col 3:16 and singing with the comment:

> *In Col 3:16, he (Paul) identifies two key elements of worship: teaching and admonishing that centers on the word of Christ, and singing praise. He couples that with two norms for worship: wisdom and thanksgiving.*[40]

Garland observes in the context of his discussion of this text that *the worship of the early Christians placed a premium on the spoken word in contrast to the perfunctory rituals or mysterious ceremonies.* Referencing observations by Marva J. Dawn regarding music in the church worship assembly he raises concerns regarding singing that is not befitting to the loftiness of the spoken word of God and becomes entertainment.[41]

James G. D. Dunn, *Colossians*, 1996

Dunn sets the singing and addressing one another clearly in the context of the worship assembly of the church. Like others he sees Col 3:16 and Eph 5:19 as parallel texts addressing the same topic of the congregation's worship of God and Christ, the celebration of God's saving activity in Jesus, and mutual edification.

> *The elements of Christian worship commended are not altogether surprising: "the word of Christ," teaching and admonition, and singing and thanksgiving, elements which have been a feature of typical Christian worship from the beginning till now. But this is in fact one of only a handful of passages that give us some insight into the content and character of earliest Christian worship and enable us to say anything at all about it (the most obvious*

---

[39] Garland, *Colossians, Philippians*, Kindle location 5370f.
[40] Garland, *Colossians, Philemon*, Kindle location 5379ff.
[41] Garland, *Colossians, Philemon*, Kindle location 5379-5414.

others are 1 Cor. 14:26 ... Quite how the elements are related to each other is not made clear: Is it a coordinated series, the instruction explaining how the indwelling takes place, the singing as the means of (cf. Eph. 5:19) or the response to the instruction? Or is it an uncoordinated series, the elements appearing in different combinations in different gatherings? Unfortunately, we cannot tell, though the first clause is certainly the principal clause. Nevertheless, for those with liturgical interests the details are of more than usual interest. The failure to mention or refer to any leaders here (prophets or teachers) may be significant ... as indicating a responsibility for worship shared by all ...

... In this context the ἐν ὑμῖν may also signify "among you," indicating an element of preaching/teaching in the communal gatherings of the Colossian Christians for worship and instruction (e.g., Masson 147 n. 5; Bruce, Colossians, Philemon, and Ephesians 157; Pokorný 173 n. 80; Fee 649) ...

That a corporate context is envisaged, a sharing of the word of Christ within the gathered assembly, is confirmed by the next clause, where the "indwelling" of the word is further described or the complementary activity indicated: "in all wisdom ... teaching and warning each other." The strong echo of 1:28 ("warning everyone and teaching everyone in all wisdom") can hardly be accidental (see on that verse). The most significant difference is that whereas 1:28 described the apostolic mission of proclaiming the gospel (though as a task shared with others, Timothy at least), here warning and teaching are seen as a corporate responsibility (Fee 649) ....

The third element of Christian worship is singing: "psalms, hymns, and spiritual songs" ...

... As its application to the first-century BCE Psalms of Solomon and the discovery of 1QH and 11QPs^a (with six further psalms) have confirmed, the practice in Jewish circles of composing new psalms for use in worship continued into the New Testament period ...

> *... We should also note that in Eph. 5:18–19 such singing is understood to be the result of being filled with the Spirit, in some ways like the uninhibited singing of those who are drunk (Eph. 5:18; cf. Acts 2:13–18), but expressive of a very different Spirit (see my Jesus 238). Whether glossolalic singing is envisaged is difficult to determine ...* [42]

Michael F. Bird, *Colossians,* **2014**

> *Importantly, the mechanism by which this word of Messiah is communicated is through instruction (teaching and admonishing each other) and in worship (singing psalms, hymns, and spiritual songs), and all of this is to occur in the context of thanksgiving. If we regard the impartation of the word of Messiah as the goal of teaching, admonishing, and singing, then we are led to the conclusion that teaching is meant to take on a worshipful character while musical praise is to take on a didactic role in order to comprehensively impart the word. Christian teaching is not meant to be dry, but soaked in thankful praise. Similarly, singing is not purposed to be doctrinally benign but should comprise a pointer to the truth of Jesus Christ. In the background to all of this is the notion that whatever Christians do in worship, teaching, work, leisure, or life, they do in the name of the Lord Jesus, giving thanks to God the Father through him. That is indicative of the binitarian nature of early Christian worship in making the Father and Son the objects of religious devotion. Jesus, the true image of God, who reconciled the believers to God, remains the fountain from which all thanksgiving overflows and is the one in whom all worship of the Father takes place.* [43]

---

[42] Dunn, *Colossians and Philemon*, pp. 236-240.
[43] Bird, *Colossians and Philemon*, Kindle locations 2547-2558.

Martin Kitchen, *Ephesians*, 1994

Paul's letter to the Ephesians makes a specific point about thanksgiving or giving thanks in worship which relates especially to Eph 5:19.[44]

Everett Ferguson, *The Church of Christ: A Biblical Ecclesiology for Today*, 1996

In his internationally acclaimed study of the church as it is reflected in the New Testament Ferguson observes regarding the "activities in the assembly":

> *Singing was closely related to prayer in ancient times (1 Cor 14:15; James 5:13) and so belongs to the daily religious life as well as to the assembly. The same elements of prayer noted above are applicable to singing. The distinctiveness of Christian song is that it, like prayer, is done "in the name of the Lord Jesus Christ" (Eph 5:19; cf. Col 3:16-17), that is, with reference to him in worship of him. Although Ephesians 5:19 and Colossians 3:16, which provide rich sources for thee discussion of early Christian singing, have as their literary context the Christian life in a larger sense, the statements are drawn from practices on church. The practice of assembly is to influence the entire Christian life.*[45]

Ferguson appends an interesting and informative footnote to this discussion, fn. 94 on p. 268. He is aware that Eph 5:19 may *appear* to be a "minimal claim" addressing the Christian life in general regarding what takes place in the assembly. But Eph 5:19 informs and influences the Christian lifestyle.

> *As in 1 Cor 14, the assembly is the literary setting but something from outside the assembly is used to reinforce the teaching (vv. 7-11), so in Eph 5 and Col 3, although the literary setting is the Christian life, something from the assembly is used to reinforce the point. I have hereby consciously made minimal claim for these verses. Many commentators see the evidence from the context that these texts refer to the assembly; e.g. Eduard Lohse,*

---

[44] Kitchen, *Ephesians*, p. 99.
[45] Ferguson, *The Church of Christ*, p. 268.

Colossians and Philemon (Philadelphia: Fortress, 1971, pp. 149-153; Rudolf Schnackenburg, Ephesians: A Commentary (Edinburgh: T. & T. Clark, 1991, pp. 237-238.[46]

Anthony Lee Ash, PhD University Southern California

In his commentary on Philippians, Colossians, and Philemon Dr. Ash addresses Col 3:16 which most scholars see in parallel with Eph 5:19. He observes that Col 3:16 reflects a picture of the *harmonious community at worship, teaching and admonishing one another.*

Some Church of Christ Scholars who are published on this topic

The following scholars, all highly qualified professors in Christian universities specializing in New and Old Testament studies all set Eph 5:19 and Col 3:16 in the context of the early Christian church worship assemblies: Everett Ferguson (PhD Harvard University); Jack Lewis (PhD Harvard University, PhD Hebrew Union College); Rubel Shelly (PhD Vanderbilt University); Earle West (PhD Indiana University); James D. Bales (PhD UCAL, Berkley); J W Roberts (PhD University of Texas).

Paul and the Corinthian Church 1 Cor 14:13-33

In his detailed discussion of abuses in the church worship assembly introduced at 1 Cor 11:17 with the Lord's Supper, Paul twice discussed singing and hymns sung in the assembly. These we find at 1 Cor 14:15 and 1 Cor 14:26.

1 Cor 14:15-17 *What am I to do? I will pray with the spirit and I will pray with the mind also;* <u>*I will sing with the spirit and I will sing with the mind also.*</u> [16] *Otherwise, if you bless with the spirit, how can anyone in the position of an outsider say the "Amen" to your thanksgiving when he does not know what you are saying?* [17] *For you may give thanks well enough, but the other man is not edified.*

1 Cor 14:26 *What then, brethren?* <u>*When you come together, each one has a hymn,*</u> *a lesson, a revelation, a tongue, or an interpretation. Let all things be done for edification.* [27] *If any speak in a tongue, let there be only two or at most three, and each in turn;*

---

[46] Ferguson, *The Church of Christ*, p. 268. Italics mine, IAF.

and let one interpret. ²⁸ But if there is no one to interpret, let each of them keep silence in church and speak to himself and to God.

It is universally accepted that these two texts fall under the discussion of a Christian worship assembly in which Holy Spirit inspired activity was involved.

Summary of Singing in the Worship Assembly

One can safely assume from a study of scholarly research and publications over the past 50 years that it is the overwhelming consensus of recognized scholars that the singing or hymnody that is reflected in 1 Cor 14, Eph 5:19, and Col 3:16 is in the context of a church, house church, or congregation meeting for formal Lord's Day worship. The singing is set in a liturgical framework of worship in which the participants or congregants are worshipping God and Jesus in their weekly Lord's Day assembly, and in this process are being edified, encouraged and built up in their faith, preparing them for a lifestyle of daily worshipping and serving God and Jesus through their Christian walk.

In the next chapter we will exegetically examine the three texts that address singing in the worship assembly in an effort to determine whether they authorize singing in the Worship assembly and why this might be so.

Chapter 15: The Fellowship or *Agapē* Love Feast

Introduction

Although the *Agapē* Love Feast appears in several instances in the 1st century literature of the early church we find only one direct reference to a love feast in the New Testament, Jude 12, and another indirect reference at 1 Cor 11:17-34.

A further possible reference may be found at 2 Peter 2:13 depending on a textual variant which reads ταῖς ἀγάπαις, *tais agapais, the love feast*, instead of ταῖς ἀπάταις, *tais apatais, the sinful delusion*[1] or as in the RSV *their dissipation*, or the NIV *their pleasures* implying their *sinful pleasures*. I prefer the translation that reads *sinful appetites*.

The reading ἀπάταις, *sinful appetites* or *dissipations* in the Greek text of 2 Pet 2:13 is stronger than the textual variant ἀγάπαις, *love feast* at 2:13 which introduces an interesting development that we find referenced at 1 Cor 11:17-34 where the presumed *love* feast had degenerated into *sinful indulgence* that abused the Lord's Supper.

An interesting point is introduced in the literary and textual parallels between 2 Peter and Jude. Scholars are challenged by the age-old question, "who copied whom"! This misses the point that both may have used a common source, with Jude's scribe copying ἀγάπαις, *love*, the other, Peter's scribe, copying ἀπάταις, *sinful desire, sinful deceit*, or *dissipation*.[2]

Richard Bauckham has an interesting comment regarding this variant:

> *Although confusion of ἀπάταις and ἀγάπαις would have been a very easy scribal error, the change of pronouns makes it unlikely that the variant reading ἀγάπαις in 2 Peter is correct, or that the copy of Jude used by the*

---

[1] Zodhiates, ταῖς ἀγάπαις.
[2] This is not the place to explore the critical issues of the textual relationship between 2 Peter and Jude. I mention this interesting enigma only to comment on the reference to ἀπάταις in 2 Peter, *sinful appetite*. Furthermore, I do not support the view that the author of 2 Peter was a disciple of Peter and not Peter himself.

> *author of 2 Peter already had the corrupt reading ἀπάταις. The author of 2 Peter must have made a deliberate alteration. It is possible that he wished to exclude any reference to the agapes ... but in that case it is odd that he has done so by substituting the similar-sounding ἀπάταις for ἀγάπαις. The suggestion that he intended a deliberate pun is more likely, and he might have expected his readers to see the pun (συνευωχούμενοι ὑμῖν, "while they feast with you," would naturally suggest the agapes) even if they were not familiar with Jude's letter. The meals which were defiled by the gluttonous and riotous behavior of the false teachers could not be called ἀγάπαι, but they might be called "deceits" (the basic meaning of ἀπάταις).*[3]

Jude 12 is more direct, obviously being negative regarding what had transpired in his community regarding the celebration and abuse of the love feast:

> *[12] These are blemishes on your love feasts, as they boldly carouse together, looking after themselves; waterless clouds, carried along by winds; fruitless trees in late autumn, twice dead, uprooted; [13] wild waves of the sea, casting up the foam of their own shame; wandering stars for whom the nether gloom of darkness has been reserved for ever.*

1 Cor 11:17-34 ties in well with the reflection of Jude 12 and possibly 2 Pet 2:13 regarding the abuse of both the Agapē Love Feast and the Lord's Supper. We have above under the study of the Lord's Supper as Eucharist already commented on how the Lord's Supper had been corrupted and abused in Corinth with the result that Paul strongly advised separating the two. The result of these observations is that fairly early in the life of the church the holiness of both the Agapē and the Lord's Supper became corrupt and at least the Pauline churches separated the Lord's Supper and the Love Feast.

---

[3] Bauckham, *2 Peter, Jude*, p. 266.

Nothing more is said in the New Testament regarding the Agapē. The literature of 1st century church does however indicate that the Agapē continued to be featured in the life of some churches.

Possible Origins of the *Agapē* Love Feast
We have also noted under the study of the Eucharist, Lord's Supper, that there are some indications in Luke's Acts that the early Jerusalem church gathered together regularly for prayer, study, and fellowship, Acts 2:42-47:

> *^{42} And they devoted themselves to the apostles' teaching and fellowship, to the breaking of bread and the prayers. ^{43} And fear came upon every soul; and many wonders and signs were done through the apostles. ^{44} And all who believed were together and had all things in common; ^{45} and they sold their possessions and goods and distributed them to all, as any had need. ^{46} And day by day, attending the temple together and breaking bread in their homes, they partook of food with glad and generous hearts, ^{47} praising God and having favor with all the people. And the Lord added to their number day by day those who were being saved.*

It is reasonable as observed by most commentators on Luke's Acts that *Luke was giving a summary of life in the early Jerusalem church* indicating the beginnings of the new Jewish Christian community that continued within the boundaries of the Temple confines to gather and be taught by the Apostles. Recognizing their potential excommunication by the Jews for their faith in Jesus as the Messiah they bonded together celebrating and benevolently taking care of one another. Their participating in common meals in which they would rejoice in their new fellowship would appropriately be referred to as love feasts, hence *agápē* feasts.

But this was nothing new, for as Jews they had already an established practice of gathering together as families to celebrate the several Jewish feasts such as Purim, Tabernacles, and the Passover.

Festive occasions and feasts were also part of the Graeco-Roman cultic life so it was a natural step from their Jewish or Graeco-Roman cultic life to gather for celebratory cultic feasts. The *Agápē* love feast would not have been a new innovation to the early Christians but would have been the beginnings of a new occasion for a festival and an addition to the Lord's Supper and Eucharist celebration.

The *Agapē* in the Literature of the Early Church

Most of the information we have on the Agapē feast we find in the late first and second century's literature of the church such as the *Didache*, Ignatius, Clement of Alexandria, Tertullian, and Hippolytus.

Everett Ferguson, *Early Christians Speak*, provides an excellent summary of the early practice of the Agapē love feast:

> *It seems that a meal provided the most convenient context in which the Lord's Supper was observed by the early Christians. At least this was the case at Corinth and provided the occasion for the abuses which developed there. The Didache also sets the eucharist in the context of a common religious meal (VIII.3). The Roman governor Pliny places the Christian gathering for a common meal at a separate time from their "stated" religious assembly (VII.1). By this time in Bithynia, it would seem, the Lord's Supper was separated from the meal. Even where an ordinary meal provided the setting for the Lord's Supper, there is no reason to think the latter was not distinct in its observance and meaning.* [4]

Ferguson observes that although the terms Agapē, Eucharist, and Lord's Supper were on several occasions used synonymously they were not always in reference to the same celebration. He observes that "apparently the agápē was used for the meal, and the eucharist of the memorial for the Lord."[5]

Although not identical with Eucharist, the Agapē was nevertheless considered to be an important church function under the leadership or control of a bishop or another member of the

---

[4] Ferguson, *Early Christians Speak*, pp. 125ff.
[5] Ferguson, *Early Christians Speak*, p. 128.

"clergy" such as a deacon or appointed leader. Moral disorders during the celebration of the Agapē soon became a problem, hence the need of "official" control leading in many cases to the separation of the two meals. Although originally considered a deeply spiritual function associated with prayer, Scripture reading, and homily, the meal often degenerated into a benevolent material function in which the needy were fed a meal and the focus was placed on the meal.[6]

The *Agapē* in Contemporary Church Life

Although not as common in the contemporary church as has been the practice in the past, the "dinner on the ground" functions or similar contemporary fellowship meals are not so much a benevolent occasion but more a fellowship occasion. Many churches today hold special fellowship meals among the youth, the elderly, or special interest groups. In most cases these are more shepherding occasions than benevolent occasions.

I am reminded of an amusing yet touching occasion in a smaller rural church where my wife and I once worshipped. We did have a special benevolent case in which a particular lady, one step away from homeless, would attend our fellowship meals. She would always station herself at or near the head of the line, fill her plate full then head outside where she had a pickup truck which was her home and in which she also housed two dogs, her special companions. She would feed the dogs, stash the left-over food, and head back into the fellowship hall and get in line for another plate full of food which she would eat, and then go back for "seconds"! This aggravated some of our members until it was pointed out that in this case our fellowship meal was an *agápē* meal in which we shared our food with a needy lady and her two companions!

The congregation where my wife and I once worshiped met on Sunday evenings in small groups spread all over our extended church city community. The congregation leadership called these groups Connecting Points. Each group was left to develop their own curriculum. Some groups shared a meal each Sunday evening and then enjoyed a Bible study/discussion period followed by

---

[6] Ferguson, *Early Christians Speak*, p. 129.

prayer. We were encouraged to invite friends to these special fellowship love feasts! Their real value was that they served as shepherding occasions for friendship enrichment. In one sense they were informal *agápē* feasts through which we planned benevolent outreach opportunities especially during high occasions like Thanksgiving, Christmas, and other special festive occasions. Our group also took these opportunities to provide benevolent opportunities for the needy.

I can imagine a small house group meeting in towns like Colossae in the first century of Christianity meeting in similar *agápē* feasts and enjoying benevolent opportunities in their communities and through them witnessing for Christ. Possibly this is what Paul had in mind in his letter to Philemon, a Christian in Colossae when he wrote:

> *[4] I thank my God always when I remember you in my prayers, [5] because I hear of your love and of the faith which you have toward the Lord Jesus and all the saints, [6] and I pray that the sharing of your faith may promote the knowledge of all the good that is ours in Christ. [7] For I have derived much joy and comfort from your love, my brother, because the hearts of the saints have been refreshed through you.*[7]

---

[7] Philemon 4–7.

Chapter 16: Christian Worship in the Second Century

Introduction

Although we do not have many references in our New Testament documents relating to Christian worship assemblies, we are fortunate that Christians in the first three centuries left us numerous descriptions of their worship practices. We are indebted to Everett Ferguson who has spent many years as a church historian researching church practices and documenting them in a repository of rich resources for our study. His publications such as *Early Christians Speak*[1] in two volumes, the first volume having reached a third edition, and his magisterial study of *Baptism in the Early Church*,[2] and two volume *Encyclopedia of Early Christianity*.[3]

I will shortly return to Ferguson's profound contribution to our understanding of early Christian worship and practices, but before doing so I wish to comment briefly on another scholar's enlightened contribution to our understanding of early or primitive Christian practices—Oscar Cullmann, *Early Christian Worship*.[4] In his first chapter, "Basic Characteristics of the Early Christian Service of Worship," Cullmann discusses worship under several different categories: first, *Place and Time*; second, *The Several Component Parts*; third, *The Aim of the Service*; fourth, *The Inter-Relation of the Various Elements: Service of the Word and the Lord's Supper*; fifth, *Freedom of Spiritual expression and the Binding Character of Liturgy*; and sixth, *The Christian Character of the Service*.

The remarkable detail provided by Cullmann is beyond the purpose of this study but is well worth reading and further reflection. My main point in mentioning Cullmann's contribution to this study is that his comments and conclusions agree with those we have traced in this study and the comments we will draw from Ferguson's study in *Early Christians Speak*.

---

[1] Ferguson, *Early Christians Speak*, 3rd Edition, 1981, 1987, 1999, 2002.
[2] Ferguson, *Baptism in the Early Church*.
[3] Ferguson, *Encyclopedia of Early Christianity*.
[4] Cullmann, *Early Christian Worship*.

Nevertheless, there are one or two points I find interesting in Cullmann's study. *First*, the place of early Christian worship was most likely in-house churches on Sunday, the Lord's Day, and not on the Sabbath or the seventh day of the Torah. *Second*, Cullmann mentions the various benedictions and doxologies encountered for instance in the *Didache* (an early 2nd century document which I will shortly discuss), and the mention of the brief prayer *Maranatha, Come Lord Jesus* at the close of the Eucharist or Lord's Supper which incorporated a future component into the Lord's Supper, *"you proclaim the Lord's death until he comes,"* 1 Cor 11:26. An additional interesting feature that Cullmann identifies is the role of baptism in the worship service and its association with the public confession of faith.

Ferguson and others observe that the earliest attestation we have of early Christian assemblies comes from the non-Christian Roman governor Pliny the Younger in a letter to the Roman Emperor Trajan, ca 98–117. In his question to Trajan on how to deal with the Christians he wrote[5]:

> *They (the Christians) affirmed, however, the whole of their guilt, or their error, was, that they were in the habit of meeting on a certain fixed day before it was light, when they sang in alternate verses a hymn to Christ, as to a god, and bound themselves by a solemn oath, not to any wicked deeds, but never to commit any fraud, theft or adultery, never to falsify their word, nor deny a trust when they should be called upon to deliver it up; after which it was their custom to separate, and then reassemble to partake of food but food of an ordinary and innocent kind. Even this practice, however, they had abandoned after the publication of my edict, by which, according to your orders, I had forbidden political associations. I judged it so much the more necessary to extract the real truth, with the assistance of torture, from two female slaves, who were styled deaconesses: but I could discover nothing more than depraved and excessive superstition.*

---

[5] Pliny, *Letters*, 10.96.

One of the earliest Christian accounts of a church assembly, outside of the New Testament documents is that of the *Didache*[6]:

> *Having earlier confessed your sins so that your sacrifice may be pure, come together each Lord's day of the Lord, break bread, and give thanks.*[7]

In several places the *Didache* refers to the early church assemblies on the Lord's Day. The interesting part is the association of the Lord's Day assembly with the Lord's Supper.

Ignatius of Antioch, ca 100-117 CE, in his *Letter to the Magnesians*, 15:9, encouraged the Christians to no longer observe the Sabbath but to come to the new hope of the Lord's Day:

> *If therefore those who lived according to the old practices came to the new hope, no longer observing the Sabbath but living according to the Lord's Day, in which also our life arose through him and his death (which some deny), through which mystery we received faith, and on account of which we suffer in order to be found disciples of Jesus Christ our only teacher, how shall we be able to live apart from him for whom even the prophets were looking as their teacher since they were his disciples in Spirit.*[8]

It is apparent that Ignatius considered the practice of gathering regularly on the Lord's Day to be the time when hope would be restored.

Justin Martyr, ca, 100–165 CE, an early Christian Apologist, spoke highly of the Sunday assembly and its role in the life of the early church. I am including a fairly extensive quote from Justin as it is early in the life of the church and demonstrates well the Sunday worship service and how the Christians celebrated their faith in God, Jesus Christ and the Holy Spirit:

---

[6] *Didache*, from the Greek *didachē*, teaching. The full title reads *The Teaching of the Twelve Apostles*. The *Didache* is a brief early Christian treatise, dated by most scholars to the early 2nd century.
[7] Ferguson, *Early Christians Speak*, p. 70, notes the double reference to the Lord in this report and suggests that it may be a take on the Jewish expression "the Sabbath of the Lord," Lev 23:28.
[8] Ferguson, *Early Christians Speak*, p. 65.

And we afterwards continually remind each other of these things. And the wealthy among us help the needy; and we always keep together; and for all things wherewith we are supplied, we bless the Maker of all through His Son Jesus Christ, and through the Holy Ghost. And on the day called Sunday, all who live in cities or in the country gather together to one place, and the memoirs of the apostles or the writings of the prophets are read, as long as time permits; then, when the reader has ceased, the president verbally instructs, and exhorts to the imitation of these good things. Then we all rise together and pray, and, as we before said, when our prayer is ended, bread and wine and water are brought, and the president in like manner offers prayers and thanksgivings, according to his ability, and the people assent, saying Amen; and there is a distribution to each, and a participation of that over which thanks have been given, and to those who are absent a portion is sent by the deacons. And they who are well to do, and willing, give what each thinks fit; and what is collected is deposited with the president, who succours the orphans and widows and those who, through sickness or any other cause, are in want, and those who are in bonds and the strangers sojourning among us, and in a word takes care of all who are in need. But Sunday is the day on which we all hold our common assembly, because it is the first day on which God, having wrought a change in the darkness and matter, made the world; and Jesus Christ our Saviour on the same day rose from the dead. For He was crucified on the day before that of Saturn (Saturday); and on the day after that of Saturn, which is the day of the Sun, having appeared to His apostles and disciples, He taught them these things, which we have submitted to you also for your consideration.[9]

---

[9] Justin Martyr, *First Apology*, 67.1-7, *Early Christian Writings;* Everett Ferguson, *Early Christians Speak*, p. 66.

Summary Observations

From these few surviving citations from the early Christian writers and apologists we see several acts of worship surfacing that define the early Christian worship services or gatherings; the Christian worship services were celebrated on Sunday as the Lord's Day honoring the Lord Jesus Christ's resurrection rather than the Sabbath rest of the Jewish tradition. In fact one thing surfaces in this shift, the Lord's Day was not celebrated as a day of rest as was the meaning of the term Sabbath. Since the early Christians were living in a pagan culture and not a Jewish one such days of rest were not practiced. As Pliny indicated many Christians met early before dawn. The worship consisted of reading Scripture, a homily (lesson or sermon) on the Scripture that had been read, prayers, a religious meal in which the Christians remembered and celebrated the death and resurrection of Jesus (the Eucharist or Lord's Supper), singing or chanting hymns, and where possible, the giving of funds or food in support of the needy.

Regarding the roots of these worship practices Ferguson observes:

> *The prevailing theory of the early history of Christian liturgy is that the Christian order of worship was built up from the Jewish synagogue service of scripture teaching and prayer with the addition of the distinctively Christian rite of the Lord's Supper. The latter too has antecedents in the Jewish Passover meal and table prayers, but these were family and home observations in Judaism. The meal became part of the community assembly of Christians.*[10]

It is not surprising that the early Christian worship practices and assemblies would follow the Jewish Synagogue influence. *First*, the Synagogue liturgy was distanced from the Temple cult of animal sacrifices and ceremonies that could only be offered in Jerusalem and the Temple. The Synagogue services and liturgy were community located. *Second*, many or most of the early Christians were Jewish Synagogue converts to Christianity or

---

[10] Ferguson, *Early Christians Speak*, p. 84.

were converts from devout Gentiles who had been drawn to the monotheism, the Jewish legal system of the Law of Moses, and the high moral standards of the Synagogue. It would be a natural flow of thought from the Synagogue focus on the reading of the Law, prayers, and religious instruction, combined with the celebration of the death and resurrection of Jesus in the Eucharist Lord's Supper into the Christian accommodation of these in a Christian liturgy honoring God's redemptive activity in Jesus Christ. *Third*, the Synagogue as a social, religious, and community center opened the door to a unique Christian community center and benevolent house of fellowship.

Chapter 17: Worship Since the Second Century

Introduction

The unfortunate centuries of religious faction surrounding the theological and ecclesiastical debates that reach back into the third century CE has introduced a wide variety of liturgical practices, many of them shaped by the theological preferences of the region or age. We see this notably in the power struggles between the Roman Catholic Church, the Eastern Orthodox churches, the Protestant Reformation churches, the Church of England and Episcopalian Churches, the Wesleyan churches, the Presbyterian churches, the Lutheran Church Synods, the Anabaptist traditions, the Mennonite churches, the Baptist churches, the Church of Christ and Disciples of Christ traditions, and the more recent free open community Bible churches.[1]

Regardless of these differences a common thread today runs through the liturgies of most Christian churches, worldwide.

First, the vast majority of Christian churches today recognize that Sunday, the Lord's Day, is the common day of Christian worship celebrating the death and resurrection of the Lord Jesus Christ.

Second, most churches recognize that the purpose, focus, and direction of the worship is the Trinitarian understanding of God the Father, Jesus Christ the Son, and the Holy Spirit. Christians recognize that they are called by God into his worship for their own spiritual welfare and that the direction of that worship should be toward God and the Lord Jesus Christ.

Third, most of the traditional churches celebrate the Lord's Supper, Eucharist, Mass, or Communion on a regular cycle; mostly weekly or monthly, some quarterly. Many of the newer fellowship, community, or Bible fellowship churches may or may not celebrate the Lord's Supper.

---

[1] I openly recognize that I have been selective in the church choices reflected in this paragraph, but my purpose has been simply to illustrate how theological and ecclesiological disagreements and battles have impacted the liturgical makeup of Christian worship services.

Fourth, most churches include the Lord's Supper, prayers, the reading of Scripture, a sermon, and a weekly contribution in their liturgy.

Fifth, all in some measure or fashion include the singing of psalms, hymns, and spiritual songs, some with choirs, some acappella, some with musical instrumental accompaniment, or solo renditions of spiritual songs.

Many, if not all, have been shaped by their ecclesiastical and theological heritage, some more formal and fixed in liturgical calendar, others free flowing in form. In some the worship service is more clergy oriented and led, in others a mutual edification is adopted. It is not uncommon to speak of High Church which is more formal with an ordained priesthood, or a Low Church which is more open adopting a "priesthood of all believers" which functions without a formal priestly ordination.

One factor that has impacted worship services in many churches today has been the rapid urbanization of society and churches, both in the American and European West, and also to a large degree in Africa. People for a variety of reasons, mostly economic, have "migrated" from rural communities and rural churches to large urban societies and large urban churches, sadly in many cases, to no churches! The close-knit relationships of rural homes and smaller churches has been found in different church forms, or, sadly in many cases by isolation, loneliness, and depression. Community churches have been able to capitalize on this need for renewed associations.

Another factor that has impacted church services is the tendency of traditional churches to hold firm to traditional practices which a younger post-modern generation has left behind geographically, economically, and socially. Advanced technology such as the cellphone and social networking, video presentations such as U-Tube, and "internet distance learning, communication, and gameplaying" have replaced older traditional forms of communication and social entertainment. Today one can attend church over a cup of latte or cappuccino in isolation from a community or fellowship, and watch a closed circuit sermon all at the same time. Without realizing the danger of such moves, which do hold some positive features, our post-modern society, which is more focused on itself, has shifted the focus of worship away from God and the Lord Jesus Christ toward self. Unless we can get immediate self-gratification or what pleases and appeals to us, we lose interest.

How we navigate the future of changing interests and needs can be either a positive incentive toward worshipping God and building healthy spiritual relationships, or a negative impact which directs the focus on self-interest.

As the church has spread throughout the world the style of worship, singing, and preaching has been shaped by various cultural and sociological influences, with varying degrees of success in worship and praise activities, but Christian worship worldwide needs to maintain its biblical and theological compass intact, and remain shaped by the primary focus of our early Christian fathers and their closeness to biblical and theological roots in Christ, rather than our cultural and sociological surroundings and neighbors.

Chapter 18: Defining and Understanding a Contemporary Theology of Worship

I trust that by now when we speak of a theology of worship, we understand that we are not speaking about a *liturgical form* of worship, or simply the traditional things we do in worship because Scripture and doctrine teach such. It is much easier to do something in worship *in order to be* Scriptural than it is *in pausing to understand the reason for doing such* which lies beyond or simply deeper than being "scriptural or doctrinally correct." Now don't get me wrong! Being Scriptural when Scripture is properly interpreted is extremely important to me.

There are two major elements in our worship service in which I find this tendency to be a problem. One is in our engaging in the Lord's Supper in a *perfunctory*[1] manner! *By perfunctory I imply a superficial, hasty manner in which we spend as little time as possible to make room for the other features of the service such as a sermon or singing.* I am not denigrating preaching or singing in this comment, but all one has to do is compare the time we often spend remembering or participating in the Lord's Supper with the time we spend listening to a sermon or singing!

Now once again, before you get the wrong impression regarding my comment about preaching, I am a preacher, somewhat retired, but still a preacher at heart who likes good preaching, and even sometimes preaching that is not so good!

Turning now to my concern regarding our practice of "breaking the bread and drinking the cup" in the Lord's Supper. Too often, but not always, we begin the Lord's Supper with a short prayer or obligatory brief comment and move on. Ten minutes in most congregations and we are through and ready to sing another song! Now, once again, before you get me wrong in this statement regarding singing, I like singing at church and believe we

---

[1] By perfunctory I imply *routinely, superficially,* or *hasty manner*. The Merriam Webster Dictionary defines *Perfunctory* as a word whose origins are found entirely in Latin. First appearing in English in the late 16th century, it means "*done in a ... superficial manner,*" from the Latin *perfungi,* meaning "*to accomplish*" or "*to get through with.*"

do an extraordinarily good job in our singing. What I am calling for is a deeper reflection at the Lord's Supper than a "doctrinally required practice," a cursory prayer, and pass the plate!

Being *scripturally* and *theologically* concerned and focused with *the reason why we are worshipping*, and *who we are worshipping* is obviously of extreme importance, and certainly more important than the *doctrinal* reason we are doing it, or our need to be *culturally* and *sociologically* relevant![2]

Explaining and understanding why we are doing *what we are doing*, beyond being *doctrinal* is more theologically important than simply being *doctrinally faithful*! This gets to the heart of a theology of worship.

I might add that in my opinion while liturgical and doctrinal form and concern is important, they are not as important as understanding the theology of what we are doing! From my experience from being a missionary, minister, professor, and teacher of Scripture and theology for over 40 years that unfortunately many of our members have only a rudimentary understanding of the importance of the Lord's Supper, and no realization of its role and power as a *sacrament*[3] properly understood as related to our baptism.

Asking where Scripture enters in determining the liturgy of our worship is of profound significance. However, asking where God is involved and how the Lord's Supper relates to our relationship to God in the worship is of even deeper significance.

At the core of my concern is the reason for how and why we enter the setting of our worship. Is the worship service designed to please us and our friends, or is it to please God? Is God the direction of our worship, or are we the direction of our worship? This is not to deny that we are important in the worship since Paul is clear that in worship of God we not only address God but also address one another and are edified. What determines the

---

[2] Kindly refer back to the concerns I expressed in the opening chapters over being sociologically acceptable to our contemporary post-modern and sociologically driven culture.

[3] A reminder, *sacrament* from the Latin implies that which *binds* us to our leader, king, or Lord.

difference and delicate balance in a theology of worship is the focus and direction of our worship. Are we worshipping to address God, ourselves, or our neighbors?

Again, as I have already mentioned above, the two aspects of our worship in which we experience the greatest difficulty is in our singing and the Lord's Supper. However, our attitude in delivering and hearing the sermon can, and should also be a subject of this concern. Are we set on entertaining the congregation and our neighbors or on worshipping God? It is in an appropriate reverent and worshipful mindset that we penetrate to the core of our worship; the sovereignty, holiness, righteousness of our God who has in Christ Jesus redeemed us and saved us from ourselves and an awful future. It is when contemplating and celebrating God's loving, merciful, gracious atoning working on our lives in our worship of God that we are edified, and the congregation is lifted up. Are we drawing the congregation closer to God or to pleasing ourselves and our neighbors when we sing? Are we given to hearing God's word in the sermon or are we more concerned or impressed with the delivery of the sermon? In our prayers I have often been concerned with our penchant for making announcements to the congregation during the prayer as to why we are praying, sort of telling God the details! Surely, he knows! And if we, the congregation, do not know then tell us *before* we engage in the prayer!

I readily recognize that in many cases in my fellowship in Churches of Christ those who provide leadership in our worship services are lay persons, not specifically trained in the theology of worship, and this is good and to be encouraged, but when that is the case we should spend more time preparing for the worship than a few minutes at the front or rear of the auditorium before the service begins.

I also readily accept the fact that we can tend to over formalize our worship service and lean more on a paid ministry staff for worship leadership. In a large congregation this can be a natural tendency, whereas in a small house church planning a worship service can be, but not necessarily so, a much simpler exercise!

Since the worship assembly in which we are called to worship by God should be should be a special encounter with God and as such should be the most significant time of our Christian spiritual experience, possibly even of our lives, and since in worship we are preparing ourselves for a future "life" in the presence of our holy God and in the presence of an innumerable host of redeemed saints and angels, we might think more about the theology or focus of our worship! Is God the focus, or are we? I like the message below from Hebrews which I feel establishes the ambiance of a theology of worship!

[14] Since then we have a great high priest who has passed through the heavens, Jesus, the Son of God, let us hold fast our confession. [15] For we have not a high priest who is unable to sympathize with our weaknesses, but one who in every respect has been tempted as we are, yet without sin. [16] Let us then with confidence draw near to the throne of grace, that we may receive mercy and find grace to help in time of need. [4]

When contemplating a worshipful attitude, I am drawn to the closing comment of Habakkuk when he compared the meaningless worship of Israel, who had reduced worship to the veneration of human categories, with the worship of YHWH:

But the LORD *is in his holy temple;*
let all the earth keep silence before him. [5]

In the light of our present banal world circumstances in which we are seemingly surrounded by wars, evil, sexual immorality, and for some life with little hope, consider the comment of Ralph Smith on Hab 2:20 above;

In contrast to the idol, Yahweh is in his holy temple, let all the earth bow in hushed silence before him. So, all of the forces that oppose God will ultimately be silenced. <u>Now</u> the forces of evil still rage. The righteous is still faithful. The battle continues. <u>Yet</u> there is a power in the world "greater than armies, bombs, bribery, and torture, and it is he who thwarts the efforts of the wicked and gives to the righteous another kind of power to enable them to resist and endure." [6]

---

[4] Heb 4:14–16.
[5] Hab 2:20.
[6] Smith, *Micah–Malachi*, p. 112.

It is this supreme God who is higher and holier than all we can imagine that we have gathered to worship. Worship needs to remind us of this profound principle and truth! Worship in its real essence implies veneration and awe, not reducing the concept of holiness to our level of life. We come to be lifted up, not to reduce God down to our level. I am constantly impressed by the tantalizing expression of Marva Dawn, *dumbing worship* down to our level![7]

---

[7] Dawn, *Reaching Out*.

Addendum 1: Gordon D. Fee, *Paul, the Spirit, and the People of God*

The following quotation from Gordon Fee is long but describes precisely the thought behind the view that Col 3:16 and Eph 5:18 in the context of Holy Spirit "inspiration" refer to the church in a worship assembly. Fee writes:

"The Opening Exhortations

We begin with some observations about the opening clauses ("let the word of Christ dwell in your midst richly" and "but be filled with the Spirit") that are of considerable importance.

1. Everything about the contexts, and the language of both sentences in particular, indicate that Paul is here reflecting on the Christian community. These are not words for the individual believer, but for believers as the people of God in relationship with one another. In Colossians that is especially clear. Beginning with 3:12, everything has the community in sight, since everything is for, or in light of, "one another." Thus in the immediately preceding exhortation (v. 15), which sets the pattern for the present one, they are to let the peace of Christ rule in their hearts, since it is to this that they have been called together as one body.

Colossians 3:16 views these relationships within the context of the gathered people of God at worship, where they are to teach and admonish one another as one way that the word of Christ will dwell "in them" richly. This means that the prepositional phrase "in/among you," even though it modifies the verb "indwell" and would ordinarily mean "within you," here means "in your midst." The indwelling "word of Christ," therefore, in its two forms of "teaching and admonishing one another" and of "singing to God," has to do with the church at worship. If the community context in Ephesians is less immediately certain, it is clearly in view, since the whole passage from 4:1 through chapter 6 takes up community life, how they are to "maintain the unity of the Spirit in the bond of peace" (4:3).

2. In the same vein, it is significant to note that the compound participles, "teaching and admonishing," are the same two that Paul used in Colossians 1:28 to describe his own ministry. Here, then, is clear evidence that Paul did not consider ministry

to be the special province of either apostles or officeholders. As in the earliest of his letters (1 Thess 5:14), *these kinds of activities in the Christian assembly are the responsibility of all.*

This is in keeping with the picture that emerges in 1 Corinthians 14:26 as well. Here he admonishes in a presuppositional way that "when you come together, each one has a hymn, [etc.] ... for the strengthening of the church."

3. The primary concern of the exhortation in the Colossians passage is with the "word of Christ." In Paul this expression invariably means "the message of the gospel with its central focus on Christ." This, after all, is what the letter is all about: Christ the embodiment of God, Christ the all-sufficient one, Christ, creator and redeemer. Paul now urges that this "word of Christ," which in part he has already articulated in 1:15–23, "dwell in their midst" in an abundant way.

In so doing, they will reflect precisely what we learned about worship from 1 Corinthians 11:4–5. Part of their activity will be directed toward one another ("teaching and admonishing one another"), and part toward God ("singing to God with your hearts"). Thus the riches of the gospel are to be present among them with great richness. The structure of the sentence as a whole indicates that songs of all kinds are to play a significant role in that richness.

4. The parallel passage in Ephesians makes explicit what we would have guessed in any case, that Paul considers all this activity to be the result of their being filled with the Spirit. *Thus, however we are to understand the adjective "Spiritual" in relation to the various expressions of song, Spirit songs are at least one expression of the Spirit's presence, whose fullness will guide and inspire all of the worship in its several expressions.*

The Worship Itself

When we turn from these opening clauses to the rest of the sentences, *we learn still more about Paul's understanding of Spirit-inspired worship.*

We need to note, first of all, that where the Spirit of God is, there is also singing. The early church was characterized by its singing; so also in every generation where there is renewal by the Spirit a new hymnody breaks forth. If most such songs do not have staying power, some of them do, and these become the treasure-trove of our ongoing teaching and admonishing of one another, as well as of our constantly turning to God the Father and God the Son and offering praise by inspiration of the Holy Spirit."[1]

---

[1] Fee, *Paul, the Spirit, and the People of God*, Kindle location 2616-2639.

Addendum 2: Clinton Arnold, *Ephesians*

The citation below is from Arnold's excellent discussion of *singing* as *speaking to one another* in a *Spirit-filled manner* in a worship service. It is long but provides an excellent resource for those who do not have a copy of Arnold, *Ephesians*, at hand.

"The first participle, "speaking" (λαλοῦντες), may seem somewhat odd to English speakers to use with reference to music since music is sung, not spoken. But this manner of expression is used throughout the Bible. Moses "spoke" (ἐλάλησεν) the words of his song to the entire assembly of Israel (Deut 31:30). Deborah likewise "spoke" her song to Israel, as did David his song to the Lord (2 Sam 22:1; Ps 18:1 [LXX 17:1]).

The audience of the singing is "one another" (ἑαυτοῖς). Although this is the reflexive pronoun, it should not be translated that way. Here it has a reciprocal function—a usage that is not uncommon for this pronoun (see 4:32; Col 3:13; 1 Thess 5:13; 1 Pet 4:8). *The singing of praise is always directed to God as the primary audience and recipient, but there is also a horizontal dimension.*[1] The people of God hear one another singing praise to God, and their hearts are encouraged and strengthened. In Col 3:16, Paul even ascribes a teaching function to the worship: "Let the word of Christ richly dwell within you, with all wisdom teaching and admonishing one another with psalms and hymns and spiritual songs" (NASB).

The form of the music covers a wide range and represents significant diversity. Paul may have deliberately chosen words that convey different cultural forms. There has been a great deal of discussion—and disagreement—among commentators on whether the terms here are essentially synonymous and represent a rhetorical way of expressing variety without being precise, or whether the readers would recognize certain kinds of musical forms based on the words chosen. Either way, the terms suggest a variety of musical forms should be used. Nevertheless, there does appear to be a discernible difference between the terms, especially the first two, that can be identified.

---

[1] Emphasis mine, IAF.

The term "psalm" (ψαλμοῖς) was used primarily in the context of Judaism. This term serves as the title for the LXX version of the 150 songs of the Hebrew *Tehillim*, the book of "praises," and appears 72 times throughout the collection. One can find the term in a number of Second Temple Jewish texts, such as in the first-century Psalms of Solomon. By contrast, "psalm" is far less frequent in Gentile texts of Graeco-Roman paganism. For instance, the term never appears in the numerous inscriptions of Ephesus.

The term "hymn" (ὕμνοις), on the other hand, was commonly used of poetic ascriptions of praise to the various gods and goddesses throughout antiquity. Some of the best known are the "Homeric Hymns"—an anonymous collection of thirty-four different hymns of praise to various deities composed in the same style that Homer used in writing the Iliad and the Odyssey. Numerous other poets wrote hymns of praise to the Greek deities. Many of these were sung in the cultic praise of the gods at their various temples. During the NT era, there were guilds of hymn writers who employed their skills at crafting hymns. In fact, an inscription discovered at Ephesus refers to a guild of hymn writers … who wrote their hymns in honor of "the most holy goddess Artemis." Another Ephesian inscription lists the members of a religious society and refers to one as a "hymn writer" … Although the term "hymn" appears occasionally in Jewish texts (including thirteen times in the LXX), it was more common in Greek religious circles.

The final expression Paul uses here, "songs" (ᾠδαῖς), was a more general term and was equally at home in Jewish or Gentile circles. It appears numerous times in the LXX (although only seven times in the NT) and is frequent in Graeco-Roman literature. This is the noun form of the verb for "singing" ( ) that Paul uses in the next line. A funerary inscription found in Ephesus refers to a group of mourners who honored the deceased "with tears and songs…"

Paul probably used the combination of the three terms to commend a variety of forms and musical styles in his multicultural churches, which were comprised of Jews and Greeks. He affirms Jewish forms (psalms) as well as Greek forms (hymns) in the worship of these communities.

The one common denominator of all is that they should be "spiritual" (πνευματικαῖς). The adjective should be understood as qualifying all three nouns. There is no grammatical or contextual reason to limit it to the last word ("songs"). They are "spiritual" in that the Holy Spirit is viewed as actively inspiring the composers as they write their songs of praise to the risen Christ and what he has accomplished by his work on the cross. This, of course, is not the same sense as inspired revelation that would become part of Scripture, but it does stress the work of the Spirit in leading people to worship. *Then it is in this context of corporate worship that the Spirit fills and strengthens God's people.*"[2]

---

[2] Arnold, *Ephesians*, Kindle locations 9758-9786.

Addendum 3: Peter O'Brien, *The Letter to the Ephesians*

This short citation from O'Brien's *Ephesians* is an excellent resource on singing Spirit-inspired psalms, hymns, and songs with the heart.

"Speaking to one another in Spirit-inspired psalms, hymns and songs singing songs and making music with your heart to the Lord."

Given the frequent repetition of keywords, cognate terms, and synonymous expressions in Ephesians, the parallelism of this verse suggests that the two halves should be taken closely together. 'Speaking in psalms and songs' is the same as 'singing songs and making music', a point which is underscored by means of the chiastic relationship between the nouns 'psalm' and 'song' of the first clause and the verbal forms of the same words in the second. Accordingly, the apostle is not referring to two separate responses of speaking in songs (v. 19a) and singing (v. 19b), but is describing the same activity from different perspectives. Each clause, then, has its own particular focus and emphasis:

(1) The first has a horizontal and corporate dimension with its reference to believers addressing one another , presumably in formal worship but also on other occasions, in Spirit-inspired psalms, hymns, and songs (v. 19a). This is akin to Colossians 3: 16, which may be based on Ephesians 5: 19, *where members of the Colossian congregation are to teach and admonish one another in psalms and hymns*. In Ephesians the more general verb 'speak' replaces the specific 'teach and admonish' (of Col. 3: 16), but the sense appears to be the same: the apostle has in view mutual instruction, edification, and exhortation which take place in a range of songs prompted by the Spirit. That such hymns can be described as 'spiritual' says nothing about their spontaneity; instead, the focus is on the source of their inspiration, namely, the Holy Spirit. And the fact that believers address one another in these psalms and songs shows that Paul has intelligible communication in view, not meditation, unknown speech, or glossolalia.

It is not possible to distinguish sharply between the three terms, 'psalms', 'hymns', and 'songs'. They are the most common words used in the LXX for religious songs, and occur interchangeably in the titles of the psalms. The first, 'psalm', is employed by Luke of the Old Testament psalms, though it came to be used more generally of a song of praise (1 Cor. 14: 26; Col. 3: 16) of which the Old Testament psalms were probably regarded as spiritual prototypes. The second term, 'hymn', 1493 denotes any 'festive hymn of praise' (Isa. 42: 10; cf. Acts 16: 25; Heb. 2: 12). In its two New Testament occurrences it refers to an expression of praise to God or Christ (Col. 3: 16 and here). The third word, 'song', is used in the New Testament of the song in which God's acts are praised and glorified (cf. Rev. 5: 9; 14: 3; 15: 3). Although firm distinctions cannot be drawn between the terms, nor can an exact classification of New Testament hymns be made on the basis of the different words, taken together 'psalms', 'hymns', and 'songs' describe 'the full range of singing which the Spirit prompts'. Through these songs members of the community who are continually filled by the Spirit will instruct, edify, and exhort one another.

(2) The focus of the second clause is singing with one's whole being to the Lord Jesus. The two participles, 'singing songs' and 'making music', should be considered as one unit, since they are conjoined by 'and', and together, rather than separately, they are followed by the one qualifying expression: in your heart to the Lord. Both verbs, 'sing' and 'make music', pick up their cognate nouns from the previous clause."[1]

---

[1] O'Brien, *The Letter to the Ephesians*, pp. 394-396.

Addendum 4: *Exegetical Studies on Singing in Worship*

Introduction

In this addendum we will briefly examine two major texts that relate to the Lord's Day worship assembly and singing.[1] There are other relevant texts, but these three will serve the purpose of focusing on singing in the Lord's Day worship assembly.

We will engage in a biblical critical exegetical examination of the texts in which I intend to begin by examining the texts in their individual contexts such as their literary context, their historical context, their sociological and religious contexts, and finally their grammatico-historical contexts. Following this examination, we will identify the major theological emphases or principles in the texts so that contemporary Lord's Day worship situations may be evaluated by those theological principles.[2]

Since this addendum may be circulated as a separate article I have in some cases included full biographical.

1 Cor 14:13-26; 37-40

1 Cor 14:13 Therefore, he who speaks in a tongue should pray for the power to interpret. 14 For if I pray in a tongue, my spirit prays but my mind is unfruitful. 15 <u>What am I to do? I will pray with the spirit and I will pray with the mind also; I will sing with the spirit and I will sing with the mind also.</u> 16 Otherwise, if you bless with the

---

[1] It will not be my purpose to offer a *detailed* biblical critical exegetical examination of these texts. The reader is encouraged to refer to major critical studies referenced in the course of the study and in the bibliography.

[2] For models of such a hermeneutical process I recommend the following major texts on exegetical and hermeneutical studies; Craig L. Blomberg, *A Handbook of New Testament Exegesis*, Grand Rapids: Baker Academics, 2010; Anthony C. Thiselton, *Hermeneutics*, Grand Rapids: Wm. B. Eerdmans, 2009; Gordon D. Fee, *New Testament Exegesis: A Handbook for Students and Pastors*, Louisville: Westminster John Knox Press, 2002; John H. Hayes and Carl R. Holladay, *Biblical Exegesis*, Louisville: Westminster John Knox Press, 2010; I. Howard Marshall, *New Testament Interpretation: Essays on Principles and Method*, Grand Rapids: Wm B. Eerdmans, 1977; Walter C. Kaiser Jr. and Moises Silva, *Introduction to Biblical Hermeneutics: The Search for Meaning*; Zondervan, 2009.

spirit, how can anyone in the position of an outsider say the "Amen" to your thanksgiving when he does not know what you are saying? [17] For you may give thanks well enough, but the other man is not edified.

[18] I thank God that I speak in tongues more than you all; [19] nevertheless, in church I would rather speak five words with my mind, in order to instruct others, than ten thousand words in a tongue.

[20] Brethren do not be children in your thinking; be babes in evil, but in thinking be mature. [21] In the law it is written, "By men of strange tongues and by the lips of foreigners will I speak to this people, and even then they will not listen to me, says the Lord." [22] Thus, tongues are a sign not for believers but for unbelievers, while prophecy is not for unbelievers but for believers. [23] <u>If, therefore, the whole church assembles and all speak in tongues, and outsiders or unbelievers enter, will they not say that you are mad?</u> [24] But if all prophesy, and an unbeliever or outsider enters, he is convicted by all, he is called to account by all, [25] the secrets of his heart are disclosed; and so, <u>falling on his face, he will worship God and declare that God is really among you.</u>

[26] What then, brethren? When you come together, each one has a hymn, a lesson, a revelation, a tongue, or an interpretation. Let all things be done for edification ... [37] <u>If anyone thinks that he is a prophet, or spiritual, he should acknowledge that what I am writing to you is a command of the Lord. [38] If any one does not recognize this, he is not recognized.</u> [39] So, my brethren, earnestly desire to prophesy, and do not forbid speaking in tongues; [40] but all things should be done decently and in order.

The *primary* context of this pericope is a pastoral epistle from the Apostle Paul ca 53/54 CE to the church in Corinth in which Paul addressed problems mentioned to him in a letter from "Cloe's people," and other members who were apparently a group of concerned brethren in Corinth, 1 Cor 1:10-13;

> *[10] I appeal to you, brethren, by the name of our Lord Jesus Christ, that all of you agree and that there be no dissensions among you, but that you be united in the same mind and the same judgment. [11] For it has been reported to me by Chloe's people that there is quarreling among you, my brethren. [12] What I mean is that each one of you says, "I belong to Paul," or "I belong to Apollos," or "I belong to Cephas," or "I belong to Christ." [13] Is Christ divided? Was Paul crucified for you? Or were you baptized in the name of Paul?*

One *initial problem* was division within the congregation over who baptized them (1 Cor 1:10-17). Another serious problem related to a brother living in an immoral relationship with his father's wife (1 Cor 5:1-13). Yet another was the abuse of the Lord's Supper in which the poor were being neglected in favor of the wealthy (1 Cor 11:17-22). *More pertinent to our discussion was the unruly exercise of spiritual giftedness in the worship assembly* including prophetic outpouring, ecstatic speaking in tongues, praying and singing in tongues not understood by all the congregation (1 Corinthians, chapters 11-14).

The *immediate context* to the discourse we are examining (1 Cor 14:13-26) related to issues when speaking, praying, prophesying, and singing under the influence and power of the Holy Spirit in the Lord's Day church worship assembly.

The worship assembly discussion actually began in 1 Cor 11:2 and continued through 1 Cor 14:40.

The divisions among the brethren appeared on a number of fronts mostly due to certain of the Corinthians considering themselves to be super spirituals or more important than others either due to Spirit empowered giftedness, or wealth. This led to abuses by some in their worship assembly in regard to eating the Lord's Supper (1 Cor 11:17-34) and other conduct in the congregational worship service.

Following his discussion of the Lord's Supper, and without leaving the context of the church meeting together in a worship assembly, Paul turned to the issue of the appropriate use of Holy Spirit giftedness in the assembly. He opened the discussion with this comment at 1 Cor 12:1ff:

> *[1] Now concerning spiritual gifts, brethren, I do not want you to be uninformed .... [4] Now there are varieties of gifts, but the same Spirit; [5] and there are varieties of service, but the same Lord; [6] and there are varieties of working, but it is the same God who inspires them all in everyone. [7] To each is given the manifestation of the Spirit for the common good. [8] To one is given through the Spirit the utterance of wisdom, and to another the utterance of knowledge according to the same Spirit, [9] to another faith by the same Spirit, to another gifts of healing by the one Spirit, [10] to another the working of miracles, to another prophecy, to another the ability to distinguish between spirits, to another various kinds of tongues, to another the interpretation of tongues. [11] All these are inspired by one and the same Spirit, who apportions to each one individually as he wills.*

After an extended discussion on the unity of the body of Christ and the use of Spirit giftedness to mutually edify one another at 1 Cor 13:1, Paul introduced his famous chapter on love as the primary gift Christians should seek as the essential solution to the division developing in the congregation. At chapter 14:1 he emphasized this by exhorting the Corinthians first to have love for one another, their aim being to encourage others to use whatever spiritual gifts they had, whether speaking in tongues, prophesying, praying, or singing, *to edify one another*.

A primary meaning of the Greek word for love, *agápē*, is not simply an emotional love but *a cognitive planned desire for the good and well-being of the other*. It is generally "Spoken more especially of good will toward others."[3] It is fundamentally directed toward desire for the good of the other person. Regarding the difference between an emotional love for another and a planned concern for the other note Ethelbert Stauffer's comments

---

[3] Cf. the discussion of ἀγαπάω, *agapáō* and ἀγάπη, *agápē* in Zodhiates, *The Complete Word Study Dictionary, New Testament*.

on ἔρως and *agápē* in Kittel's *Theological Dictionary of the New Testament*.[4]

Paul's point was that tongue speaking,[5] referring to ecstatic utterances without an interpreter, would not edify anyone since *no one would understand the speaker*. Paul's whole point in this discussion of speaking, prophesying, praying, and singing under the influence of the Holy Spirit was *that the abuse of the Spirit giftedness was creating confusion and disarray in the Corinthian worship assembly. The point was that any form of communication should be clearly understood by all.*

At 1 Cor 14:26 Paul addressed singing in the worship assembly but interestingly here he does not use the words *adō* and *psallō*! He uses several expressions that have obvious reference

---

[4] Ethelbert Stauffer, *agápē* in Kittel's *Theological Dictionary of the New Testament*. Discussing the early Greek difference between ἔρως and *agápē* Stauffer observes, "The specific nature of ἀγαπᾶν becomes apparent at this point. Ἔρως is a general love of the world seeking satisfaction wherever it can. Ἀγαπᾶν is a love which makes distinctions, choosing and keeping to its object. Ἔρως is determined by a more or less indefinite impulsion towards its object. Ἀγαπᾶν is a free and decisive act determined by its subject. Ἐρᾶν in its highest sense is used of the upward impulsion of man, of his love for the divine. Ἀγαπᾶν relates for the most part to the love of God, to the love of the higher lifting up the lower, elevating the lower above others. *Eros* seeks in others the fulfilment of its own life's hunger. Ἀγαπᾶν must often be translated "to show love"; it is a giving, active love on the other's behalf."

[5] This is not the place to engage the spirit inspired giftedness of tongue speaking. I merely observe in this discussion that tongue speaking referred not only to uttering unknown ecstatic utterances of joy and praise to God, but also referred to speaking in a language not known by the speaker. A classic case of such tongue speaking would be Acts 2:5ff, *"Now there were dwelling in Jerusalem Jews, devout men from every nation under heaven. ⁶ And at this sound the multitude came together, and they were bewildered, because each one heard them speaking in his own language. ⁷ And they were amazed and wondered, saying, "Are not all these who are speaking Galileans? ⁸ And how is it that we hear, each of us in his own native language? ⁹ Parthians and Medes and Elamites and residents of Mesopotamia, Judea and Cappadocia, Pontus and Asia, ¹⁰ Phrygia and Pamphylia, Egypt and the parts of Libya belonging to Cyrene, and visitors from Rome, both Jews and proselytes, ¹¹ Cretans and Arabians, we hear them telling in our own tongues the mighty works of God."* For a fuller discussion of tongue speaking cf. Thiselton, *The First Epistle to the Corinthians*; Fee, *The First Epistle to the Corinthians*; Blomberg, *1 Corinthians*.

to singing in the assembly. "*What then, brethren? When you come together, each one has a hymn, a lesson, a revelation, a tongue, or an interpretation. Let all things be done for edification.*" Each one has a *hymn*, ψαλμός, *psalmós,* a noun related to the generic word *psalm,* understood here as *a unique song sung in honor or praise of God.* Hence, Delling observes "in 1 C. 14:26 ψαλμός means a Christian song in general."[6] Whatever the case, the song of praise *should be intelligible and sung in respectful consideration of others.*

Apparently, some were breaking into the worship service with songs intended to be of praise to God but either no-one understood them, or different songs were being sung at the same time, either inspired or not! The singing, preaching, teaching bringing revelations and interpretations, *all being uttered together* were confusing some and turning the worship into a sideshow! Note Paul's comment following verse 26:

> *If any speak in a tongue, let there be only two or at most three, and each in turn; and let one interpret. ^{28} But if there is no one to interpret, let each of them keep silence in church and speak to himself and to God. ^{29} Let two or three prophets speak, and let the others weigh what is said. ^{30} If a revelation is made to another sitting by, let the first be silent. ^{31} For you can all prophesy one by one, so that all may learn and all be encouraged; ^{32} and the spirits of prophets are subject to prophets. ^{33} For God is not a God of confusion but of peace.*

Of particular import to our discussion is 1 Cor 14:13-17:

---

[6] Delling on ψαλμός in Kittel, *Theological Dictionary of the New Testament.* There is considerable discussion regarding whether these songs were prepared beforehand or were spur of the moment spirit inspired songs. Whatever the case, the difference is irrelevant to our discussion of this text at this point.

¹³ Therefore, he who speaks in a tongue should pray for the power to interpret. ¹⁴ For if I pray in a tongue, my spirit prays but my mind is unfruitful. ¹⁵ What am I to do? I will pray with the spirit and I will pray with the mind also; I will sing with the spirit and I will sing with the mind also. ¹⁶ Otherwise, if you bless with the spirit, how can anyone in the position of an outsider say the "Amen" to your thanksgiving when he does not know what you are saying?

My point here is that just as praying *in the worship assembly* should be intelligible, *so should singing.* At this stage of our study we will not discuss whether this singing should be vocal and *acappella* other than to emphasize that the singing should be *intelligible* and *edifying with the purpose of edifying the church and not for self-gratification or self-satisfaction* (1 Cor 14:5, 17, 26).

Paul's observation at the close of this long discourse at 1 Cor 14: 26, 37-40 centers the discussion on *appropriate behavior in the context of the worship assembly*, "*²⁶ What then, brethren? When you come together, each one has a hymn, a lesson, a revelation, a tongue, or an interpretation. Let all things be done for edification ... all things should be done decently and in order.*"

Adding an interesting dynamic to worshipping appropriately was Paul's stress that this worship function, whatever it may be was that it should be done in a manner centered on God and not the congregation's personal wishes and interests. Paul inserts 1 Cor 14:24, 25 into the discussion, "*²⁴ But if all prophesy, and an unbeliever or outsider enters, he is convicted by all, he is called to account by all, ²⁵ the secrets of his heart are disclosed; and so, falling on his face, he will worship God and declare that God is really among you.*"

Theological Summary of 1 Cor 14:15-40

Since this study is intended to present *a theology of worship* it is appropriate that at this point we should draw together whatever theological principles Paul had in mind in this section of his epistle to the Corinthians, and then consider what this would say to a theology of worship.

Overriding the conversation is the principal idea that worship should be directed primarily toward God and not toward the desires of the worshippers.

It is apparent from the above brief exegetical survey of 1 Cor 11:1-34 and specifically 1 Cor 14:15-26 that Paul was concerned over the Corinthian Lord's Day worship assembly having degenerated to an emphasis on the behavior of the *haves* and *have-nots* both financially and spiritually first in the behavior of the women in the assembly, then during the Lord's Supper and the abuse of the poor, then in the exercise of their Spirit empowered giftedness. The Corinthian worship service was not focused on God but on the participant's self-interest and self-gratification. This included a range of issues, one of which related to their congregational singing. *This singing should be intelligible, meaningful, and edifying to all.* It should be sung with *the Spirit and understanding*! That the process of the worship should be toward God is clearly indicated by verse 25, *"falling on his face, he will worship God and declare that God is really among you."*

The preliminary theological principle we draw from 1 Cor 14:13-26 is that singing in worship should be *toward God, vocal, intelligible, meaningful* and *edifying to all*.

Eph 5:15-20

We begin by examining the general flow of thought in this pericope by setting it in its paranetic context. Because the days are evil, and the Christians are to live in such a manner as to bring glory to God in Christ and the in church. We will note that the pericope is dominated by *three imperatival* **not ... but** *expressions* followed by five present plural modal (imperatival[7]) participles:

1. The *first imperative* **not ...but**; the Christians must *look carefully* how they live, **not** as unwise men **but** as wise.
2. The *second imperative* **not ... but**; they must **not *be foolish*** like their pagan neighbors **but *understand*** what the will of the Lord is.

---

[7] Participles do not have a mood such as an imperatival or indicative mood but gain their mood from their related verb.

3. The *third imperative* **not… but**; they must **not** *get drunk* like their neighbors **but** must *be filled* with the Spirit.
   a. They should *address* one another in psalms, hymns, and spiritual songs.
   b. They should *sing making melody* with their heart.
   c. They should *give thanks* to the Lord on every occasion.
   d. They should *be submissive* to one another in their general household lifestyle.

5:15, 16. "*Look carefully then how you walk …*" The expression *look carefully*, βλέπετε οὖν ἀκριβῶς, is introduced by οὖν, a logical inferential conjunction which connects this pericope back to vss. 13 and 14, "*but when anything is exposed by the light it becomes visible, for anything that becomes visible is light. ¹⁴ Therefore it is said, "Awake, O sleeper, and arise from the dead, and Christ shall give*r *you light."* This expression stresses the point that behavior, both appropriate and inappropriate is visible to all; emphasizing that good behavior is obviously readily seen by all, and is therefore important to bringing glory to God in a pagan neighborhood, "*therefore look carefully how you walk or live,*" περιπατεῖτε, *peripateite*, a second person plural present tense verb from περιπατέω, *peripateō*, *walk*, or metaphorically, *live* implying a continuous lifestyle.

Paul is laying the foundation for the remainder of this larger pericope (Eph 5:15-6:9) stressing the thought that if Christians are going to so live that they bring glory to God they need to think *carefully* about several pertinent Christian lifestyles. Unlike their pagan neighbors who are careless about their ways, Christians need to think *wisely*.

The expression, **not** *as unwise men* **but** *as wise*, introduces the first **not … but** *imperatival* structure we noted in the structural diagram above. This is the first of three such **not … but** constructions which break the pericope into three sections, each with a specific behavior in mind. Here the thought Paul stresses is *do not live* as *unwise* men (people) but as *wise* men (people), *making the most of the time* (ἐξαγοραζόμενοι, *exagoradzomai*, literally *buying up* the time) *for the days are evil.*

5:17. The second imperative structure "*therefore* **do not be foolish** but **understand** ..." introduces the second **not ... but** expression and the second concern or behavior of the pericope which contains two new additional imperatives. Paul connects the second **not ... but** back to vs. 15 by the preposition διὰ, *dia*, in syntax with demonstrative pronoun in the accusative τοῦτο, *touto*. This is translated in the RSV as *therefore* which leads into the next clause, *therefore do not be*. Peter O'Brien notes that "Hoehner thinks that διὰ τοῦτο ('*on account of this*') draws the foregoing discussion of vv. 15 and 16 to a conclusion" thus introducing *a new and independent thought*. O'Brien likewise sees the second **not ... but** being introduced by διὰ τοῦτο, *dia touto*, suggesting that Paul introduces *a new independent thought* growing out of the primary statement of vs. 15 to "look carefully."

> *The general exhortation of v. 15, which urges the Christian readers to be very careful how they live, is further explained by this second contrast: they are admonished not to be foolish but to understand what the Lord's will is. Although this exhortation is parallel to v. 15b (not as unwise but as wise), it is not simply a restatement of the former: there is a development of thought in v. 17 and a slightly different focus on the Lord's will.*[8]

O'Brien, in a footnote,[9] adds that "it is better, however, to regard v. 17 with its introductory διὰ τοῦτο ('on account of this') as providing *a further exhortation* based on v. 15: because it is necessary to walk ἀκριβῶς ('carefully')."

Regarding the clause introduced by διὰ τοῦτο, *therefore*, Hoehner writes:

> *"On account of this do not become foolish."* As in 1:15 διὰ τοῦτο, *"on account of this,"* concludes the foregoing discussion. In this text Paul is drawing a conclusion not from the immediately preceding clause, "be-

---

[8] O'Brien, *Ephesians*, p. 383.
[9] O'Brien, *Ephesians,* Italics mine, IAF.

cause the days are evil," but from his discussion beginning in verse 15. Paul has summoned believers to walk wisely, taking advantage of every opportunity because the days are evil. For this reason he warns them not to become foolish. It is a restatement of 15b with slightly different words.[10]

The point in this discussion is that διὰ τοῦτο, *therefore*, either points back to the thought of vs 15, "*Look carefully then how you walk ...*" or looks forward introducing a new independent thought, the second, in Paul's three admonitions. There is then in διὰ τοῦτο, *therefore*, a "new development" in emphasis or thought, or a second emphasis of the first admonition to *look carefully how you walk*. Clinton Arnold translates the διὰ τοῦτο as "because of this ..." He observes[11] regarding *therefore*, διὰ τοῦτο, *dia touto*:

The phrase "because of this" (διὰ τοῦτο; 5:17) draws out an inference based on 5:15–16 and the central exhortation, "give attention to walk wisely." Paul develops it with the second contrastive (μὴ ... ἀλλὰ) set of sentences, here containing a negative command ("don't!") and a positive command. The core of the summons is to avoid foolishness by knowing the will of the Lord. These two imperatives serve as a bridge and are both semantically dependent on the acquisition of divine wisdom and the divine Spirit.

In keeping with Hoehner, Arnold considers the clause following *therefore* to connect back to vs 15, *introducing a new category of thought*:

Part of what it means to live wisely is to discern how God would want believers to think and live in every unique situation that confronts them and in every opportunity that presents itself. "Because of this" (διὰ τοῦτο) connects this appeal with the central idea of 5:15–16: "give careful attention to walk wisely." This is more likely than seeing it refer to the immediately preceding

---

[10] Hoehner, *Ephesians*, p. 695.
[11] Arnold, *Ephesians*, Kindle locations 9488-9492.

phrase, "because the days are evil" (5:16b), in light of the contrast in thought between "wise" and "unwise" (5:15–16).[12]

The second instruction of **do not ... but** is interesting in that this clause, like the previous one, includes two imperatives, "**do not** *be foolish* **but** *understand* what the will of the Lord is." "*Do not be*" is derived from γίνεσθε, a present imperative verb, middle or passive, second person plural of γίνομαι, *ginomai*, meaning *to be* or *to become*. *Do not be* is then joined by the third present imperative second person plural *but understand*, συνίετε, *suniete*, that is, "understand what the will of the Lord is."

The preposition and demonstrative pronoun construction διὰ τοῦτο (*because of*) either looks back to vs. 15 (the initial imperative "*look carefully* how you live …") or looks forward introducing a second admonition, *no not be foolish* like the Gentiles and *understand what the will of the Lord is*." My point is that the second **do not ... but** construction introduces *a new and independent imperative* to the initial imperative *look carefully how you walk*, and introduces a new thought which is not *simply* related to the expression *the days are evil* but *begins a new flow of thought, do not be foolish but understand what the will of the Lord is*.

The role διὰ τοῦτο, *dia touto* plays in this pericope is important in that it stresses *a new different imperatival thought* to the pericope and instruction to look carefully how you walk.

5:18. *And* **do not get drunk** *with wine, for that is debauchery; but* **be filled** *with the Holy Spirit*

The two imperatival thoughts of vs 18 are introduced by the conjunction καὶ, *and*, which can be variously translated according to context and structure. Depending on intention they can be either coordinating or emphatic epexegetical. To different degrees and in a variety of ways with different degrees of emphasis καὶ can be read as either *but*, *and*, *also*, *indeed*, *namely*, *that is*, etc. Hoehner correctly points out that the καὶ, *and*, may be an *explicative conjunction*, or what some call an *epexegetical conjunction* which makes a stronger statement than simply *and*. Hoehner

---

[12] Arnold, *Ephesians*, Kindle locations 9574-9579.

suggests two possibilities, *that is* or *namely*.[13] I prefer to translate the καὶ as *indeed*, thus reading vs 18 as "*indeed*, do not get drunk with wine, for that is debauchery; but be filled with the Spirit ..." Paul would then be saying "look carefully how you live, not as foolish men but as wise men ... *indeed* (or *that is*, or *namely*) do not get drunk with wine ... but be filled with or by the Holy Spirit." Thus **not ... but** introduces the third and last **not ... but** clause which is as in vs 17 a *new independent imperatival statement* that goes back to vs 15.

The context or meaning of the expression **do not** *be drunk* has been open to some discussion. Some have suggested a reference merely to pagan debauchery of drunkenness which would have been common in the pagan Roman or Greek culture. Others have suggested that this could have reference to the Dionysian cult of worshipping the god of winemaking and drinking, Dionysius, which was fairly common in that part of the ancient world. Objections to the latter view are that Paul does not specify the Dionysian cult practice, but neither does he specify any other community practice, yet the context does imply a communal practice. I lean partially toward the Dionysian cult practice but do not rule out any other form of community drunken debauchery.[14]

The major point in Paul's argument is the contrast of being *filled with wine* and under the influence of the wine, and *being filled with the Holy Spirit and under the influence of the Spirit*.

However, being filled with the Holy Spirit has led to considerable discussion as to whether this filling is *with* or *by* the Holy Spirit.

One possible way of considering this is the contrast of being *under the power or influence of wine* or *under the power and influence of the indwelling Holy Spirit*. Being under the influence of wine leads to debauchery. Being under the influence of the Holy Spirit leads to addressing one another or speaking to one

---

[13] Hoehner, *Ephesians*, p. 699.
[14] Cf. the discussion of this in the major commentaries of Ephesians, in particular O'Brien, Arnold, Hoehner.

another in psalms, hymns, and spiritual songs. This seems to imply that the Holy Spirit is the power, instrument, or influence of the practice.

Hoehner suggests that we should see ἐν πνεύματι, *en pneumati*, in an instrumental sense (the expression is in the locative, instrumental, or dative case) of "by the Spirit" or "by means of the Spirit."[15]

Peter O'Brien expresses this as:

> *To be admonished, 'Be filled by the Spirit', then, means that Paul's readers are urged to let the Spirit change them more and more into the image of God and Christ, a notion which is consistent with Pauline theology elsewhere. This explanation accords well with the parallel passage in Colossians, 'Let the word of Christ dwell in you richly as you teach and admonish one another in all wisdom by means of Spirit-inspired psalms, hymns and songs, singing thankfully to God with your whole being' (Col. 3: 16). It also synchronizes with the preceding context of Ephesians 5: 15-17, where believers are urged to walk wisely (v. 15) and to understand what the Lord's (i.e., Christ's) will is.*[16]

Clinton Arnold writes:

> *Throughout the letter, Paul frequently refers to the ministry of the Holy Spirit in their lives (1:3, 13, 14, 17; 2:18, 22; 3:16; 4:30; 6:17–18). In the previous chapter he spoke of how the Spirit is involved in the process of renewing the minds of each believer (4:23). Now he gives some insight as to how believers can receive the Spirit's work in full measure. In a continuation of his language related to the temple, Paul speaks of believers "be[ing] filled" with the Spirit. He associates this infilling with the corporate community of believers coming together for worship. As they sing, worship, and give thanks, God responds with his empowering touch.*[17]

---

[15] Hoehner, *Ephesians*, pp. 703f.
[16] O'Brien, *Ephesians*, pp. 392-393.
[17] Arnold, *Ephesians*, Kindle locations 9446-9448. Italics mine, IAF.

Arnold introduces the situation where this influence takes place with a statement that is acknowledged by most scholarly commentaries of Ephesians and Colossians as a reference to a worship service. *"He (Paul) associates this infilling with the corporate community of believers coming together for worship."*

A previous chapter of this book discusses this point in detail and documents scholarly conclusions. However, I will now briefly describe *how* or *why* scholars have drawn this conclusion which primarily has to do with the parallel terminology in Col 3:16 and Eph 5:18 of *mutual teaching, instruction, singing psalms, hymns, and spiritual songs*, the *communal nature of these thoughts*, and *the involvement of the indwelling word of the Lord and the indwelling/inspiration of the Holy Spirit* in this discussion, and the use of *the reciprocal pronoun one another* (ἑαυτοῖς) at Eph 5:19.

5:19, 20. The second personal plural pronoun ἑαυτοῖς, heautois, indicates a reciprocal community activity "… addressing one another in psalms and hymns and spiritual songs, singing and making melody to the Lord with all your heart, [20] always and for everything giving thanks in the name of our Lord Jesus Christ to God the Father.

The encouragement to *address one another* in psalms, etc. is the first of *three modal participles* describing or explaining the result of being filled with the Holy Spirit. The result of being filled with the Holy Spirit is that Christians should be *addressing one another*, *singing* to *one another*, and in everything *giving thanks* to God the father.

First, the instruction to *speak (addressing, λαλοῦντες, lalountes) to one another* in psalms, hymns, and spiritual songs (Eph 5:19), and to be *teaching and admonishing* (διδάσκοντες καὶ νουθετοῦντες, *didaskontes kai nouthetountes*) *one another* in psalms, hymns, and spiritual songs (Col 3:6), *involves some form of corporate setting*, most likely a worship service in which the Holy Spirit would be active (cf 1 Cor 14). The reciprocal pronoun ἑαυτοῖς, *heautois* implies such a community activity. Such teaching, admonishing, encouraging, and instructing *one another* is precisely the kind of action one would expect to experience in a 1st century Christian worship service in which the Christians would be filled with the Holy Spirit.

Second, I mention that throughout this pericope, Eph 5:15-21 the verbs are all in the *second person plural* which leads one to assume that Paul has a *communal involvement* in mind. It is not a private or personal experience that Paul is discussing but a plural community experience. Likewise, the pronoun ἑαυτούς, *one another*, best understood in this context as a reciprocal pronoun is *plural*, not singular, implying a communal setting.

Third, as previously mentioned, most scholars discussing the parallel nature of Col 3:16 and Eph 5:18 note that experiencing the *word of Christ dwelling in one richly* (Col 3:16), and one being *filled with the Spirit* (Eph 5:18) are parallel texts in which Paul is addressing a community regarding a *communal worship experience*.[18] Scholars have noted that the terminology used by Paul in these two texts; the mutual teaching and admonishing one another, and speaking to one another, the dwelling richly of the word of Christ in the Colossians (which is the preaching of the gospel message), the Holy Spirit inspirationally enriching the singing of psalms, hymns, and spiritual songs, and Paul's use of the plural reciprocal pronoun (ἑαυτούς, *one another*), all speak clearly to *a communal setting as in the church gathered for worship*.

It is imperative when doing an exegesis of any text that one maintain the text within its original situational, cultural, and theological context, in this case a 1st century church in which the Holy Spirit was actively present in the life of the church as well as the lives of the Christians. For instance, in Antioch, *when the congregation was assembled for worship* the Holy Spirit spoke to them instructing them to set Barnabas and Paul apart for the mission to the Gentiles. At 1 Cor 14 the Holy Spirit was visibly and audibly active in the life of *the congregation in the worship as-*

---

[18] Snodgrass, *Ephesians*, Kindle location 7076f; Arnold, *Ephesians*, Kindle location 9599ff; O'Brien, *Ephesians*, pp. 389ff; Moo, *The Letters to the Colossians and to Philemon*, Kindle location, 5356ff; Bird, *Colossians and Philemon*, Kindle location, 2516ff; Garland, *Colossians and Philemon*, Kindle locations 2516f, 4928ff, 5371ff.

sembly. It is surely apparent that in the life of a 1st century "charismatic" church, as the Ephesian church, the Holy Spirit would be active. Several commentators have noted the Ephesian epistle simply bristles with Holy Spirit activity.[19]

At Eph 5:18 we find the Holy Spirit filling the lives of those present (ἀλλὰ πληροῦσθε ἐν πνεύματι *but be filled by the Spirit*) as they sang. It should be no stretch of imagination or interpretation to assume that the church in Ephesus would be gathered in worship, as in Acts 13:2 and 1 Cor 14, when the Holy Spirit was actively filling their lives, and the word[20] of Christ was dwelling and working in them richly (Col 3:16)! It would be surprising under the circumstances mentioned in the text if the Ephesians were not gathered in worship when the filling by or with the Holy Spirit in the plural sense took place.

Fourth, by bringing the three words for the singing together, *psalms*, *hymns*, and *spiritual songs*, Paul is using terms that normally in the New Testament, the Old Testament, and Jewish tradition have a corporate worship setting in mind. Much has been written in the relevant literature regarding the use of these three words; the consensus is that Paul is deliberately using three words that cover a wide range of spiritual singing interests, referenced in both the Jewish and Greco-Roman contexts. It is a widely accepted consensus that psalms, ψαλμός *psalmós*, does not necessarily refer to the Psalms of the Jewish Psalter but can also refer to a wide range of Spirit inspired Christian songs either known by Christians at large, or Spirit inspired songs sung during a "charismatic" worship service.

Clinton Arnold reflects a widely accepted view;

> *In the new covenant era, we often see the Spirit active in the hearts and lives of God's people during times of worship. It was during a time of worship that the Spirit gave key direction to the church at Antioch: "While they were worshiping the Lord and fasting, the Holy Spirit*

---

[19] The Spirit, referring to the Holy Spirit, is mentioned 11 times in 6 chapters.
[20] Here we should understand the mention to the word of Christ referring to the message regarding Christ or in other words the gospel referring to Christ, his death, burial, and resurrection (1 Cor 15:1-5).

said, 'Set apart for me Barnabas and Saul for the work to which I have called them'" (Acts 13:2).[21]

Along similar lines, O'Brien observes;

> *"given the frequent repetition of keywords, cognate terms, and synonymous expressions in Ephesians, the parallelism of this verse suggests that the two halves should be taken closely together. 'Speaking in psalms and songs' is the same as 'singing songs and making music', a point which is underscored by means of the chiastic relationship between the nouns 'psalm' and 'song' of the first clause and the verbal forms of the same words in the second. Accordingly, the apostle is not referring to two separate responses of speaking in songs (v. 19a) and singing (v. 19b) but is describing the same activity from different perspectives. Each clause, then, has its own particular focus and emphasis:*
>
> *(1) The first has a horizontal and corporate dimension with its reference to believers addressing one another, presumably in formal worship but also on other occasions, in Spirit-inspired psalms, hymns, and songs (v. 19a). This is akin to Colossians 3: 16, which may be based on Ephesians 5: 19, where members of the Colossian congregation are to teach and admonish one another in psalms and hymns ...*
>
> *(2) The focus of the second clause is singing with one's whole being to the Lord Jesus. The two participles, 'singing songs' and 'making music', should be considered as one unit, since they are conjoined by 'and', and together, rather than separately, they are followed by the one qualifying expression: in your heart to the Lord. Both verbs, 'sing' and 'make music', pick up their cognate nouns from the previous clause.*[22]

Thus, we can safely assume that it would not be out of place to find these three words, psalms, hymns, and spiritual songs in the context of a worship service.

---

[21] Arnold, *Ephesians*, Kindle locations 9758-9786.
[22] O'Brien, *Ephesians*, pp. 394-396. Italics mine, IAF.

Fifth, Arnold[23] mentions that ἑαυτοῖς, normally a *reflexive* pronoun, can and should in this case be seen as a *reciprocal* pronoun.[24] Again we note that this reciprocal pronoun is in the second person plural implying a communal reciprocal action. This implies that the Ephesians would be singing reciprocally to one another in a communal setting and the natural place for this to occur would be in a situation involving the communal sharing of the indwelling word of Christ (Col 3:16) and speaking to one another in spiritual songs (Eph 5:19) involving the activity of the Holy Spirit inspired fellowship. It would seem most likely that this would be a congregational worship service where God and Christ would be worshipped, and the Lord's Supper would be shared!

Most scholars hold that the best understanding of Col 3:16 and Eph 5:19 is that they are parallel texts expressing the same sentiment in different terminology. The terminology of both Eph 5:19 and Col 3:16 thus clearly supports a liturgical context within a church in a formal worship assembly. The plural verbs and pronouns in both texts, the presence and activity of the Holy Spirit in worship assemblies as reflected in the New Testament, the cultural and theological context of "charismatic" experience in 1st century churches, the inference of mutual edification in the worship assembly, and the teaching and speaking to one another in spiritual songs is best understood in the context of a communal worship assembly.

5:19. The expression *addressing one another* in psalms, and hymns, and spiritual songs singing and making melody to the Lord with all your heart and being subject to one another involves five descriptive or modal participles following the imperative to be filled by the Spirit.

Paul continues to discuss the imperative πληροῦσθε ἐν πνεύματι, *be filled by the Spirit*, with the present active plural participle, λαλοῦντες ἑαυτοῖς, "*addressing one another*" (RSV). The NIV translates this as "*Speak to one another …*" translating the participle λαλοῦντες as an imperative. This is possible but

---

[23] Arnold, *Ephesians*, Kindle locations 9758-9786.
[24] Cf. also Zodhiates.

loses the balance of the five participles following the imperative verb, πληροῦσθε, *be filled*. Paul follows this first modal participle with four more present participles *singing*, *making melody*, *giving thanks*, and *being subject*, all modifying or explaining the desired effect of the Christian being filled with the Spirit.

Clinton Arnold makes the following astute observation regarding the varied interpretations of this participle:

> *The regular act of gathering together with other believers to worship God and sing praise to his name is one of the means by which believers are filled with the Spirit.*
>
> *At this juncture, Paul employs a series of five present participles to clarify the means by which believers can be filled with the Spirit. These do not exhaust the various means of being filled with the Spirit, but Paul presents them as crucially important. Because of the ambiguity of participles, which are capable of a variety of interpretations, there have been four different ways scholars have interpreted their functions in this context:*
>
> *1. The most common interpretation has been to understand the participles as indicating result, that is, "be filled with the Spirit and the result will be that you worship...."*
>
> *2. Another less common view is to interpret the participles as having an imperatival sense. In other words, "be filled with the Spirit. Speak to one another ... sing ..." (NIV; NJB; TNIV [translates all but the first participle as imperative]).*
>
> *3. Still others have taken the participles as attendant circumstance. This interpretation takes the participles as not dependent on the imperative "be filled," but as actions that occur in conjunction with the main verb. The translation would be something like, "be filled with the Spirit as you worship ..." (NRSV).*
>
> *4. The final possibility is to take the participles as expressive of means, that is, "be filled with the Spirit by means of worshiping...."*

> *It is this last view, the participles taken as the means of being filled by the Spirit that makes the best sense in this context ..."*
>
> *... Rather, the text is simply asserting a connection between being filled with the Spirit and the church gathering together for corporate worship. This is not a mechanistic approach, but rather a recognition that God meets his people and strengthens them by his Spirit as they corporately worship him and praise his name. There is some level of precedence that can be seen for this in the OT. Saul, for example, is filled with the Holy Spirit as he joins in the worship of a procession of prophets (1 Sam 10:5–6, 10). Perhaps even more significant, in light of the "filling" language of this text, is a passage that describes the temple of the Lord being filled with the glory of God during a time of worship ...*[25]

Peter O'Brien agrees with Arnold,

> *"Of the five participles (vv. 19-21) that follow the exhortation to be filled by the Spirit, and which describe the results of that infilling, the first three have to do with singing: 'speaking [with psalms, hymns, and songs]', 'singing', and 'making music' (v. 19). The verse may be structured as follows: Speaking to one another in Spirit-inspired psalms, hymns and songs singing songs and making music with your heart to the Lord.*
>
> *Thus, we may safely conclude that what Paul was stating was that being filled with or by the Spirit will result in our singing spiritual songs to the Lord, making music with our hearts.*[26]

5:19b. The next clause of 5:19 has been at the heart of discussions since the early years of the history of the two sister movements of the Stone-Campbell Restoration Movement, that is, Churches of Christ and the Instrumental Christian Churches! This discussion even surfaces today within some Churches of Christ who have traditionally for over 200 years been of the

---

[25] Arnold, *Ephesians,* Kindle locations 9701-9732.
[26] O'Brien, *Ephesians*, p. 394

acappella persuasion. The issue of instrumental accompaniment has been reintroduced by some who feel the need for instrumental music in the worship service in order to make the service more appealing to some. Seeking to keep pace with the burgeoning growth of Bible and community churches, some propose introducing an instrument into the worship assembly in order to reach out to the unchurched in a significantly increasing sociologically secular oriented postmodern society. Apparently, Marva Dawn's *Reaching Out by Dumbing Down* has not reached their reading list! Nevertheless, as I reflected on this concern in my opening chapter one realizes that Churches of Christ have for several reasons lost their evangelistic zeal or competence, and some are exploring new approaches in reaching the unchurched. On its own, reaching the unchurched is a noble and desirable concern, but this surely does not justify adopting a means of worship that for over 150 years has been considered by most Churches of Christ to be unbiblical.

The question regarding the use of an instrument to accompany singing in the worship assembly circles around whether there is possible permission for the use of an instrument accompanying the singing in Eph 5:19 and Col 3:16, or whether instruments are excluded in these two texts by the silence of the texts, or the specific mention of singing vocally in the texts. The issue involves the question whether there is or is not textual justification for introducing an instrument. Do Christians have the option of either singing with an instrument, or not singing with an instrument?

One additional quirk to this discussion is that since there is no condemnation of an instrument in this text, and since instruments were used in the Temple liturgy, some assume that they have the freedom to use an instrument in the Christian worship assembly! And in the words of Bilbo Baggins of the Hobbits, the road goes on and on! They offered animal sacrifices for the atonement of sin in the Temple, but in the Christian age and assembly we do not, for Jesus has already offered the sacrifice for the forgiveness of sins and no further sin sacrifice is necessary. Furthermore, contrary to Roman Catholic doctrine, the Eucharist,

Mass, or Lord's Day meal is not a sacrifice but a memorable celebration of the *hapax, once for all time sin sacrifice on the cross by Jesus.* The old covenant or previous system was annulled at Jesus' death and a new covenant introduced in which Jesus entered once into the holy sanctuary, heaven, to offer a sacrifice for sin. Cf. Heb 7:22, Heb 8,and Heb 9:12.

It will not be my intention in this exegetical study of Eph 5:19 and brief reflection of Col 3:16 to pass judgment on the practice of singing accompanied by an instrument of the Christian worship assembly, for that is more a theological or hermeneutic question than an exegetical one. My purpose has and will be to seek to understand what the text said in its original setting and then leave the hermeneutic question of how to interpret this in a contemporary culture and age.

I wish I could be absolutely true in this statement, but unfortunately since I do have some deep opinions regarding how one should sing in the worship assembly I find it extremely difficult to not reflect negatively on how I feel we should react to this in a contemporary situation while attempting to stay within the biblical text especially when exploring a theology of singing and a theology of worship, so please bear with me as I lead you through an exegetical study of the remainder of the text. You may disagree with me regarding the application of the text but my purpose at this point is simply to be more biblical critical exegetically than to be hermeneutic in the application of the meaning of the text in the contemporary church. Again, I am sensitive to judging people! The Lord did not commission me to be a judge, but to be a teacher or preacher. Note Jesus' instruction on this to his disciples at Matt 1:24-30. And, yes, I do know that Paul instructed the church in Corinth to judge a brother who was living in open adultery, the context was a clear disobedience to moral instruction taught in both the Old Covenant and the New Covenant.

We return now to Paul closing out this third and last **not ... but** clause of **not** *being under the influence of wine* in a drunken stupor **but** *being filled by or with the Spirit.* His point is that Christians should be "*addressing one another in psalms and hymns and spiritual songs <u>singing and making melody to the Lord with all your heart</u> ...*"

This exhortation opens with a present plural modal or descriptive participle *addressing <u>one another</u>* introducing *how* one experiences the imperatival instruction of being filled with the Spirit, Eph 5:19b. The five present participles (enumerated in Eph 5:19 and 20) that follow the imperative *be filled* all explain *the results* of being filled with the Spirit in the Christian's life. Under the influence of the Spirit Christians *sing* spiritual songs and *make melody* to the Lord *with all their heart*.

Three salient points surface from *within* the text: Christians *sing psalms to <u>one another</u>*, *they sing to the Lord*, and *they make melody <u>with their hearts</u>*. That is not difficult to understand! The text is quite clear! As a result of the influence of the Spirit, 1) Christians *sing to one another* implying a communal setting! 2) Their singing is *to* or *toward* the Lord. 3) They make melody *with their heart*!

O'Brien has succinctly pointed out that there is a vertical worshipful dimension to this text, Christians sing to the Lord. But there is also a horizontal communal dimension in this singing in which Christians address and encourage *one another* in this community setting.[27] O'Brien notes that although this might imply two separate actions of singing, the context calls for two *perspectives* within the *one action*:

> *In the light of this exegesis, then, v. 19 describes the singing of psalms, hymns, and songs by those who are Spirit-filled from different, though closely related, perspectives. The two clauses of v. 19 refer not to two separate responses or activities, but to one and the same action, each with a slightly different focus. To start with, the 'audiences' are distinct. According to v. 19a, believers speak in psalms, hymns, and songs to one another, reminding each other of what God has done in the Lord Jesus Christ. A further distinction is the purpose of this singing, namely, to instruct and edify members of the body. In a sense, this singing has a horizontal and corporate focus to it. In v. 19b, the singing and making music are directed to the Lord Jesus. This activity thus has a*

---

[27] O'Brien, *Ephesians*, p. 394.

vertical focus and a personal dimension, for believers praise the Lord Jesus 'with their whole being'. It is in and through singing and making music, by which other members of the body are instructed and edified, that praise is offered to the Lord Jesus. The same singing has a twofold function and purpose.[28]

Snodgrass likewise observes:

Singing, then, has two audiences. Christians sing to each other, reminding each other about God's character and work in Christ, but they also sing to the Lord as a way of offering praise to him. In the parallel in Colossians 3:16 singing is addressed to God, but "Lord" here in Ephesians 5:19 clearly refers to Christ.[29]

Regarding the *communal aspect of this singing* we have already on several occasions discussed the reciprocal action in the plural pronoun ἑαυτοῖς, *one another*, which can be either a reflexive or reciprocal plural pronoun. Arnold observes:

The audience of the singing is "one another" (ἑαυτοῖς). Although this is the reflexive pronoun, it should not be translated that way. Here it has a reciprocal function—a usage that is not uncommon for this pronoun (see 4:32; Col 3:13; 1 Thess 5:13; 1 Pet 4:8).[30]

Both Col 3:16 and Eph 5:19 are clear that this singing is primarily *to* the Lord and *to* God. At Eph 5:19 the construction is in the dative case τῷ κυρίῳ, *tō kuriō*, which implies *with regard to* or *toward the Lord*. At Col 3:16 the construction is likewise a dative case, τῷ θεῷ, *tō theō, to God*. The audience is therefore, primarily the Lord Jesus and God the Father. Singing has a Trinitarian dimension, inspired by the Holy Spirit and directed toward God and Jesus Christ.

The construction of *"singing and making melody to the Lord with all your heart ..."* is interesting and pivotal to the understanding and interpretation of this clause. Unfortunately, the syntax of this expression is often overlooked. The Greek syntax of

---

[28] O'Brien, *Ephesians,* pp. 396-397.
[29] Snodgrass, *Ephesians*, p. 291.
[30] Arnold, *Ephesians*, Kindle locations 9746-9748.

ᾄδοντες καὶ ψάλλοντες, *adontes kai psallontes*, combines two participles joined by a coordinating conjunction *καὶ* in a *hendiadyl*[31] construction. In such constructions the second part of the construction qualifies the first part of the construction, thus singing and making melody refer to one action in which making melody describes the singing, hence *singing melodiously* to the Lord.

O'Brien supports the hendiadyl construction even though he does not use the term.

> *"The two participles "singing songs" and "making music" should be considered as one unit, since they are joined by "and", and together rather than separately they are followed by the one qualifying expression "in your heart to the Lord."*[32]

Getting closer to the heart of the discussion Arnold observes:

> *The two participles (ᾄδοντες καὶ ψάλλοντες, adontes kai psallontes) represent the verbal forms of two of the three nouns and are functionally equivalent expressions to "speaking with songs and psalms" (λαλοῦντες ἐν ᾠδαῖς καὶ ψαλμοῖς, lalountes en ōdais kai psalmois). While the first term clearly means "singing," some have argued that the second term implies the use of stringed instruments. It is true that the original meaning of the verb (ψάλλω, psállō) referred to the plucking of strings, but it certainly does not carry that meaning into all of its usages. Barth tries to support this view by contending that the Jerusalem temple worship would have been accompanied by instruments (e.g., Ps 150),33 but that is not something required by this verb. Hoehner rightly concludes, "the main point is the verbalizing of praise through singing."*[33]

What we have in this construction is that the Christians should be addressing one another in psalms and hymns and spiritual songs, singing melodiously to the Lord *with all the heart*.

---

[31] *Hendiadyl* from *hendiadys* syntactically meaning saying one thing through two things.
[32] O'Brien, *Ephesians*, p. 394.
[33] Arnold, *Ephesians,* Kindle locations 9789-9796.

Two points surface in this expression, 1) Christians sing melodiously *to the Lord*. We have already above discussed the hendiadyl construction here so there is no need to repeat the joining of these two participles in one sense. 2) They make melody *with all their heart*.

The Greek actually reads τῇ καρδίᾳ ὑμῶν τῷ κυρίῳ, *tē kardia humōn tō kuriō*, *with the heart to the Lord*. Τῇ καρδίᾳ is a noun in the locative, dative, or instrumental case which can either mean *in* the heart, or *for* the heart, or *with* the heart. *First*, the singing melodiously is not simply *in* the heart, since singing is *in the active voice*, otherwise it would be silent singing! *Second*, neither is the singing melodiously *with reference* to the heart, it is singing *with the heart* in reference to the voice. We sing with our voice, but with the heart, *heartfelt* singing! Obviously, the singing is *with reference to the voice but it is <u>with</u> the heart*, the voice is the *instrument* with the heart being the *agent* or the instrument!

We occasionally hear some argue that Eph 5:19 does not mention any instrument! *Read again!* Τῇ καρδίᾳ, *with* the heart (instrumental case) indicates the instrument! The heart here is clearly best understood as in the *instrumental* case noun, identifying the instrument making the melody pleasing to one another and to God, which is *the heart*! Singing without the heart is dead singing!

In passing we will note that several commentators observe that there is no mention in Eph 5:19 of a *musical* instrument, implying something like a harp or flute, but this does not exclude the heart as the instrument providing the melody of the singing. What makes the singing melodiously acceptable is that it is sung with the heart. In 1 Cor 14:15 singing and praying are sung and prayed *with* the Spirit and *with* understanding, *Spirit* and *understanding* are the instruments that make the singing acceptable.

Arnold observes:
> *The singing of praise includes profound heart involvement (τῇ καρδίᾳ). Modern readers may be tempted to think only in terms of an emotional response, which is clearly included in this expression, but it is not limited to that. As we noted at 3:17, the heart is the center of the*

> *person, equivalent to the idea of the "inner self." It includes one's intellect and ability to reason and choose.*[34]

O'Brien agrees with Arnold;

> *The focus of the second clause is singing with one's whole being to the Lord Jesus. The two participles, 'singing songs' and 'making music', should be considered as one unit, since they are conjoined by 'and', and together, rather than separately, they are followed by the one qualifying expression: in your heart to the Lord. Both verbs, 'sing' and 'make music', pick up their cognate nouns from the previous clause. The additional words 'with your heart' do not specify an inward disposition (NIV: in your heart), as though the apostle is referring to silent worship in contrast to 'with your voices'. Rather, heart here signifies the whole of one's being. The entire person should be filled with songs of praise, thereby expressing the reality of life in the Spirit.*[35]

In support of his view that there is no mention or inference of a musical instrument in the singing and making melody with the heart to the Lord O'Brien cites Hoehner in a footnote,

> "For the view that ψάλλω means to make music by singing, without any suggestion of musical accompaniment, see BAGD, 891; and Hoehner."[36]

Although Snodgrass is not as specific as Arnold and O'Brien regarding the use of an instrumental noun following the instruction to sing, or describes the singing as being with the heart. Snodgrass, observes that singing is an instrumental case noun. He observes:

> *Whether any difference is intended between psalms, hymns, and spiritual songs is difficult to say. In all probability no clear demarcation is intended. That people are to sing in their heart is not a request that people sing with feeling or emotion. Rather, "heart" refers to the controlling center of one's being: "Sing with your whole being"*

---

[34] Arnold, *Ephesians,* Kindle locations 9796-9799. Italics mine, IAF.
[35] O'Brien, *Ephesians,* p. 396. Italics mine, IAF.
[36] O'Brien, *op. cit.*, Kindle location 14651.

> *(which certainly includes the emotions). The issue is the integrity with which one sings, not the feeling. Words are not merely sung, they express the reality of the life in the Spirit.*[37]

Lincoln does not specifically address the expression *singing with the heart* but comments in such a manner that it is reasonable to assume that the expression *with* the heart is parallel to *with* the Spirit. Speaking syntactically and not theologically, the Spirit is the "instrument" (no disregard for the Spirit) filling the Christian as they sing and give thanks, so is *the heart* the "instrument" with which the Christians sing.

> *The second participial clause builds up the sentence in the writer's characteristic style by employing the verbal forms of two of the previous nouns—ᾠδή, "song," and ψαλμός, "psalm." Although its original meaning involved plucking a stringed instrument, ψάλλω here means to make music by singing (cf. also 1 Cor 14:15; Jas 5:13), so that there is no reference in this verse to instrumental accompaniment (cf. the discussion in BAGD 891; pace Barth, 584). If the singing involved in the first participial clause has a horizontal and corporate dimension, that of the second clause has a more vertical and individual focus. The singing is now directed to the Lord, who, as in v 17, is Christ (a change from Col 3:16 where the singing had been addressed to God) ... Believers who are filled with the Spirit delight to sing the praise of Christ, and such praise comes not just from the lips but from the individual's innermost being, from the heart, where the Spirit himself resides (cf. 3:16, 17, where the Spirit in the inner person is equivalent to Christ in the heart).*
>
> *In addition, believers who are filled with the Spirit will give thanks. The writer still has in view primarily thanksgiving in public worship.*[38]

---

[37] Snodgrass, *Ephesians*, p. 291.
[38] Lincoln, *Ephesians*, p. 346. Italics mine, IAF.

Bruce comments on this pericope in passing but does make an interesting observation regarding the expression *with*. Interestingly *with the spirit* (τῷ πνεύματι) and *with the mind* (τῷ νοΐ) in 1 Cor 14:15 are both in the *instrumental* case:

> *The verb translated "making melody" (Gk. psallo) means originally plucking the strings of a lyre or similar instrument, but this etymological sense is probably not intended here; we may take it in the sense of singing psalms which it has in 1 Corinthians 14:15 and James 5:13. (It is, in fact, the word from which "psalm" is derived.) The context in which it occurs in 1 Corinthians 14:15, "I will sing with the spirit, and I will sing with the understanding also," chimes in well with the apostle's insistence here, that such melody, to be acceptable to the Lord, must spring from the heart. We may also compare Colossians 3:16, "singing with grace in your hearts unto God," where "grace" (Gk. charis) means thanksgiving. Nothing yields worthy praise more spontaneously than a thankful heart.*[39]

5:20. Paul now turns to the fourth participle describing the results of being filled with the Spirit, "always in everything *giving thanks* (εὐχαριστοῦντες, *eucharistountes*) in the name of our Lord Jesus Christ *to God the Father*." Note that Paul has not left the context or discussion of being filled with the Spirit and of worship *toward* God, for *thanksgiving is also the result of being filled with the Spirit and is thus also directed toward God*. The *immediate* context is being filled with the Spirit. The larger context is *be careful how you walk*. The list of five participles and their relationship to being filled with the Spirit is interesting and meaningful:

---

[39] Bruce, *Ephesians*, Kindle locations 1948-1955. Italics mine, IAF.

> "... be filled with the Spirit, [19] <u>addressing</u> one another in psalms and hymns and spiritual songs, <u>singing</u> and <u>making melody</u> to the Lord with all your heart, [20] always and for everything <u>giving thanks</u> in the name of our Lord Jesus Christ to God the Father. [21] <u>Be subject</u> to one another out of reverence for Christ.

One may be tempted to consider a change in context in these clauses relating to *being filled with the Spirit,* but the context is the same. They fall under Paul's third **μὴ ... ἀλλὰ, not ... but** construction, relating to *being filled with the Spirit.* The result of being filled with the Spirit is that one *sings* and *makes melody* with the heart when worshiping, the Christians always in everything *give thanks*; the Christians *submit* to one another in the family setting out of reverence to the Lord Jesus.

One should observe carefully that in the larger context of Eph 5:13-20 Paul builds his argument of looking carefully how you walk around *three independent constructions,* **not ... but**, each developing a separate independent thought; 1) *not as unwise men but as wise, making the most of the time, because the days are evil.*, 2) *do* **not** *be foolish,* **but** *understand what the will of the Lord is,* 3) *And do* **not** *get drunk with wine, for that is debauchery;* **but** *be filled with the Spirit.*

Exegetical Summary of Eph 5:15-20.
This pericope develops the thought that Christians need to be careful about how they practice their Christian faith in a world that is mostly pagan in persuasion and lifestyle.

Paul encouraged Christians to "look carefully and buy up the time" in the sense that their time is valuable and opportunities rare; they should make the most of their daily lives as a vehicle to "speak" to their pagan or worldly neighbors.

He carefully structured the pericope around three Greek **mē ... ἀλλὰ, not ... but** constructions *each introducing a new deliberation to the instructions on how to make the most of their time* in order to impact their neighbors.

Into these three **mē ... ἀλλὰ, not ... but** constructions he inserts *five present plural imperatival verbs* and *five present modal* *plural participles* that explain how one should carry out the **do not ... but** imperative verbs which they describe.

The *first* **mē ... ἀλλὰ**, **not ... but** construction reads *do **not** be foolish **but** be wise* making the most of the time. In this first clause the imperatival verb is ***look carefully*** *how you live*.

The *second* **mē ... ἀλλὰ**, **not ... but** construction includes the second and third imperatival verbs ***do not be*** *foolish*; ***but understand*** *what the will of the Lord is*.

The *third* **mē ... ἀλλὰ**, **not ... but** construction includes the fourth and fifth imperatival verbs ***do not get drunk*** *with wine which is debauchery but **be filled** with the Spirit*.

Each of the three **mē ... ἀλλὰ**, **not ... but** clauses introduce a separate thought or deliberation. The second **do not ... but** clause is introduced by the expressive demonstrative pronoun construction *διὰ τοῦτο, therefore, which sets it apart from the first* **do not ... but** clause. The third **do not ... but** clause is introduced by the epexegetical coordinating conjunction *καὶ, kai,* meaning *indeed,* or *namely, to wit, even which sets it apart from the first and second imperatival clauses* introducing a third deliberation or thought.

In the third **do not ... but** clause Paul introduces the *five present plural modal participles*, *speaking* to one another, *singing* and *making melody* to one another, *giving thanks* to the Lord Jesus Christ and God, and *submitting* to one another out of reverence for Jesus Christ. Each of these modal participles modifies or explains how one carries out the fifth imperatival verbal clause, *be filled* with the Spirit.

The Spirit inspired context of worship in the first century (cf. the Corinthian congregation and 1 Cor 14 in which the singing and praying was in the context of "charismatic"[40] worship) is the setting in which the singing melodiously as a result of being filled by the Spirit normally took place in the first century of Christianity.

---

[40] I use *charismatic* in the normal sense of persons functioning under the *charisma* or *giftedness* of the Holy Spirit and not in the sense of modern Pentecostal churches.

The plural nouns, adjectives, verbs, and participles in Eph 5:19, 20 and the third **not ... but** expression in conjunction with the *reciprocal* pronoun ἑαυτοῦ, *heautoú, one another* imply a *reciprocal* practice *of mutual edification and behavior in the context of communal worship service.*

Translation or Reading of Eph 5:15-20

Working through the above exegetical study of this pericope I propose the following reading which takes into consideration the three **not ... but** sections, the five imperatival verbs, and the five participle expressions in Eph 5:19, 20:

> *Be careful how you live your daily lives,* **not** *as unwise men* **but** *as wise men, making the most of the time, because the days are evil. Because of this,* **do not** *be foolish,* **but** *understand what the will of the Lord is. Notably,* **do not** *keep getting get drunk with wine, for that is debauchery;* **but** *be constantly filled with the Spirit, speaking to one another in psalms, hymns, and spiritual songs, singing melodiously with your heart to the Lord, always and for everything giving thanks in the name of the Lord Jesus Christ to God the Father, being subject to one another out of reverence to Christ.*

AUTHOR

Ian A. Fair (PhD)
Professor Emeritus of New Testament
and New Testament Theology
Graduate School of Theology
College of Biblical Studies
Abilene Christian University

TEACHING & SPECIALIZATION	SEMINARS AND WORKSHOPS
Revelation	Revelation
Romans	Romans
Prison Epistles	Matthew
Synoptic Gospels: Matthew	Strategic Planning
1 & 2 Thessalonians	Leadership
Leadership	Unity in Diversity

Education

Ph.D. in Systematic Theology, University of Natal, South Africa
Dissertation: *The Theology of Wolfhart Pannenberg as a Reaction to Dialectical Theology*
MA in New Testament Theology, University of Natal, South Africa
Thesis: *The Resurrection of Jesus in Three Contemporary Theologians*
BA Honors in Bible and Theology, University of Natal, South Africa
BA in Bible, Abilene Christian University, Abilene, Texas, USA.

Books by Dr. Ian Fair published by HCU Media
(available in paperback & Kindle Formats)

Conquering in Christ: Commentary on the Book of Revelation

Ephesians: Studies in the theology of Paul's Letter to the Ephesians

Paul's Epistle to the Galatians

Philippians: A Remedy for the Spiritual Blahs

A Biblical Theology of Worship

WHO WE ARE

HCU Media LLC

Publishing in support of

Heritage Christian University – Ghana (HCU Ghana)

www.hcuc.edu.gh

HCU media has been established to support the publication of materials, both paper and electronic, created by faculty and friends of HCU Ghana. These materials will be offered initially in the USA & Ghana but may become available globally via other outlets.

www.ingramcontent.com/pod-product-compliance
Lightning Source LLC
Chambersburg PA
CBHW051523020426
42333CB00016B/1757